POTENTIALS OF
DISORDER

MANCHESTER
UNIVERSITY PRESS

New Approaches to Conflict Analysis

Series editor: Peter Lawler,
Senior Lecturer in International Relations,
Department of Government, University of Manchester

Until recently, the study of conflict and conflict resolution remained compara-
tively immune to broad developments in social and political theory. When the
changing nature and locus of large-scale conflict in the post-Cold War era is also
taken into account, the case for a reconsideration of the fundamentals of conflict
analysis and conflict resolution becomes all the more stark.

New Approaches to Conflict Analysis promotes the development of new theoretical
insights and their application to concrete cases of large-scale conflict, broadly
defined. The series intends not to ignore established approaches to conflict analysis
and conflict resolution, but to contribute to the reconstruction of the field through
a dialogue between orthodoxy and its contemporary critics. Equally, the series
reflects the contemporary porosity of intellectual borderlines rather than simply
perpetuating rigid boundaries around the study of conflict and peace. *New
Approaches to Conflict Analysis* seeks to uphold the normative commitment of the
field's founders yet also recognises that the moral impulse to research is properly
part of its subject matter. To these ends, the series is comprised of the highest
quality work of scholars drawn from throughout the international academic
community, and from a wide range of disciplines within the social sciences.

Potentials of disorder

Edited by Jan Koehler
and Christoph Zürcher

Manchester University Press

MANCHESTER AND NEW YORK

distributed exclusively in the USA by Palgrave

Published by Manchester University Press
Oxford Road, Manchester M13 9NR, UK
and Room 400, 175 Fifth Avenue, New York, NY 10010, USA
www.manchesteruniversitypress.co.uk

Distributed exclusively in the USA by
Palgrave, 175 Fifth Avenue, New York,
NY 10010, USA

Distributed exclusively in Canada by
UBC Press, University of British Columbia, 2029 West Mall,
Vancouver, BC, Canada V6T 1Z2

British Library Cataloguing-in-Publication Data
A catalogue record for this book is available from the British Library

Library of Congress Cataloging-in-Publication Data applied for

ISBN 0 7190 6241 1 *hardback*

First published 2003

11   10   09   08   07   06   05   04   03   10   9   8   7   6   5   4   3   2   1

Typeset in Photina
by Servis Filmsetting Ltd, Manchester
Printed in Great Britain
by Bookcraft (Bath) Ltd, Midsomer Norton

CONTENTS

NOTES ON CONTRIBUTORS

Pavel K. Baev is Senior Researcher at the International Peace Research Institute (PRIO), Oslo.

John Borneman is Professor of Anthropology at Princeton University. From 1991 to 2001 he taught at Cornell University and has been guest professor at the University of California, Berkeley, Stockholm, Bergen and Senior Fulbright Professor at Humboldt Universität zu Berlin.

Barbara Christophe is researcher and lecturer at the University of Frankfurt in the department of Political Science.

George Elwert is Professor of Social Anthropology and director of the Institute of Ethnology at the Free University, Berlin.

Christian Giordano is Head of the Department of Anthropology and Director of the Interfaculty Institute of Central and East Europe (IICEE) at the University of Fribourg.

Kristóf Gosztonyi works with the Return and Reconstruction Task Force of the Office of the High Representative of the United Nations for Bosnia and Hercegovina OHR.

Hannes Grandits is lecturer and researcher at the Department for Southeast European History at Graz University and the Center for the Study of Balkan Societies and Cultures.

Enver Kisriev works in the Department of Sociology at the Russian Academy of Science, Institute of History, Archaeology and Ethnography in Makhachkala, Dagestan.

Jan Koehler is researcher at the Institute for Ethnology and Social Anthropology at the Free University, Berlin.

Carolin Leutloff is a PhD candidate at the Max-Planck Institute for Social Anthropology in Halle/Saale, Germany.

Norbert Mappes-Niediek is a journalist who has worked for a number of influential newpapers including *Die Zeit* and *Freitag*.

Xavier Raufer is Professor at the Institute of Criminology, University of Paris.

Olga Vassilieva graduated from the Moscow Physical Technical Institute. She is an expert on inter-ethnic conflicts in the post-soviet space.

Christoph Zürcher is Assistant Professor at the Department of Political Science, Institute of Eastern European Studies at the Free University, Berlin.

ACKNOWLEDGEMENTS

Many people and organisations have contributed to this book.

We are grateful to the Heinrich-Boell-Foundation, Berlin, for supporting a first conference on the subject, held in Berlin in June 1999. We are also grateful to the Free University, Berlin and to the Institute of Eastern European Studies of the Free University, Berlin for their support. We gratefully acknowledge the help of Sybill De Vito-Egerland. Gesa Walcher and Miriam Abu-Sharkh did a marvellous job with the conference organisation. Graham Stack and Erica Richardson mastered the Sisyphus work of language editing nine contributions of non-native speakers. We would like to thank Akhmed Tikhomirov for inspiration, Horst and Karin for the shelter; Kristóf Gosztonyi, Hannes Grandits and Georg Elwert have contributed to this volume much more than just their chapters. Finally, we would like to thank Holm Sundhaussen. The inspiration for this project is his.

Introduction: potentials of disorder in the Caucasus and Yugoslavia

Jan Koehler and Christoph Zürcher

Conflict after empire

ORGANISED INTER-GROUP violence has been linked to primordial instincts, to the struggle for power and profit, to the ambitions of ethnic entrepreneurs, and most often to uncertainty and fear. Here violence is linked to institutions. It is asked which institutions foster violence, and which institutions, on the contrary, provide for procedures that turn 'either-or-conflicts' into 'more-or-less' conflicts. It is asked which institutional arrangements lead to societal fragmentation, and which can integrate society even when state power is virtually absent. The implosion of the Union of Soviet Socialist Republics (USSR) and the Federal Yugoslav Republic provide ample material for this endeavour.

Judging by historical and contemporary evidence, the collapse of multi-ethnic empires is almost inevitably a conflict-prone process. The implosion of the central state and its hierarchies turns imperial peripheries into peripheries without empires. The former centrally administered society fragments into multiple societies, which have to (re-)build state administrations, (re-)draw boundaries and (re-)invent loyalties. They have to establish new institutional arrangements for self-regulation in order to ensure security, political participation and economic development after empire. These institutions have to be inscribed into a political space, whose boundaries are often ill-defined and contested. And there has to be an understanding of who is legitimately in charge of designing these institutions, and to whom these new rules of the game are going to apply.

The implosion of the socialist empires forced the societies of the post-socialist spaces to redefine the most basic institutions that govern social life. They had, in short, to embark upon a process of competitive and contested polity building.

All the societies of the collapsed empires faced this challenge. Not all societies, however, managed to find a non-violent solution. Those administrative units of the collapsing empires with a multi-ethnical population faced particular problems: the ambitions and fears of two or more ethnic groups had to be

1

addressed, separatist tendencies had to be avoided, growing antagonism along ethnic lines needed to be defused and the attempts of ethnic entrepreneurs to conquer the state by using ethnicity as a mobilising resource had to be blocked. Some of the post-socialist societies have successfully managed these tasks and have avoided violence; others have succeeded in polity building, but only at the price of conflict and violence. And some have completely failed – they have lost the state and internal violence has become endemic.

Thus, it is not only violence that needs to be explained but, in a more general sense, the different response of the post-socialist societies to the conflicts that followed the collapse of the central state.

This volume deals with the institutional framework in post-socialist, after-empire spaces. The volume consists of nine case studies and two contributions of a more theoretical nature. Each of these analytical narratives sheds some light on the micro-politics of organised violence. All case studies are taken from the Caucasus and Former Yugoslavia. This has allowed, implicitly, and at times directly, the use of a comparative approach in order to identify those institutions which had an impact on the organisation of violence, and on the organisation of non-violent stability, respectively. Comparing cases from the Caucasus and Former Yugoslavia can be a rewarding endeavour for two reasons: first, both regions have produced ample material for the study of violent conflicts. Secondly, both regions share a number of structural similarities. All cases are thus embedded in a relatively similar context, which makes it easier to identify the relevant factors.

In the Caucasus, there have been four major violent conflicts. The first to erupt was, in 1988, the quarrel between Armenians and Azeris over Nagorno-Karabakh, an autonomous province within Azerbaijan but mainly populated by Armenians (on this war see Koehler and Zürcher's Chapter 8 in this volume). The quest of the Armenians of Nagorno-Karabakh to join Armenia led to a large-scale conflict and massive ethnic cleansing on the territories of Armenia and Azerbaijan. The conflict is still not resolved and Nagorno-Karabakh's status remains undecided.

The status of Georgia's breakaway autonomous provinces of South-Ossetia and Abkhazia is also undecided; both provinces broke away when their host state, the Georgian Soviet Republic, became the independent sovereign Republic of Georgia (see Baev's Chapter 7 in this volume). After heavy fighting, which caused massive refugee flows, the two conflicts are frozen, at least for the time being.

The fourth major Caucasian conflict is the Chechen war for independence. When the USSR broke apart in 1991, the Chechens reacted by declaring their independence, thus unilaterally seceding from the Russian Federation. This move eventually triggered the first Chechen war (1994–96), which Russia lost on the battlefield. Since October 1999, Russia has again engaged the Chechen guerrillas, trying to re-establish its state authority. Surprisingly, Chechnya's neighbour, the republic of Dagestan, has avoided internal turmoil and has opted to stay within the Russian Federation. Kisriev's Chapter 6 in this volume discusses the factors that caused the very different response to the Soviet breakdown by these two republics which share many structural similarities.

In Yugoslavia, there were also four major violent conflicts: the first to start and to end was the short campaign of the Yugoslav army against the breakaway republic of Slovenia in June 1991. This is the only conflict from this sample that qualifies as a typical inter-state war. The second was the violent clash in Croatia between Croats and Serbs. In August 1991, the fighting began in those regions of Croatia where Serbs formed an absolute or relative majority of the population. Intensive fighting took place in eastern Croatia and in the Krajina. The Serbian militias that had been organised well in advance, were armed mainly from the stock of the Yugoslav Army, which actively took part in the fighting. Grandits and Leutloff provide in Chapter 1 in this volume a detailed account of the organisation of violence in the Krajina.

The third Yugoslav conflict was the war in and about Bosnia and involved fierce fighting between Serbs, Bosniaks[1] and Croats, with changing local alliances between adversaries in the course of the war (see Gosztonyi's Chapter 2 in this volume on consequences of the war for so-called 'Herceg-Bosna').

The most recent war so far in former Yugoslavia was the war over Kosovo, which was fought on the one hand between Serbs and Kosovo-Albanians in Kosovo, and on the other hand between NATO and Serbia. Raufer's Chapter 3 in this volume treats one aspect of the Kosovo wars, namely the intertwining of political violence and organised crime. Mappes-Niediek's Chapter 5 in this volume takes a broader perspective and sheds light on the process of restraint and eventual escalation of violence focusing on the organisational potential of the local population and the state in place.

All of these conflicts are often labelled 'ethno-political conflicts'. This term implies that at the core of the organisation of violence lies the political aspirations of ethnically defined groups. This is certainly not wrong: the slow decline and eventual collapse of the Soviet and the Yugoslav empires was partly triggered, partly accompanied by the quest for national sovereignty, put forward by the ideologists of many nationalities in the crumbling empires.

However, the label 'ethno-political' is in some respects more deceptive than revealing. While all of these violent conflicts may have been fuelled by the aspirations of ethnically defined groups and their leaders, all were framed and shaped by the administrative–territorial borders of the crumbling empires. At the core of these conflicts lies the struggle over the status of territorial units, which formerly belonged to federal states. Thus, the label of 'status conflict' is probably more adequate than the label of 'ethno-political conflict'. Status conflicts arise when the main objective of one conflict group is to unilaterally upgrade the status of its territory or its administrative unit or when an existing status is downgraded by the central power. The objective can be to form an autonomous unit within the host state, to form an independent, sovereign state, or to join a neighbouring state.

The fault line of all hot conflicts in the two regions can be traced back to the system of ethno-federalism of the USSR and Yugoslavia: both the USSR and Yugoslavia were asymmetric federations – that is, they consisted of territorial units with different status. On the first level, there were, in the case of the USSR, fifteen federal republics, while Yugoslavia consisted of six federal republics. First-order units were, according to the Soviet constitution, sovereign states and possessed all institutional prerequisites for statehood. They had political institutions, political symbols, a constitution, borders and a titular nation. *De jure* they even had the right to have their own armed forces. Within these first-order units, there were units of the second order, which were subordinated to the first-order units. While these second-order units enjoyed lesser privileges than the first-order units, they nevertheless possessed similar institutional prerequisites for statehood. Overall, there are eleven second-order units in the Caucasus.[2] Three of them (Abkhazia, Adjaria and South-Ossetia) were autonomous republics within Soviet Georgia; Nagorno-Karabakh was a second-order unit within Soviet Azerbaijan. Seven second-order units are within the Russian Federation. These are Chechnya, Adygeya, Dagestan, Ingushetia, Kabardino-Balkaria, Karachaevo-Cherkesia and North-Ossetia.

Yugoslavia had only two second-order administrative units, Kosovo and Voivodina, both within Serbia. In 1989, Milosevic removed the autonomous status of both units, a move which created a dramatic backlash in Kosovo, leading to the establishment of a parallel shadow administration and aggravated the Kosovo-Albanians' quest for more autonomy or even independence. After the implosion of the USSR and Yugoslavia, the first-order subjects of the federations became independent and were quickly recognised by the international community. Thus, Georgia, Armenia and Azerbaijan of the former USSR, and Serbia, Bosnia-Herzegovina, Croatia, Slovenia, Montenegro and Macedonia of Yugoslavia became newly independent states. (Serbia and Montenegro together form the successor state of Yugoslavia) (Table 1).

The sovereignty and territorial integrity of these newly independent states was from the beginning challenged by the secessionist ambitions of the second-order units, the former Autonomous Republics. Thus, Russia was confronted with breakaway Chechnya, Georgia with breakaway Abkhazia and South-Ossetia, Azerbaijan with breakaway Nagorno-Karabakh and Serbia with breakaway Kosovo. In all these cases, the administrative borders of the USSR and of the Yugoslav Federation provided the template for the secessionist movements, while the bureaucracies of the second-order units provided the organisational resources for the secessionist movements. Only the armed secessionist movements in Croatia (the Serbs of the Krajina) and in Bosnia-Herzegovina (the

Table 1 *Administrative units in the Caucasus and former Yugoslavia, selected (ethnic, religious and titular) identity groups*[a]

Administrative unit / republic	Population	Titular identity group	(%)	Largest other identity groups	(%)
North Caucasus					
Chechnya[b] (Russian Federation)	836,000	Chechen	(73)	Russian	(27)
Dagestan (Russian Federation)	1,802,188	None		Avar	(28)
				Dargin	(16)
				Kumyk	(13)
				Russian	(09)
				Lezgin	(11)
				Tabasaran	(04)
				Nogay	(02)
				Rutul	(01)
				Aghul	(01)
South Caucasus					
Abkhazia (Georgia)	525,061	Abkhaz[c]	(18)	Georgian	(46)
				Armenian	(14)
				Russian	(13)
Adjaria[d] (Georgia)	392,432	Adjarian	(63)	Georgian (non-Muslim)	(23)
				Russian	(08)
				Armenian	(04)
South-Ossetia (Georgia)	98,527	Ossetian	(66)	Georgian	(29)
				Russian	(02)
Nagorno-Karabakh (Azerbaijan)	189,085	None		Armenian	(77)
				Azeri	(22)
Former Yugoslavia[e]					
Bosnia-Herzegovina	4,359,895	None		Muslim	(44)
				Serb	(31)
				Croat	(17)
				Yugoslav	(05)
Croatia	4,784,265	Croat	(78)	Serb	(12)
				Yugoslav	(02)
Macedonia	2,159,503	Macedonian	(65)	Albanian	(22)
				Turkish	(04)
				Roma	(03)
				Serb	(02)
				Other	(04)
Serbia and Montenegro (Yugoslavia)[f]	11,101,833	Serb	(63)	Albanian	(14)
		Montenegrins	(06)	Hungarian	(04)
				Other	(13)

Table 1 continued

Administrative unit / republic	Population	Titular identity group	(%)	Largest other identity groups	(%)
Slovenia	1,965,116	Slovenian	(91)	Croat	(03)
				Serb	(02)
Kosovo[g]	1,974,747	None		Albanian	(82)
				Serb	(10)
				Muslims	(03)
				Roma	(02)
				Montenegrin	(01)

Notes

[a] The figures are, unless otherwise indicated, from the census of 1989 (Goskomstat 1991). They do not reflect the considerable migration flows, particular in Chechnya (Russians, leaving for Russia, Chechen refugees to Ingushetia or Russia), Abkhazia (Georgians, fleeing or forced to leave) and South-Ossetia (refugees, mainly leaving for North-Ossetia).

[b] Exact figures are available only for the Chechen-Ingushetian Republic, which split into two republics in 1992. Figures are based on the authors' estimates.

[c] Other sources give 8 per cent (Pirtskhalava 1997). Evidently, the percentage of the Abkhaz population is highly politicised.

[d] The data on Adjaria is not very reliable; Adjarians were counted as Georgians (324,813 – 83 per cent of the overall population), as they are distinguished by religion which was not adequately reflected in the census. The approximate number of Adjarians, according to estimates, is around 250,000. With thanks to Gia Tarkhan-Mouravi for sharing this information with the authors.

[e] Figures refer to the census of 1991. Unless otherwise indicated, the data is taken from Heller (1997).

[f] Data is from Gosztonyi 1998.

[g] Figures for 1991 are based on estimates of natural population growth and migration since the census of 1981 conducted by the Federal Institute for Statistics of Yugoslavia (quoted in Judah 2000: 313).

Croats and the Serbs) did not follow the template of the administrative borders, but rather the patterns of ethnic settlements and ethnic geography.

Notably, there has been no 'classical' inter-state war, with the possible exception of the short campaign of the Yugoslav Army against Slovenia. The form of violence witnessed in the Caucasus and in Former Yugoslavia has typically not been organised and executed by state armies, and the violence has typically been confined within the borders of the state or polity where it has its roots. Although some of the neighbouring states assigned considerable resources to the support of their secessionist ethnic brethren (Serbia supported the Serbs in the Krajina, and later in Bosnia; Bosnian Croats were supported by Croatia; Armenia supported Nagorno-Karabakh Armenians), all avoided straight, official intervention, thus avoiding outright escalation on the one hand and stigmatisation by the international community on the other hand (Gosztonyi 1998).

Violence is organised either between the state and an identity group, or between two identity groups rather than between states. However, with regard to the Caucasus and Yugoslavia during the first years after the end of the empires, the notion of 'state' is misleading. The successor states of the USSR and Yugoslavia often had to organise their state capacities from scratch. The violent contest between 'secessionist rebels' and 'states' thus resembles, especially in the Caucasus, the competition between two upstarts competing for the same market. With the wars of Azerbaijan against the breakaway Nagorno-Karabakh and Georgia against the breakaway Abkhazia and South-Ossetia, the 'rebel upstarts' proved to be much more efficient in organising violence than the 'upstart states' they challenged. Consequently, the 'rebels' won on the battlefield.

In all conflicts, the borders between privately organised, entrepreneurial violence and publicly organised, state-sponsored violence were somewhat permeable. The armed conflicts in the Caucasus and in Yugoslavia may have been fought in the name of the state and of ethnicised groups, but the fighters were more often than not private entrepreneurs. In all cases not only state actors were involved in the organisation of violence, but also a myriad of non-state actors, like paramilitaries, warlords, criminal gang leaders, militias and self-defence units, and the distinction between state actors and non-state actors was blurred. Grandits and Leutloff's account of organised violence in the Krajina, Mappes-Niediek's of Kosovo, Koehler and Zürcher's of Nagorno-Karabakh and Baev's of the internal war in Georgia underline this point.

Christophe in her Chapter 10 in this volume shows that the key actors in the ethno-political conflicts in post-Soviet Caucasus are not ethnic groups, but instead patrimonial networks with particular interests. These networks are in turn an institutional legacy of the 'socialist production state'. This socialist mode of production required the total penetration of society by the state. As a result the Soviet state constantly overstretched its capacities. In order to compensate for the resulting institutional weakness, the state vested power in personal networks rather than institutions. Patron–client networks were used as a means of governance. After the collapse in 1991, these networks filled the institutional vacuum – patrimonial networks, using symbols and discourses of ethnicity, took over what was left of the state. This, however, must be seen as a sign of weakness rather than a sign of strength of nationalism: nationalism proved to be too weak to overcome the patrimonial networks dominating society and regulating conflicts over the distribution of resources. In this sense the weakness, not the strength of Transcaucasian nationalism proved to be harmful. Nationalism can be crucial in overcoming informal practices and ousting patrimonial networks, as was the case in the Baltic States. As a rule in the Transcaucasus, it merely served as an additional resource for patrimonial, private networks.

The exception, as argued by Koehler and Zürcher's Chapter 8 in this volume, is the period of Armenian 'war-nationalism'. For the period of perceived existential crisis, otherwise competing patrimonial networks were temporarily integrated, an integration facilitated by the imitation of core functions of statehood through nationalist mobilisation.

Organisers of violence may develop a vested interest in the sustainability of organised violence for economic motives. Conflicts which started as struggles for ideological–political goals may then turn into 'markets of violence', a term used by Georg Elwert's Chapter 12 in this volume to describe a situation where violence becomes a means for profit making and warlords become entrepreneurs of violence. Elwert argues that violence requires logistics and logistics requires investments: one can steal weapons but one still needs to buy fuel. In environments where violence is profitable the invisible hand of the market rewards those who economically organise violence; this means that entrepreneurs in markets of violence must trade in goods with a very high value per weight, such as drugs, gold, diamonds or weapons; they must recruit a cheap 'labour-force' (fighters) through the spreading of fear and the destruction of alternative labour ('burn the crops and blame the enemy'); and they must tap humanitarian aid to sustain the market of violence. By understanding the economic rationale of markets of violence, conclusions can be drawn about how to stop violence: raising the costs of violence can be achieved by closing the borders for supply, denying access to financial markets and eventually establishing a monopoly of violence by external powers.

Raufer's Chapter 3 in this volume also stresses the importance of what he calls an often-overlooked aspect of the Kosovo war, namely the symbiosis of political and private violence, the latter being interested only in economic profit. His chapter focuses exclusively on Albanian organised crime and omits the political context of the Kosovo conflict. This view from a criminologist reminds scholars of organised violence that the linkages between political violence and organised crime deserve more systematic research.

Yugoslavia and the Caucasus are 'conflict regions' that are characterised by a remarkably similar environment. First, when the central states collapsed in 1989 (Yugoslavia), and 1991 (USSR), respectively, both regions fell victim to the most dramatic mode of state weakness – state collapse. State weakness breeds uncertainty and fear and opens windows of opportunity for political entrepreneurs, all of which increase the risk of violent conflicts.

Secondly – banal but highly important – both regions were flooded with cheap weapons after the collapse of empires. Each successor state of the two empires received its share of weapons, and rebel upstarts simply stole or bought weapons from the crumbling central armies.

Thirdly, both regions score relatively high on risk-increasing factors, such as history of mutual grievances, rough terrain and complex, intermingled patterns of ethnic settlement. These are the factors, among others, that the literature has identified as having a negative impact on prospects for ethno-political stability.[3]

8

Fourthly, there is the institutional legacy of the Socialist system. The most important of the bits of imperial wreckage that continue to shape events is the socialist system of ethno-federalism. As a peculiarity of Soviet and Yugoslav federalism, all first-order units (the fifteen federal republics in the USSR and the six federal republics of Yugoslavia) and some of the second-order units (autonomous republics within federal republics) were ethnically defined. Although Yugoslav federalism was originally very much a copy of the Soviet system, there were some differences. The USSR was *de facto* and *de jure* more centralised than Yugoslavia. A Yugoslav Federal Republic enjoyed more privileges than a Soviet Republic did. On the other hand, in the USSR there was an informal system of quotas that assigned a more than proportional share of key posts within the republic to members of the titular nation. This was not applied in Yugoslavia. The relatively high percentage of Serbs in key position within Kosovo (10 per cent Serbian population) and Croatia (17 per cent Serbian population) was indeed an issue of complaint for Kosovo-Albanians and Croats.

The most important aspect of this system of ethno-federalism was, however, that in both Federations, the federal units each had their titular nation; ethnicity thus became 'territorialised'. After the breakdown of the federal states, this linkage of a territory to an ethnic group provided an excellent breeding ground for a wave of secessionism, since the socialist ethno-federalism had provided the titular nations with a clear-cut territory, a state bureaucracy, mass media, an education system and national symbols. These were assets that considerably reduced the cost of secessionism. Giordano reminds us in his Chapter 4 in this volume that the territorialisation of ethnicity is not only the legacy of socialist federalism but started earlier with land reforms motivated by emerging nationalist political elites in the Balkan region.

All four factors – state weakness, cheap and readily available weapons, the presence of risk-increasing factors and the legacy of the socialist ethno-federalism – help explain the emergence of organised violence. And since all factors are common to both regions, the comparability of the case studies presented here is increased.

The rich empirical material that these regions have produced can be structured in different ways. First, in both regions, hot conflicts have emerged on the ruins of collapsed ethno-territorial, socialist federations. By comparing Yugoslavia and the Caucasus as macro-regions and highlighting the similarities, we are able to highlight the risk potential of the socialist legacy, most notably, of the system of ethno-federalism.

A second comparison could be designed for addressing the different processes of conflict escalation in these two regions: organised violence in Yugoslavia proved to be more intense and more contagious than in the Caucasus. Organised violence in Yugoslavia has torn a country to pieces – Bosnia-Herzegovina – and only international intervention has put it back together again, albeit in a rough and ready way. Violence in Yugoslavia has been organised on a larger scale and, as inappropriate this may sound with regard to individual suffering, in all of these wars, has led to even worse atrocities than in the Caucasus. Comparing the Caucasus with Yugoslavia may help to find an answer to the question of why the Caucasus has so far avoided following the worst-case scenario. Two factors are apparent which help explain the different outcomes.

The first factor pertains to the way the federal centres reacted to the secessionist ambitions of the subjects of the Federations. In Yugoslavia during the 1980s, the most powerful of the Republics, Serbia, tried to usurp the position of the dwindling federal Yugoslav centre. This alienated the other republics, which feared Serbian hegemony. Thus they intensified their struggle for secession, while the Serbian-dominated centre tried to hold the federation together by force. When this became apparently impossible, Milosevic tried to secure a 'greater Serbia' – at the expense of the territorial integrity of Croatia and later Bosnia-Herzegovina.

By contrast, in the USSR, the most powerful of the Republics, Russia, opposed the Soviet centre. It was mainly the democratic movement in the Russian republic that prevented the centre from holding the Union together by force. Russia was, until 1991, the natural ally of the secessionist Union Republics. The Russian Republic under Yeltsin thus checked the hegemonic aspirations of the Soviet centre, which explains the relative ease with which the centre let the republics go during 1990–91.

Secondly, size matters. After the demise of the USSR, Russia became by far the most powerful of the successor states. Russia still had, despite the period of dramatic state weakness after 1991, the means to protect the vital interests of the state, to protect Russian minorities living outside Russia and to scare off challengers. Russia thus, by and large, avoided ethno-political violence within its territory and refrained from large-scale interventions outside its territory. The bloody war in Chechnya is the exception. In Yugoslavia, Serbia and Croatia emerged as two states with relatively similar capacities. Therefore, neither had the means to scare off the other or decisively win. The results were the bloody wars in Croatia and Bosnia.

The chapters in this volume are, however, mainly concerned with the third aspect, namely with the micro-politics of organised violence. Most chapters in this volume deal with the question of how conflict potential was either defused or transferred into organised violence, taking into account the relatively similar environment of Yugoslavia and the Caucasus. If there is a common question in all of the case studies, it is the question of which institutions provided incentives for the organisation of violence, and which institutions, on the contrary, discouraged the organisation of violence. The task that the contributors to this volume have taken up in empirical case studies is to identify those particular institutional frameworks that have blocked or promoted organised violence. The findings of the case studies (a synopsis of which is presented in Chapter 13) should therefore be of interest to both area specialists and scholars of conflict and peace.

Explaining violence: institutions at work

Violence, although here by no means the 'black hole' of irrationality and atavism as often portrayed, nevertheless retains a great deal of contingency. In almost every social situation, violence can be one of the strategies that actors chose in order to obtain their goals. Violence is a socially ubiquitous phenomenon, and therefore there are an unlimited number of possible factors and combinations of factors that can trigger violence. The understanding of violence by the social sciences is also seriously hampered by the fact that there are only few empirical studies on the processes of violence available; such empirical expertise seems to be, however, of special importance, since violence is a phenomenon of human interaction in which discourse and action may radically differ – the narratives on the phenomenon may conceal rather than describe the process itself.[4] This point is demonstrated by Kisriev in Chapter 6 in this volume; according to his assessment of the post-Soviet power games in Dagestan the public ethno-nationalist discourse 'does not reveal but hides the structures of power'. The same point is stressed by Koehler and Zürcher in their account in Chapter 8 of the war in Nagorno-Karabakh.

In their search for explanations of violence, many scholars focus on factors which increase the risk of violence. Among the most often quoted are such factors as cultural differences; a history of mutual grievances and ancient hatreds; group cohesion and the strength of group identity; patterns of settlement and ethnic demography; defendable borders and rough terrain; the degree of state violence and group discrimination; external support and access to weapons. While it is certainly not denied that these factors can and do increase the risk of organised violence (and many chapters in this volume illustrate the importance of some of these factors) the listing of such factors is considered to be of only limited explanatory value.[5]

Organised stability and organised violence are always multi-factoral phenomena, and it may be very difficult to isolate the right factor or the right combination of factors that have actually triggered violence. Therefore, the question of 'what causes violence' may be of less heuristic value than 'how and when violence is organised'.

For organised violence to emerge, it takes certain social situations in which actors think that the relative costs of violence are smaller than the relative costs of non-violence. There may be a myriad of such situations, each requiring a tailored approach, but they all boil down to two words: fear and opportunity.

Fear and opportunity are likely to emerge when trained and institutionalised patterns of interactions between groups are subject to rapid change, and when the perpetuation of these patterns seems endangered or unlikely. In an ideal world, the ideal state provides institutions that guarantee inter-group stability. The state provides mediating structures between groups, checks aggressive claims and protects weaker groups. State institutions regulate access to resources and to political power. The state guarantees a continuous information flow between groups by providing impartial media[6] and, lastly, the state defends its monopoly over violence.

The disintegration of the state structures that had, for seventy and fifty years, respectively, provided inter-ethnic accommodation is the key to the explanation of organised violence in Yugoslavia and in the Caucasus. It was the state collapse that has pushed the societies of these two regions into a state of fear and uncertainty and has opened up windows of opportunity for political entrepreneurs. State weakness, and its most extreme manifestation, state collapse, has been acknowledged by many authors as the key variable for explaining conflict.[7] Michael Ignatieff summarises the causal chain thus:

> Note here the causative order: first the collapse of the overarching state, then Hobbesian fear, and only then nationalist paranoia, followed by warfare. Disintegration of the state comes first, nationalist paranoia comes next. Nationalist sentiment on the ground, among common people, is a secondary consequence of political disintegration, a response to the collapse of state order and the inter-ethnic accommodation that made it possible. Nationalism creates communities of fear, groups held together by the conviction that their security depends on sticking together. People become 'nationalistic' when they are afraid; when the only answer to the question 'Who will protect me now?' becomes 'my own people'. (Ignatieff 1998: 45)

Fear and opportunity, the two inevitable companions of state weakness, often trigger violence. State weakness opens up large windows of opportunity for political entrepreneurs. It is precisely through these windows that ethnic entrepreneurs enter the political scene. State weakness, or state collapse, unblocks access to resources and power: established institutions that have regulated access to and distribution of resources crumble or collapse, and new ones have yet to be designed. Elites thus inevitably engage in a competition, which is no longer framed by existing, accepted institutions. A key resource in power struggles can be ethnicity. Political entrepreneurs thus often turn into ethnic entrepreneurs – they appeal to real or perceived threats and injustices in order to mobilise support, that is, they instrumentalise ethnicity and fear. Instrumentalism explains ethno-political conflict by the political ambitions of ethnic entrepreneurs.[8] Ethnification of politics is thus a result of a strategic decision of elites in search of a new power base or a new legitimisation. Successful ethnic entrepreneurs often portray themselves as the best safeguard against an aggressive, threatening 'Other' while at the same time making sure to establish the means of internal coercion to punish those that do not perceive the imminent danger to the collective and the necessity of action (something which results in acts of violence frequently blamed on the enemy). Not every social situation favours the entry of ethnic entrepreneurs into the political scene. Ethnic entrepreneurs often take centre stage only when state weakness and fears of coming anarchy lead people to believe that the only viable answer to the question 'who will protect me' becomes 'my ethnic kin'. A breeding ground for ethnic entrepreneurs is the situation when an ethnic group starts to think that their mistrust of the other group is justified, the warnings of their leaders thus correct. When the group believes that its fears of the other group are rational and well founded, it tends to enhance its support for radical leaders. This 'rationality of fear' (de Figueiredo and Weingast 1999) can quickly spiral into ethnic violence, as it has in numerous cases in Yugoslavia and in the Caucasus.

A detailed account of the rationality of fear is provided in Grandits and Leutloff's Chapter 1 in this volume. Their chapter examines the role of discourses of violence and threat and the exploitation of 'violent events' for conflict escalation. After 1990, Serbs and Croats were competing over access to the resources needed for institution building and state building. Fear proved to be the key resource. Fear in turn triggered ethnic mobilisation. Within a year, an 'unprofessional' riot of Serbs in the Krajina region developed into a professional war between Serbs and Croats in Croatia, in which several thousand died and several hundred thousand people were forcefully expelled from their homes. The authors stress the relevance of institution building and the role of changing perceptions in the process of escalation.

The instrumentalist approach is obviously highly plausible, and it is hard to think of an ethno-political conflict where ethnic entrepreneurs did not play a crucial role. The list of Yugoslav and Caucasian ethnic entrepreneurs is long and prominent: Milosevic in Serbia, Tudjman in Croatia, Elchibey in Azerbaijan, Dudaev in Chechnya, Ardzinba in Abkhazia and Gamsakhurdia in Georgia. They have all pursued politics of ethnification and used a rhetoric which centred on the rights of their ethnic group to sovereignty, on the threats that the group faced from other groups and on the undivided loyalty that the group was entitled to receive from individual members.

There are other perils in state weakness. When state institutions fail, private organisers of violence get more leverage. They develop private interests and acquire the means to pursue their interests. The official leaders of the state may no longer be able to control them, even if they wished to. Thus, even if leaders commit themselves to peace, they are no longer able to deliver, a dilemma demonstrated in Koehler and Zürcher's analysis in Chapter 8 in this volume of drawbacks in the Nagorno-Karabakh peace process. Such situations are referred to as 'commitment problems' (Fearon 1998; Walter 1999). In such a situation, leaders might prefer a preventive strike to a shaky settlement which, they think, cannot hold. Again, the wars in Nagorno-Karabakh, Bosnia and Croatia provide insights into the mechanism of the commitment problem.

Meaningful conflict resolution must take steps towards minimising the commitment problem. However, in his intriguing Chapter 2 in this volume, Gosztonyi describes how well intended 'soft interventions' by the international community sometimes have the opposite effect. The end of the Cold War, he argues, saw the emergence of a new, 'soft' type of intervention, based on democratic principles and an aversion to overt engagement. Under certain circumstances, 'soft' intervention seems to effect a decentralisation of power and responsibility rather than its centralisation. Herceg-Bosna is such a case. External 'soft' intervention contributes to a diffusion of power, when four conditions are met: the external intervention is relatively restrained; the interveners target pre-existing political structures instead of appointing new ones; there is a willingness on the side of the interveners to hold the representatives of the local political structures responsible for certain policy failures and human rights abuses; and there is a strong common sentiment among the recipients of the foreign intervention that the aims of the intervention are not just. These conditions, in turn, create an incentive structure, which make it rational for local elites to appoint weak leaders and to create an institutional 'jungle' in order to diffuse responsibility. In time, the local elite loses the ability to commit themselves and to deliver – both preconditions for instability.

Institutions and the potential of disorder

Taking into account general risk factors, the institutional legacy of socialist ethno-federalism and state weakness causing fear and opportunity go a long way towards explaining organised violence. However, questions remain. Most important (in the sense of it being heuristically the most rewarding to ask) is probably the search for factors explaining the variation.

Why do some potential conflicts not erupt into violence, even if the underlying structures and proximate causes are remarkably similar to cases where violence has erupted? What are the factors that block ethnic mobilisation? What does it take to remove the market for ethnic entrepreneurs? Why do some multi-ethnic societies fragment, but others hold together, while both have to deal with state weakness, fear and opportunity? Under what conditions can ethnic entrepreneurs conquer the state? And under what conditions can they consolidate it?

Answers have been sought in the institutional framework of the post-socialist societies of the Caucasus and of Yugoslavia. We assume that stability and violent conflicts in inter-group relations are social outcomes that have been produced by the combined effect of many institutions, state or non-state, formal or informal, self-enforcing or externally enforced.

Institutions are, according to the classical definition of Douglass North, 'the rules of the game in a society or, more formally, are the humanely devised

14

constraints that shape human interaction' (North 1990: 6). Institutions are trained patterns of human interaction, which are codified in contracts and rules, or which root in shared norms, values and codes of behaviour. Because institutions are trained, repeated and 'sticky' patterns of interaction, they stabilise social expectations and help reduce transaction costs. By focusing on the existing institutional framework, actors are placed in the context that structures their actions. Thus, the 'pathological social systems' (Lake and Rothchild 1998: 6–7) that make violence both probable and individually rational become the central unit of analysis.

Institutions perform three functions which are relevant for the organisation of stability/violence.

First, institutions are accepted, trained and sometimes enforced patterns of interaction, which can frame conflicts. Conflict potentials can thus be defused. The breakdown of such a framework may enable the risk factors to 'go active'. As a rule all societies have institutions in place that specialise in conflicts in a way that contains violent dispute by fostering compromises in favour of alternative conflicts (Hirschman 1994). On a smaller social scale or in remote stateless societies cross-cutting networks of loyalty and services of institutionalised mediators or councils of elders may sufficiently provide for this. In complex societies these institutions provide for (due) procedures in the classic understanding of Luhmann: they exclude the actual power of the antagonists and channel the decision power over the conflict to a third party, implement a set of rules independent from everyday-life reality and guarantee a meaningful and applied result (Luhmann 1983: 38–53, 100–106).

Secondly, the institutional framework provides the incentive structure for local actors and thus determines their strategic action. Institutions can thus not only diffuse violence, but they can also produce violence, if the incentive structure is 'badly' designed.

Thirdly, institutions have distributional effects. They determine the access to resources crucial for organising violence and determine the relative position of actors.

All three functions of institutions are of consequence in the probability of organised violence emerging.

Institutions matter. The institutional arrangement of a society produces incentive structures for actors, defines the windows of opportunity for political entrepreneurs and establishes the constraints in which actors are locked. Challenging widespread state-centric approaches, it is argued here that the institutional framework consists not only of the institutional legacy of the 'official' state institutions of the socialist systems, but also of the 'shadow' institutions that have emerged as a response to the organisational deficits of socialism. Attention should also be paid to locally rooted norms and conventions that have survived in niches not occupied by the socialist state. These three analytically distinct sets of institutions form together a hybrid, eclectic, locally distinct framework, which structures actors' incentives, opportunities and constraints.

'Official' institutions

Official institutions are understood to be the legacy of the socialist systems. The relevancy of socialist ethno-federalism has already been underlined. It has left behind territories, equipped with titular nations, territorial bureaucracies, territorial media, proto-democratic institutions, such as parliaments (soviets), and an ethno-territorial elite that was ready to take over this legacy. In the case of Yugoslavia and the USSR, these borders thus formed a template for status conflicts. Other residues of empire are not territorial, but functional (Rubin and Snyder 1998: 6). These include military organisations, economic networks of supply and production, networks of party or business nomenclature or parts of bureaucracies that have survived the collapse. Some of them have adapted to post-imperial circumstances. They became the new locus of power and formed the functional backbone of the newly assembled polities. The rise of Milosevic, for example, can be understood only by taking into account his taking over and skilful manipulation of the Serbian Communist Party. Most of the authors in this collection stress the importance of surviving socialist institutions. But while Milosevic's takeover of the Party structure led to escalation, there are also cases when the takeover of post-socialist institutions, on the contrary, led to stabilisation. Kisriev on Dagestan and Koehler and Zürcher on Nagorno-Karabakh (Chapters 6 and 8 in this volume) show that the 'old' Soviet institutions, and primarily the rubber-stamp parliaments, were vital for the reconstruction of statehood, once they were allocated real power.

Another often-overlooked official institution is property rights. Giordano in his Chapter 4 deals with the link between nationalism, agrarian policy and property rights on land. Laws on land were and still are often used as a strategy for cultural homogenisation and 'purification'. Emerging nation states claim the management of property rights on land and often use it to change ethnic composition. Giordano compares over time and across borders the link between land reform and nationalism in south-eastern Europe in 1900, between the two world wars and after 1989.

'Unofficial' institutions

Here, 'unofficial' (or shadow) institutions are those which were not part of the socialist state design, but which emerged as a reaction to the organisational voids in the system. Institutions that survived the socialist modernisation also belong in this category.

These unofficial institutions went largely undetected by political science and 'sovietology', which focused mainly on 'official' state institutions, but they proved to have a significant impact on the way polities reassembled after the implosion of the central state. A typical example of a shadow institution is the endemic second economy and the highly sophisticated administrative corruption, both of which are common features of post-socialist societies (Kordonskii 1995).[9] Another widespread unofficial institution of socialist systems, which has retained its importance and functionality beyond the collapse, is the networks of patronage (Willerton 1992). In areas where the state lacked the resources to penetrate the periphery with bureaucratic institutions, it had to rely on personal networks for governance and control. After the collapse of the central state, networks of patronage became, in many places, the most cohesive institutional structure, substituting state tasks and concentrating political power and economic resources.

Other unofficial institutions are based on local know-how and local traditions, which retained their functionality during and after the socialist period. For many Caucasian and Balkan societies networks of trust based on a notion of extended kin groups are important structuring elements.[10] Political power is vested, to a large extent, in these structures, a fact that could be easily overlooked, since many powerful clans occupied important positions in the socialist hierarchies. This does not mean, however, that the 'modern' bureaucratic state system has replaced a 'traditional' clan system. Instead there was a parasitic exploitation of the bureaucratic hierarchies by the clan system (cf. Willerton 1992: 191–222).

In large parts of the Caucasus and the Balkans, specific forms of local regulation of justice, solidarity and conflict regulation exist, which do not depend on a modern state bureaucracy, even though they might depend on it in their functionality to regulate conflict on the monopoly of violence of the state. Codified traditional value systems (e.g. *adat* – the 'law of the mountains' in many remote parts of the Caucasus) existed together with the Soviet, and later, Russian legal systems.[11] Detecting and describing such local institutions is crucial for understanding post-socialist spaces – from the Balkans to Central Asia, the Caucasus and the multi-ethnic provinces of China. It is precisely this hybrid, eclectic combination of official and unofficial institutions that forms the institutional framework which governs post-socialist, and in fact most political spaces after modernity. Today it is obvious that socialist self-perception and western analysis both dramatically underestimated the residual power of 'the local'. A better understanding of this simultaneous functioning of different codes and value systems is by no means only of 'folkloristic' value, but helps to understand the capacity of a society to deal with conflicts and state building.

Kisriev's Chapter 6 in this volume on Dagestan offers a stunning demonstration of this. Dagestan is notable for its ethnic diversity and, even by post-Soviet standards, its dramatic economic deprivation. Dagestan's ethno-political stability against all odds is something that needs to be explained. Kisriev argues that Dagestani society has avoided the pitfall of ethnic unrest owing to a functional integration of official and unofficial institutions. In a spontaneous and highly political balancing act the political elite has successfully institutionalised mechanisms of restraint, cooperation and power sharing. These institutions draw heavily on traditional, trained societal mechanisms of conflict mediating and inter-group cooperation. Of crucial importance in overcoming the dangers of an ethnic security dilemma proved to be the traditional *dzhamaat*, a cross-cutting, non-ethnically defined village community.

Another view on the perspectives for stability is offered by Vasilieva's Chapter 9 in this volume. She analyses the integrative potential of cooperative movements at the republican, the regional and the inter-state level for the Caucasus. A major finding of the analysis is that cooperative movements had the strongest impact on the republican level, while they remained marginal at the regional and inter-state level. Within republics, cooperative movements were effective only when they became institutionalised procedures of power sharing within parliament or alternative bodies with legislative power.

If the local know-how of building cooperatives as networks of solidarity fails to integrate with official institutions it may instead be disruptive, as shown in Grandits and Leutloff's and Mappes-Niedieck's Chapters 1 and 5 on Kosovo and Christophe's Chapter 10 on Georgia in this volume.

Elwert's Chapter 12 offers insights into the economics of ending violence. He argues that violence can be ended by raising the costs of violence. This can be achieved by closing the borders for supply, denying 'rebels' access to financial markets and eventually by external powers establishing a monopoly of violence.

Finally, Borneman's Chapter 11 addresses the question of reconciliation after ethnic cleansing. Reconciliation is seen here as a project of departure from violence by breaking the vicious circle linking the present to the pains of the past. Common futile strategies for survivors include the perpetuation of violence by revenge and/or the group's engagement in a further purification of its principles – usually connected with nostalgia for autochthony, obsession with origins and clear demarcation of itself from other groups. Such a turn inward, an inner purification, not only appears to complete, in a putatively voluntaristic spirit, the ethnic cleansing initially perpetrated on the group, but it also institutionalises a further 'cleansing' of the group by enforcing endogamy on its members. Reconciliation, says Borneman, is an inter-subjective process, an agreement to settle accounts that involves at least two subjects who are related in time. They are related in a temporal sense not in that they necessarily have a shared past or a shared future. Consensus about what was shared in the past or what will be shared in the future – in modern parlance, a 'collective memory' – is not necessary for reconciliation, and its expectation may in fact awaken counterproductive drives to recover a lost whole or to produce a harmonious community. Instead, in order to reconcile, different subjects must agree only to share a present, a present that is non-repetitive. Politics of intersubjectivity may be reached through the retribution of justice in judicial processes holding perpetrators publicly accountable for their deeds.

The case studies presented here reinforce the argument that focusing on the micro-politics of conflict and examining social institutions on the ground is essential for the analyses of conflict. Generally speaking, the search for rules governing social processes is complicated by two factors when dealing with collective violent conflict: (1) the widening divide between the rationale of action and the normative narratives assigning sense to deed *ex post* and (2) the increasing relevance of informal institutions.

'This is not about religion', Barnett R. Rubin is quoted as saying about the building of a post-Taliban order in Afghanistan. 'It's about a fight for the post-colonial state system' (Eurasia Insight 2001). Aside from the grand tale of good and evil, war always involves institutionalised interests not directly connected to or coinciding with the normative story.

Also for the post-socialist conflicts dealt with in this book the differentiation between the normative framing of the conflict and the rules guiding the incentives of relevant actors is essential. The normative framing of a conflict by the parties and other interested observers is by no means just a fancy, an irrational story of good and evil told by otherwise rational war-mongers in order to appease their children and rid themselves of bad dreams. Making sense of violence (perpetrated or endured) is but one crucial function of normative frameworking and has strong implications for the chances of post-violence rapprochement and healing. However, of much more immediate practical influence for the organisation and channelling of violence is the mobilising power of the normative story. In terms of mobilising young people to fight, kill and die it may come second only to the organisation of fear.

Despite the intimate interrelation between the normative and the practical levels in the organisation of violent conflict, the differentiation between them is crucial for our understanding of conflict as a dynamic process; this differentiation is of particular importance when the rules set by the normative story are not in tune with the incentives governing the practical level and may lead to the failure of the overall operation (as in the abortive attempts to kick-start independent statehood on a nationalist grand scale in Georgia and Azerbaijan as referred to in Christophe's Chapter 10 and Koehler and Zürcher's Chapter 8 in this volume). In order to come to terms with state weakness leading to violent conflict or resulting from sustained conflict, analysing the dysfunctions of the official institutions is insufficient. The ability of society to penetrate, exploit or replace weak or even defunct official institutions with informal rules, drawing on local social or cultural know-how is of decisive importance in grasping patterns of difference and similarity in post-socialist development. The post-colonial (here: post-socialist) state system referred to above by Rubin is emerging from the hybrids of the official rump institutions of the state and informal networks of trust, capable of negotiating power and resources along channels considered criminal in any functioning state.

Detecting potentials of disorder requires therefore that both official *and* unofficial institutions are addressed in order to identify the real incentive structures of local actors. Actors in conflicts usually veil their real incentives behind a discourse of seeming – but false – clarity. Particularly in situations of insecurity and potential violence, political protagonists put great effort into establishing discourses of 'unambiguity' and creating a façade of clear codes for defining friend and foe, truth and justice. This discourse veils the typical post-socialist condition of hybrid institutions. It also veils the fact that key players are most successful when they command various social languages and can thus exploit different institutional settings – official, unofficial or even international. Both the official and informal levels have – when institutionalised and not contingent – their own normative discourses and logic of action. These discourses may compete with each other, or may be compatible. In any case all four levels of 'the rules of the game'– the official and the unofficial normative discourses and the official and the unofficial practice – have to be addressed in order to gain a thorough understanding of the potentials of order and disorder in weak states. The editors hope that this volume presents a fruitful first attempt.

NOTES

1   The term 'Bosniak' denotes the Muslim population of Bosnia, whereas Bosnian refers to the citizens of Bosnia-Herzegovina.
2   Here autonomous republics (ASSR) and autonomous *oblasts* (AO) are both treated as second-order units.
3   For useful overviews of factors which can increase the risk for ethno-political violence, see van Evera (1994); Gurr and Harff (1995); Brown (1997).
4   A series of papers addressing this issue is published in Elwert, Feuchtwang and Neubert (1999).
5   For a criticism of what he calls 'mainstream' research on violence from a sociological viewpoint, see von Trotha (1997). Trutz von Trotha argues that a sociology of the causes of violence is not the same as a sociology of violence itself and presses for a paradigmatic change in the research on violence, replacing the etiological 'why?' with the phenomenological 'how?' For a discussion of the problems both 'new' and 'mainstream' research on violence pose for the empirical work of social science, see Koehler (1998).
6   Exchange of information between groups is crucial. Once an information failure emerges, groups are no longer able to judge the intentions and the real capabilities of the other group. They might miscalculate the costs of a preventive strike, be it predatory or strictly defensive, and engage in organised violence. See Lake and Rothchild (1998).
7   On the importance of state weakness for explaining ethno-political conflict, see Fearon and Laitin (1996); Brown (1997: 5).
8   For empirical evidence see Rothchild (1986); Gagnon (1994); Brass (1995); Glazer and Moynihan (1995); Laitin (1995); Tishkov (1997).
9   The general theory of venality (Elwert 1985) would have to be adapted for socialist societies where, in most cases, favours and privileges replaced fiscal relations.
10 In particular for the Balkans the relevancy of institutions of loyalty based on an emic

20

concept of extended kinship (e.g. the *zadruga*) has been intensely discussed and sometimes branded more of a myth than a social reality (Todorova 1990; Kaser 1995: 36–60). However, the line of argumentation presented here is not concerned with the question of whether local institutions 'survived' by tradition, are invented or reactivated. Networks of loyalty based on kinship or ethnicity may also well be consequences of organisational shortcomings of the state. A convincing example is demonstrated by Verdery on how the economy of shortages fostered ethnic networks in Romania (Verdery 1993).

11   As a case in point see Koehler (1999) on legal pluralism in Svanetia, Georgia.

REFERENCES

Brass, P. (ed.) (1995), *Ethnic Groups and the State* (London).
Brown, M. E. (1997), 'The causes of internal conflict: an overview', in M. Brown, O. Coté, S. Lynn-Jones and S. E. Miller (eds), *Nationalism and Ethnic Conflict. An International Security Reader* (Cambridge, MA and London), 3–26.
de Figueirdo, R. and B. R. Weingast (1999), 'The rationality of fear: political opportunism and ethnic conflict', in B. F. Walter and J. Snyder (eds), *Civil Wars, Insecurity, and Intervention* (New York), 261–303.
Elwert, G. (1985), 'Märkte, Käuflichkeit und Moralökonomie', in B. Lutz (ed.), *Soziologie und gesellschaftliche Entwicklung* (Frankfurt), 509–526.
Elwert, G., S. Feuchtwang and D. Neubert (eds) (1999), *Dynamics of Violence. Processes of Escalation and De-Escalation in Violent Group Conflicts* (Berlin).
Eurasia Insight (2001), 'Examining the origins of the September 11 attacks 9/25/01', *Eurasia Insight* (6 October), www.eurasianet.org/departments/insight/articles/eav092501a.shtml (accessed 26 January 2002).
Fearon, J. D. (1998), 'Commitment problems and the spread of ethnic conflict', in D. A. Lake and D. Rothchild (eds), *The International Spread of Ethnic Conflict. Fear Diffusion, and Escalation* (Princeton), 107–127.
Fearon, J. and D. Laitin (1996), 'Explaining inter-ethnic co-operation', *American Political Science Review*, 90:4 (December), 715–735.
Gagnon, V. P. (1994), 'Ethnic nationalism and international conflict: the case of Serbia', *International Security*, 19 (Winter), 130–166.
Glazer, N. and D. P. Moynihan (eds) (1995) *Ethnicity: Theory and Experience* (Harvard).
Goskomstat (Gosudarstvennyi Komitet SSSR po Statistike) (1991), *Natsional'nyi sostav naseleniya SSSR. Po dannym vsesoyuznoi perepisi naseleniya 1989* (Moskva).
Gosztonyi, K. (1998), 'Militarised disputes in the post-socialist era', in J. Koehler and S. Heyer (eds), *Anthropologie der Gewalt. Chancen und Grenzen der sozialwissenschaftlichen Forschung* (Berlin), 159–178.
Gurr, T. R. and B. Harff (1995), *Ethnic Conflict in World Politics* (Boulder).
Heller, W. (ed.) (1997), *Migration und sozioökonomische Transformation in Südosteuropa* (München).
Hirschman, A. O. (1994), 'Wieviel Gemeinsinn braucht die liberale Gesellschaft?', *Leviathan*, 2, 293–304.
Ignatieff, M. (1998), *The Warrior's Honor. Ethnic War and the Modern Conscience* (New York).
Judah, T. (2000), *Kosovo. War and Revenge* (New Haven and London).
Kaser, K. (1995), *Familie und Verwandtschaft auf dem Balkan. Analyse einer untergehenden Kultur* (Wien, Köln and Weimar).

Koehler, J. (1998), 'Einleitung. Soziologisches Sprechen und empirisches Erfassen – Explaining Violence', in J. Koehler and S. Heyer (eds), *Anthropologie der Gewalt. Chancen und Grenzen der sozialwissenschaftlichen Forschung* (Berlin), 9–20.

Koehler, J. (1999), 'Parallele und integrierte Rechtssysteme in einer postsowjetischen Peripherie: Swanetien im Hohen Kaukasus', in E. Alber and J. Eckert (eds), *Settling of Land Conflicts by Mediation. Schlichtung von Landkonflikten – ein workshop* (Berlin), CD-ROM.

Kordonskii, S. (1995), 'The structure of economic space in post-perestroika society and the transformation of the administrative market', in K. Segbers and S. de Spiegeleire (eds), *Post-Soviet Puzzles. Mapping the Political Economy of the Former Soviet Union*, 1 (Baden-Baden), 157–205.

Laitin, D. (1995), 'Marginality: a microperspective', *Rationality and Society*, 7:1 (January), 31–57.

Lake, D. A. and D. Rothchild (1998), 'Spreading fear: the genesis of transnational ethnic conflict', in D. A. Lake and D. Rothchild (eds), *The International Spread of Ethnic Conflict. Fear Diffusion, and Escalation* (Princeton), 3–33.

Luhmann, N. (1983), *Legitimation durch Verfahren* (Frankfurt/M.).

North, D. (1990), *Institutions, Institutional Change and Economic Performance* (Cambridge).

Pirtskhalava, G. (1997) *The Population of Georgia* (Tbilisi).

Rothchild, D. (1986), 'Inter-ethnic conflict and policy analysis in Africa', *Ethnic and Racial Studies*, 9:1 (January), 66–86.

Rubin, B. R. and J. Snyder, 'Introduction', in B. R. Rubin and J. Snyder (eds), *Post-Soviet Political Order. Conflict and State Building* (London and New York).

Tishkov, V. (1997), *Ethnicity, Nationalism and Conflict in and after the Soviet Union. The Mind Aflame* (London).

Todorova, M. (1990), 'Myth-making in European family history: the zadruga reconsidered', *East European Politics and Societies*, 4:1, 30–76.

van Evera, S. (1994), 'Hypotheses on nationalism and war', *International Security*, 18:4, 5–39.

Verdery, K. (1993), 'Ethnic relations, economies of shortage, and the transition in Eastern Europe', in C. M. Hann (ed.), *Socialism. Ideals, Ideologies, and Local Practice* (London and New York), 172–186.

von Trotha, T. (1997), 'Zur Soziologie der Gewalt', in T. von Trotha (ed.), *Soziologie der Gewalt. Sonderheft Kölner Zeitschrift für Soziologie und Sozialpsychologie*, 49:37 (Opladen and Wiesbaden), 9–56.

Walter, B. (1999), 'Introduction', in B. F. Walter and J. Snyder (eds), *Civil Wars, Insecurity, and Intervention* (New York).

Willerton, J. P. (1992), *Patronage and Politics in the USSR* (Cambridge).

1

Discourses, actors, violence: the organisation of war-escalation in the Krajina region of Croatia 1990–91[1]

Hannes Grandits and Carolin Leutloff

Introduction

O N 6 MAY 1990 the second and final round of the first free multi-party elections since the end of the Second World War were held in Croatia. At that time it was still a socialist republic within the Yugoslavian Federation. The results of the elections were quite surprising. It was expected that the former Communist Party would lose its absolute political predominance, but the decisive victory of the nationalistic Croatian Democratic Community (HDZ), led by Franjo Tudjman, was remarkable.[2] This party became the new leading political force after forty-five years of socialist autocracy. The HDZ was able to form the new government in the Croatian federal parliament (Sabor) without other parties. Two weeks later, on 20 May 1990, the Serbian Democratic Party (SDS), the small nationalistic party of the Serbs in Croatia, which had only a few representatives in the newly elected Sabor, suspended its contacts with the parliament.[3] Their withdrawal from formal politics in Croatia was one of the first signs of the growing conflict between Croats and Serbs within Croatia's official political life.

The background of this move by the SDS can be summed up as follows: the first two weeks after the elections brought a completely new orientation to the political scene in Croatia. After coming to power, the leaders of the HDZ immediately began to launch initiatives for increasing the autonomy of Croatia within Yugoslavia or, if this could not be achieved, Croatia's full independence. But they were threatened by the aggressive policy of the president of Serbia, Slobodan Milosevic. Using Serbian nationalistic movements, Milosevic was on the way to realising a more centralised, Belgrade-dominated concept of Yugoslavia. The HDZ, as well as almost all other Croatian political parties, feared a Belgrade-organised military intervention by the Yugoslav National Army (JNA) in Croatia. There were constant rumours that actions had already been planned in Belgrade to 'restore order' in Croatia and put down all democratic efforts and 'national' aspirations by such a military intervention. Under these circumstances 'Serbophobic'

tendencies became increasingly popular in Croatian society and began to dominate public and political discourse. This anti-Serbian attitude was also one of the
key factors in the electoral success of the nationalist HDZ.

But there were also opposing developments, which tended to lessen national
antagonisms; thus, after the elections the leader of the SDS, Jovan Raskovic,
wanted to disassociate himself from the nationalistic proponents on his own side.
He stressed that he saw a positive future for Serbs in Croatia, if the political
leaders of both sides would be willing to cooperate and try to eliminate the
growing 'national phobias' among the people (*Vjesnik* 1990a: 5). Shortly after
the elections Raskovic and Tudjman began to discuss the possibility of a 'historic
compromise' for future coexistence between Croats and Serbs after the fall of the
Communist Party in Croatia.

However, the first Croat–Serbian attempts at cooperation, between the HDZ
and the SDS, were soon overshadowed by violent events. On the first Sunday after
the elections in the Maksimir Stadium in Zagreb, a football game between the
football clubs Dynamo Zagreb and Crvena Zvezda (Red Star) Belgrade ended with
a major brawl between the Croat and Serb fans. The police became increasingly
involved. The riot later moved from the stadium to the centre of the city. More
than one hundred people were seriously hurt. Then, just a few days later, there
was an attempted assassination of a local SDS functionary in Benkovac, a small
ethnically mixed town in south-western Croatia. This event politically radicalised
the SDS. Since it was not known who was responsible for this act of violence, the
SDS functionaries interpreted it as a political move against their party. In reaction, as already mentioned, they suspended their collaboration in the newly
elected parliament until responsibility for that event could be established.

These violent events would soon be followed by other smaller incidents.
Attempts to contain hostile Croat and Serb interpretations of the situation in the
country became increasingly complicated. Also influential politicians became
increasingly uninterested in this approach, since the media and the public discourse tended more and more to accept only 'clear' and nationally one-sided
explanations. In the course of 1991 this conflict escalated into a war and, by its
end in 1995, thousands of people had been killed and hundreds of thousands
made refugees.

In this chapter we attempt to investigate the interplay between hostile and
threatening public discourses, the action of political leaders, and subsequent
violent events in the Serbo-Croatian conflict in Croatia. Special attention will be
given to the changing interpretations of the threatening situation within the
communities involved and to the role of institutional reform and institutional
formation in the process of societal transformation. The leader–follower-
oriented perspective was chosen to avoid the hypothesis that conflict escalation
was inevitable.

The analysis of the year before the outbreak of open war in June 1991 is subdivided into three sections focusing on distinct phases in the development: first the popularisation and institutionalisation of national front-lines, secondly, the mobilisation for violent conflict resolution and, finally, the importance of the potential of war. Clearly these aspects overlapped in the course of conflict escalation but, as will be shown, their respective importance changed over time.

Popularisation and institutionalisation of national frontlines

On 30 May 1990, three weeks after the elections, the HDZ sponsored a big celebration on the occasion of the official inauguration of the new Croatian parliament. This day, declared as the 'Dan Hrvatske Drzavnosti' ['Day of Croatian Statehood'], developed into the biggest Croatian festival since the 1970s. (*Vjesnik* 1990b: 3) It was an impressive event not only in Zagreb, but also in the whole country. These festivities expressed first of all the end of the communist system and the introduction of a multi-party democracy but also the celebration of the Croatian 'ethno-nation' (Sundhaussen 1994). The new ruling party had thus converted their national programme into the new official position of the federal state.

This programme was represented by several 'Croatian' symbols. One of the crucial symbols was the 'Sahovnica', the red and white chessboard flag, which later became the official Croatian national flag. But the 'Sahovnica' as well as many other Croatian symbols also recalled the fascist wartime Croatian state which was formed by Nazi Germany in the Second World War.[4] Because of their Second World War connection, these symbols could also be read as a threat to the Serbs living in Croatia.[5]

In the light of this, those Serbs of Croatia who felt alienated by these symbols did not participate in the celebrations. On a political level all SDS members of parliament boycotted the official ceremonies. However, most of the members of parliament of Serbian nationality in the SDP-SKH (the former Communist Party) were present at the official celebrations. At that time, hostile boundaries between Serbs and Croats were not yet so well established.

In socialist times, ethnic or national affiliations were known in neighbourhood situations as well as at work places and other spheres of everyday life. However, up to 1990 everyday inter-ethnic relations were depicted as being to a large extent harmonious, and it was often asserted that ethnic affiliations were not at all important for the people (Nyström 1987; Siber 1988; Dugandzija 1991; Denich 1994a). But at the time of the election campaign and especially after the elections in May 1990 discussions about possible 'cultural and material discrimination' and also about violent aggression – especially those put in the context of the Second World War – were of growing importance (Grandits 1998; Zakosek 1998b). The people became involved in a process of increasing national self-consciousness and consequently also one of ethnic segregation (Elwert 1995a: 114–115).

Feelings of being endangered on both the Serbian and Croatian side were in fact evident in some ethnically mixed regions at that time, and they began to increase, as the following interview illustrates. When asked who after the elections in 1990 had been more frightened in the Kordun (an ethnically mixed region in south-western Croatia), the Serbs, because the HDZ had come to power in Croatia, or the Croats, because here the Serbian-dominated SDP (former Communist Party) was in power at the regional level, S. Livada, a sociologist who came from that region, answered:

> Both sides were frightened. On the one side was a movement with really dangerous intentions [he refers here to the ruling HDZ], on the other side a structure came into being, I think here of the Serbs in the Kordun, which had no longer any kind of political centre. In former times this had been the Central Committee of Croatia or the Central Committee of Yugoslavia, but both were already dissolved at that time. Because of the danger they were facing or they thought themselves to be in, the political structure of the Serbs now turned exclusively to a monstrous power, the Yugoslav National Army. (Livada 1995: 19)

In this statement, reference to the missing political centre of the Serbian community in Croatia and the broken relationship to Croatian governmental institutions are of particular interest.[6] In this way Livada explains the strong movement of the 'Serbian structure' in Croatia towards a new orientation, to the JNA. At the same time the JNA was subjected to transformation from a Yugoslav to a Serbian-national institution.

This political institutional deficit of the Serbs in Croatia and the new orientation of Serbian political life from Yugoslav to Serbian national institutions form the background for the enormous popularisation of the nationalistic Serbian SDS in the summer of 1990. Not until then was a network of local SDS organisations, extending over all regions with Serbian settlements in Croatia, organised. In all communities with a large proportion of Serbian inhabitants – for the most part ex-communist SDP functionaries were still governing the local affairs – founding ceremonies of new SDS branches took place in June 1990.

After the elections of April–May 1990 the ex-communist SDP in Croatia was increasingly shifting from their former Yugoslav orientation into a Croatian nationalist one, very much in reaction to the strong centralist and Serbian-nationalist developments in Belgrade. Consequently, the ex-communists successively lost the support of their functionaries and voters of Serbian nationality. This was an important precondition for the success of the SDS politicians in Croatia.

Also significant was the ceremonial organisation of the SDS gatherings: often several times a week, so-called '*mitings*' were held by the SDS in the course of the founding of new local branches of the party. They were attended by several hundred, and sometimes even several thousand Serbs. The key person in these foundation ceremonies was Jovan Raskovic, the leader of the SDS and charismatic main speaker in most of these meetings. In these very emotionalised mass gatherings, the speeches of the SDS leaders, and in particular of Raskovic, were full of national pathos and historic myths. These views fell on fertile ground and were really able to generate a following for the SDS movement. The principal political core of Raskovic's speeches, not to prevent a possible independence of Croatia at all costs, but to fight for the official acknowledgement of the special individual and collective rights of the Serbs in Croatia, was pushed into the background by his emotional nationalistic rhetoric.

Already during these emotional days of the political mobilisation of large parts of the Serbian population for the SDS, the local SDS mayor of Knin, Milan Babic, began his 'Initiative of Knin', which soon came to be of prime importance for the 'Serbian question' in Croatia. His plan aimed for a reorganisation of the local administration borders in the south-west of Croatia. The Knin area should become a newly established administrative unit containing all Serb-populated villages of the region. Knin was proposed as the centre of this administrative district, with the name 'District of Northern Dalmatia and Lika' ('Opcina sjeverne Dalmacije i Like'). On 28 June 1990, the Serb holiday 'Vidovdan' (this day is also one of the most important Serbian national holidays commemorating the legendary Kosovo battle), an assembly of SDS regional leaders, quickly organised by Babic, adopted this proposal as an 'official' resolution. In this way a project was initiated which would soon become the centre of the violent escalation of the conflict in Croatia.

But at the end of June, the public discourse in Croatia did not take much notice of the occurrences in Knin. The people were primarily interested in the presentation of the first draft of the first post-communist constitution by the HDZ. When this draft was presented in a working meeting of the Sabor, which also took place on the Serb holiday of 'Vidovdan' on 28 June 1990, it became obvious that the HDZ wanted with this constitution 'to give Croatia a new identity' (*Vjesnik* 1990c). This new identity was built upon 'breaking free from socialism' and was an increasingly 'Croatian' one. Croatia should be the state of the Croatian nation. In this draft, which dealt with various aspects of the social and political transformation, the Serbs were labelled as a national minority. Under communist rule they had always been a 'titular nation' within the Social Republic of Croatia. Thus the Serbian politicians in Croatia perceived this plan to declare the Serbs a 'minority' as an act of discrimination and a massive undermining of their status.

The coincidence of these two events on 28 June 1990, the presentation of the draft of the first constitution and of the resolution in Knin, marked the first official antagonistic moves of national(-istic) Croatian and Serbian political projects and were firmly linked to the process of Croatian state building. The reorganisation of old and the foundation of new state institutions formed the background for ethnicised competition for participation in the new state. The question of the ways in which power could be allocated became the prime political question and source of conflicts.[7]

Cautious and compromise-oriented institutionalisation policies might well at that time have calmed emotions and reduced the danger of violent conflict. But another path was chosen by initiatives which promoted political radicalisation and the consequent mobilisation of competing groups. In this short period after the democratic elections, the political positions were thus quickly transformed into differences and became irreconcilable antagonisms leading to nationalistic mobilisation of the respective populations and subsequently to violent conflict.

The mobilisation for violent options of conflict resolution

> Barricades were built on the outskirts of villages in case the Croats would come at night, four or five armed men, who would come and kill people . . . That was the reason why the barricades were built, to block off the Serbian villages from the Croatian ones. In my town the Serbs were in the majority, but half way to Knin there was a village mainly inhabited by Croats. We built up our barricades in this direction, because the people were frightened. ('J' from Knin 1996: INT)[8]

This recollection from a 1996 interview refers to circumstances in the Knin area in August 1990, barely two months after the above-mentioned political confrontation over constitutional provisions and administrative jurisdictions. The situation escalated in some of the regions in south-western Croatia where a high percentage of the total population was Serbian. Part of the Serbian people had taken up arms. What had happened? To better understand the perspective of the Serbian people who participated in this uprising we can gain perspective from an interview dealing with those critical days in August 1990:

> Then we saw many people from our village with arms. Hunting rifles, but not weapons from the army. They gathered in the village centre and discussed, what to do at night. They were frightened that the Croats would come at night to kill Serbs. They also told my father that he should go to the barricades, but he said that he did not have a gun. One of the neighbours gave my father a kind of rifle with ammunition and told him, that he should go to a certain place. He did go, since he did not want to get into a quarrel with the neighbour.
>
> My mother began to cry – what should she do with the little children? My father left a long knife by the door. We usually used it to slaughter the pigs in autumn. He told us, that we must use it, if someone should come. We were very nervous and scared during the night. I stayed at home with my mother, while my father was at the front. To have this weapon in the house and to be scared at the same time, that was really a horrible time. Of course, I had never had a weapon before – CDs and a television yes, of course. ('S' from Knin 1996: INT)

28

In this and the other interview with two Serbs, who later fled from the region of rebellion, the 'taking up of weapons' has been described as an act of self-defence, which resulted from intense fear (Elwert 1995b: 130–131, 1997: 91–92). They pointed out that fear of extremists made life really unsafe in the region. They felt endangered just for the reason that they were of Serbian ethnicity. The strong meaning that the ethnic identification came to represent indicates the extent of national mobilisation (Scheffler 1995).

However, a deeper analysis of this fear leading to the national mobilisation reveals that it did not necessary correspond to a real threat. Rather it represented a reaction to perceptions of threat as an interpretation of reality not necessarily closely linked to external 'objectifiable' criteria (Nicklas 1991).

In this setting it is absolutely necessary first to point out the most important initiatives of those strategic actors and their clients, who were the main driving forces of the threat messages. These people can be called 'ethnic' or 'national' entrepreneurs (see Bailey 1970: 44–57). These ethnic entrepreneurs propagated a discourse of the conflict promoting escalation into a violent conflict. In their discussions the use of violence was always legitimised by representing it as being defensive. The Serbs would have to defend themselves or they would soon become victims of violent acts coming from the others. This was their message. In the escalating conflict, the majority of the affected population followed the interpretations presented by their leaders. In this way, the former dominant local or even Yugoslav self-definition was successively replaced by a widened national one.

Generally in the Krajina region this process of strategic escalation of violence was strongly connected to the 'Knin initiative', which was driven by the SDS mayor of Knin, Milan Babic, step-by-step. While his SDS colleague but opponent Raskovic was partly engaged in negotiations with official representatives of the new Croatian government, Babic worked on his ambitious project to unify Serbian communities. He visited different settlements with a Serbian majority. By that summer Obrovac, Dvor, Vojnic, Donji Lapac, and all communities in the region of Knin, had agreed to the unification (Silber and Little 1995: 105). However, many communities, especially those where the SDP was still in power, were not immediately ready to support the Knin initiative. On the contrary, it would not have been surprising if the project had failed. In these cases, to 'win over' these communities, Babic, together with his closest followers, started to strategically use violence in the emotionally heated atmosphere. Thus he succeeded in creating support without democratic legitimisation. These methods are shown very vividly in the following description of the village Titova Korenica:

> In Korenica . . . the SDP [the former Communist Party] members composed the majority in the regional assembly. They did not want to join the union of Babic. Instead of this they invited Tudjman's Minister for Regional administration, Slavko Degoricija, into the region. They wanted to negotiate about internal investigations and plans to develop the tourist potential of the Plitvice National Park . . . Babic anticipated this

meeting by sending forty armed men from Knin into the city in the night before Degpricija was supposed to arrive. In the following weeks, the SDS organised demonstrations in Korenica until the SDP representatives were chased away from their positions. (Silber and Little 1995: 106)

During that summer, while questions of the transformation from socialism and the consequences of the possible independence of Croatia from Belgrade dominated media in Croatia, Babic and his followers, at that time not really taken seriously by Zagreb, continued to work on their plan. Their objective of autonomy from the Croatian government and administration became increasingly clear. It also became increasingly apparent that this was supported by Belgrade.

The next step in Babic's plan was the call for a 'people's assembly' of Serbs, who lived in regions of the Krajina, the area in Croatia with a high proportion of Serbian population. On 25 July 1990, a 'Serbian National Council' was founded in Knin and it decided to hold a referendum in August about the autonomy of the 'Serbian Krajina'.[9]

Parallel to this first step of building up a parallel political institution, Milan Martic, the chief of police in Knin and associate of Babic, encouraged the predominantly Serbian police of Knin to disobey the authority of the newly elected government of Croatia. Initially the officers refused to wear the newly introduced uniforms. Milan Martic legitimised this by pointing out that police forces of Serbian nationality should not be forced to wear the same badges and uniforms 'which were worn by Croatian fascists at the time of the criminal NDH state' (BBC/CRF-TV 1996).

The government in Zagreb was provoked by the acts of the police in Knin, but they still counted on mediation of the conflict. They sent a high-ranking delegation to Knin. It consisted of the Croatian Minister of the Interior, his deputy and the chief of police of Sibenik, which was the direct superior of Martic. They tried to normalise the situation by making concessions to the police in Knin in order to bring them into line. But this action ran counter to that of the leadership of Martic and Babic in Knin. The delegation was confronted with a tumultuous situation shortly after the beginning of the negotiations. An agreement could not be reached and soon it became an open disagreement. At the same time more than a thousand people were organised by Babic and Martic to gather in front of the police station where the negotiations were taking place. They loudly 'supported' the position of 'their' police. Finally, the delegation was forced to hastily leave Knin (BBC/ORF-TV 1996; *Vjesnik* 1990d). This first attempt at a peaceful agreement with the protesting police, which could have led to a wider dialogue, and possibly a compromise between the Croatian and Serbian protagonists, had failed.

When some weeks later the Croatian Ministry of the Interior sent special police forces to reclaim control of the police station and to disarm the disobedient police of Knin, an open revolt began in the villages of Krajina. It was organised under the energetic leadership of SDS activists led by Babic and Martic and soon got called the 'Balvan revolution'. The name derives from the building of barricades from tree trunks which, during the revolt, were manned by armed guards to 'protect' the Serbian villages.

Let us turn here again to the motives of the local Serbian population in participating actively in this armed 'Balvan rebellion'. As explained above, the Serbian population has to be seen as behaving in a scenario of threat. Following the fact that 'Croatian special forces were sent to punish Serbs', as the Krajina Serb leader claimed, the situation appeared increasingly dangerous to them and formed a new, somehow 'second reality' (Rösel 1997: 165). In this reality the present developments were constantly mixed with the experience of the Croatian Serbs in the Second World War, when Serbs were violently persecuted by the Croatian Ustasha. In the interpretation of the Serbian people the violence suffered during the Second World War threatened to be repeated. This increased the fear of the imminent use of violence. Thus, the historical situation was projected onto the current situation.

Paradoxically, because of the authoritarian suppression of nationality issues by the Yugoslav communists, these unresolved issues became more explosive. Especially after the collapse of communist rule at the end of the 1980s, stories about the atrocities in the Second World War began to circulate again. They were often based on the experiences of the older generation. This situation is reflected in the views of the above-cited respondent who described the Ustasha crimes as 'national events', experienced by his grandfather in the Second World War:

> My grandfather was in the Partisan army of Tito . . . he knew many problems between Serbs and Croats during the Second World War. He told me that at the beginning of the Second World War, the Croats killed 520 Serbs not far from our house, only twenty to twenty-five kilometres away. Civilians, girls, young children, etc. . . . I know, that Croats, Ustasha, killed at least 10,000 people in our area within a radius of about a hundred kilometres. I do not know why . . . In Glina, about sixty miles from our home, I am not sure, but there were about 1010 or 1012 people shot by Ustasha, that means shot by Croatian soldiers . . . ('B' from Vojnic, Kordun region 1996: INT)

In these detailed explanations, it is striking that the exact locations of the crimes, and even the numbers of victims, could be given. Although it is possible that these details were really given by the grandfather, as most of the Serb families did have victims of the Ustasha terror during the Second World War among their relatives, it is more probable that the informant knows about these events from the media, which were increasingly controlled by nationalists.[10]

Since the end of the 1980s, the Yugoslav population was permanently influenced by actualised pictures of the enemy and by historical myths with little opportunity to verify the information given (Sundhaussen 1994: 418). In the

Krajina the rhetoric of the SDS constantly re-emphasised that with the 'return' of the symbols of the Ustasha period, e.g. as with the introduction of the new police uniforms, it could be 'assumed' that the return of the fascist policy of the ethnic cleansing of Serbs would soon follow. The fear of a 'new genocide' was therefore increasingly based on synchronised representations of the present and the past, which were one-dimensionally described along friend–enemy schemes opposing Serbs and Croats.[11]

Smaller acts of violence, which slowly began to increase in number, intensified fears even more. Often ethno-political entrepreneurs consciously planned this violence. In this way they, along with their initial small group of supporters, created loyal relationships along ethnic lines. Thus through these acts of violence the ethno-political entrepreneurs, which at the beginning represented only a small minority of the proclaimed 'nation', eventually created a frame of conflictual relationships manifested in notions of protection and obedience. National unity was manifested by a reliance on force (for comparison, see Scheffler 1995:33 and Waldmann 1999).

In this context, the extreme fear of violence was often linked to the social expectation of self-defence. To defend one's home and family was accepted as the norm in a perceived situation of threat. It was propagated and even expected that men would take up arms in Krajina in 1990.

The readiness to use violence for self-defence is a widespread attitude. Still, the question may be asked whether people act in situations of conflict totally without any reference to so-called 'cultural dispositions'.[12] This matter can be examined by reference to two levels of meaning. First the symbolic level can be investigated, in which 'culturally immanent pictures' may be awoken which recreate a special tradition and which may effect the escalation of violence (Elwert 1989). Secondly, one should investigate the 'level of action', which may relate to traditional patterns of behaviour.

The culturally immanent pictures in connection with the armed self-defence of Krajina society are partly taken from a culture of armed self-defence, which has characterised life in this region at different stages and in different forms: as border peasant soldiers up to the end of the nineteenth century, during Partisan battles in the Second Word War and during the communistic organisation of territorial defence. The first particularly represents a regional characteristic.[13]

In 1990, in the situation of threat, the Krajina–Serb group consciousness was strengthened by those culturally specific characteristics. A tradition of taking up arms for self-defence was present in the form of historic pictures, which were at the same time deprived of their context. They functioned as symbols which were used in a specific way to strengthen the demarcation of nationality and to influence social attitudes and expectations. Present value systems could be modified and/or – in the actual situation of threat – constructed anew.[14] However, the credibility of the special meaning which was given to the pictures was bound to special constellations. In the summer of 1990, as discussed here, these pictures gained plausibility only with the situation of immanent threat and the rapid weakening of the state power monopoly (Grandits and Promitzer 2001b).

A discussion of the actualisation of a traditional pattern of action, involving the readiness to defend oneself, is much more difficult (Kaser 1996: 132). A culture of armed self-defence in the sense of a social organisation of border peasant soldiers of the Austro-Hungarian Empire could not survive after the dissolution of the system at the end of the nineteenth century. Perceptions of a tradition of taking up arms for self-defence survived as a kind of a male ideal, which in former times was bound to patriarchal–militaristic structures, and which still may have had some influence on the process of socialisation and in this form was a reference point for the use of special cultural immanent pictures (Grandits and Halpern 1994).[15]

Despite the fact that cultural and social expectations to take up arms could be found in wide sections of the population, this certainly does not mean that it had universal power. Many individuals refused to be mobilised voluntarily. But with the development of the conflict and the expansion of a militaristic–administrative infrastructure, these individuals were increasingly put under pressure. Withdrawal from armed resistance was soon defined as being shameful and dishonourable by the public. From the summer of 1991 many people were mobilised by force. This left little scope for withdrawal from participation in the armed conflict. This situation was reflected in an interview: 'They have all been mobilised by the Krajina-army. If they had refused, they would have been declared as deserters and would have been imprisoned' ('J' from Knin 1996: INT).

From rebellion to war: the importance of the potential of war

Until now the focus has been primarily on the local level of the conflict constellation and perception. But to understand how this conflict developed into a broader regional war it is essential to discuss how it was embedded in a broader context. As noted, the struggle for power between the centralist Serbian political elite in Belgrade and the Croatian policy makers in Zagreb, who aimed for a more federal-based sovereignty or national independence, represented a necessary precondition for the successful ethno-national mobilisation in all of Croatia. The developments in Krajina were used for, and increasingly influenced by, tactical and strategic considerations from outside powerful protagonists. The local frontlines and ambitions were instrumentalised for their political plans.

On the side of the Krajina Serbs, the Milosevic-led regime in Belgrade, and to a growing degree also the JNA, became increasingly important in the local conflict.[16] The integration of the Krajina into 'larger structures' and the building up of a potential for war, i.e. a sufficient supply of weapons, the maintenance of a functioning wartime economy, etc. was fundamental for securing such a pre-condition for war and one of the most important consequences of the 'Balvan revolution' (Orywal 1996: 40–41). These efforts were also a main reason for the incipient conflict – at both a regional and a supra-regional level – which from now on became triggered by the same actions: the repeated attempts at disarm-ing the progressively growing armed forces.

First of all, the 'Balvan revolution' itself had been triggered by the attempt of Croatian special forces to disarm the rebellious policemen in Knin. The failure of this move was caused by the involvement of the JNA. JNA combat aircraft forced the Croatian police helicopters, which had been sent to Knin, to return to Zagreb and JNA units stationed in Krajina are reported to have marched out of their barracks. Both actions were interpreted as a sign for the rebellious Krajina Serbs that they could count on the support of the Yugoslav National Army in the future (*Tanjug* 1990; *Vjesnik* 1990d).[17]

This first armed confrontation shocked public life in Croatia. It also influenced the public discourse on both sides of the conflict. The argument that weapons and the organisation of defence had really become necessary because the other side seemed ready to act violently became increasingly persuasive. The following statement of Milan Babic, the radical leader of 'Serbian Krajina', illus-trates this very vividly. After SDS functionaries had just handed out weapons from police magazines and from official military Territorial Defence (TO) reserv-ist depots to the people, Milan Babic told the press:

> The Croatian government wages a psychological war through its Ministry of the Interior and its Police headquarters in Sibenik against the Serbian people in Croatia. Now an ultimatum was delivered to us, that the people should return their weapons, that the barricades should be removed and that all weapons should be registered. That means that the Serbian people should be disarmed. I do not have the moral right to request from my people not to defend themselves from any form of terrorism, including when it is coming from the Croatian government. (*Politika* 1990)

In this statement, Babic denies the legitimacy of the official administration in Croatia and at the same time he refers to the fact that the Croatian Serbs have a necessity and a right to organise an armed self-defence. In the following months he devoted all his efforts to organising this 'self-defence'.

After the events of 17 August 1990 the authorities of the Croatian republic, referred to in the above quotation, tried to prevent the arming of the Serbian pop-ulation in Krajina and attempted to 'restore order' and reassert their authority. Initiatives to disarm the population began. But these attempts were met with resistance and aggravated the whole situation. For example, on 28 September 1990 special forces of the Croatian police began to confiscate the weapons of mil-itary reservists, mainly in villages with a high proportion of Serbs. This resulted in demonstrations and clashes between the police and Serbian civilians (*Archiv der Gegenwart* 1990: 35182; *Vjesnik* 1990e). The unrest and disturbances not only worsened the atmosphere in the region, but also encouraged extremists on both sides, supported by the media, to outdo each other in the creation of threatening scenarios.[18] In such an atmosphere of distrust and fear, disarmament hardly became possible. On the contrary, the arming of the Serbian people in the insurgent region as well as the organisation of local combat units proceeded with the support of the JNA based in the Krajina region.[19]

The arming of the Croatian combat forces has to be seen in a much larger dimension.[20] After the HDZ took over power in Croatia, the Croatian government, as it was just a federal-component government within Yugoslavia, had only a relatively small police force with almost no heavy weapons at its disposal.[21] Most of the heavy weapons belonged to the JNA. The JNA's supreme command was the joint Yugoslav state presidium in Belgrade, which consisted of representatives of all Yugoslav republics and autonomous provinces. Soon after the elections, the HDZ decided to expand its police force and, in addition, to secretly build up their own Croatian army. Thousands of Croatian men were enrolled in the armed forces through the first months after the HDZ took power in Croatia.[22] Weapons were bought abroad and illegally smuggled into the country.

The arming of Croatia's military did not remain a secret to the leaders of the JNA and the socialist elite in Belgrade. However, for months they did not intervene. But on 9 January 1991, at a meeting of the Yugoslav state presidium in Belgrade a resolution to launch an offensive against Croatia surprisingly became the main topic. The leading commanders of the JNA together with Milosevic's people in the presidium wanted the state presidium to give an order to the JNA to react against the 'illegal and secret formation' of a new Croatian army. They called the formation of an independent Croatian army an aggressive act against the Yugoslav Federation. The resolution for a military intervention was even discussed a second time in the Yugoslav state presidency, but in the end did not get a majority. The whole initiative ended up as a compromise with further negotiations. Veljko Kadijevic, the Yugoslav minister of defence and highest officer of the JNA, and Tudjman agreed that the JNA would end their alert if Croatia followed its obligation to hand over the people 'responsible' for the smuggling of weapons.[23]

At about the same time Milosevic and the leading figures in his Serbian political circle came to the realisation that the unity of Yugoslavia could no longer be 'saved' and they changed their strategy on the Yugoslav question. From now on they no longer in principle opposed the independence of Croatia and Slovenia; but they felt that Croatia should not be allowed to keep those parts of its republic which the Belgrade authorities regarded as Serbian territory. These areas 'must stay in Yugoslavia at any cost'.[24] Within these conflicts about the future of Yugoslavia, the rebels of the Serbian Krajina now attained enormous strategic importance in the struggles for power.

It seems reasonable to return here to the local context in the Krajina. The uprising had meanwhile become increasingly institutionalised and its own 'official' political and military administration had been built up. Already on 1 October 1990, the 'Serbian National Council' in Knin, presided over by Milan Babic, proclaimed the autonomy of the regions under their control.[25] A few months later in February 1991 the declaration of independence of the 'Republic of Serbian Krajina' followed. The secession from Croatia and the building up of a new state structure were justified by Croatia's ambitions to separate from Yugoslavia.[26] At the beginning, the territory of the 'Republic of Serbian Krajina' encompassed only the immediate region of Knin.

The support of Belgrade for the Krajina rebels, as fighters for the 'Serbian cause' in Yugoslavia, had meanwhile been growing constantly. In return, the Serbian regime in Belgrade had gained much control over the aims and strategies of the Krajina Serbian insurgents. This was also the time when so-called 'volunteers', different heavily armed paramilitary individuals and groups from Serbia and other Yugoslav regions, increased their presence in the Krajina.

Further developments in Krajina in the spring and summer of 1991, can be characterised by two combined processes: the mobilisation and the regulation of violence. As a reaction to individual acts of violence – some of which were strategically calculated, others seemingly 'unplanned' – an increasing part of the population was won over to support the use of force. This was the time of nationalistic hard-liners and extremists claiming radical solutions. Conciliatory politicians, arguing for negotiations and non-violent solutions, rapidly lost influence. The regional authorities began to tolerate acts of violence against members of the other ethnic group. Until the escalation into war in June 1991 this development was reflected in public discussions associated with a series of bloody clashes. They dominated the media on both sides and helped to unify public opinion. Fierce fighting broke out between special forces of the Krajina Serbian and the Croatian police for the control of strategic centres.

On 2 and 3 March 1991 in the ethnically mixed town of Pakrac in western Slavonia, Krajina Serbian special forces came into the town, took over a police station and disarmed the sixteen Croatian policemen stationed there. The following night in a large-scale police operation, Croatian special police forces stormed the police building and forced out the Krajina Serbian forces (Borba 1991; *Politika* 1991; *Vjesnik* 1991a).

In Plitvice, a thinly populated tourist area about 150 km south-west of Zagreb, a similar occurrence ended with the first casualties of the conflict. In the fighting, one soldier on each side was killed and at least twenty fighters were very seriously injured. The JNA intervened on the order of the Yugoslav state presidium. JNA troops separated the fighting forces and installed a buffer zone between them. In the following weeks, the JNA reinforced its presence in the region and grew in importance (*Profil* 1991; *Vjesnik* 1991b).

As a consequence of these strategic violent events more soldiers and weapons were sent to all areas of conflict. Smaller clashes, which followed in several places, had an effect on the conflict constellation in the region as a whole. Consequently the Croatian population in ethnically mixed or in the vicinity of predominantly Serbian areas 'sensed' danger and organised a defence against attacks from the 'Serbian terrorists' (*Danas* 1991a). Barricades were built and patrols organised. The same happened in the predominantly Serbian villages in Croatia outside the territory of the Republic of Serbian Krajina.

Particularly affected by this national panic were the Serbian or ethnically mixed villages in eastern Slavonia. One of these villages, Borovo selo, became the place where the next significant violent event broke out in early May 1991. After a series of smaller incidents – initially provoked by nationalistic HDZ radicals – two Croatian policemen were detained in the village. Two buses full of Croatian policemen moved into the village of Borovo selo to 'free' their colleagues. Their arrival had been expected and a large number of Serbian fighters waited in ambush, among them were also 'volunteers' from the Chetnik movement of the ultra-nationalist Vojislav Seselj in Serbia. They began to fire on the buses. Twelve Croatian policemen were killed and more than twenty seriously injured. The number of Serbian fighters killed has not been made public (Borba 1990; *Danas* 1990: 7–9; *Der Standard* 1990: 3, Silber and Little 1995: 158–160).

After the incident at Borovo selo was publicised, the conflict took on a new dimension. The dead bodies of the policemen were omnipresent in the Croatian media. The Serbs were collectively referred to as Chetniks or terrorists and were declared to be enemies of the Croatian state. Reciprocally, on the Serbian side, Croats were collectively labelled as 'Ustasha who were again attacking Serbian villages' and were proclaimed enemies of the Serbian people. Consequently, the chances for initiatives to reach some kind of non-violent compromise were enormously diminished.

When the war began in Croatia at the end of June 1991, after Croatia's declaration of independence and with a large military offensive from the Krajina Serbs, long-lasting preparations on both sides had preceded this escalation of violence. Supported and/or directed by their allies, the JNA as well as nationalistic volunteer militias from Serbia, the Krajina Serbian troops tried to take over those parts of Croatia they claimed as Serbian and to successively expel the Croatian population. To get an impression of the dimensions of the potential for war which was built up by the warring factions, one need only look at the list of combat troops, which were fighting each other soon after the outbreak of war.[27]

At that time the militia of the 'Republic of Serbian Krajina' had, according to Milan Martic, 35,000 men under arms. The 'Knindze', the so-called army of the Krajina, which had partly developed out of the former territorial defence, consisted of hundreds of combat units. In addition volunteers and paramilitary units from Serbia (Cetniks, Arkanovci, etc.) also played an important role in the fighting.

The official size of the JNA in Croatia was 60,000–70,000 soldiers (it is difficult to estimate how many Croatian soldiers left the army before or after the fighting started). In addition about 20,000–25,000 JNA soldiers were transferred from Slovenia to Croatia and 10,000–15,000 were stationed at the Serbian and Bosnian borders with Croatia.

The Croatian police (Mupovci) consisted, with their regular and reservist members, of 45,000 men, the 'Zbor narodne garde' (new Croatian army), had about 30,000 soldiers but at that time still limited resources of arms. In addition, many armed civilians and several paramilitary units were also involved in the fighting.

Conclusion

This analysis has tried to show why, after the decade-long, basically harmonious, everyday inter-ethnic life of Croats and Serbs in Croatia, the 'Balvan revolution' took place in the Krajina region in the summer of 1990, and why in the course of the following year this rather amateur local revolt was able to escalate into a brutal war between Serbs and Croats.

The first section focused on the popularisation and institutionalisation of boundary-maintenance mechanisms in Croatia in 1990. The HDZ, which formed the government after the first free multi-party elections in Croatia, increasingly integrated its nationalistic position into the newly developing post-socialist state machinery. Political antagonisms, which in the breakdown of the socialist system and the following temporary power vacuum seemed inevitable, aroused national conflicts between Croats and Serbs about the form and character of the new institutions of the developing national state. These conflicts became manifest in serious disputes over the character of the new constitution and new power relations within the police. The emerging leaders of the Serbian population in Croatia feared that the takeover of the government by the Croatian nationalistic HDZ would be followed by discrimination against Serbs. They passionately demanded explicit acknowledgements of their special claims. The Croat population feared a Belgrade-organised intervention of the JNA against the new democratically elected first post-socialist government in Croatia. It was feared that this would be accompanied by a wave of repression and a return to the socialist one-party system.

Soon two deeply antagonistic positions on the 'national question' were confronting each other in political life. Masses of the Serbian, as well as the Croatian, population could in this way be won over to radical nationalistic positions. In the beginning these positions were abstract, but slowly they began to become relevant in everyday life.

In the second section, the readiness of the Serbian people in the region around Knin to participate in the so-called 'Balvan revolution' was discussed. It was shown that the people in Krajina explained their participation in the rebellion as a necessary and inevitable act of self-defence for the protection of their rights, their property, and even their lives which they felt were threatened by Croatian extremists and by the newly elected Croatian authorities. But these feelings of being threatened and the closely connected readiness to use violence were very much caused by specific discourses of conflict scenarios and programmed violent incidents, which were often produced by political entrepreneurs.

Political leaders, intellectuals and the media not only on the Serbian, but also on the Croatian side, projected historical conflicts between Croats and Serbs into the developing situation. By this means, they were very successful in stirring up fear among the people, which pushed them to an even greater degree towards confrontational national self-definitions and prepared them for violence. In this constellation, the discursive projection and instrumentation of specific cultural images of virility, especially of traditional male role expectations, became one of the important aspects in mobilising the people for conflict. The images were taken partly from the perceived heroic history of Krajina society. This analysis of the escalation of violence has also shown the difficulty in finding the dividing line between the voluntary mobilisation of the population and the sequential social-role expectations in the use of force.

It has to be stressed that the strategic use of force and violence were probably the most important means of winning over the people to a confrontational mode that promoted the ensuing conflict. The strategic use of violence was able to powerfully transform the interpretation of the conflict in the respective societies.

However, that the 'Balvan revolution' of the Krajina Serbs could lead within several months to a large-scale war was, besides the strategic employment of violence, predominantly a consequence of the instrumentalisation of the regional conflict into a trans-regional confrontation of interest. The third section dealt with this decisive element. Only the accumulation of a potential for warfare, i.e. the necessary supplies of weapons, trained soldiers, the maintenance of a functioning war economy, and, further, the evolution of an institutional infrastructure, made it possible that this local conflict could develop into a war. Initiatives from outside, for the Krajina Serbs, especially from Serbia and from the now Serbian-dominated JNA, were of crucial importance in the outbreak of war in the Krajina region in Croatia.

NOTES

1 Many colleagues helped us with their comments and criticisms in the writing of this chapter. We are especially grateful to Joel M. Halpern for his work on the final draft.
2 On the elections, see Grdesic *et al.* (1991) and Siber (1997); for analysis on the background to the new political elite, see Dejan (1993) and Zakosek (1998a).
3 In the 1990 election the great majority of Serbs in Croatia did not vote for the Serbian nationalistic SDS, which had candidates in only a few electoral districts. Instead they voted for the former Communist Party, which ran under the new name SDP-SKH. For details of

the election results, including regional differences, see *Vjesnik* (1990a). Some 581,663 or 12 per cent of the 4,784,265 people living in Croatia in 1991 were ethnic Serbs (according to the population census of 1991), see *Republicki zavod za statistiku* (1992: 9).

4   The Sahovnica has been the symbol for the kingdom of Croatia since the Middle Ages. From 1102 this kingdom was ruled by the kings of Hungary and from 1526 it was part of the Habsburg Empire. Between 1941 and 1945 the Sahovnica became the official flag of the first Croatian national state, the 'Independent State of Croatia' (NDH). In the Communist post-war period this flag was therefore also seen as a symbol for this Second World War Croatian quisling state.

5   The Second World War 'Independent State of Croatia' was governed by the fascist Croat-centric Ustasha movement. Between 1941 and 1945 mass persecution, expulsion and murder made hundreds of thousands Serbs victims of the Croatian Ustasha state (which at that time also encompassed Bosnia-Herzegovina).

6   For the background of the strong attachment of Croatian Serbs to the Communist Party in the post-war period see Roksandic (1991: 157).

7   This mechanism is theoretically described in the articles of Nagel (1994), Neckel (1995) and Wimmer (1995). They point out that as soon as a state distributes resources by ethnic categories, or as soon as a group does not have the same access to citizens' rights and therefore is not able to access resources, the members of the group may try to become members of the privileged group or, if that is not possible, may postulate an ethnic identity which differs from the identity of the major nation. Ethnicity, respectively, nationality may win increasing importance very fast.

8   Most of the interviews with Serbs from the Krajina quoted in this text were made by Carolin Leutloff in the course of fieldwork in Former Yugoslavia on identity aspects of Krajina-Serb refugees in 1996, one year after their flight from Croatia. For results of this research see Leutloff (1998).

9   The 'Krajina' encompassed the region close to the north-west border of Bosnia, large parts of the northern Dalmatian hinterland, and the regions of Lika, Krbava, Kordun and Banija. Historically these territories belonged to the so-called 'Vojna Krajina', or 'military border', which was for centuries a multi-ethnic defence zone of the Austro-Hungarian Empire against the Ottomans, until it was dissolved and reintegrated into Croatia in 1881. In 1990 Croatian Serbs tried to ideologically re-establish the meaning of 'Krajina' (see, for example, Grandits and Promitzer 1997). See especially also n. 13.

10 For theoretical input see Halbwachs (1985: 35): 'The national group I belong to was in the course of my life the scene of a special number of events from which I think that I would remember them, but which I only know from newspapers or from evidence of those who were actually involved in these events. These events take a special place in the memory of one nation. When I vitalise them again I am forced to fully rely on the memory of others, which does not complete my own memory, but which are the only source of what I want to remember.'

11 For the dynamic of parallel existing perceptions of official and unofficial historicisations in Krajina, see Denich (1994b).

12 Compare critical reflections concerning this matter, which draw attention to the Balkans in general, in Höpken (1997).

13 In the course of the sixteenth and seventeenth centuries the most southerly Croatian regions of the Austro-Hungarian Empire which bordered with the Ottoman Empire were organised as a separate Military Border territory (the Croatian expression was 'Vojna krajina' or even 'Krajina'). The population was attracted to settle into this dangerous region by several privileges. In return they had, as border-men, the duty to defend the Military Border. Over the centuries the Military Border society functioned according to

military needs. It was different to the neighbouring Croatian feudal regions; armed defence was a major criterion of social organisation and this gave its inhabitants a very special identity. Only after the dissolution of the Military Border system and after the reunification of the Military Border with Croatia in 1881 did these differences began to disappear. About the history of the Military Border and its society, see especially Kaser (1997). The population of the Military Border had a different confessional (orthodox and catholic) as well as ethnic background. But the orthodox and catholic border-men were unified in the same social structure for centuries. At the end of the nineteenth century after the dissolution of the Military Border these different backgrounds began to be transformed into national self-definitions. Compare in this context Promitzer (1998).

14　Compare the reflections in the context of symbolic systems by Bausinger (1990) and the concepts of Erdheim (1992: 201–270).

15　With respect to the modernisation of patriarchal structures in former Yugoslavia in the period after the Second World War see especially the works of Joel Halpern, e.g. Halpern (1967, 1980).

16　For the connection between the state and actors level in ethnic conflicts, see Elwert and Gosztonyi (forthcoming).

17　The confrontational agitation of the political entrepreneurs (Babic, Martic) may have already started after agreements with the leadership of JNA. At this point one may ask if the JNA was acting according to 'instructions', possibly from Milosevic. It can only be speculated if the leaders in Krajina only realised the possibility of the situation escalating and took advantage of it, or if the conflict was stirred up after agreement on plans developed in Belgrade.

18　For the media war, see the published round table discussions of Croatian and Serbian intellectuals in Zagreb in 1993 during the war in *Erasmus* (1994). See also the contributions on the 'war of the media' in Popov (1996).

19　The news magazine *Profil* (1990) describes the atmosphere of the situation at the end of September–beginning of October: 'During Friday night Serbs in different villages of Croatia attacked police stations to arm themselves. In the following hours Croatian special police forces tried to collect the arms in the police stations to prevent them from being taken by militant Serbs. Protests in Petrinja, Glina and Dvor na Uni were quashed by heavily armed Croatian police forces with tear-gas and truncheons . . . After two policemen were hurt on Wednesday, 100,000 Croats demonstrated in the streets of Split, screaming: "give us weapons".'

20　See here also the detailed report of the Croatian Defence Minister of 1990–91: Spegelj (1999) and Tus (1999). For the point of view of the JNA command, see the memoirs of the Yugoslav defence minister of 1991 Kadijevic (1993).

21　The territorial defence forces (Teritorijalna odbrana – TO), a people's militia in reserve, were, along with the police forces, under the command of the individual republics of Yugoslavia. However, they were mostly disarmed during a broad action of the JNA in May 1990.

22　Nationality was of course very important in the recruitment of soldiers in the very beginning of this process. That the Croatian military forces were very much based on party membership was later openly declared in an interview by Spegelj, the former Minister of Defence. To give an example, during the establishment of military forces in Slavonia, about 40 per cent were members of HDZ, 30 per cent members of other Croatian parties and another 30 per cent did not belong to any party (Promitzer 1991: 20). After the HDZ assumed power, it was very difficult, if not to say impossible, for police forces of Serbian ethnicity to start a career; some policemen of Serb ethnicity were dismissed from their duties. In communist times, belonging to the Serb ethnic group had on the contrary been a decidedly significant advantage.

23 See the political memoirs of the last Serbian and the last Croatian president of the Yugoslav state presidium of that year; both were at that time directly involved (Jovic 1995; Mesic 1992). At that time, international pressure was exerted on Kadijevic to refrain from the use of violence (Kadijevic 1993).

24 This was described in detail by the then Milosevic protégé and at that time Serbian representative on the Yugoslav State committee, Borisav Jovic, in a TV interview in the documentary '*Bruderkrieg*' (BBC/ORF-TV 1996).

25 This happened on the basis of a referendum which was organised by the SDS in the second half of August. This referendum was held in Croatian communities with a Serbian majority and in those districts with a significant Serbian population share. It was announced that 560,000 voted for Serbian autonomy, while only 144 voted against it. At the same time the Serbian population was asked to resist in all ways the 'Terror of the Ustasha-like administrations' (*Archiv der Gegenwart* 1990: 35182).

26 On 21 December 1990 the new Croatian constitution was agreed in the Croatian Sabor. In it, the resignation of Croatia from the Yugoslav Federation and the announcement of independence were to be proclaimed, as soon as two-thirds of its members approved and a majority of voters in Croatia agreed to this action in a referendum.

27 During the escalation of war in July 1991, a detailed map of the towns and villages in which fighting took place was created by the Serbian opposition weekly magazine *Vreme*. Compiled by a military expert, it encompassed a detailed list of armed forces which were engaged in the fighting in Croatia (*Vreme* 1991: 4–5). Another detailed military expert estimate of the number of troops mobilised against each other can be found in *Danas* (1991b: 18–19).

REFERENCES

Archiv der Gegenwart, 60 (1990), 35182.

Bailey, F. G. (1970), *Stratagems and Spoils. A Social Anthropology of Politics* (Oxford).

Bausinger, H. (1990), 'Symbolfragen in der Volkskunde', *Tübinger Korrespondenzblatt*, 37, 3–7.

BBC/ORF-TV (1996), *Bruderkrieg* (Part II) (Vienna, London [documentary-video-cassette/ORF – BGM Ariola], 1996).

Borba (1990), 5–9 May (Belgrade).

Borba (1991), 3–5 March (Belgrade).

Danas (1990), 7 May (Zagreb).

Danas (1991a), May (Zagreb).

Danas (1991b), 16 July (Zagreb).

Dejan, J. (1993), 'Politicki stavovi i pozicije hrvatskih saborskih zastupnika u mandatu 1990–1992', *Politicka misao*, 30:4, 53–73.

Denich, B. (1994a), 'Unmaking multi-ethnicity in Yugoslavia: metamorphosis observed', *Anthropology of East Europe Review*, 11, 43–54.

Denich, B. (1994b), 'Dismembering Yugoslavia: nationalist ideologies and the symbolic revival of genocide', *American Ethnologist*, 21:2, 367–390.

Der Standard (1990), 4 May (Vienna), 3.

Dugandzija, N. (1991), 'Domet nacionalne zaokupljenosti', in S. Bahtijarevic and M. Lazic (eds), *Polozaj naroda i medjunacionalni odnosi u Hrvatskoj. Sociologijski i demografski aspekti* (Zagreb: Institut za drustvena istrazivanja Sveucilista).

Elwert, G. (1989), 'Nationalismus und Ethnizität. Über die Bildung von Wir-Gruppen', *Kölner Zeitschrift für Soziologie und Sozialpsychologie*, 3, 440–464.

Elwert, G. (1995a), 'Boundaries, cohesion and switching. On we-groups in ethnic, national and religious form', in B. Brumen and Z. Smitek (eds), *Bulletin of the Slovene Ethnological Society*, 24 (Ljubljana: Mediterranean Ethnological Summer School), 105–121.

Elwert, G. (1995b), 'Gewalt und Märkte', in W. Dombrowsky and U. Pasero (eds), *Wissenschaft, Literatur, Katastrophe. Festschrift zum 60. Geburtstag von Lars Clausen* (Opladen), 130–131.

Elwert, G. (1997), 'Gewaltmärkte. Beobachtungen zur Zweckrationalität der Gewalt', in T. Trotha, *Soziologie der Gewalt, Kölner Zeitschrift für Soziologie und Sozialpsychologie: Sonderheft 37* (Opladen), 86–101.

Elwert, G. and K. Gosztonyi (forthcoming), 'Gewalt und Ethnizität', in *Die 'zweite nationale Wiedergeburt'. Nationalismus, nationale Bewegungen und Nationalstaatbildung in der spät- und postkommunistischen Gesellschaft*, (Mannheim).

Erasmus (1994), 'Casopis za kulturu demokracije', 5 (Zagreb).

Erdheim, M. (1992), *Die gesellschaftliche Produktion von Unbewußtheit. Eine Einführung in den ethnopsychologischen Prozeß* (Frankfurt/M.).

Grandits, H. (1998), 'Über den Gebrauch der Toten der Vergangenheit als Mittel der – Deutung der Gegenwart – Betrachtungen zum Krajina-Konflikt 1991–95', in J. Koehler and S. Heyer (eds), *Anthropologie der Gewalt. Chancen und Grenzen der sozialwissenschaflichen Forschung* (Berlin), 179–186.

Grandits, H. and J. Halpern (1994), 'Traditionelle Wertmuster und der Krieg in Ex-Jugoslawien', *Beiträge zur Historischen Sozialkunde* 3, 91–102.

Grandits, H. and C. Promitzer (2001a), '. . . denn ein Kampf zwischen Serben und – Kroaten würde beide vernichten – Serben in Kroatien', *Ost-West Gegeninformationen*, 3, i–x.

Grandits, H. and C. Promitzer (2001b), '"Former Comrades" at war: historical perspectives on "ethnic cleansing" in Croatia', in J. M. Halpern and D. Kideckel (eds), *Neighbors at War. Anthropological Perspectives on Yugoslav Ethnicity, Culture and History* (Pennsylvania), 125–144.

Grdesic, I., M. Kasapovic, I. Siber and N. Zakosek (1991), *Hrvatska u izborima'90* (Zagreb).

Halbwachs, M. (1985), *Das kollektive Gedächtnis* (Frankfurt/M.).

Halpern, J. (1967), 'The process of modernization as reflected in Yugoslav peasant auto-biographies', *Essays in Balkan Ethnology*, 1, 109–126.

Halpern, J. (1980), 'Memories of recent change: some East European perspectives', in I. Volgyes, R. Lonsdale and W. Avery (eds), *The Process of Rural Transformation. Eastern Europe, Latin America and Australia* (New York), 242–268.

Höpken, W. (1997), '"Blockierte Zivilisierung"? Staatsbildung, Modernisierung und eth-nische Gewalt auf dem Balkan', in *Leviathan*, 25, 518–538.

Jovic, B. (1995), *Poslednji dani SFRJ* (Belgrade).

Kadijevic, V. (1993), *Moje videnje raspada – vojska bez drzave* (Beograd).

Kaser, K. (1996), 'Zum Problem der Erhaltung von Gewaltvorstellungen am Beispiel der ehemaligen österreichischen Militärgrenze', in E. Hardten *et al.* (eds), *Der Balkan in Europa* (Frankfurt, Berlin and New York).

Kaser, K.(1997), *Freier Bauer und Soldat. Die Militarisierung der agrarischen Gesellschaft an der kroatisch-slawonischen Militärgrenze 1535–1881* (Wien, Köln and Weimar).

Leutloff, C. (1998), '"Du gehörst weder hierher noch dahin. Du bist im Niemandsland." Zum Wandel des Selbstverständnisses von Krajina-Serben nach dem Exodus im August 1995', *Magisterarbeit, Institut für Ethnologie FU-Berlin.*

Livada, S. (1995), interviewed by Drago Hedl, in *Erasmus* 13, 19.

Mesic, S. (1992), *Kako smo srusili Jugoslaviju. Politicki memoari posljedneg presjednika predsjednistva SFRJ* (Zagreb).

Nagel, J. (1994), 'Constructing ethnicity: creating and recreating ethnic identity and culture', *Social Problems*, 41:1, 154–175.

Neckel, S. (1995), 'Politische Ethnizität. Das Beispiel der Vereinigten Staaten', in B. Nedelmann (ed.), *Politische Institutionen im Wandel. Kölner Zeitschrift für Soziologie und Sozialpsychologie, Sonderheft 35* (Opladen), 217–236.

Nicklas, H. (1991), 'Psychologie des Unfriedens. Ergebnisse der psychologischen Friedensforschung', in *Friedensforschung – Eine Handlungsorientierung zwischen Politik und Wissenschaft* (Darmstadt), 149–164.

Nyström, K. (1987), 'The Serbs in Croatia: a dual identity', *Nordic Journal of Soviet and East European Studies*, 4:3, 31–52.

Orywal, E. (1996), 'Krieg und Frieden in den Wissenschaften', in E. Orywal (ed.), *Krieg und Kampf. Die Gewalt in unseren Köpfen* (Berlin).

Politika (1990), 21 August (Belgrade).

Politika (1991), 3–5 March (Belgrade).

Popov, N. (ed.) (1996), *Srpska Strana Rata. Trauma i katarza u istorijskom pamcenju* (Belgrade).

Profil (1990), 9 October (Vienna).

Profil (1991), 8 April (Vienna).

Promitzer, C. (1991), 'Vom Krieg zum Bürgerkrieg', *Ost-West Gegeninformationen*, 7:8.

Promitzer, C. (1998), 'Grenzen und ethnische Identitäten. Eine theoretische Annäherung am Beispiel der habsburgischen Militärgrenze 18./19. Jh.', in D Roksandic (ed.), *Microhistory of the Triplex Confinium* (Budapest), 111–124.

Republicki zavod za statistiki (1992), *Popis stanovnistva 1991, Narodnosni sastav stanovnistva hrvatske po nasjelima. Republika Hrvatska, Dokumentacija 881* (Zagreb).

Rösel, J. (1997), 'Vom ethnischen Antagonismus zum ethnischen Bürgerkrieg. Antagonismus, Erinnerung und Gewalt in ethnischen Konflikten', in T. Trotha, *Soziologie der Gewalt, Kölner Zeitschrift für Soziologie und Sozialpsychologie: Sonderheft 37* (Opladen), 162–182.

Roksandic, D. (1991), *Srbi u Hrvatskoj* (Zagreb).

Scheffler, T. (1995), 'Ethnoradikalismus: Zum Verhältnis von Ethnopolitik und Gewalt', in G. Seewann (ed.), *Minderheiten als Konfliktpotential in Ostmittel- und Südosteuropa* (München), 9–47.

Siber, I. (1988), *Psihologijski aspekti medunacionalnih odnosa* (Zagreb 1988).

Siber, I. (1997), *The 1990 and 1992/93 Sabor Elections in Croatia: Analyses, Documents and Data* (Berlin).

Silber, L. and A. Little (1995), *Brüderkrieg. Der Krieg um Titos Erbe* (Graz, Wien and Köln).

Spegelj, M. (1999), 'Prva faza rata 1990–92: Pripreme JNA za agresiju i hrvatski obrambeni planovi', in B. Magas and I. Zanic (eds), *Rat u Hrvatskoj i Bosni i Hercegovini 1991–1995* (London, Zagreb and Sarajevo), 39–65.

Sundhaussen, H. (1994), 'Ethnoradikalismus in Aktion: Bemerkungen zum Ende Jugoslawiens', in *Geschichte und Gesellschaft*, 20. 402–423.

Tanjug (1990), Newsagency message, 18 August.

Tus, A. (1999), 'Rat u Sloveniji i Hrvatskoj do Sarajevskog primirja', in B. Magas and I. Zanic (eds), *Rat u Hrvatskoj i Bosni i Hercegovini 1991–1995* (London, Zagreb and Sarajevo), 67–91.

Vjesnik (1990a), 11 May (Zagreb).

Vjesnik (1990b), 31 May (Zagreb).

Vjesnik (1990c), 29 June (Zagreb), 1.

Vjesnik (1990d), 18 August (Zagreb).

Vjesnik (1990e), 28 September–4 October (Zagreb).

Vjesnik (1991a), 3–5 March (Zagreb).

Vjesnik (1991b), 29 March (Zagreb), 3.

Vreme (1991), 29 July (Belgrade), 4–5.

Waldmann, P. (1999), 'Societies in civil war', in G. Elwert, S. Feuchtwang and D. Neubert (eds), *Dynamics of Violence* (Berlin), 59–80.

Wimmer, A. (1995), 'Interethnische Konflikte. Ein Beitrag zur Integration aktueller Forschungsansätze', *Kölner Zeitschrift für Soziologie und Sozialpsychologie*, 47:3, 466–472.

Zakosek, N. (1998a), 'Elitenwandel in Kroatien 1989–1995', in H. Sundhaussen and W. Höpken (eds), *Eliten in Südosteuropa. Rolle, Kontinuität, Brüche in Geschichte und Gegenwart* (München), 279–288.

Zakosek, N. (1998b), 'Ekstremizam kao normalnost', *Erasmus*, 24, 15–18.

2

Non-existent states with strange institutions

Kristóf Gosztonyi

Introduction

THE SEPARATIST CROATIAN Republic of Herceg-Bosna is an especially opaque phenomenon even taking into account the usual obscurity of Bosnian events. As fighting erupted in Bosnia-Herzegovina, Croatian Forces under the command of the Herceg-Bosna authorities fought together with the fledgling troops of the Bosnian government against the Serb aggression. Rivalries between Bosnian Croats and Bosniaks, which seemed to have been present from the beginning cf their alliance (Halilovic 1997), led to increasingly violent clashes in January 1993 and to full-scale war four months later. At the height of this war (28 August 1993) the Croat Community of Herceg-Bosna transformed itself into a Republic and declared its independence. Military losses and international pressure compelled Franjo Tudjman, the President of the Republic of Croatia, to pressure Bosnian Croats to sign a peace agreement with the Bosnian central government in the spring of 1994, the so-called 'Washington Agreement'.

Until the signing of the Washington Agreement, Herceg-Bosna was a 'normal' secessionist pseudo-state with a dubious and authoritarian leader, Mate Boban, a more or less efficient and hierarchical wartime administration, and an increasingly centralised military corps (the HVO). In the course of the peace talks, Mate Boban was forced to resign and Krezimir Zubak, a previously unknown politician, took his place.

At the time of commencing fieldwork in February 1996, the impression gained from discussions differed strongly from the one-man-dominated para-state which had been described previously. Herceg-Bosna, though always a disputed and dubious political unit, seemed to be an obscure and undefined entity which gained a clear shape only if nationalist issues were touched upon. If asked about power holders, the names of politicians, military leaders and criminals were mentioned repeatedly, but none of them seemed to be anything other than second- or third-rank as far as political power was concerned.

46

So what happened? How was this amorphous and decidedly nationalistic political monster created? It may be argued that a general lesson can be learned from the Herceg-Bosna case.

Hypothesis

The major problem of Herceg-Bosna is that to the outside world it says that it is *not* a state, but it actually *acts* like a state and says it is to its population. This line of thought leads to an examination of the interaction of an outside agency (the international community) with the local political structures.

The impact of changes induced by the simple interaction between a hegemonic external agency and local structures can be extremely far-reaching. A total transformation of political systems can result. Usually an increase in centralisation and bureaucratic control is expected as a consequence of this development. This phenomenon has been repeatedly observed by scholars and is part of the common- sense knowledge of social sciences (Bierschenk 1984; Evers and Schiel 1988; Spittler 1981; Sigrist 1979, etc.).

These external interventions have been characterised by an authoritarian and undemocratic mindset. The end of the Cold War saw the emergence of a new, 'soft' type of intervention, based on democratic principles and an aversion to overt engagement. International engagement still has unintended effects. However, under certain circumstances, recent interventions seem to effect a decentralisation of power and responsibility rather than its centralisation. Herceg-Bosna is such a case.

Modern (peacekeeping) interventions take place in a political universe, the determining factors of which are: (a) traditional '*Realpolitik*', (b) democratic principles, (c) human rights and (d) an aversion to overt engagement owing to domestic political concerns.

It may be argued that under such circumstances a diffusion of power can take place in the political entity under pressure. This is what happened in Herceg-Bosna. Four conditions seem to contribute to such a diffusion of power owing to outside pressure:

- A relatively restrained foreign intervention.
- A tendency on the side of the interveners to address pre-existing political structures (instead of appointing new ones) or to accept new political structures legitimised by 'democratic' elections.
- A willingness on the side of the interveners to hold the representatives of the local political structures responsible for certain policy failures and human rights abuses.
- A strong identity and a common sentiment among the recipients of the foreign intervention that the aims of the intervention are not just.

If the above conditions are present, the diffusion of power and responsibility takes place as an effect of the following four mechanisms:

- The appointment of weak leaders (this strategy is conscious and rational on the level of group interests).
- The conscious dismantling of personal power by some politicians.
- The loss of legitimacy of politicians who bow to external pressure.
- The conscious creation of an institutional 'jungle' in order to diffuse responsibility.

The historical genesis of Herceg-Bosna will be briefly described first, and subsequently, its current amorphous condition will be treated in detail.

Herceg-Bosna: a normal separatist state

The first free elections in Bosnia-Herzegovina in 1990 resulted in a clear victory for the ethnic parties. The distribution of the votes between the national parties is almost identical to the national distribution of Bosnia-Herzegovina: 43 per cent Muslims, 31 per cent Serbs, 17 per cent Croats and 6 per cent Other (most of whom described themselves as being Yugoslavs).

When war broke out in 1992 the three leading national parties took over the state and organised the spontaneously forming defence groups into a structured military system. For the Croats the leading national party was the Croatian Democratic Community of Bosnia-Herzegovina, the HDZ BiH – a party closely connected to the ruling Croatian party, the HDZ.

Extremist forces within the HDZ BiH linked up and were supported by extremist groupings in Croatia planning to establish a Greater Croatia through the annexation of parts of Bosnia-Herzegovina. As a result of this hard-line conspiracy within the HDZ, the Croatian Community of Herceg-Bosna (HZ HB) was founded on 18 November 1991. The aim of the HZ HB was to protect the interests and historical territories of all Croat people, though it still claimed to be committed to a unified Bosnia-Herzegovina. The founding document already listed the regions of which it claimed to be composed and mentioned the town Mostar as its seat (*Narodni List HZ Herceg-Bosna* 1991).

The president of the newly founded HZ HB was Mate Boban. Soon afterwards, in February 1992, in a *coup*-style takeover Boban also became the president of the HDZ BiH and begin the cleansing of the party of liberal, pro-Bosnian elements. This coup thus marked a change in Bosnian–Croat policies concerning their Bosniak allies. Another significant event in this respect was the assassination of Bla Kraljevic, the leader of the paramilitary organisation the HOS (Hrvatske ombrambene snage – Croatian Defence Forces). He was killed in the summer of 1992 near Mostar and his organisation was disbanded following this. What was remarkable about the murder is that Kraljevic and the HOS, a military group of the extreme right, supported the continued alliance of Croats and Bosniaks against the Serbs.

The first significant clashes between the Bosnian Croat Army (HVO) and the Bosniak-dominated Bosnian government forces (ARBiH) erupted in Central Bosnia in the beginning of 1993 and were followed by a counter-offensive of the ARBiH somewhat later. The heavily outnumbered Croats suffered heavy losses.

Throughout these skirmishes the situation around Mostar and in Herzegovina remained relatively calm. Nominally the HVO and ARBiH were still allies in this region. This changed on 9 May 1993 when the HVO launched a full-scale, but not very successful attack on the mainly Bosniak-dominated east side of Mostar.

A nine-month-long bloody war ensued between the former allies. During this war even those areas which until then had escaped such atrocities were ethnically cleansed. The result was three, nationally homogeneous regions – one Serb, one Croat and one Bosniak. At the height of this war, 28 August 1993, the Croatian Community of Herceg-Bosna was transformed into the Croat Republic of Herceg-Bosna and its independence was declared. Croatia reacted positively.

For the rest of 1993 the Croats continued to suffer heavy losses especially in Central Bosnia, where the previously numerous Croats were now surrounded in a few embattled enclaves. Additionally foreign and domestic Croatian pressure was increasing on President Tudjman to change his policies towards Mate Boban and Herceg-Bosna. In February 1994 Mate Boban was forced to resign. His place was taken by 'an anonymous politician, Kresimir Zubak' (BOSNET 4 March 1994).

Still in February a ceasefire was brokered between Bosniaks and Croats and on 1 March 1994 the Washington Agreement was signed. The Agreement envisaged the foundation of a Federation based on Swiss-style cantons (four Bosniak, two Croat, two Mixed and a special Sarajevo district). The Federation would eventually join in a confederation with Croatia. 'Zubak said after taking office that a confederation with Moslems was "possible, even desirable"' (BOSNET 4 March 1994).

This marks the beginning of intense international involvement in the Bosnian War and also of the amorphous state of Herceg-Bosna. Before addressing this topic, however, the political structures of Herceg-Bosna prior to the diffusion of political authority in this entity will be examined.

Political structures in Herceg-Bosna until the end of the war

In the period until the fall of Mate Boban, Herceg-Bosna was a normal separatist state emerging from the chaos of the dissolution of the former Yugoslavia. Herceg-Bosna had, it seems, a functioning party apparatus and at its head an authoritarian leader, Boban. To demonstrate the difference between the emerging political authority and organisation (until February 1994) and the later state of 'disbanded' political control in Herceg-Bosna, two aspects of para-state politics have to be examined. First, the increasing unification and bureaucratisation of control over spontaneously formed military defence units and secondly, the political leadership and the relation of Herceg-Bosna to Croatia.

Unification and bureaucratic control of paramilitary units

Paramilitary units already began to be formed at the end of the 1980s as tensions between the federal partners of the Yugoslav state were increasing. In the initial period of the war, the military landscape was truly confusing. A report of the Hague War Crimes Tribunal summarises the situation accurately:

> The Croatian Defence Council forces in Bosnia and Herzegovina are supported by the Croatian Army, local Croatian police, volunteer civilians and 'special forces' like the military wing of the Croatian Party of Rights (named after the former Ustashas of the Second World War, who also fought against the Serbs in the Krajina area). Other Croatian armed civilian forces operate essentially in local areas. (Report of the Hague War Crimes Tribunal: The military structure of the warring factions and the strategies and tactics they employ 1995)

In this initial phase of the war, there were still no efficient command structures; the relationship between the different units was not yet established. The subsequent evolution towards a unified command structure affected the different paramilitary groupings – the local Croat police, 'special forces' and local forces of armed citizens – in different ways.

Whereas the bringing together of police forces and the local militias under a unified command structure seems to have been relatively easy, the 'disciplining' of the 'special troops' deserves particular attention. In all the theatres of war in the former Yugoslavia a cleansing of such troops and of their individual leaders has taken place. In Croatia it occurred towards the end of the first war year in 1991 and the beginning of 1992. The Serb insurgent para-states (i.e. the Republika Srpska Krajina in Croatia and the Republika Srpska in Bosnia) and the Bosnian government all cleansed their militaries in the course of 1992 and 1993. 'These heroes were either killed, put in jail, or disciplined', wrote the war reporter, Vladimir Jovanovic (1995).

However, not all 'special troops' suffered the same fate. Only 'those paramilitaries disloyal to the ruling elite were caught by a wave of never solved murders'. Cooperative special troop leaders continued to participate in the fighting, and were occasionally redeployed for 'special tasks' such as ethnic cleansing or to break the 'remnants of the democratic opposition and independent media' (Jovanovic 1995).

Concerning Herceg-Bosna the elimination of Bla Kraljevic, the leader of

HOS, fits into this same pattern. Other 'special troop' leaders, such as Mladen Naletilic Tuta, continued to exert influence and actually became one of the most powerful military leaders of Herceg-Bosna. Unlike Kraljevic, however, Tuta supported a split between the Croats and Bosniaks.

Thus, until the beginning of 1994, Herceg-Bosna seems to fit in the general pattern of all the warring parties. All these states increasingly began to unify their initially loose military units under a joint command and were thereby eliminating troublesome, independent-minded paramilitary units and their leaders. This process could not be completed in a short space of time and it is still ongoing. Additionally, it was probably never intended to be a completely finished process; semi-independent paramilitaries were a useful tool for doing the 'dirty work' of ethnic cleansing and terrorising the political opposition.

Nevertheless, it may be concluded that a movement towards the centralisation of power took place in Herceg-Bosna. If it was successful with regard to the armed forces it can be assumed to have been even more successful concerning other branches of the wartime administration of Herceg-Bosna. The next section examines the political leadership in Herceg-Bosna and the relations of Herceg-Bosna with Croatia.

Political leadership and the relations of Herceg-Bosna with Croatia

As has been already stated, Mate Boban was a leader with authority. His steady rise, first to the post of the President of the Croatian Community of Herceg-Bosna, then the President of the Bosnian HDZ and finally to the head of the self-proclaimed Croat Republic of Herceg-Bosna, shows his strong ambitions. In the course of his advance he reshaped the politics of the Bosnian Croats and of the HDZ BiH, though he received strong support for this project from the Croatian President, Tudjman and his Defence Minister, the Herzegovinian Gojko Susak, who died in April 1998.

Boban therefore must have held significant authority and even after his forced resignation he remained an influential figure in Herceg-Bosna until his death in the summer of 1997. His portrait hangs in the office of the Mostar Municipal Board of the HDZ. Without any doubt in 1992–93 he shaped Bosnian Croat politics. President Izetbegovic bitterly accused him of wanting to establish a 'Bobanistan'. Clearly he also saw Boban as wielding great power.

The actions of Boban supported Izetbegovic's views. In the course of 1993 he participated in the Geneva talks, and met for a round of secret negotiations with Karadjic where they attempted to carve up Bosnia and Herzegovina between Croats and Serbs. In other words, the actions of Boban indicate that he was an authoritarian leader with real power who was also treated that way by other politicians.

The further important question concerns the relationship of Croatia to

Herceg-Bosna. It seems that President Tudjman had at least four instruments available to put pressure on Boban and Herceg-Bosna: the structure of the HDZ, personal networks through his Herzegovinian Defence Minister Gojko Susak, the military and financial aid Croatia was giving to Herceg-Bosna and the networks of the Croatian secret service (SIS) and its Bosnian–Croat counterpart the HIS.

Particularly in this period the Croatian leadership viewed Herceg-Bosna as its own territory. Even more revealing about the Croatian influence on Herceg-Bosna in this period is the fact that facing mounting foreign and domestic pressure added with the deteriorating military situation in Central Bosnia, President Tudjman was able to force Boban to withdraw from his position as President of Herceg-Bosna at the beginning of 1994.

To summarise, Herceg-Bosna in the period before the beginning of 1994 was a nationalist para-state emerging from the chaos of the dissolution of the former Yugoslavia and later of Bosnia-Herzegovina. The disorderly, spontaneously formed units of this new state were, however, rapidly being transformed and integrated into an increasingly centralised, though never internationally recognised state. All this occurred under the leadership of an authoritarian leader, Mate Boban, who was able to shape the policies of the state and, it would seem, to enforce his decisions. He was treated accordingly by foreign statesmen. Moreover, the structures of the para-state Herceg-Bosna were being merged into Croatian structures of power, with Croatia being able to exert significant influence on Herceg-Bosnian events.

The question is, therefore, how did the breakdown of power, or at least the decentralisation of power, which is currently experienced by diplomats and foreign statesmen trying to deal with Herceg-Bosna, occur?

Mysterious Herceg-Bosna

Kresimir Zubak, the new President of Herceg-Bosna, stated after taking office in February 1994 'that a confederation with Moslems was "possible, even desirable"' (BOSNET 4 March 1994).

There was, however, little movement towards the implementation of the Federation of Bosnia and Herzegovina. The superstructure of the Federation was established but it remained without any effective power and without any institutions on the ground. No steps were made either towards the dismantling of Herceg-Bosna, 'a direct negation of the idea of the Federation'. Cooperation between Bosniaks and Croats was reduced to occasional joint military actions against the Serbs.

Some movement came with the signing of the Dayton Peace Agreement on 10–11 November 1995. The *Dayton Agreement on Implementing the Federation of Bosnia and Herzegovina of 10 November 1995* confirmed the abolition of Herceg-Bosna and set deadlines for the establishing of the cantons as agreed in the

Washington Agreement. The dismantling of Herceg-Bosna was a complicated process of transferring the competencies of the para-state to the Federation and/or to the cantons.

Under the Dayton Agreement, Herceg-Bosna was to disappear within two weeks of the signing of the Agreement. But Herceg-Bosna was not dismantled. Croat officials referred to the fact that the institutions of the Federation were not yet functioning. A transfer of competencies would thus leave Croat areas in an administrative vacuum. Facing mounting international pressure various distracting and confusing steps were taken and some competencies were formally transferred to new ministries or cantons.

Finally, 'Kresimir Zubak, the former President of the Muslim–Croat Federation and a Croat member of the three-man Bosnian presidency [announced] that the Bosnian Croat para-state of Herceg-Bosna ceased to exist on 17 December, the same day that the Bosnian republican government transferred its functions to the federation' (Sito Sucic 20 December 1996). A little over one month later, on 27 January 1997, representatives of all Bosnian Croat associations met to set up a new Croat Community of Herceg-Bosna. The new community replaced the banned para-state of the same name (Sito Sucic, 28 January 1997). Obviously Herceg-Bosna had not ceased to exist.

Since 1997 further significant improvements have taken place, and cantons have been established. The establishing of the ethnically pure Croat cantons posed no problems. The establishing of the two mixed cantons, however, proved to be more difficult. In order to meet the Dayton Agreement deadlines all cantonal assemblies did hold meetings, though not very productive ones. Whole cantonal sessions could be spent with the discussion of such interesting topics as to what the flag of the canton should be. Unfortunately the mixed cantons may prove as powerless as the Federation as a whole.

While a number of joint institutions – among others a joint police force – have been established, and one can see signs of increasingly coordinated joint action, in practice they still function as separate institutions. Thus, in a joint Federal Ministry the Croat head would give instructions to the Croat officials and the Bosniak head to the Bosniak officials.

As of 1999, the institutions of the Federation still did not function satisfactorily. The top-to-bottom strategy of establishing common institutions in Bosnia-Herzegovina is not a success. The orders of these institutions, which can be established only under significant international pressure, are not carried out. The blockade occurs on the one hand on an institutional level, e.g. the re-establishment of Herceg-Bosna, and on the other hand by individual level actors like policemen, administrative clerks, etc. who refuse to carry out the instructions issued by institutions which they do not consider legitimate.

Even though progress has been made in implementing the Federation, the general picture is still one of two separate para-states. The joint Croat–Bosniak institutions of the Federation wield little authority. But do the Herceg-Bosnian authorities hold power? Naturally, Herceg-Bosnian authorities are more powerful than any of the Federal institutions, but there is no centralised power or responsibility which would be usual for modern states.

However, the following indicators show the lack of coherent command structures, which are then discussed in greater detail:

- There is no strongly coordinated strategic action. Herceg-Bosna politics are mostly only able to act reactively, or to act in order to achieve simple objectives.
- The occasional total breakdown of hierarchical structures.
- An unconscious recognition of the loose command structures by the international community, as their representatives go to negotiate at a municipal levels.

Lack of strategic action

In addition to the usual political divisions within a party (e.g. hard-liners versus moderates) which usually appear at all levels of the party as vertical splits, and regional divisions, which are also quite frequent in most political organisations, in Herceg-Bosna a very strong division or chasm in a hierarchical sense may also be found. The leadership is frequently simply unable to impose its decisions on the hierarchically subordinate units.

A comparison with the Bosniaks is revealing. In the summer of 1997 the Office of the High Representative of the UN to Bosnia and Herzegovina (OHR), the main international organisation tasked with the implementation of the Dayton Agreement, increased its pressure on the Bosniak East-Mostarian leadership to evict some 150 Bosniak families from Croat houses near the former confrontation zone, but within ARBiH-held territory, the Bosniak leadership conceded. They had committed themselves to vacating the area in an internationally brokered agreement a few months earlier. Evacuating the 150 families was very unpopular among the population, but the leadership nevertheless went ahead with the project and succeeded. In the general scheme of Mostar politics, the Bosniak side appeared once again sufficiently cooperative, while the Croats remained the 'bad guys'. Compared with the Bosniak structures, the Croat side was unable to sacrifice short-term nationalist goals or achievements in order to gain longer-term political benefits.

Breakdown of hierarchic structures

An example of the breakdown of hierarchic structures occurred in early October 1998, when Bosniaks attempted a return to the strategically crucial village of Tasovcici. The reason for Tasovcici's strategic importance lies in its location on the major road leading from the Croatian Coast to Mostar. Additionally, there is a bridge of similar military importance spanning the Neretva. Immediately after the return took place, tensions flared and two days later the returnees were attacked with hand-grenades by a Croat mob after a demonstration organised by the Mayor of the Municipality. The attacks left one Bosniak dead and several wounded and increased international political pressure on the Croat side tremendously.

Probably because of the expected negative repercussions for the cause of Herceg-Bosna, a number of high-level Bosnian Croat politicians went to see Sir Martin Garrod, the Head of the Southern Office of OHR, in order, basically, to beg him to remove the Bosniak returnees from Tasovcici. They said they feared incalculable consequences if the returnees stayed. While they were still in discussions with Sir Martin, the first reports about the attacks on the returnees arrived. In the following days, the Croat Interior Minister of the Canton, who was one of the delegation asking Sir Martin to remove the returnees, completely lost control over the police administration of the municipality responsible for Tasovcici. The police there openly defied his instructions which were aimed at a de-escalation of the situation.

Recognition of loose command structures by the international community

Even though most international officials believed there was a clandestine and tightly organised hierarchy in Herceg-Bosna, when faced with a political problem in a certain Croat-controlled area, they usually try negotiating with all levels of decision making. Thus they approached the Croatian President, Franjo Tudjman, they held discussions with the Bosnian Croat leaders, i.e. Kresimir Zubak and later Ante Jelavic, as well as with cantonal and usually also municipal (!) heads. If there was a tight hierarchy within Herceg-Bosna, there would have been no need for high-level international representatives, such as, for example, the OHR Deputy High Representative Hanns Schumacher, to negotiate with the Mayor of the Croat-dominated Municipality of Stolac concerning the return of Bosniaks in the spring of 1997. The fact that high-level international officials repeatedly negotiated with mayors of municipalities reveals that they 'unconsciously' realised the true power of such low-level politicians within Herceg-Bosna.

Institutional anarchy

It is very difficult to show the partial absence of power in Herceg-Bosna, which has been hypothesised here. It is difficult to show the decentralisation and disintegration of power owing to the confusing presence of an administrative and party hierarchy which has created the impression of an organised political entity.

To a certain extent Herceg-Bosna does present a normal picture – roads are built, business permits are issued, etc. Other aspects of a functioning state are, however, absent.

Another difficulty in proving the absence of centralised power is the possibility that an unknown strong man or a grouping of power holders might control events from behind the scenes – a conspiracy theory. Additionally, the politics of the region are full of lies, deceit and confusion.

Owing to these difficulties and a general lack of information the evidence presented here is sketchy and is drawn from a variety of sources. Furthermore, a major part of the argument is based on indirect evidence. Conflicts of interest between certain groupings or individuals who are suspected of having determinate power or authority may reveal hidden structures.

It is important to clarify what is meant by a 'lack of power'. It is clear that no social system has an unambiguously hierarchical and centralised power structure. What will be shown here is that a number of individuals and groupings can be found which all hold certain powers in Herceg-Bosna. The relative status of these actors, regarding the amount of influence and authority they wield, is that of more or less equals, it is anarchy within an oligarchy.

Several different social actors, in the widest sense of the word, are usually suspected of wielding or having wielded power in Herceg-Bosna, namely:

- the state of Herceg-Bosna, or in other words the administrative organisation of that state;
- the HDZ;
- Croatia, i.e. Franjo Tudjman or Gojko Susak, the now deceased Croatian Defence Minister;
- criminals like Mladen Naletilic Tuta;
- the general population.

However, on several occasions all them have been proven incapable of imposing their will on the other power factors. Decision making frequently tends to become collective, carried out by bodies of the Assemblies of Municipal Boards of the HDZ. Finally, a number of power holding actors (organised crime, municipal boards of the HDZ, the general population, etc.) have the capability to block certain political developments. This capability can function as an effective veto.

The question is, then, how did this decentralisation of power occur? The phenomena of power decentralisation described above need to be connected to the actions of the international community. In this concluding section, an attempt is made to show how the international intervention caused the decentralisation of power in the region.

The international community

It has been shown that in the course of its historical evolution, Herceg-Bosna, emerging from the total chaos of the initial phase of the Bosnian war, entered a stage of increasing centralisation of power. This occurred from the beginning of 1992 until the end of 1993 under the leadership of Mate Boban.

Following the signing of the Washington Agreement, a change in the leadership of Herceg-Bosna took place. This period of Herceg-Bosnian history was characterised by a decentralisation of power and decision making, though its main nationalist goals remained untouched. It was also argued that modern international pressure is effective, though its effects are often not immediately obvious. Usually they manifest themselves only with a certain time lag.

The dissolution of power in Herceg-Bosna occurred as an unintended result of international pressure. However, this is not easy to establish as the kind of social mechanisms which are supposed to be operative in the process of power decentralisation are difficult to describe. The conditions for a Herceg-Bosna style dissolution of power, as discussed already, are outlined below:

- Owing to a relatively restrained international intervention (the unwillingness to suffer losses, etc.) the main instruments of enforcement are positive and negative economic sanctions. Military threats or sanctions are rare.
- The willingness on the side of the interveners to address pre-existing political structures (instead of appointing new ones) or to accept new political structures legitimised by 'democratic' elections.
- The willingness on the side of the interveners to hold the representatives of the local political structures personally responsible for certain policy failures and human rights abuses. With regard to this aspect of the international intervention, the main instrument available to the international community has been the Hague War Crimes Tribunal and more generally the United Nations (UN).
- A strong identity and a common sentiment among the recipients of the foreign intervention that the aims of the intervention are not just.

How did Croat and local Herceg-Bosnian politicians react to the approach of the international community as described in the first three conditions, given the strong common identity in the region as referred to in the fourth? The following mechanisms were suggested in the introduction:

- the appointment of weak leaders (this strategy is conscious and rational at the level of group interests);
- the conscious blurring of the chain of command or even dismantlement of personal power by some politicians;
- the loss of legitimacy of politicians who bowed to external pressure;

- the conscious creation of an institutional 'jungle' in order to diffuse responsibility.

The reality of these social mechanisms as a response to international pressure can only be surmised, because these strategies are formed on the basis of considerations not explicitly formulated. It would be naive to expect politicians to acknowledge having concealed their channels of authority or even that they consciously dismantled their personal power. Therefore, the different mechanisms proposed above as being a response to international intervention and as contributing to the current state of the dissolution of effective power, are elaborated upon through relevant examples.

Appointment of weak leaders

Two Croat leaders, Kresimir Zubak, the first President of the Federation of Bosnia and Herzegovina, and Mijo Brajkovic, the former Mayor of West Mostar, seem to fall into this category. Both were previously relatively unknown and both had a reputation for being moderate. It seems that neither of them was usually capable of enforcing agreements made with the representatives of international institutions. Weak political leaders often find themselves caught in a rather uncomfortable situation: on the one hand they are pressured by the international community, and on the other by their own national hard-liners.

Obscuring command structures and dismantling personal power

The Hague War Crimes Tribunal wrote the following concerning the blurring of command structures, particularly with regard to the unclear hierarchical relationship between different military units and between certain units and the national leadership: 'such a structure and the strategies and tactics employed help to blur the chain of command and conceal responsibility. This concealment may well be intended by some of the parties to provide a shield of plausible deniability.'

According to the United Nations High Commissioner for Refugees (UNHCR) Officers who served in the area during the Bosniak–Croat War soon after the establishing of the Hague War Crimes Tribunal, the Mayor of the west Herzegovinian town of Capljina began to refer international officials to his Deputy, Krunoslav Kordic when approached about the concentration camp for Bosniaks. Markovic claimed he was not responsible.

The reaction was the severance of formal chains of command to Bosnian Croats and a switch to an increasingly clandestine manipulation of Herceg-Bosnian politics. It is difficult to imagine that the dismantling of official channels of authority would not also result in a consequent loss of power.

A similar concealing, blurring and conscious dissolution of organised command can be suspected as having taken place at all levels of politics. However, the observation that decision makers do occasionally conceal authority, even at the cost of effectively dismantling the chain of command, can be accepted as valid for the situation with which Herceg-Bosna is currently confronted.

Loss of legitimacy for 'compromisers'

If leaders were strong prior to their contact with international actors, their compromising attitude would probably make them weak. A 'compromising' attitude means here a tendency to give in to pressure from international actors. The loss of power for such a 'compromiser' would probably happen gradually. Increasingly their subordinates would refuse to execute orders which they considered unjustified or harmful to national goals.

In a number of instances Herceg-Bosnian Croat police refused to execute the orders of Croat politicians, for example participating in Joint Police Patrols with Bosniaks in Mostar or prosecuting the individuals who evicted non-Croats from West Mostar (i.e. the Croat part of the town). The case of Ivan Prskalo, the Mayor of Mostar, provides another example. With regard to the expulsions 'Prskalo assured the city council during its December 14 session that these criminal acts [i.e. the expulsions of non-Croats from their apartments in West Mostar] would cease. The next day the expulsions continued' (BOSNET 1997).

By the same token, weak leaders can be forced to adopt more nationalist attitudes. Brajkovic, the former Mayor of West Mostar was originally regarded as a moderate. After he called for the infamous 'peaceful' demonstration against the European Union Administrator of Mostar, Hans Koschnick which, some foreign diplomats say, he could not avoid, he completely lost all credibility in the eyes of international actors. He is now generally known as a Croat hard-liner. He had nothing more to lose with regard to the international community.

Conscious creation of an institutional 'jungle'

This is the mechanism for which it is most difficult to provide 'hard' evidence. The argument that a confusing set of institutions, committees and subcommittees can easily be used by Herceg-Bosnian politicians eager to divert attention from themselves rests on two clues and on the general plausibility of the notion.

International officials told me repeatedly in interviews that they were convinced that when local politicians wanted to obstruct constructive negotiations they often forced the foundation of a working group of 'experts'. Such meetings were truly frustrating and rarely came up with anything constructive. Another hint as to the conscious use of an 'institutional jungle' to conceal responsibility is even more vague. It seems that Herceg-Bosnian institutions are restructured and their personnel changed with a confusing frequency. The names of certain functionaries turn up again and again in different positions.

It has to be noted, however, that the presence of such a highly complex institutional structure as prescribed in the Dayton Agreement, combined with the institutional reality of Herceg-Bosna is in itself sufficient to completely blur competence.

In summary, the above mechanisms of avoiding compromise when faced with international pressure can only be successful given the current form of restrained international intervention and by the presence of a strong common identity in Herceg-Bosna. The restrained character of international intervention is important in opening up the avenues of local resistance mentioned above, because its sanctions are relatively 'soft', and it shows little commitment to completely purging the Herceg-Bosnian political elite and replacing it with one more acceptable to international actors. The problems of such a relatively weak approach were already apparent to Holbrooke during the negotiations. Accordingly he pushed for a stronger mandate of international organisations implementing the Dayton Agreement, e.g. for the International Police Task Force to have real policing functions and not just the role of monitoring the performance of the local police, and also for the NATO-led Implementation Force (IFOR) to have a more robust mandate (Holbrooke 1998).

Past interventions often did not have such constraints. Soviet occupation of Eeastern European countries replaced the entire ruling elite of those countries with communist cadres favourable to Soviet interests. Also US interventions in South America, for example, did not have many constraints. Economic pressure was frequently supplemented with all kinds of subversive US activities. With ruthless strategies interveners thus either created their own elite or gave a compromising, opportunistic new elite such powers that it could stabilise its position regardless of public acceptance.

Given the current restrained interventions on the one hand, and a strong identity and a common rejection of the aims of the intervention by the population being subjected to the intervention on the other, the Herceg-Bosnian style of resistance can be surprisingly effective. The reason for the success of resistance in areas with strong common identities when faced with a restrained intervention lies in the social sanctioning of potential collaborators. This way opportunistic elites, who would be willing to accept the resources of the foreign interveners to build up their own power base, are discouraged. This discouragment can take the form of 'shaming' collaborators, boycotting cooperation with them or can even include violent sanctions against them.

REFERENCES

Bierschenk, T. (1984), *Weltmarkt, Außenabhängigkeit und Staatsformation in Südostarabien* (Saarbrücken and Lauderdale).

BOSNET (Bosnian Electronic Network) (1997), 7 January. Subject: BosNet Report: A Decisive Year Part 2., Online-publication, web 15 January 2002, www.bosnet.org/archive.

BOSNET (Bosnian Electronic Network) (1994), 4 March. Subject: Bosnet News – 3 March. Source: Reuters, www.bosnet.org/archive.

Evers, H. D. and T. Schiel (1988), *Strategische Gruppen. Vergleichende Studien zu Staat, Bürokratie und Klassenbildung in der Dritten Welt* (Berlin).

Halilovic, S. (1997), *Lukava Strategija* (Cunning Strategy) (Sarajevo).

Holbrooke, R. (1998), *To End a War* (New York).

Jovanovic, V, (1995), 'Paravojske jedinice' (Paramilitary units), *Monitor*, 14 April.

Narodni List HZ Herceg-Bosna (Official Gazette of the Croatian Community Herceg-Bosna) (1991), September.

Sigrist, C. (1979), *Regulierte Anarchie. Untersuchungen zum Fehlen und zur Entstehung politischer Herrschaft in segmentären Gesellschaften*, (Frankfurt/M.).

Sito Sucic, D. (1996), 'Herceg-Bosna said to be officially dismantled . . .' *OMRI Daily Digest*, 20 December.

Sito Sucic, D. (1997), 'Step closer to establishing Croatian community of Herceg-Bosna?' *OMRI Daily Digest*, 28 January.

Spittler, G. (1981), *Verwaltung in einem afrikanischen Bauernstaat* (Wiesbaden).

United Nations Security Council (1994), *S/1994/674* – 27 May 1994, Final Report of the Commission of Experts. Established Pursuant to Security Council Resolution 780 (1992), www.his.com/~twarrick/commxyu4.htm#III.A (19 January 2002).

3

A neglected dimension of conflict: the Albanian mafia

Xavier Raufer

The Albanian mafia: a real mafia at the heart of the Balkans?

A T THE END of 1999, the Kosovo daily newspaper *Koha Ditore* decided to break the law of silence: 'Drugs are flowing into Kosovo where we are witnessing the birth of a powerful mafia network', the province is gradually becoming 'a Colombia at the heart of Europe' (*Koha Ditore* 23 December 1999). On 10 March 2000 the special UN human rights investigator returned from a ten-day tour of the Balkans. What Jiri Dienstbier said is, if possible, even clearer: 'Kosovo is in chaos', the province has become 'a mafia paradise' (RFE/RL Newsline 21 March 2000).

This is not the first time that the term 'mafia' has served to describe organised crime at work throughout the albanophone area in the Balkans. But this debased word has lost so much force that now it describes any band of hoodlums. Whereas a real mafia is, on the contrary, a precise, very definite criminal entity having little in common with the 'milieu' of villains which is normally found almost everywhere in the world.

The real mafia

A mafia is a permanent secret society uniting a coalition of 'families' bound by blood or marriage; it is closed, endowed with elaborate hierarchies and rules from which one deviates only at the risk of one's life. A merciless law of silence (*omertà*) is made to surround it. A gang can be joined through affinity or friendship; but a mafia may be joined only by family or clan co-option, after an initiation. Mafias pass over but the 'family' endures – some have been in existence for centuries, whereas, if its boss is dead or locked up, a gang does not survive for long. Mafias recruit only on the basis of race or sex; thus, by cousinhood or clan. Initiation into the Cosa Nostra is only for those who are Sicilian, born in Sicily and male. Even if they are implicit, these rules always exist in a mafia. Able to resist the worst repression, a mafia is a state within a state with territory, subjects, laws and armed forces. 'The mafia family never dies out. You arrest two or three of them but the family remains, and if there are not enough children it co-opts even more daring men and gives them its daughters as wives' (Bocca 1993). The Cosa Nostra survived twenty years of fascism. The Chinese Triads have resisted fifty years of communism, ten of which were the 'Cultural Revolution' that claimed 30 million victims.

Is the Albanian–Kosovan–western Macedonian agglomeration a 'mafia' in the strict sense of the word? Taking strict definitions let us see if the proven facts in our possession confirm the diagnosis or not.

A real mafia? The circumstances of its appearance

Several visible signs show that Albanian crime has attained a high degree of organisation and sophistication. If this stage in itself is not enough for one to speak of a mafia, discussion is none the less eminently necessary. The signs are in the multi-criminal activity. The Albanian villains traffic in drugs, illegal migrants, arms, stolen vehicles, contraband cigarettes and alcohol. They devote themselves to pimping and burglary on a grand scale, kidnapping for ransom, contract killings, audio and video pirating, falsifying official documents (visas, etc.) and laundering criminal money.

The impressive capacity to conduct highly complex transnational operations

The secret mass transfer of migrants from the Albanian coastline to nearby Italy is anything but spontaneous and disorderly. According to a number of first-hand accounts – and the best Albanian and Italian experts – it is, on the contrary, a concerted operation aimed at making Puglia a criminal outpost in the Balkans for the European Union. At the point of departure ships are 'requisitioned' by disciplined, well-armed teams – not by panic-stricken, destitute hordes. Passengers are carefully selected on the basis of future possibilities of 'agreement' and of their hard currency funds; once on board, order is assured by armed criminals who melt into thin air in sight of the Italian coast.

There are other examples of international cooperation practised by Albanian organised crime:

- From Tirana a front company situated in Albania buys and then has delivered from the US safes, top-quality alarm and security systems. Subsequently, expert burglars from gangs come from Europe and America to train using these 'demonstration' materials.
- In the field of burglary, specialised gangs have teams variously qualified

depending on the difficulty of the target. Among them are elite elements whose operations are accompanied by a wealth of security and protection.

Consummate protection

Even more internalised than at the disappearance of the communist regime, two-thirds of the agents of the very paranoid Albanian GPU (the Sigurimi or Secret Police) were sacked; a number of them soon joined the local criminal clans. These individuals all go under the cover of pseudonyms, nicknames and false identities. Worse still, according to their local origins, Albanian hill-dwellers speak dialects crossed with slang which – even in the nearby valleys – their neighbours understand poorly. Take these difficulties together (pseudonyms and dialect) and imagine the difficulties for Italian or Swiss police who have to decipher the transcripts produced from telephone tapping.

Reliable evidence of criminal sophistication

Michael Lauber, head of the Financial Intelligence Unit (FIU) and until 2000 head of the Centre for Organised Crime/Crime-Analyses of the Federal Police Office in Switzerland, has stated: 'The Kosovars and Albanians operate in the greatest secrecy. It is very difficult to get information from them during inquiries because they are grouped in small closed clans – almost in families comparable to the old model of the Italian mafia. Besides, they are experts in the art of using new technologies such as laptops, mobiles and the Internet' (*Le Matin-Dimanche* 15 August 1999).

An officer of the Italian ROS (the elite operations section of the Italian gendarmerie, specialising in high-risk anti-mafia actions) has said: 'The Kosovo Albanians are among the most dangerous drugs and arms traffickers. These men are determined, violent and capable of the worst. They can mobilise in a few hours a host of men at arms and have at their disposal enormous amounts of ready money. To keep in trim they burgle homes and businesses every night while constantly being on the move from one part of Lombardy to another' (*Corriere della Sera* 15 October 1998).

These facts and testimony reveal a high level of criminal professionalism, but this still does not allow us to speak of a mafia in the strict sense. Two decisive elements are lacking.

A clan society: Kanun, *honour and vendetta*

In Albania, and even more so in the mountainous north of the country, there survives in an almost chemically pure form (owing to the constant isolation of the country throughout the twentieth century) a traditional Mediterranean clan society, respectful of ancestral traditions of honour and vengeance. For most of the mafias these rules and laws are implicit, passed down by word of mouth. But in Albania the code of honour or *Kanun* is written down and the brochure that contains it is on sale in newspaper kiosks.

Complex organisation, iron discipline

Up to this point all the elements which would allow us to qualify a sophisticated trans-national criminal organisation as a mafia have been listed. Only one, deciding factor is lacking, which in itself allows us to confirm or disqualify the mafia claim: the mode of organisation. For, in Corsica for example, a clan society and a very active criminal scene have produced – for the lack of an appropriate organisational model or the will to apply one – only a circle (*milieu*) rather than a mafia.

Starting at the base of the pyramid, among Albanian criminals the basic cell is a team of four to ten men from the same clan and the same village, often from the same biological family. Specialising in a distinct kind of criminal activity (pimping, burglary, various types of trafficking, etc.) and most often very 'professional', the team obeys a boss blindly. Several teams operate on a territory, in a given sector. In emigration, coordinating the activity of the basic cells is done by a 'liaison coordination officer' who operates most often under the cover of a cultural or folkloric activity. Throughout Europe the police diagnosis is the same: these teams live discreetly, without attracting attention; they systematically practice countersurveillance of the forces of order. The actions they demonstrate often have a military precision.

To 'work' in a cell is to belong to a distinct criminal clan; the conditions of access to this criminal clan are strict, codified, ritualised. There is one code, the *Kanun*, and one biological cadre, an extended family. There is a hierarchy in which the ties of blood win out over those of marriage – for example, tactical coordination among local teams is entrusted to a man who can have entered the criminal clan only through marriage; but for strategic planning, between branches of activity or extended geographical areas and the criminal directorate situated at home, the coordinator must belong to the clan by blood and the biological family. At the intermediate level, the second-in-command controls a geographical area or a branch of activity. Depending on place and time, the various elements of the criminal clan act separately or come together in a flexible and decentralised manner. At the apex is a boss, assisted by a directing council which determines major policies and acts as arbiter in crises. Overall the organisation is adaptable, flexible and capable of evolving. With regard to tradition and the *omertà*, personal initiative is possible – even recommended; mutations and adaptations are even better since the obedience of the troops is assured and the scorn of the bosses for the law of the country in which they operate is absolute.

Finances of the Albanian mafia

It is hard to estimate the 'turnover' of one of a secret and ferocious criminal society. Especially when the only police force which could, under the circumstances, be effective, that of the Republic of Albania, prefers most of the time to steer clear of such dangerous entities. We should note, however, that in the Croatian journal *National* (No. 287, May 2001) the Croatian minister of the interior, Mr Sime Lucin, estimated the fortune of one of the main Serb gangsters, Stanko Subotic Cane, at US$ 500 million. And Cane's main line of activity is only trafficking in cigarettes, which is much less lucrative than drugs. Besides which it is known that most of the heroin transported along the Balkans route passes through the hands of Albanian mafia groups; that this traffic has taken off since summer 1999 (before then only 5–10 kg of heroin was being seized; since then, from 50 kg to nearly 1 metric tonne); and that 1 kg of 'good' heroin from the Golden Crescent (Afghanistan, etc.) brings a wholesale price, in western Europe, of US$ 80,000–100,000. This gives some idea of the scale of profits made by the Albanian mafia.

The deciding distinction made by Italian experts

In autumn 1999 the Italian Directorate for Anti-Mafia Investigations (DIA) transmitted to its supervising authorities a confidential report entitled 'Strategic and tactical importance of Albanian criminal organisations'. Let us recall that the DIA brings together – for a good reason – the best experts on mafia phenomena who have been confronted for years by the most ferocious and intractable criminal families in the European Union. These are specialists in observation and penetration – one might say dissection – who, moreover, have long been planted on the criminals' patch, in Albania itself. Nobody is better qualified than they to differentiate between a real mafia and a simple criminal gang.

In a text showing a high degree of analytical subtlety the DIA experts flag up from the outset a trap which must not be fallen into – and into which the Albanian mafia intends to make us fall, by urging us to confuse the disorder and chaos reigning in Albania for almost a decade and the reality of the mafia in that country. In fact for the DIA nothing would be more wrong than to confuse the Albanian mafia with 'the groups of looters leaving their trails throughout the country without being disturbed, groups with no equivalent in any European country', this 'multitude of hardened gangs operating at the local level with no link between them' which functions 'under a regime of reciprocal non-interference, without one being able to pick out [among them] dominant cells, and devoting themselves to acts of pillage pure and simple' (DIA 1999). Gangs 'whose fragmentation reflects the social and political break-up of the [Albanian] nation' (DIA 1999).

The Albanian mafia and these anarchical gangs do not mingle. Worse, these gangs embarrass the local mafias, men of order who prefer to reach agreements with politicians in their pay and corrupt an apparently repressive police rather than evolving among the looters who threaten their profits and the peace of their (biological or criminal) family. However, on the day when, inevitably, the Albanian disorder is resolved, when an apparent calm reigns in Tirana, the usual optimists will proclaim the 'Good News' of the death of the local mafia. But on the contrary, that will be the sign that this mafia has finally imposed order on the anarchic gangs who simply cause trouble prejudicial to 'business'.

But what do the DIA experts say about the Albanian mafia itself? 'Today we can speak of a true Albanian mafia in a state of permanent evolution; it is developing in a criminal context capable of making remarkable qualitative leaps . . . The actual criminal level of the Albanian mafia has no equal in any country in the Mediterranean basin, not even in Turkey' (DIA 1999):

- The Albanian mafia in Italy 'has at its disposal there a formidable network of accomplices and supporters used to squeal on members of rival groups and assist in assassinations' (DIA 1999).
- Putting down international roots: 'The Albanian [mafia] groups operating abroad work in conditions of perfect criminal sophistication and territorial integration in the states where their members have been planted (Germany, Spain, Italy, the Netherlands, Switzerland)' (DIA 1999). There is 'a perfect osmosis between Albanian mafiosi residing in Italy and those living in their country of origin' (DIA 1999). We should note that certain 'globalised' Albanian mafia clans are based outside the albanophone area, for example in Turkey.
- Unity of criminal law, competition for territory: 'Groups active in Italy operate in competition and are often locked in a struggle with each other, reflecting the cleavages which exist in Albania' (DIA 1999).
- Centralisation of decision making: 'Murders committed in Italy are often a consequence of incidents which happen in Albania linked with the redistribution of the Italian, and therefore European, heroin market' (DIA 1999).
- Law of silence: 'The very pronounced mafia character of the Albanian [criminal] associations follows equally from the behaviour of its members after an arrest. There is never, even in confidence, any revealing of the features of the group to which they belong. The response is unchanging: my [biological] family is in danger in Albania' (DIA 1999).
- Finance and money laundering: 'The Albanian criminal groups show a remarkable aptitude in the matter of financial management and a theoretical ability to carry out recycling' (DIA 1999).

All the characteristics are definitely there. Albanian organised crime is a mafia, of the first rank. It is also a mafia whose activism is growing in its primary base in Europe, in Italy. Early in January 2000 the DIA published another report, this one public, intended for parliamentarians. It is entitled 'Vitality of the Italian mafia, the rise of the Albanian mafia'. In this study the latter is described as 'particularly aggressive and determined', the experts underline that it 'has succeeded in planting its networks and logistics in the great metropolises of northern Italy and on the Adriatic coast' (DIA 2000).

Kosovo, guerillas, mafia: causality or symbiosis?

Since the public appearance of the Kosovo Liberation Army (UCK) during 1996 the accusations and rumours have not ceased. The UCK is a narco-guerrilla force financed by heroin from the Balkans route. In an interview given to the weekly *Der Spiegel*, Norbert Spinrath, president of the association of German police officers, returning from a stay in Kosovo, declared: 'The UCK is a criminal organisation . . . the UCK sequesters, steals, loots, kidnaps, blackmails, pressurises witnesses and carries out assassinations.' In short it 'behaves like a mafia' (*Der Spiegel* 15 December 1999). Shortly afterwards, Walter Kege, head of the equivalent Swiss general intelligence police, affirmed that they have information indicating a link between drug money and the UCK. In January 1999, La *Repubblica*, a heavyweight and respected daily, ran the following headline: 'Heroin sold in Milan finances the Kosovo Liberation Army.'

As early as March 1998 commissioner Olivier Gueniat, head of the Neuchâtel criminal investigations department, warned: 'Drugs are financing ethnic war' (*Le Temps* 28 March 1998). He was referring to the war in Kosovo. Confirmation came in June 1998 when an international police operation out of Italy arrested ninety villains and broke up eight networks of drugs traffickers of which 'one group of Albanians from Kosovo was smuggling arms destined for their province which was rebelling' (AFP 9 June 1998). In total, in that single haul, 100 kg of heroin and cocaine was seized. The base of the networks is in Milan where the drugs traffickers have as cover a vast infrastructure of cafés, restaurants, garages and various companies.

But even if it seemed serious to the European media the suspicion of drugs trafficking hanging over the UCK – 'drugs are financing the guerrilla' – does not have much meaning insofar as it transfers onto the Balkan situation blueprints and values peculiar to western Europe but unknown in eastern Europe, especially in the albanophone area of the Balkans.

Our, western European, society is individualist. The individual is practically the only motor and actor in social life. Getting involved in a party, acting as a militant in a union, taking up a religion or joining an association are personal acts relevant to the political, social or religious conscience of an individual. In the albanophone area of the Balkans this is absolutely not the case. War, guerrilla, clans and the like should be less compared to western European society but rather to, say, Lebanon during the civil war (1975–90). In the south of that country and at that time, it was not individuals who joined Amal or Hezbollah – in the same way as westerners join Republican or Socialist Parties – but whole villages, families or clans. In a society of this type the individual is nothing outside their extended family.

Returning to the albanophone area of the Balkans the clan dimension has always been a reality, and how it disguises itself according to circumstance simply a masquerade to amuse the gallery. When some western Marxist–Leninists of the 1960s idolised Enver Hoxha as a pure, tough revolutionary they missed the point that in 1962, of fifty-eight members of his Central Committee, twenty-eight came from the same clan and eight had married among themselves. The Albanian Communist Party resembled a tribal coalition – it was an affair of the extended family.

The search for material proof of a significant drugs traffic organised by the UCK itself is most likely in vain. There is no hope of finding a 'smoking gun' here. It may be unpalatable, but the UCK evolved in the bosom of a criminal economy, bathing in nourishing plankton of felony. This classic division of labour was explained by an (anonymous) American official posted to Kosovo as thus: 'The Albanian mafia has played a key role in the rise of the UCK. The latter needed money, smuggling routes and contacts in the Kosovan diaspora; in exchange, the UCK gave these "patriotic" gangsters political legitimacy.' As a result throughout Europe, from Oslo to Prague (with Princ Dobroshi), and across to Milan (with Agim Gashi – see below for profiles), mafia cells and networks are financing 'The cause', buying arms on behalf of the guerrillas. Even criminals in obscurity, those without rank, cooperate. In Barcelona, it is a group called the 'Vanguardia', a gang which burgles companies in the region and uses its booty to finance the UCK.

There remains the case of the high-level (i.e. 'political' and 'military') staff of the UCK. Even though there certainly seem to be a number of clues pointing to the assumption that they are hand in glove with the important figures in the mafia it proves difficult to carry out investigations among some of them, as 'L'Humanité' emphasises: 'What would happen if one were to find out that Hashim Thaci, the man on whom the international community has staked everything to rebuild the province, is implicated in almost all this traffic? It was without doubt in order to avoid this embarrassing question that Bernard Kouchner decided to filter out all enquiries directed against the latter.' But in spite of these hurdles the mafia connections among some of the UCK leaders are well established, a notch above the army itself and outside of Kosovo proper, in fact what is known allows us to speak of serious criminal involvement.

Among the sixteen Kosovar delegates to the Rambouillet conference in February 1999 was Xhavit Haliti, presented as a member of the political bureau of the UCK. Close to Hashim Thaci (the political head of the UCK) this man is influential in the Albanian diaspora in Switzerland and Germany. But this former adviser to Enver Hoxha under the Stalinist regime is nowadays linked to the special services and to the Tirana government, and is above all the link between Hasim Thaci and another Thaci (or Thaqi, according to records), first name Menduli, one of the heads of the Albanian community in Macedonia.

All experts on the Balkan criminal scene are categorical that the Albanian parties in Macedonia emanate directly from the local mafia. Several of their leaders (Midhat Emini and Husein Haskaj) have already been convicted of arms trafficking. These experts warned the French government about this in good time, before the Rambouillet meeting. They added that leaders of these parties, like Menduli Thaci and his colleague Abdurahman Haliti, have since 1994 directed an armed community militia forming in reality a criminal bloc bound up with corrupt elements of the SHIK, the Albanian secret service, and the local mafia. This bloc operates throughout the 'Golden Triangle' on perfect terms with the heads of the UCK, thanks to the diligence of *consigliere* such as Xhavit Haliti.

After Xhavit Haliti there are evidently plenty of others in the shadows. To identify them and reveal their mafia connections would allow us to draw a criminal web at the centre of which, unsurprisingly, the heads of the Albanian mafia reign. And potentially more or less near to the centre of the web one would also be able to identify certain Kosovar politicians or military chiefs. But this last point is at best secondary; in the region there is no lack of candidates ready to get rich quick.

The two 'godfathers' of the Albanian mafia

In northern Europe: Princ Dobroshi

On 23 February 1999 Princ Dobroshi, 35, was arrested in Prague by a police special unit, the Czech equivalent of RAID. At the wheel of a BMW, the man was parking in front of the Hotel Atrium. A little later his right-hand man, Murati Limani, was in turn questioned at his home in Prague. In Dobroshi's apartment a Croatian machine-pistol, a Chinese telescopic rifle with a silencer, a Czech handgun and a banknote counter (of the kind used in banking establishments) were found. This is the usual arsenal of a drugs trafficker, which is exactly Princ Dobroshi's trade. He is a big-time drug trafficker and for the Norwegian police, Dobroshi 'controls the Scandinavian drugs market'; to be exact, the northern path of the Balkans route (Turkey–Balkans–Czech Republic–Nordic countries). Dobroshi has imported hundreds of kilograms, even tonnes of heroin into Scandinavia. Arrested in Norway in 1993, Dobroshi was sentenced at the end of 1994 to fourteen years in prison for drugs trafficking. He escaped in January 1997 from the Ullersmo prison in Oslo after bribing a guard (who was paid FF

120,000 to turn a blind eye). He got as far as Croatia where plastic surgery made him unrecognisable. He moved to Prague in 1997.

For several months a joint operation (codenamed 'Cage') between Czech, Norwegian, Danish and Swedish police targeted the Dobroshi network, forty-two members of which were questioned up to February 1999. But when its boss was arrested the 'family' quickly made it known that it would hand over the sum of FF 4 million to whomever in the Czech Republic could set him free.

Significantly, a note by the BIS (the Czech special services) stated that part of the drugs money went towards buying arms for the UCK (*Lidove Noviny* March 1999). And when the Czechs decided to extradite Dobroshi, the Norwegian police eventually chose to take him back to Oslo in a private plane as 'it would be too dangerous to transport him on a commercial flight due to his close links with the UCK' (*The Norway Post* 13 April 1999). Dobroshi was returned to his cell in Norway in August 1999.

In southern Europe: Agim Gashi

In July 1998, the special anti-mafia unit of the Italian *carabinieri*, the ROS, launched operation 'Africa'. It was aimed at dismantling an important Albanian mafia clan trafficking heroin worth 'hundreds of millions of dollars' (*The Philadelphia Inquirer* 15 March 1999). In all, 124 arrests were made, most of them Albanians, but also Italians, Germans, Tunisians, Spaniards and Turks. At the head of the 'family' was Agim Gashi, 33, an Albanian from Pristina (in Kosovo) where at the beginning of the 1990s he directed a drugs trafficking network under the cover of beauty parlours and estate agencies.

In January 1992 Gashi settled in the suburbs of Milan and married an Italian. At that time the Albanian criminal clans were active in Milan – but not yet in drugs. Their speciality then was enslaving children who were forced into begging, into becoming pickpockets or prostitution for paedophiles. Violent and pitiless, the Albanian gangsters quickly imposed themselves on the low life of Milan, and from prostitution soon moved into drugs trafficking. Gashi ruled over this traffic. From 1995 he owned beauty parlours and perfume shops in London and companies in Hungary, Germany and Norway. In Italy itself Gashi established close professional links with the Ndrangheta, the Calabrian mafia. It was a case of importing cargoes of drugs into Italy; his associate Avni I. Ademer, a wholesaler specialising in trade with Turkey, every day hid tens of kilos of heroin in his containers of nuts and cotton goods, etc.

Gashi lived the high life in a luxury villa on the outskirts of Milan, but nevertheless, as a good 'patriotic bandit' did not forget his country. 'When war broke out in Kosovo', as Carlos De Donno, commander of the *carabinieri* intelligence unit, remarked, 'Kosovar criminals planted in Italy suddenly took an interest in arms trafficking. Up till then they only trafficked in drugs' (*The Philadelphia*

Inquirer 15 March 1999). Since then the activity in Italy of the Albanian mafia and that of the overseas elements of the UCK merged, everybody lent a hand, as telephone tapping operated by the ROS proved (*Corriere Della Sera* 19 January 1999). Gashi was in talks with arms dealers from Bulgaria, Romania and Albania to buy automatic weapons, rocket launchers and grenades. In these 'business' transactions it should be noted that Gashi spoke Serbo-Croat.

Having been convicted and receiving a heavy sentence in Milan in March 1999, Gashi sows less fear. Which doubtless explains why, at the end of February 1999, his cousin and associate Ekrem Gashi was assassinated in Pristina; in the purest mafia tradition, his Mercedes was riddled with bursts of automatic gunfire.

Why was the Albanian mafia able to spread in Europe at this point?

Forgetting the criminal dimension

In April 1999 the 'seventy-eight-day war' broke out in Kosovo. A criminologist should not expound on the political or military dimension of such a conflict but should warn of the risk, if it exists, and then analyse the possible criminal consequences of the conflict. With a mind to the future the criminologist should also think preventively and see how best to integrate the notion of respect for the law into the 'specifications' of future international operations or peacekeeping actions.

What happened prior to the NATO military intervention in Kosovo?

In Europe (in France and Great Britain, but also in the United States) official experts or products of the academic world (criminologists, police, intelligence officers, etc.) warned the coalition's political and military leaders about the very specific nature of the conflict in the Balkans, peculiarities, complex and deeply rooted in history, which are impossible to fully expound upon here. But briefly, these experts insisted on:

- The hybrid nature of the conflicts in the region. These Balkan conflicts have always had a military dimension, of course, but also a strong criminal element.
- The presence in the region of authentic mafias – especially the Albanian mafia. One degree lower, these experts did not fail to emphasise the existence in the Balkans of powerful organised crime, which was rich and well armed.

Truth obliges us to say that no heed was taken of these warnings. Diplomats continued to carry on their diplomacy, politicians their policy, and the military made war. The result of this disastrous neglect of the criminal dimension of the conflict in the Balkans is that, since then, trafficking in drugs, stolen vehicles and human beings has exploded in the region and from there has spread to western Europe.

As mentioned above Interpol notes that seizures of heroin along the Balkans Route, which were until the beginning of 1999 from 1 to 5 kg on average, have gone since the summer of 1999 to 50 kg and sometimes even 1 metric tonne of pure heroin per seizure!

Preventing such catastrophes tomorrow

What can be done to avoid international intervention fostering the spread of criminal networks – for which Europe will pay the price for a long time? What could be the role of the United Nations, in particular that of the UN Bureau for the Control of Drugs and Prevention of Crime, in the domain of crisis prevention?

One must be realistic, there will be more such serious international crises in the future, in the absence of a world order which is clear, lasting, stable and acceptable to all. In these conditions military interventions and peacekeeping missions will again be necessary. What can be done so that, in case of need, the criminal dimension of a given region can be taken into account?

In this case, clamouring for the establishment of the rule of law is not enough. Asking for the application of the law is a rhetorical demand if one does not know what laws are in question and what crimes are most likely to be committed – in short, if one ignores the criminal reality of the region concerned. In fact laws and legal procedures have, always and everywhere, one aim: to check and punish specific crimes. As long as one has no serious idea about the nature of these crimes one cannot speak seriously of restoring the rule of law. So what is to be done?

Civil and military officials tend to neglect the advice of experts – naturally, put forward in secrecy – when faced with the intense media bombardment to which they are submitted. In a time of grave crisis and serious criminal danger the warning must therefore be strong and come from the top. The community of nations should therefore have at its disposal a crime observatory allowing it to carry out with authority, responsibility and independence a criminal diagnosis of the region concerned. The mission of this observatory would be dual:

- To provide the leaders of the United Nations and the forces of order with precise and neutral information on the criminal situation in the region concerned.
- To make sure that this information is taken into account by political and military leaders involved in the operation.

This observatory could also appraise needs in terms of judges and precise juridical texts, if a crime wave was to follow intervention. It is all the more important to have this type of 'crime X-ray' tool since the forces of justice are slow – bound as they are by laws, rules and procedures – and since, on the contrary, criminal societies are essentially opportunist and fast-moving.

Kosovo provides a clear example: since the arrival of NATO forces, from the beginning of July 1999 at the latest, the mafias were at work throughout the province. Eighteen months after the start of the NATO intervention, Kosovo and Albania had no effective reciprocal extradition agreement allowing Kosovar criminals captured in Albania to be taken back to Kosovo, and to send back the former Albanian mafias arrested in Kosovo, without complex juridical wrangling.

In concrete terms we can see that from the point of view of crime the international community is confronted by problems which are serious but few in number and similar in nature. Prior to the establishment or re-establishment of the rule of law it seems important to define a few great anti-criminal principles of universal import and accepted by all. The anti-terrorist struggle provides a concrete example here, great progress has been made in this area when the international community decided in its entirety that certain acts (indiscriminate attacks, hijacking aeroplanes, massacres, etc.) were ideologically, politically and morally unjustified and would henceforth only be considered serious crimes and inexcusable terrorist acts. These sorts of rules must be created and approved in the course of the struggle against organised international crime.

REFERENCES

Bocca, G. (1993), *L'enfer: enquête au pays de la mafia* (Paris).
Corriere Della Sera (1998), 'How the Albanian mafia helps the guerilla fighters of Kosovo' (15 October).
Malcolm, N. (1998), *Kosovo. A Short History* (London).
Ministry of the Interior of Italy (1999), Directorate for Anti-Mafia Investigations (DIA), *Strategic and Tactical Importance of Albanian Criminal Organisations* (Rome) (confidential report).
Ministry of the Interior of Italy (2000), Directorate for Anti-Mafia Investigations (DIA), *Vitality of the Italian Mafia, the Rise of the Albanian Mafia* (Rome).
RFE/RL Newsline (2000), 21 March 2000, 'UN envoy decries situation in Kosova', Online-publication, web 10.01.2002
www.rferl.org/newsline/2000/03/210300.asp.

4

Land reforms and ethnic tensions: scenarios in south east Europe

Christian Giordano

Introduction: 'Staatsnation' and the 'purity myth'

BOTH IN WESTERN and eastern Europe the specific combination of territory, language, creed with citizenship and/or nationality, is generally perceived as an invariable and inviolable heritage of individual and collective 'identities' (Conte 1995: 138). It is a widespread belief that can be found even in the most common aspects of everyday life. This belief reaches its political–institutional achievement in the concept of *Staatnation*. This German term of French origin (Pierré-Caps 1995: 56) is based on the doctrine according to which each 'nation' must have its own territorial State and each State must consist of one 'nation' only (Altermatt 1996: 53). It is not surprising that the past century has been marked by repeated efforts to make individual national territories more and more ethnically and culturally homogeneous, especially in south east Europe where the principle of *Staatnation* was applied much later than in western Europe; that is, only after the downfall of the imperial multi-ethnic states. Connected with this 'logic of purity' land reforms played a significant role in this part of Europe.

Land reforms and 'ethnic recomposition'

It is well known that, in very broad terms, a land reform implies a redefinition of property rights on land through State legislative acts. The definition of land regimes are basic duties that *Staatsnationen* claimed from the very beginning, almost without exception. Hence, land reform as a legislative instrument is the cornerstone of any territorial policy that pursues the heightening of national cohesion and unity.

In substance, land reforms in the south east European *Staatsnationen* was meant to achieve the following goals:

- To carry through an 'act of justice' mainly by retrenching the latifundist regime in order to apportion 'the land to the peasants'. Land reforms were intended to find a solution to the 'social question' which, given the specific socio-economic situation in south east Europe (as in several other societies), is above all an 'agrarian question'.

- To create an economic basis for the rise or growth of a rural 'middle class' or 'fifth estate' of wealthy peasants who could rapidly modernise agriculture, which was considered indispensable to a successful industrialisation policy.
- To 'nationalise' the state's territory by 'ethnicising' landed property: that is, preferably apportioning it only to the members of the 'titular nation'.

This last point, which is generally not officially stated in land redistribution policies, often becomes the heart of reform action (Warriner 1969: 11).

As far as south east Europe is concerned, the exigency of land reform rose primarily as the need to resolve the 'social question' which in this area is more an 'agrarian question', as mentioned above. From the beginning of the twentieth century onwards, the rural masses' indebtedness and impoverishment, usury, overpopulation and unemployment in the farmlands, emigration, an extreme fragmentation of small and medium-sized property holding, and the persistence of latifundia, led to further precarious living conditions in south east Europe's rural regions. A lame and at times entirely off-the-mark industrialisation process, which was absolutely incapable of employing the agricultural work force surplus, heightened an already dire critical situation. Added to this was the international recession between the two world wars, which brought down both agricultural produce prices and exports.

In most of Europe's south eastern countries, these economic factors have created a widespread atmosphere of social tension that has often broken out into bloody revolts such as the well-known case of the Romanian farmers in the spring of 1907 (Castellan 1994: 51). This endemic rebelliousness, reinforced by sweeping historical events such as the Russian Revolution, summoned the phantom of bolshevisation among the big landowners in south east European societies. Even the more conservative classes saw the pressing need to bring about land reform that would abate friction, protests and conflicts through land redistribution. It is therefore no coincidence that major land reforms with a liberal background were undertaken between the two world wars. The two main goals of the reform process seemed to be an 'equitable' property redistribution and agricultural modernisation. For these same reasons, some western European observers and experts were pleased by projects which tended towards deep socio-economic changes in the backward rural areas of Europe's south-east regions (Ancel 1930; Mirkovitch 1934).

However, under the influence of increasing nationalism, this attitude changed rapidly and land distribution's ethnicisation became the main characteristic of several land reforms in this region. In this way land reforms turned into legislative actions of a more political than socio-economic nature, which aimed at changing the ethnic diversity of historically mixed regions along with disputed, changeable, uncertain and essentially unstable boundaries. From this geopolitical point of view, owing to the ethnic homogenisation and recomposition processes involved, land reforms were conceived increasingly often as a major remedy to the 'variable geometry' of national territories which had always ailed Europe's south-eastern States. Two examples clearly show the 'ethnicisation' of land reforms in south east Europe.

From the 'social question' to the 'national question' in Romania and Yugoslavia: the power of 'ethnicity' in land reforms

Romania

Undoubtedly Romania, after the actual liberation from Ottoman dominion in 1859, was the south eastern European country that had undergone the greatest number of land reforms. In terms of expected modernisation outcome, some of them should be considered to be among the most advanced, on paper at least (Roberts 1969; Hitchins 1994).

The first reform dates back to the period directly following the unification of the two Principalities, which became known as the 'Old Kingdom', until the end of the First World War. Since this reform concerned the expropriation of ecclesiastical property, it was a 'secularisation law' regarding mainly land that had belonged to monasteries since the Middle Ages, some of which were abroad (Holy Sites, Mount Athos, Sinai). This landed property accounted for more than a quarter of the country's land expropriated in December 1863. However, the then Prime Minister Mihail Kogalniceau, a great promoter of reforms that he deemed essential, aimed at a broader project based on two points: the abolition of compulsory labour and the establishment of private small holdings. In a country dominated by latifundism and boyars, the land reform law, strongly supported by Kogalniceau, caused uproar and was promulgated in August 1864 only after a bitter political struggle, the aftermath of which even included constitutional change. The law that came into force in 1865 released farmers from compulsory labour and 500,000 families were able to take possession of over 2 million hectares which they already farmed (Castellan 1994: 43). However, the boyars kept one-third of the land, the best obviously (Roberts 1969: 11), and were lavishly compensated by the State to whom the new small land owners reimbursed their dues in thirty-five annuities. However, the expected results of the land reform were quickly undermined, for several reasons. In the first place, too little land was assigned to too many candidates even though many farmers were excluded from the redistribution and went on working in semi-serfdom on the boyars' estates. Secondly, a demographic increase caused devastating overpopulation in the rural areas. Thirdly, the inheritance practice based on equally divided portions gave rise to alarming property fragmentation (Mitrany 1930: 161; Roberts 1969: 11; Castellan 1994: 44). Owing to these circumstances, the new land-owners quickly ran into debt and because of the inadequate banking system of the times were compelled to borrow from boyars, large tenants, or usurers at exorbitant interest rates. Another strategy was to transfer the land back to the former owners and toil again on the estates, basically as before. Either way, researchers agree that within a few decades neo-serfdom had been established and that in Romania around 1905 the gap between large and small property ownership exceeded that of any other European State, including Russia (Creanga 1914; Mitrany 1930: 63; Roberts 1964:6). As Mitrany aptly states, Romanian rural society and economy at the beginning of the twentieth century were a distinctive mixture of feudal serfdom and capitalism (Mitrany 1930: 80). The farmers' chronic discontent, which flared up in recurrent uprisings culmi-nating in 1907, is not surprising. The 1907 uprising came very close to being a full-blown national revolution. Its traumatic effect on the regnant house and the country's elites may be seen as a recurrent intention to sanction the new land reform. Avowed by King Ferdinand in a famous speech to the Romanian troops at the height of the First World War in April 1917, the new land reform was promulgated between 1918 and 1921 (Roberts 1964: 23). This second land reform also aimed chiefly at solving the country's greatest social problem, i.e. the age-old land question (Castellan 1994: 77). In fact, the law stated that landed property could not be over 100 ha. Any land exceeding this, expropriated from the big landowners through state compensation, should be redistributed on repayment in lots of 5 and 8 ha (Mitrany 1930: 136; Castellan 1994: 77). Consequently, 2.8 million hectares of the Old Kingdom's territory (one-third of it) went from the boyars to the farmers. However, Romania's borders after the First World War had changed considerably. In contrast to Hungary, which terri-torially had lost the most in central and eastern Europe after the First World War, Romania was the greatest winner. After the Treaty of Versailles in 1920, Romania more than doubled its area and had a 70 per cent population increase. Through this expansion, Romania had gained regions such as Transylvania, the Banat, Bukovina and Bessarabia that were very unlike the Old Kingdom. If the Old Kingdom had been a quite homogeneous entity, the new 'Greater Romania' was a rather more heteroclite state, socio-economically and even more so ethni-cally. Owing to distinct historical processes, Transylvania, the Banat, Bukovina and Bessarabia had very different socio-economic structures and relations even in rural areas. Moreover, large minority groups lived in these regions of the country. Ukrainians (also known as Ruthenians) were mainly in Bukovina and Bessarabia, while Hungarians, Germans (Saxons and Swabians), 'Szekler', Serbians and others, were in Transylvania and the Banat.

As far as the land reform was concerned, the government in Bucharest was compelled to apply distinct standards for each region because of their marked diversity; single laws were therefore promulgated and applied in specific regional contexts. Within this remarkably complex socio-economic, ethnic and legislative framework, according to 1921 official data, a total of 6 million ha were expropriated; 4 million were apportioned to 1.4 million farmers while 2 million became State property or were assigned to the municipalities (Castellan 1994: 78).

At first sight, the reform appears imposing. A strong modernisation drive could be hoped for, indeed, even a solution to the 'land question' in terms of the 'social question'; but this was not so. Before the Second World War, agriculture did not progress much and rural living standards were among Europe's lowest (Castellan 1994: 79). Moreover, according to the 1930 census, 6,700 big landowners still held 24 per cent of the land while 2.5 million indigent farmers owned only 28 per cent. Notwithstanding the unmistakable increase in the size of the average holding, which had been yearned for and was almost unanimously held to be the basis of the nation's stability and socio-economic development (Ancel 1926: 178), the average holding was again slowly declining owing to rural overpopulation, which in turn caused extreme land fragmentation as a consequence of the inheritance practice in force (Roberts 1969: 53; Castellan 1994: 78). Both politicians' and expert evaluations of the reform were often as trenchant as Ion Michalache's, an influential leader of the National Farmer's Party, who in 1922 stated that: 'The ruling class made only such concessions as were necessary to assure its own existence. The reforms have been a kind of safety valve' (Michalache 1922: 5, 29, quoted in Roberts 1969: 30).

It is worth noting that Michalache, even with his slightly overstated and drastic attitude, like most Romanian authors overlooked the problem of the relationship between land distribution and ethnic groups. In spite of this intentional or unintentional reticence, it is now well known that Romanian land reform in the regions obtained after the First World War, primarily in Transylvania, became a 'thorny branch', as David Mitrany phrased it, within the troubled 'Greater Romanian' minorities issue (Mitrany 1930: 211). The promulgation of specific regional laws was perceived, especially by Transylvanian Hungarians, as the premise for an unchecked discrimination against non-Romanians. Likewise, a subtle indeterminateness and inaccuracy in the legislative acts, which cannot be examined thoroughly in this context, were considered deliberate and therefore aimed at establishing a land reform with a nationalistic bias (Mitrany 1930: 211). Indeed, certain aspects of the law postulated a tendency to exclude minorities from the reform's inherent advantages. In fact, in the acquired territories, especially the frontier ones, the land had to be assigned to veterans, and war orphans or widows who were obviously national Romanians (Teichova 1988: 43; Sterbling 1995: 91). This measure paved the way for a 'colonisation' of Transylvania. In fact, the lands on a controversial border were to be entrusted to loyal citizens (Sterbling 1995: 91). According to some Romanian politicians, for example Octavian Goga, land reform should be regarded as 'the most powerful means in the Rumenisation process of Transylvania' (Mitrany 1930: 181). Almost concurrently the French geographer Jacques Ancel, without hiding his partiality for the 'colonisation' cause, literally wrote about the Romanian farmers' 'agrarian re-conquering' of Transylvania (Ancel 1926: 178). According to the authoritative historian Seton-Watson, in the regions acquired by the Old Kingdom, particularly in Transylvania, the land reform brought about a 'territorial Rumenisation' that finds its match in several other central and eastern European countries (Seton-Watson 1986: 79).

However, some further consideration of this point is necessary. The 'territorial Rumenisation' process enacted through the land reform was a reaction against the agrarian colonisation of the Hungarian government, which began at the end of the nineteenth century and lasted until the First World War. The Hungarian government had established a special fund of 3 million florins to aid national Hungarian farmers settle in the Transylvania districts which had a significant non-Hungarian population (Mitrany 1930: 214). In 1911 the fund had bought over 7 million florins' worth of property. Moreover, in the case of municipally owned landed property fragmentation and privatisation in Transylvania, settlers of Hungarian descent, if necessary brought from other regions, were granted privileges. Romanian farmers living in the same areas were, to a large extent, excluded from this land distribution (Mitrany 1930: 215). Mitrany also highlights how this intrinsically 'ethnic' colonisation policy created a desire for retaliation among Transylvania's Romanian population who then took a sort of revenge through Romanian land reform (Mitrany 1930: 215).

In Transylvania, class division almost coincided with ethno-national division (Mitrany 1930: 214). Therefore, it is not surprising that after the First World War land reform favoured the Romanian population (mostly farmers) while this was not the case for the Hungarians since most Transylvanian big land owners were Hungarian and would have been expropriated regardless of their nationality. However, the land reform was undoubtedly applied more rigorously in this region than in the Old Kingdom; Hungarian big landowners were more commonly affected than Romanian boyars. Nonetheless, farm labourers and small land owners of Hungarian descent rarely experienced impartial application of the reforms although the law guaranteed equal treatment. The simple fact of being from the 'enemy nation', therefore not the 'titular nation', could have been a discriminatory element in land redistribution (Seton-Watson 1986: 79). For example, Mitrany reports that Romanian authorities in charge of applying the land reform laws in Transylvania even expropriated several Hungarian small landowners, the official reason being that a church or a school was going to be built on that property (Mitrany 1930: 217).

The land reform was undeniably perceived in nationalistic terms as pursuing the ideal of a cultural and territorial 'Rumenisation' in the whole region (Mitrany 1930: 175), although in Transylvania there was no fully fledged ethnic persecution of minority groups related to the land reform (Mitrany 1930: 218).

The Hungarian and Saxon population also reacted loudly against this project and their spokespeople persistently denounced the shady and sometimes blatantly corrupt methods by which land expropriation and distribution were enacted with the intention of modifying this crucial frontier area's ethnic composition (Connert 1928: 262).

The land reform in 'Greater Romania' after the First World War, which should have modernised the rural areas, reducing the gap between Romania and western European countries, also failed for economic reasons. Nonetheless, it became a controversial issue among the various nationalities. It poisoned inter-ethnic relations, which had been strained for centuries owing to conflicting class interests, mainly between Hungarian big land owners and the mainly Romanian farmers which represented Transylvanian social life.

In conclusion, although the land reform discussed so far did not incite civil war and can definitely not be considered a form of 'ethnic cleansing', it may be said that it encouraged the nationalism of different ethnic groups, deepening enmities which were already present.

Yugoslavia

The centuries-old Ottoman domination in Europe ended in 1913 after the second Balkan War. The 'sick man on the Bosphorus' held only a small territory, namely present-day European Turkey. Serbia and Montenegro united after the First World War into the Kingdoms of Serbia, Croatia and Slovenia, which in turn became the Kingdom of Yugoslavia in 1929, and took over most of the 'liberated' regions; i.e. northern Macedonia and Kosovo. However, the Ottoman legacy was burdened with problems. In the first place, Serbia and Montenegro had an archaic social and economic system, a consequence of the breakdown of the original imperial patrimonialism based upon the *timar* institution. The sultan, as absolute ruler and sole owner of the land, entrusted military commanders with collecting tributes and recruiting soldiers. In exchange for these bureaucratic duties, the sultan allotted them non-hereditary lands called *timar*. The *timar* included the *ciftlik*: lands and real estate that the *timariot* (*timar* controller) could exploit directly for his family's needs. Between the sixteenth and eighteenth centuries, while centralised power was waning, the military commanders seized inalienable property that belonged to farmers and repeatedly appropriated lands of the *timar* on a hereditary basis. Therefore, the *ciftlik* areas were significantly increased although several remained quite small and would never become large landed estates. Furthermore, the *ciftlik* were privatised, *de facto* becoming allodial lands. Nineteenth-century reforms, despite Koranic law, gave a legal foundation to this unsettled situation and the term *ciftlik* became synonymous with private property. While striving to modernise and lead their countries closer to European standards, Serbia, Montenegro, and later Yugoslavia encountered the problem of dismantling this semi-hereditary structure that was unanimously considered unjust and utterly obsolete. The most obvious solution to this problem was to promote land reform. This was also the authoritative opinion of eminent foreign experts, such as the renowned French geographer Jacques Ancel, who knew the region well having been *in situ* during the First World War (Ancel 1930: 1). According to all these western experts, researchers as well as travellers and dip-lomats, the *ciftlik* was perceived, on the one hand, as a symbol of a fearful admin-istration and low economic productivity, and, on the other, as the bulwark of an agrarian system based on semi-serfdom: social relations that implied exorbitant taxes as well as arbitrary and iniquitous services for the peasants (Schultze-Jena 1927: 50). Present-day researches have re-examined this institution and have reached more discriminate conclusions (Adanir 1979); however in those days the *ciftlik* represented, figuratively speaking, an insult to civilisation. In light of this outlook, land reform was launched in an area whose economic situation was deplorable to say the least (in northern Macedonia and Kosovo) taking into account not only the *ciftlik* but also a fifty-year span of political instability marked by uprisings and wars. Therefore, these two regions were characterised by massive land abandonment and the utter insecurity of a territory overrun by bands of irregular troops halfway between a liberation warfare and simple ban-ditry. Overall, Yugoslav land reform required an elaborate series of measures which pivoted, however, on colonisation. In fact, by the end of the second Balkan War (1912–13) a conspicuous migratory trend ensued, more or less forced, mainly towards Turkey or Albania. The migration was of *ciftlik* owners of Turk or Albanian descent who left the country anticipating changes to the rural prop-erty regime. Around 1913–14 indigenous families of Slav ancestry had already begun an unforeseen takeover of the deserted lands or were buying them at low prices (Roux 1992: 191). The governments of Serbia and Montenegro immedi-ately tried to check this tendency. A law concerning the peopling of the 'liberated' regions, which provided for the state management of all deserted lands plus all lands lacking a property title, was promulgated in Montenegro in February 1914. This law may be considered a prologue to the land reform itself, the prom-ulgation of which took an incredibly long time (from 1919 to 1934) owing to numerous additions and amendments. These few data provide evidence for the Yugoslav government's significant efforts to modernise agriculture in the two peripheral and economically backward regions mentioned above.

Undoubtedly, the pillar of this complex reform action was the decree dated 24 September 1920 that regulated the new southern regions' 'colonisation', whereby colonisation meant the granting of State lands to farmers. This project had two main aims:

* land redistribution to the most poverty-stricken indigenous rural population through the subdivision of *ciftlik*;

- the settlement of farmers from other areas of Yugoslavia on deserted and former State or municipal properties (Ancel 1930: 58).

The allocated plots were between 4 and 5 ha, congruent with family unit size. According to the reform's promoters, this amount of land would be enough to guarantee an entire family's subsistence. However, most of the land in Macedonia and Kosovo was unproductive and the allocated plots soon proved to be inadequate (Ancel 1930: 60). This already suggests that the first stages of the reform were indeed superficial, chaotic and irrational. Moreover, there were no plans for the subsequent establishment of any infrastructure. In 1923, the Yugoslav government, to cope with the operation's tangible shortcomings, undertook road, canal and rural housing construction, swampland drainage, a fight against malaria, professional training for farmers and the promotion of cooperatives (Roux 1992: 192). To complete the reform process, further government decrees enacted between 1931 and 1934 concerning colonisation demanded the migration of numerous farmers into Macedonia and Kosovo from other regions of the country (Roux 1992: 193).

At the time, several western European experts of rural problems were impressed by the accomplishments and regarded them as evidence of effective modernisation. In his book on colonisation in Macedonia, Jacques Ancel praised the Yugoslav land reform in relation to the wonders worked in Old Serbia and Kosovo (Ancel 1930: 2).

However, the Yugoslav land reform was not only a means to promote socio-economic development as it appeared to the enthusiastic foreign observers of the time. Nowadays it is well known that an ethnic homogenisation project linked to a clearly nationalistic policy, adopted particularly by Serbia since the second half of the eighteenth century, lurked behind the 'progressive' façade. In fact, in 1878 Serbia had been able to expel Albanians from the Upper Morava River basin, a territory assigned to Serbia by the Treaty of Berlin (Roux 1992: 187). Later, Nikola Pasic (Serbian Prime Minister from 1909 to 1918) took up this notion of 'de-Albanising' and simultaneously 're-Slavising' the south of future Yugoslavia. He hoped to complete this project within twenty years (Roux 1992: 187). This plan was resumed in the Yugoslav land reform after the First World War and, as mentioned above, concerned only the southern regions of the new State, i.e. a region known to be a territory with vast areas of Albanian predominance. From a present-day standpoint, influenced by ideals of multi-culturalism, such an undertaking might seem monstrous. At the time however, projects of ethnic homogenisation by agricultural colonisation, i.e. more or less forced migrations, were deemed wholly appropriate if not expedient in increasing the political stability of a region, as in the specific case of the Balkan area. The 'normality' of such procedures, which we might define 'post-imperial', has been skilfully highlighted by Rogers Brubaker (Brubaker 1996: 10, 148–178). Corroborated by the international community's approbation and firmly believing in the historical right due to their nation as well as the presumed recentness of the Albanians' settlement in that territory, Serbians and Montenegrins had no doubts concerning the legitimacy of changing the ethnic composition of these two regions since, according to them, their nation held historical rights over Macedonia and Kosovo which the Albanians had only recently settled. Albanians were seen as invaders or occupiers because for centuries they had collaborated with Ottoman powers often as high-ranking civil service officials. Moreover, Albanians were regarded as 'Turks' in the first place owing to their Islamic faith and secondly because their national identity had only recently become apparent; at the turn of the twentieth century Albanians as a nationality obtained only vague regional and international acknowledgement. The same religious faith plus a real similarity in some everyday behaviour, especially publicly, could have given rise to fabricated narratives that were easily utilised by nationalistic policies aimed at a shift in the ethnic composition of the southern regions. Therefore, Macedonia and Kosovo, the latter acclaimed as the 'cradle of the Serbian nation', had to be 'liberated' not only from Ottoman domination but also from the intolerable and unmanageable foreign, i.e. non–Slav, population. The true logic behind the land reform lies here.

It was not so much the need to modernise Yugoslavia's south as the eagerness to strengthen the 'national element' by re-Slavising the two regions which counted (Roux 1992: 191). Consequently, the *ciftlik* liquidation was not principally a programme to abolish unjust and entirely corrupt, archaic semi-patrimonialism; it was a scheme to seize the land of a class of landowners who were regarded as 'alien' because of their ethnic background. The predominance of an 'ethnic logic' instead of a 'social logic' behind the elimination of *ciftlik* is confirmed mainly by the fact that most *ciftlik* in Macedonia and Kosovo were expropriated merely and tacitly because their owners were not of Slav origin, although their *ciftlik* were below average size; therefore, this was quite unlike the redistribution of large estates (Roux 1992: 194). As Ancel also notes, just before the land reform the *ciftlik* owners in southern Yugoslavia were not like the rich absentee '*beg*' who lived in Istanbul yet collected a specific income in kind from their landed property (Ancel 1930: 60). In southern Yugoslavia they were average farmers mainly of Albanian descent whose land was tilled by servants (Ancel 1930: 60; Roux 1992: 194), and not a class of 'landlord-capitalists' with a 'parasitic' mentality (Bobek 1962). In fact, only 37 of the 6,973 *ciftlik* catalogued by the administrators of the land reform exceeded 500 ha while 75 per cent were below 50 ha and half of this percentage was not above 20 ha (Roux 1992: 194). Although this data indicates the presence of a nascent rural middle class, the ideal aim of several land reforms, *ciftlik* were declared state property without exception and subsequently allotted free of charge to tenants of Slavic stock leaving the former owners with a quota from 5 to 15 ha (Roux 1992: 194). The 'ethnic' project of the '(re)Slavisation' of Albanian lands in the southern regions, chiefly in Kosovo, is even more unmistakable in the colonisation policy. Agrarian colonisation was a remarkable undertaking charged with symbolic consequences particularly in Macedonia, the so-called 'cradle of the Serbian nation'. The goal was to re-establish the supposed primordial Slav nucleus through the settlement of immigrants from other areas of Yugoslavia. More than 100,000 ha, over one-quarter of Kosovo's agricultural land, was apportioned to between 12,000 and 14,000 families, according to different sources (Roux 1992: 195). In order to evaluate the real extent of the reform, the further 60,000 ha apportioned to 14,000 local allotted families must also be taken into account.

In line with the prevailing 'Yugoslavist' ideology of the time and propagated by the renowned geographer Jovan Cvijic, a confirmed believer in the historical ethno-national fusion amongst southern Slavs (Cvijic 1918), the newcomers hailed from various regions of the country. The settlers' geographic origin shows that the vast majority, 76.4 per cent, came from Montenegro and Serbia, 11 per cent from Bosnia and Herzegovina, 1.2 per cent from Vojvodina, while 4.4 per cent arrived even from Croatia (Roux 1992:196). Since the authorities wished to avoid the dispersion of the immigrants, they were settled in specific colonisation areas from which Albanians were banned. In fact, if the latter owned any land within these areas, they were expropriated and then compensated either with low-quality lands far away from towns or with inadequate indemnities (Roux 1992: 195). A veritable ethnic segregation strategy came to the fore.

However, this was not the only discrimination connected with the agrarian colonisation that Albanians from that area had to endure. In Metohija (nowadays western Kosovo, near the present border with Albania) only 0.4 ha of agricultural land per person were left to farmers of non-Slav origin. Concurrently, agrarian courts of law would rarely uphold any appeals filed (Roux 1992: 195).

This ethnic struggle over territorial appropriation went awry and the Yugoslav land reform's implicit nationalistic policy fell short. One of the main reasons for the fiasco in Kosovo was certainly the demographic issue owing to the rural class' high birth rate, especially among the Albanians. This phenomenon with the settlers' arrival plus the small chance of internal or external emigration at the time brought about rural overpopulation in the region. A national and international drop in produce prices, meaning lower incomes for farmers, made things even worse.

It is not surprising that around 1930 inter-ethnic relations worsened, giving rise to strong tensions between Slavs and Albanians culminating in a violent atmosphere strewn with clashes and atrocities (Roux 1992: 199). The political and intellectual elites saw this crescendo of inter-ethnic clashes as proof of the land reform's political weakness and the need for more drastic measures to push back Albanian expansion in the 'cradle of the Serbian nation'. At this time, more definite projects, which indeed correspond to present-day 'ethnic cleansing' or 'ethnic purification', arose and multiplied for the active 'transfer of Albanians'

(Grmek, Gjidara and Simac 1993). The strongest supporter of this new policy which should have strengthened the (re)Slavisation of Kosovo, which was started but not completed by the land reform, was certainly Vasacubrilovic, an eminent representative of the Serbian intelligentsia, professor at Belgrade University's Literature Department, besides being a cabinet member of several Yugoslav governments after the Second World War (Grmek, Gjidara and Simac 1993: 149). In his famous conference on 'The expulsion of Albanians' held at Belgrade's Serbian Cultural Circle on 7 March 1937, Vasacubrilovic proved the relationship between the land reform's ethno-political failure with particular regard to colonisation on the one hand, and the need to relocate Albanians on the other (Gasparini 1999: 1). The closing statements of this text, which the 'ethnic cleansing engineers' of present-day former Yugoslavia regard as 'sacred', is worth quoting verbatim:

> Compte tenu de tout ce qui vient d'être dit, ce n'est pas par hasard que, dans l'analyse de la colonisation du sud, nous partons de la conception selon laquelle le seul moyen efficace pour résoudre ce problème, c'est le transfert massif des Albanais. La colonisation graduelle n'a pas eu de succès chez nous, pas plus que dans les autres pays. Lorsque le pouvoir d'Etat désire intervenir, dans l'intérêt de son propre élement, dans la lutte pour la terre, il ne . . . peut réussir que s'il s'agit brutalement. Sinon, l'aborigène installé sur sa terre natale et qui . . . est acclimaté est toujours plus fort que le colon. Dans notre cas, il faut d'autant plus tenir compte que nous avons affaire à une race rude, bien implantée, résistante, et féconde, dont feu Cvijic disait qu'elle est la plus expansive dans les Balkans. De 1870 à 1914, l'Allemagne a dépensé des milliards de marks pour coloniser graduellement ses territoires de l'Est, en achetant des terres aux Polonais, mais la fécondité des mères polonaises a eu dessus sur l'organisation et l'argent allemands. (Quoted in Grmek, Gjidara and Simac 1993: 184)[1]

This drastic programme, as with similar ones by Serbian intellectuals and politicians, remained a dead letter owing to the upcoming Second World War which led to Yugoslavia's 'first dismemberment' in the Spring of 1941 when eastern Macedonia and most of Kosovo were annexed to 'Greater Albania' under Italian control. As was to be expected, the trend shifted since the assimilation and expulsion policy was subsequently directed against Slavs, especially against farmers who had settled since the 1920s. Under Marshal Tito's establishment of the 'second Yugoslavia', pre-war boundaries were reinstated but the 'Albanian issue' was only 'set aside' until the 1980s when strong inter-ethnic tensions flared up again in Kosovo: the beginning of the present tragedy. Since the mid-1980s the 'transfer of Albanians' issue, devised between the two world wars as an extension of the land reform, reoccurred peremptorily in the Balkans, bringing with it hatred and bloodshed.

In conclusion, the Yugoslav land reform was surely not a prior instance of 'ethnic cleansing' but it certainly was a relevant factor contributing to the escalation of ethnic tension in the southern regions, especially in Kosovo.

Undoubtedly it can be interpreted as a primary historical antecedent to the conflicts at the end of the twentieth century consequent on Yugoslavia's 'second dismemberment'.

Comprehending land reform experiences in south east Europe: some theoretical comments

First of all, analysis of the two cases examined indicates how land reforms enacted in Romania, and Yugoslavia between the two world wars were reputedly legislative acts to solve both the 'social question' and the 'agrarian question'. Actually, they were decreed to 'nationalise' the territory of regions with centuries of ethnic complexity in an attempt to turn the territory into a mono-ethnic space. Therefore, land reforms were extremely expedient for the exasperated and opposed nationalisms that clashed at that time in south east Europe.

The outcome of the three processes examined was to some extent to introduce the socio-political premises for the development of highly antagonistic 'ethnic discourses' and simultaneously induce 'autoethnification' and 'heteroethnification' processes. Until then, these phenomena had surfaced unplanned and irregularly, although it would be deceptive and misleading to assume that relations between the different groups were untroubled before the land reforms. In all two cases, a rising 'diversity', experienced and perceived daily, caused several problems among the different communities sharing the same space.

Owing to the new ways of acquiring land, a vital resource at the time, an atmosphere laden with inter-ethnic tension began to crystallise in these cases leading to an escalation of reciprocal physical and symbolic acts of violence. At length, land reforms with their 'inclusion' and 'exclusion' policies greatly encouraged or emphasised 'ethnic differences' and boundaries between 'us' and 'them' verifiable to date in the regions mentioned. In such cases, land redistribution through 'ethnic' criteria is an important 'historical precedent' that works its way into present inter-ethnic relations from the deepest strata of collective memory. Therefore, it is not surprising that distribution and colonisation laws concerning such a basic resource as land have caused strong 'collective traumas' by being enacted as already explained. To this day, after several generations, reciprocal feelings of mistrust, fear and hostility in areas that are still predominantly agricultural are reinforced and nourished by these 'collective traumas'. A study of 'potentials for conflict and disorder' from a historic–anthropological point of view wishing to overcome the instantaneous and mechanistic approach of a structural and functionalist type cannot put aside a sort of 'dramatological' analysis of the 'flow of events', i.e., the 'conjunctural cycle' distributed along the '*longue durée*' (Braudel, 1977: 47). Therefore, what Marshall Sahlins has called the 'structure of the conjuncture' must be reconstructed (Sahlins 1981). In other words, starting from certain historical events, apparently not very significant at the time, but in the end crucially relevant, how such dramatic changes, which have repercussions to this day on the collective representations of 'otherness' and on the social relations between ethnic communities, are produced.

At this point, however, there is also the question of how the socialist political regimes, which for fifty years ruled over Romania and Yugoslavia, faced the ethnic polarisation: a pre-war legacy partly owing to the land reforms.

First, it must be emphasised that searching for a uniform and coherent 'method' used by all regimes under Soviet influence to resolve their specific 'national question' would be a fruitless task. Each regime developed its own peculiar policy; hence, even the 'historical patterns' are different. Therefore, present 'potentials of conflict and disorder' cannot be drawn from assumed elements of an abstract and monolithic socialist order, which existed only in the minds of western Sovietologists and Party officials' ideology. The circumstances in Romania, and Yugoslavia instead reveal that socialism applied two different 'policies' in each case:

- 'Increasing' the contrast between majority and minority. This was the case of Romania under Ceausescu, who with his peculiar national-communism tried vainly to 'obliterate' Transylvania's and the Banat's minority groups, especially the Hungarians, by means of repressive measures. During the socialist era inter-ethnic tensions were further sharpened but never reached the point of open hostilities mainly because the repressions were acknowledged for what they really were: the outcome of the personal policy of a tyrannical 'conductor' rather than the collective will of the 'titular nation'.
- 'Promoting' a contradictory and opportunistic strategy of the institutional recognition of ethnic diversity. This was the case in Tito's Yugoslavia, where such a policy played permanently and ambiguously upon the institutionalised difference between 'nations' and 'nationalities'. Owing to a fully apparent federalism with a deliberately inert institutional framework, which made all ethnic groups discontented in the end, pre-war problems and obsessions stemming also (but not only) from the land reform were hauled over and augmented from pre-socialist to post-socialist eras.

Looking back, socialism chose inadequate, grievous and often deliberately counterproductive strategies to 'manage' ethnic diversity. The existing tensions, rifts, and conflicts were aggravated or postponed. In the cases examined, among the elements that determine present 'potentials of conflict and disorder' there are processes, such as those instigated by the land reforms, which date back to pre-socialist times. Socialism was never a true break from the past, although to regard it as a mere 'freezer' of history would be a serious oversight. This is one more reason that further justifies the analysis of the 'structure of the conjuncture' so as to understand the 'logic' underlying the unexpected but foreseeable escalation of ethnic disputes in south east Europe since 1990.

NOTE

1   'Taking into consideration all aspects, it is not far-fetched that in analysing southern colonisation we have reached the conclusion that the only effective way to solve this problem is a mass transfer of Albanians. Gradual colonisation was not as successful here as in other countries. When the State wants to intervene to safeguard its own interests, its own land, it can only do so by acting ruthlessly. If not, the aboriginal, settled and acclimatised in his native land, is always stronger than the coloniser. In our case, we must also bear in mind that we are dealing with a tough race, deeply rooted, hardy and prolific; as Cvijic notes, it is one of the most widespread in the Balkans. From 1870 to 1914, Germany spent billions of marks buying land from the Poles to gradually colonise its eastern territories but the fertility of Polish mothers defeated German organisation and capital.'

REFERENCES

Adanir, F. (1979), *Die makedonische Frage. Ihre Entstehung und Entwicklung bis 1908* (Wiesbaden).
Altermatt, U. (1996), *Das Fanal von Sarajevo. Ethnonationalismus in Europa*, (Zürich).
Ancel, J. (1926), *Peuples et nations des Balkans* (Paris).
Ancel, J. (1930), *La Macédoine, son évolution contemporaine* (Paris).
Bobek, H. (1952), 'The main stages in socio-economic evolution from a geographical point of view', in P. L. Wagner and M. W. Mikesell (eds), *Readings in Cultural Geography* (Chicago).
Braudel, F. (1977), 'Geschichte und Sozialwissenschaften. Die "longue durée"', in C. Honegger (ed.), *Schrift und Materie der Geschichte. Vorschläge zur systematischen Aneignung historischer Prozesse* (Frankfurt/M.), 47–85.
Brubaker, R. (1996), *Nationalism Reframed. Nationhood and the National Question in the New Europe* (Cambridge).
Castellan, G. (1994), *Histoire de la Roumanie* (Paris).
Connert F., (1928), 'Zur Frage der Agrarreform in Siebenbürgen', *Nation und Staat*, 1:4, 262.
Conte, E. (1995), 'Terre et "pureté ethnique" aux confins polono-ukrainiens', in E. Conte and C. Giordano (eds), *Paysans au-delà du mur. Etudes Rurales*, Nos 138–140 (Paris), 53–85.
Creanga, G. D. (1914), *Grundbesitzverteilung und Bauernfrage in Rumänien*, (Berlin).
Cvijic, J. (1918), *La peninsule balcanique* (Paris).
Gasparini, A. (1999), Presentation in 'Towards a new Balkan order', *ISIG Magazine*, Nos 1–2, 1–5.
Grmek, M., M. Gjidara and N. Simac (eds) (1993), *Le nettoyage ethnique. Documents sur une idéologie serbe* (Paris).
Hitchins, K. (1994), *Rumania, 1866–1947* (Oxford).
Mirkovitch, B. B. (1934), *La Yougoslavie politique et économique* (Paris).
Mitrany, D. (1930), *Land and Peasant in Rumania* (New York).
Pierré-Caps, S. (1995), *La multination. L'avenir des minorités en Europe centrale et orientale* (Paris).
Roberts, H. L. (1969), *Rumania. Political Problems of an Agrarian State* (New Haven).
Roux, M. (1992), *Les Albanais en Yougoslavie. Minorité nationale territoire et développement* (Paris).

Sahlins, M. (1981), *Historical Metaphors and Mythical Realities* (Ann Arbor).

Schultze-Jena, L. (1927), *Makedonien. Landschafts- und Kulturbilder* (Jena).

Seton-Watson, H. *Eastern Europe Between the Wars 1918–1941* (Boulder and London).

Sterbling, A. (1995), 'A qui appartient la terre Transylvaine?', in E. Conte and C. Giordano (eds), *Paysans au-delà du mur. Etudes Rurales*, Nos 138–140 (Paris), 87–101.

Teichova, A. (1988), *Kleinstaaten im Spannungsfeld der Grossmächte. Wirtschaft und Politik in Mittel- und Südosteuropa in der Zwischenkriegszeit* (Wien).

Warriner, D. (1969), *Land Reform in Principle and Practice* (Oxford).

5

'Freedom!': Albanian society and the quest for independence from statehood in Kosovo and Macedonia

Norbert Mappes-Niediek

THE POLITICAL STORY of the Albanian conflicts has been widely discussed and documented in numerous publications (see, for example, the Independent International Commission on Kosovo 2000). But to understand the Kosovo and Macedonian wars, one needs to travel up into the mountains south of Vitina, keep on driving even when there is nor more asphalt on the road and enter one of the large compounds in the hills. In S, for example, one would be received by AR, a friendly man of sixty years with no incisors, and his wife, dressed in colourful baggy trousers, shyly waving from behind. Politics is not an issue for these hard-working people, life has made them wise and they feel no hatred towards any other nation. Their oldest son is a physics teacher at Vitina grammar school, the second and third sons are electricians, and a further, younger son is a student in Austria. Dad formally collects all the money that the sons earn and M, the oldest, decides on what to spend it. They hate being interrogated by the police, the corrupt municipality officials and the visa problems they face when they want to travel to Ljubljana, which is vital for them as they hold an exclusive licence for the import of electric counters from Slovenia. The Rs want to live freely and in peace, and they are ready to fight for it.

Focusing on the shortcomings within the Albanian societies of former Yugoslavia might lead to a serious misunderstanding of the situation. These societies are indeed always at risk of conflict; however, at least the Kosovo war in 1998 and 1999 was caused to a much greater extent by outside factors. The Kosovo Albanian society may be blamed only for its failure to avoid conflict and its poor capacity to manage problems that were generated elsewhere. Once it had begun, the conflict was extremely difficult to stop, and instead of dying out or continuing on a small scale, it tended to spill over into neighbouring areas inhabited by Albanians. The explanation for this phenomenon is one which can actually be found within these societies.

From 1986 onwards, when a wave of nationalist feelings accompanied the rise of Slobodan Milosevic, Kosovo Albanians became its mainly innocent and almost accidental victims. After the Pristina rallies in 1981, nothing had happened in Kosovo to stir up nationalist feelings among Serbs. In fact, the percentage of Serbs in the Kosovo population was declining, owing both to the much higher birth rate among Albanians and the emigration of Serbs. The 'exodus', as Belgrade media liked to call the steady Serb emigration, was above all a consequence of the high unemployment and the poor economic status of the southern province. As opposed to Albanians, Serbs in Kosovo found it easy to leave the impoverished area and to settle somewhere in Serbia proper or in other, more prosperous parts of what was then Yugoslavia. Back in 1974 when there was a change in Yugoslavia's constitution, a feeling of alienation spread among Kosovo Serbs who from then on were no longer privileged; they started to feel like foreigners in what they considered their own country. To be fair, it was certainly hard for Serbs to live in a rapidly changing society with different values, a different religion and a different language; and the notorious priority Albanians give to family life certainly contributed to the isolation of the minority, which in 1991 was about 10 per cent of the Kosovo population. Nevertheless, there was never a perceivable political strategy to expel Serbs from Kosovo or even to create an 'ethnically pure' province. The incidents of the years to come – e.g. the killing of soldiers by an Albanian in Prokuplje or the smear story of the Serb who had a bottle forced into his anus by an Albanian – were all invented or at least exaggerated and misused. Outside interested political circles, there are not even reports of any particular hostility of Albanians towards their Serb neighbours. The alleged rape of Serb women by Albanian men simply did not take place, as the Croatian academic Branko Horvat has shown in detail (Horvat 1989: 148–167). In fact, the conflict started in Belgrade. Kosovo was the first and easiest means of feeding the aspirations of the new Serb nationalists and this was the most important factor. 'Srbija cela, a ne u tri dela' (Serbia is one, not separated into three), was the slogan. Serbia and its position in Yugoslavia was the target, not Kosovo.

The second most important factor was the policy of the international community. The Badinter Commission, inaugurated by the then European Community to regulate the succession of the dissolved Yugoslav Federation, decided to recognise – and thus grant the status of sovereign states to – the six former republics of the Socialist Federal Republic of Yugoslavia (SFRJ), if they applied. Although ethnically mixed and, in the east European sense of the word, 'nationally' divided, Bosnia was recognised. Kosovo was not, although it had been, as a former 'Autonomous province', a constitutive part of the federation and thus equal to the republics. After the Dayton Peace Accord in late 1995, the blockade of economic sanctions against the Federal Republic of Yugoslavia (SRJ) was not lifted. Albanians, undoubtedly the first victims of Serb nationalism, suffered most from the sanctions as their province belonged to the SRJ as its poorest part. Seen from a different point of view, Belgrade was deprived of all means of calming the conflict with the Albanians. Even if Milosevic had wanted to, he had nothing to offer them. Albanian representatives were told by western diplomats they should make do with their status, while at the same time the SRJ was gradually redefined as a 'rogue state'. This approach sought to seal a lid on the steam-pot rather than to diminish the heat: a recipe for an explosion. No strategy, not even a positive option existed for the Kosovo Albanians. For them gaining independence was the only plausible aim.

The small political elite of Kosovo was badly prepared to meet these serious challenges. The Albanian communist establishment in Pristina opposed the loss of autonomy in 1989–90, but was unable to retaliate. Using familiar party structures, Belgrade replaced uncomfortable leaders such as Azem Vllasi with faithful lapdogs such as Rahman Morina. Before they were dismissed, most of the Albanian communist leaders had been forced to crack down on 'nationalists' and movements of unrest among their fellow citizens. As a result, they were all unpopular. The Yugoslav federation was already weak, and Kosovo had no true allies among the other nations gaining independence. Once autonomy was lost, Kosovo Albanian leaders – with very few exceptions – found themselves ousted. Their immediate and natural reaction was not to accept the unilateral constitutional changes. Nobody really expected them to accept the changes; Belgrade did not even try to convince anybody in Kosovo of their worth. From now on, the Albanians were simply the enemy and had to be kept down. The declaration of independence from the dissolving Yugoslavia was a logical and uncontested consequence. The loss of autonomy came with a wave of strong anti-Albanian propaganda, and not even the most loyal Albanians could feel invited to cooperate in the new structures. Thus, even unification came from outside. The only non-communist party, the Democratic League of Kosovo (LDK), founded in December 1989, became the natural backup system for the Albanian communist elite, who were the only ones with at least a little political experience. The 'Autonomous province' deserved its name only from 1974, when the constitution was changed, and historically it was the only political body Kosovars had ever run themselves. There were no dissidents, there was no old bourgeoisie, and there was no political emigration. The thin layer of politically educated people came from rural families and they were brought up during communism. University teaching in Albanian started only in 1970. In 1945, Kosovo had had an illiteracy rate of 74 per cent.

The ousted Kosovo Albanian leaders were so desperate that they could not even find a leader. Those who had been in office were compromised, and those who had not were incapable. Mahmut Bakalli, head of the Kosovo Central Committee in 1974, has told how Ibrahim Rugova, president of the Kosovo Albanian Writers' Association, became the leader of LDK. When they had to leave the Party premises, a building was needed. They found the small pavilion of the Writers' Association close to the Pristina stadium. 'Rugova was elected for practical reasons. The seat of the newly founded Democratic League was the building of the Writers' Association. He is a serious and quiet man, so he was elected' (Petrovic 1996: 26). Whatever was needed to form an independent state was now provided. A constitutive assembly was formed and a referendum was organised, spontaneously supported by all political and civil authorities in every town and village.[1] When the first unofficial elections had taken place, the job was done. The shy and friendly Rugova lacked any political sense, let alone experience. In his whole political 'career', he has stubbornly kept repeating his political mantra that Kosovo was an independent state. During the first years, it was the policy to act as if the goal of independence had already been achieved. Like ousted monarchs, Kosovo Albanian leaders acted as 'legitimists' and simply ignored the new authorities, claiming they were the only legitimate authority. This kind of behaviour may be typical of emigrants who have nothing in hand but an abstract legal position. But the LDK leadership acted inside the country, and everybody could see their weakness. Two attempts to gather the newly elected parliament were inhibited by the police. Its authority was transformed into an unofficial 'council of parties'. Instead of forming a state, Kosovo Albanian leaders pretended to have one.

From the outside, the 'Independent State of Kosovo' was frequently viewed as something comparable to Mahatma Gandhi's movement of civil disobedience. Indeed, Rugova is a deeply peaceful person who detests violence and war. Born into a rural family in the village of Istok, he was awarded a scholarship and studied literature in Paris, where he heard Roland Barthes, a famous existentialist (Carlen, Duchene and Ehrhart 1999: 51). Pacifism was and still is a rare phenomenon in Kosovo. Albanians are a Balkan people with a long tradition of war and heroism. Virtues and values are deeply patriarchal, as is typical in formerly cattle-breeding societies, and to be a man, one has to carry a gun. Islam, the predominant religion among Kosovo Albanians, has no specific sympathy to ideas of non-violence – unlike Hinduism in India. Even communist Yugoslavia was not at all pacifistic, on the contrary: war was intensely glorified in hundreds of films about the partisans. Rugova's so-called 'Gandhi strategy' had no roots in Kosovo Albanian society. Rugova, once a member of the communist party himself (Carlen, Duchene and Ehrhart 1999: 70), has no charisma and is not persuasive. His pacifist approach was accepted only because there was no alternative. Serbia, aware of the mood in Kosovo, concentrated large numbers of police and army in the province. Nobody could even think of open resistance. Public rallies were impossible. Whenever more than three people gathered in the centre of Pristina, armed policemen would appear and disperse them. Whoever tried to speak out against the regime in public risked being terribly beaten.

As opposed to Gandhi, Rugova and the Kosovo Albanian leadership never had a plan, except that by calling their weakness pacifism, they tried to benefit from western countries' sympathy. 'Passive resistance' in India was an active strategy, including demonstrations and sabotage, aimed at destabilising the colonial regime and influencing the British public. Kosovo Albanian leaders, by contrast, never took action.[2] They chose to build a 'parallel system', as analysts put it. But even the setting up of this parallel system was hardly planned and required little organisational performance. In less than a year, most 'socially owned' firms changed into Serb hands and their managers were dismissed.[3] The Albanian party and state authority ceased to exist. In the Albanian community, nobody accepted the changes, and mere non-acceptance was the founding act of the 'Independent State of Kosovo'. In practice, Albanians in public jobs lost their money, their weapons, their offices, but kept their titles. The new, Serb-dominated authorities tended to ignore the Albanian majority of the province. The Albanian-dominated communist society of the 1980s was changed to into a virtual system of meaningless claims and pretensions.

In July 1990, most of the Albanians in public service had been asked by the new Serb authorities to sign a declaration of loyalty. Many of them refused and were immediately dismissed, and many of those who signed were fired later.[4] Unemployment was high even before this. The pressure was greatest on school and university teachers. The province's authorities, now installed by Belgrade, decided to introduce Serbian curricula and had Serbian textbooks translated into Albanian. Very few Albanian teachers remained, and Serbs were unable to teach Albanian children in their mother tongue. So school teaching simply went on as it had been before, but with two changes: ousted teachers no longer got a salary and, in many cases, the authorities kept the school buildings closed. The organisation of a 'parallel system' thus meant providing money and sometimes alternative school rooms. Transition to a modern system of education did not and could not take place. Teachers formally stayed in office for ten years, not controlled by anybody. University teachers in particular look back on this period when they taught students in their private homes as a time of heroism, and they think they deserve gratitude and at least permanent employment (Koliqi 1997).

The 'government' of the 'Republic of Kosovo', headed by the Germany-based physician Bujar Bukoshi, organised a system of tax collection to finance the few state-like authorities. In practice, taxes were collected by the LDK, as Noel Malcolm put it (1998: 349). Precise data are missing, but most of the money was almost certainly collected among young Albanians in western Europe who had left the country fleeing unemployment. The only state-like apparatus in Kosovo besides education was the health system, organised by a humanitarian foundation called 'Mother Teresa'. The organisation played an important role in keeping up some social welfare and medical treatment, although on a very low scale (Malcolm 1998: 351). In fact, many Albanian health workers kept their jobs even after 1990. In principle, there was always free access to hospitals and outpatient clinics.

Official tax collection more or less stopped, as the Serb financial authorities were unable to replace their Albanian colleagues. Not even electricity bills were paid. The infrastructure suffered from the lack of any repair and there was no longer any public construction. Of course, the Serbian state continued to pay pensions, but in fact, Albanian pensioners avoided the state bureaux in order to avoid being humiliated or shouted at. Although the official Serbian state institutions never openly refused to cooperate with Albanians, most of the citizens were reluctant to come into contact with 'the Serbs'. The atmosphere in public buildings was rude. Going into a public office, younger men risked being handed over to the police for anything suspicious, checked for weapons or beaten up. What remained of the Serbian state served the needs of the Serb and Roma minority in Kosovo. For the rest of the population, there was nothing but the police.

Both communism and the pre-modern structure of Kosovo society prevented the existence of non-governmental organisations (NGOs). Besides the state and the family, there was no third sector. While the Orthodox Church in Serbia fuelled nationalism, the Muslim community in Kosovo was completely useless for political purposes. Although more than 90 per cent of Kosovo Albanians come from a Muslim tradition, religion never had deep roots (Malcolm 1998: 134–138). Albanian nationalism has always been anti-Muslim. Its most important mythical hero is Skanderbeg, who in the fifteenth century organised the Christian resistance against conquest by the Ottomans. According to nationalists, Islam is something that has been imposed on Albanians by foreign conquerors; it is not looked upon as their 'essential religion'. Referring to the famous Kosovo battle of 1389, when a Christian army led by the Serbian Tsar Lazar was beaten by the Ottoman forces under the sultan Murat, Albanian nationalists claim their forefathers had instead fought on the Christian side. In their mythology, Lazar was an Illyrian, i.e. pre-Albanian, and 'had nothing to do with Serbs' (Rizaj 1992: 122).

After 1990, most of the state functions were taken over by the family, which had always played a very important role in Albanian societies. Even today, a considerable part of the population live in so-called 'complex households' with up to several dozen people, linked by kinship in the male line. In the countryside, family compounds form entire village quarters, each of them surrounded by walls. Villages frequently lack public places like pubs, mosques, or assembly halls as all social life remains in the family. Neighbourhood is unimportant compared with family links. When an enemy came, villagers in western Europe would gather in the market place; in Albanian villages, there is no such thing. Everybody would seek shelter within their own family walls. It is still amazing how little people know about each other, and this fosters an atmosphere in which suspicions and conspiracy theories flourish. But on the other hand, the family provides for all an individual's basic needs and gives solidarity to all members.

In rural and conservative areas, especially in western Macedonia, the state has never really replaced the authority of the family. There was opposition to female employment among religious Muslims which excluded Macedonian

Albanians from industrialisation in the 1950s. Everything else the state demanded was even more unpopular, above all taxes and military service. An Austrian scholar has defined the south-western Balkans societies as 'acephal' rather than pyramidal (Kaser 1992). At the time of the Ottoman Empire, the Sublime Porte was interested only in the regular payment of tributes and had no interest in self-organisation at a higher level (Kaser 1992: 164). Everything else was left to the families. When, after the Balkan wars, Serbia occupied Kosovo, people for the first time came into contact with the challenges of a modern state. The famous upheavals of the '*Kacaks*' in the 1920s were primarily resistance to the modern state as such, and not a national struggle (Banac 1995: 238–250). Even now, one can feel a spirit of 'freedom' in all Albanian lands. 'Freedom' is the most important slogan in all movements, against the Serbian or the Macedonian state as well as those against the government in Tirana. In all of these movements, freedom means the absence of the state, be it Serbian, Macedonian, or even Albanian. The remains of '*Kanun*', the ancient legal system still known to many people in the countryside, regulates the relations between families; part-time judges play a minor role, no police and no correctional system is needed. Even in the most developed areas, contempt for the public space is visible to any visitor. There are large private houses with some luxury, carefully cleaned and abundantly decorated with brass and false marble, but schools look like ruins, and nobody cares about rubbish collection. Sometimes families and neighbourhoods replace the absent state by self-organisation. In villages even road construction is done privately. Many people prefer it this way. Interference by the state means control, corruption and sometimes violence. Even in Albania proper with its ninety years of state tradition, state authorities are often looked upon as adhering to 'another gang'. The notion of the state as a power neutral to personal interests simply does not exist.

Everywhere in the Balkans, but especially in Albanian areas, families are the most important institution. After the collapse of the Yugoslav state authorities in Kosovo in 1990, the families functioned as the natural backup system. They had to care for the ill, the elderly and the disabled, give shelter to persecuted family members and, during the war, form important defence units. Following an old tradition, women were kept at home and the young men sent abroad to make money, while the parents, the father's unmarried brothers and the young wives were engaged in household maintenance and agriculture. Many urban families in Pristina, Peja/Pec or Skopje/Shkup keep close ties with their family houses somewhere in the countryside. Even today, a big household is a sign of wealth rather than a sign of backwardness.

Families like the Rs, in the hills above Vitina, were and still are the place where the transition to market economy has happened. While many Serbs or Macedonians were sitting in their tower blocks waiting for jobs to come, Albanian families rapidly turned into modern profit centres. From 1991 to 1992, the number of private enterprises in Kosovo increased 2.9 times (Lidhja 1996: 16). Many families can boast about ten or even more trained workers and professionals, all of them being supported by the women, wives and sisters, aunts or nieces. Inside the family everybody can rely on each other and strict obedience to the father or even the oldest brother (addressed by the title '*bac*') is common. In some parts it is the custom that all the money every family member earns is collected and guarded by the head of the family. Some families engaged in international trade and soon became wealthy. Emigration helped to find partners abroad. It is certainly true that quite a few families were involved in illegal businesses such as the drugs and arms trade and the trafficking of women; moral standards beyond the borders of the wider family are certainly low. But it can also be said that the pre-modern structure of Albanian families turned out to be more modern in its flexibility than any other structure in the area.

Family spirit is also the explanation for what is erroneously called 'Albanian nationalism'. Everywhere else in Europe, nationalism is an ideology that came about along with the bourgeoisie and industrialisation, replacing traditional bindings by a spirit of belonging to a spiritual community. Nationalism among Slav peoples in the Balkans started in the nineteenth century, often copying the ideas and myths in western nations, with Serbs producing the richest mythology and the highest aspirations of all. Like German nationalism, national ideas in the Balkans were not at all confined by state borders; most people lived in multi-ethnic empires, the Ottoman or the Austrian-Hungarian Empires, and some, like the Serbs, lived in small and emerging states. According to the German poet and philosopher Johann Gottfried Herder, publisher of Slav fairy tales and an influential thinker for East Europeans, a nation is a community based on common language, common culture and common descent (Herder 1965: 224). The State is not even mentioned. Nationalism is at first a purely spiritual, ideological phenomenon which might become political once the period of 'liberation' has begun.

Common descent, replacing the common state in western European nationalism, in German and Slav nationalism is a myth to give people the feeling of belonging together, with little respect for real relations people might have. The feeling of national solidarity, for example, led Croats in central Bosnia into a fatal trap when they took sides with Croats in Herzegovina rather than with their Muslim neighbours. In Bosnia, nationalism even split families. In Kosovo or Macedonia it did not. For Albanians, the 'national' feeling of belonging together is not a myth, but a part of their reality. Many people are able to recite the names of their forefathers for more than ten generations back, and there is an amazing awareness of to whom one is related. People feel closest to those to whom they are the closest kin. An individual sees the social world in concentric circles, the inner circle formed by his or her parents, children, brothers and sisters, outer ones by cousins, some would even feel they belong to a 'tribe' ('*fis*'), and all feel they belong to the Albanian nation, a large family united by real descent. Being itself the outer circle of a kind of family relation, national adherence can never destroy family links. There are no reports that the very few mixed Albanian–Serb families were divided by the conflict. Even the popular 'godfather' relations that imitate kinship survived the war.

But the crisis of the 1990s not only empowered families, it also significantly challenged them. Obvious police oppression was humiliating and harmed the traditional authorities. Everybody could see that even the supposedly almighty father, as head of the family, was afraid of the police. Adolescent sons sending money from Switzerland objectively became much more important for the survival of the family than their fathers. And finally, families could not compensate for everything that the state had once provided. Kosovo Albanian society is the youngest in Europe, with more than half of the population being aged under twenty-five.[5] The parallel educational system failed to provide everybody with the necessary schooling, and generation after generation was sent into unemployment and no prospects. Everybody who graduated from Pristina University was solemnly handed their diploma, but few ever got a job, either in Kosovo, or in Macedonia, let alone in western Europe. The old, mainly former communist dignitaries of the Kosovo Albanian societies got their salaries, paid by young emigrants in Switzerland or Germany, but the 'parallel system' had nothing to offer the Kosovar youth. Although most young Kosovo Albanians remained loyal to their families, a spirit of anger and of independence grew, especially among the temporary emigrants in Zurich or Munich.

In Kosovo, Rugova's attentism and passivity led to more and more divisions within the national movement (Troebst 1998: 9). Adem Demaci, a very popular former political prisoner labelled 'the Albanian Mandela', was the first to openly criticise the official policy, urging action instead. There was particular unrest among students who repeatedly ignored the LDK recommendations and demonstrated in public. The faction of 'former political prisoners', forming the so-called 'left wing' of the Kosovo political scene, gradually distanced itself from the leaders. In 1996, the 'Ushtria Clirimtare e Kosoves' (Kosovo Liberation Army/ UCK) started to kill Serb policemen. A conspiratorial organisation based above all in Switzerland and Germany and directed mainly by students, it gained more and more sympathy among the young in Kosovo. When, in 1997, people in Albania proper stood up against the semi-dictatorship of Sali Berisha, arms deposits were looted on a massive scale, and much of the booty was sold into Kosovo. The Kosovo Albanian establishment, unable to react, simply ignored the new force. Yet in 1998, when Kosovo was already at war, Rugova claimed the UCK was only an invention by the Serbian secret service. When in late February 1998 army and police units cracked down on the rebel clan of the Jashari in a village in the Drenica Mountains, the conspiratorial circle of the UCK suddenly became the synonym for overall upheaval (Halimi and Shala 2000). However, neither before nor after the Jashari massacre could the UCK be called a real army.

After the 78-day bombing of Yugoslavia by NATO forces in spring 1999, the UCK was transformed into a paramilitary 'civil protection corps' in order to keep the soldiers and officers under control and prevent them from terrorising the province. But according to regional military traditions, leaders kept their independence and did not subject themselves to political orders. For Albanians in former Yugoslavia, and not only for them, the borders of the successor states have little meaning. It was normal for everybody to continue to fight for 'freedom' in Serbian Presevo or Macedonian Tetovo. The Albanians in the neighbouring states and territories shared the desire for 'freedom'. In Macedonia, there was a fierce debate on whether the Macedonian UCK was made up of Kosovars or Macedonian Albanians. Among the Albanians nobody considered the question important. In Yugoslav times, Pristina was the cultural centre and also the only university for Macedonian Albanians, many of whom spent most of their lives in Pristina which is only 70 km from Skopje. Borders are considered artificial and unnatural, places of birth are more or less accidental, and it was the fixing of the border between Macedonia and Kosovo near the village of Tanusevci that incited the war in Macedonia.

The situation in Macedonia lifted the political veil from the events in Kosovo and showed its social nature. In Macedonia there had never been any autonomy for Albanians. Consequently there were no 'parallel institutions'. Yet the societies were and are strictly separated. The number of mixed Albanian–Macedonian marriages amounted to just sixteen in 1999 (Brunnbauer 2001: 160). Macedonians run the post-socialist state institutions, and Albanians have built up a private sector. The latter have coped much better with the transition from self-administrative socialism to capitalism. Although it is not easy to find a meaningful indicator, areas populated by Albanians are visibly wealthier than others.[6] The peace agreement of 16 August 2001, brokered by the European Union, invited Albanians to engage in state institutions, which is anything but tempting to them. Average salaries in ministries are as low as 100 Euro per month, and the private sector offers much better opportunities. A special quota allows ethnic Albanian students to enrol at Skopje University with worse marks than Macedonians, but few Albanians make use of the opportunity. With the peace agreement, Albanians achieved something they had never sought.

As opposed to Kosovo, the situation in Macedonia was not unbearable for Albanians when the violent conflict broke out. Arben Xhaferi, the 'moderate' leader of the Macedonian Albanians, was not as passive as Rugova in Kosovo. Yet the radicals soon became more popular than the elected leaders. There are two main reasons for this, first, any conflict with the slightest national connotations gathers all Albanians under one flag – right or wrong, my family. There is hardly a forum among Albanians to discuss different opinions; the press is poor and obedient to varying leaders. Second, the UCK insurgents met the spirit of 'freedom' as they promised to 'liberate' Albanians from the state rather than offering to integrate them into it. Xhaferi's party had joined the government only in late 1998, sharing power and sinecures with the national party of Macedonians, the VMRO. From the perspective of professional western observers, Xhaferi's party had achieved a lot, important positions in Albanian-dominated municipalities were for the first time given to Albanians. But those who benefited were all members of Xhaferi's party. Ordinary people in Tetovo or Gostivar did not feel proud that the head of the county hospital or the culture hall was now a compatriot. They wanted 'freedom' and felt betrayed by Xhaferi. This is not a distinction between 'moderates' and 'radicals', it is a rift between ordinary people, on the one hand, who do not want to be bothered by any state authority and, on the other, politicians who see a chance to exploit the institutions.

It is an old and sad story. Misled by the 'national' aspirations in the Balkans, western diplomats force people into new states with nobody having a clear picture of what they should look like or what they are good for. Albanians, at least, want freedom of movement all over Europe rather than a national state, and they are not interested in the heritage of corrupt and ruined socialist republics with which they never identified. But they get what others think is good for them. Since the infamous London conference on New Year's Eve 1912–13, when a handful of ambassadors generously gave birth to the independent state of Albania, little has been learned.

NOTES

1   The referendum took place on 26–30 September 1991. According to the official result, 87 per cent participated, of whom 99 per cent voted in favour (see Zajimi 1994: 145).
2   Rugova himself, typically, sees it exactly the other way round: 'C'est pourquoi, meme si cela m'honore, je n'aime pas trop que l'on parle de résistance passive, gandhienne. Je dis qu'il s'agit d'une résistance politique, non passive, donc non gandhienne' (Rugova 1994: 126).
3   Stavileci (1995: 550) mentions 250 managers.
4   According to Stavileci (1995: 551), 135,000 were fired, among them 20,000 teachers.
5   In Yugoslavia, Kosovo had by far the highest birth rate at 3.00.
6   Natalja Nikolovska, a Macedonian professor of economics, has compared house construction in Macedonian and Albanian areas and found it several times higher in the latter (Nikolovska 2001).

REFERENCES

Banac, I. (1995), *Nacionalno pitanje u Jugoslaviji. Porijeklo, povijest, politika* (Zagreb).
Brunnbauer, U. (2001), 'Historischer Kompromiß oder Bürgerkrieg? Makedonien sucht Antworten auf den albanischen Extremismus', *Südosteuropa*, 50, 159–189.
Carlen, J. Y., S. Duchene and J. Ehrhart (1999), *Ibrahim Rugova. Le frele colosse du Kosovo* (Paris).
Halimi, E. and A. Shala (2000), *Jasharet. Histori e nje qendrese* (Skenderaj).
Herder, J. G. (1965), *Ideen zur Philosophie der Geschichte der Menschheit. Erster Band* (Berlin and Weimar).

Horvat, B. (1989), *Kosovsko pitanje. Drugo i dopunjeno izdanje* (Zagreb).

Kaser, K. (1992), *Hirten, Kämpfer, Stammeshelden. Ursprünge und Gegenwart des balkanischen Patriarchats* (Wien, Köln and Weimar).

Koliqi, H. (1997), *Das Überleben der Universität Prishtina 1991–1996. Aus dem Albanischen von Teuta Abrashi* (Pristina).

Lidhja e ekonomisteve e Kosoves (1996), *Problemet ekonomike ne Kosove me veshtrim te vecante ne ekonomine private* (Pristina).

Malcolm, N. (1998), *Kosovo. A Short History* (New York).

Nikolovska, N. (2001), 'Mislewa prawa', *Dnevnik* (a Skopje newspaper) (11 April).

Petrovic, M. (1996), *Pitao sam Albance sta zele, a oni su rekli: republiku . . . ako moze* (Belgrade: Radio B92).

Rizaj, S.(1992), *Kosova dhe shqiptaret dje, sot dhe neser* (Pristina).

Rugova, I. (1994), *La question du Kosovo. Entretiens avec M.-F. Allain and X. Galmiche* (Paris).

Stavileci, E. (1995), *Kosovo und die Albaner zwischen Verleugnung und Unabhängigkeit. Ins Deutsche übertragen von Max Weber* (Pristina).

The Independent International Commission On Kosovo (2000), *Kosovo Report. Conflict – International Response – Lessons Learned* (Oxford).

Troebst, S. (1998), 'Conflict in Kosovo: failure or prevention? An analytical documentation, 1992–1998', *ECMI Working Paper* (Flensburg: European Centre For Minority Issues).

Zajimi, G. (1994), *Dimensions of the Question of Kosova in the Balkans* (Pristina).

6

Why is there stability in Dagestan but not in Chechnya?

Enver Kisriev

The formulation of the question

DAGESTAN, UNLIKE CHECHNYA has demonstrated enviable political stability. This Caucasian republic, unique in its multi-ethnic composition,[1] undergoing radical changes and similarly experiencing serious social transformations, nevertheless successfully preserved its integrity; it did not allow mass inter-ethnic clashes, social disorder and uprisings, and refrained from border disputes with neighbours. Although there were instances of serious tension in the republic (the last military actions in the Botlikhskii and Tsumadinskii mountains were in August–September 1999 – the bloody conflicts with the 'independent Islamic territory' of the villages of Karamakha and Chabanmakha, and the conflict with the armed Chechen divisions, who penetrated into Novolakskii *raion*), the course of their development and their results bears witness to the fact that in Dagestani society there are mechanisms at work which have up until now helped prevent the worst.

Particularly striking in this respect is the contrast with the political fate of neighbouring Chechnya. The Republic of Chechnya borders on Dagestan. Chechnya and Dagestan are linked through many significant episodes of history, in particular the general struggle against Russian expansion in the nineteenth century and the formation of a single state, the Imamat of Shamil', who lead the Caucasus mountain peoples' struggle against Russian colonisation for twenty-five years.[2]

Meanwhile, recent history demonstrates completely different political conduct in Dagestan and Chechnya. In Chechnya there has been a national revolution and independence has been declared, but in Dagestan it has not been possible (for internal reasons) even to approve the sham 'Declaration of State Sovereignty', which all the national republics of the Russian Federation passed in 1991 under the direction of the Kremlin. Chechnya put up an unprecedented armed resistance to the Russian army in 1994–96, whereas Dagestan constantly devoted its energies to ever greater integration with Russia.

How is this to be explained? Which historical, socio-cultural or political conditions and mechanisms secure the maintenance of internal stability in multi-ethnic Dagestani society but do not allow the single Chechen nationality[3] to aim for the unity of their own political elite necessary for the founding of an independent state? Why does the multi-ethnic, continuously in-fighting Dagestani elite nevertheless arrange a system of effective cooperation among themselves and seek close collaboration with Moscow, but the Chechen leaders, who belong to one nationality, are at odds with one another in the periods of peaceful independent development and unite only in times of direct opposition to Russia, exhibiting a monolithic and effective unity in these instances? These are difficult questions and this is an attempt only partially to clarify the relevant issues. Most attention will be concentrated on the analysis of most recent political processes in Dagestan. In the course of the analysis we try to note the essential differences between Dagestan and Chechnya within the examined parameters of ethno-cultural, historical and socio-political themes.

The structure of the new elite

The political and economic revolution which took place in the Soviet Union in the late 1980s and early 1990s may be called a 'revolution from above'. Quite clearly the famous existentialistic philosopher Karl Jaspers was not right when he formulated the idea that 'once introduced, a dictatorship cannot be removed from within' (Jaspers 1991: 218). Drawing on the experience of the political history of the first half of the twentieth century, he maintained that 'everything that we know of the terroristic state with its characteristic total planning and bureaucracy bears witness to the fundamental impossibility of stopping this almost automatically self-preserving machine, which grinds up all internal resistance'. Indeed, a leadership totalitarian in character and without the control of society cannot be changed from below, but it has turned out that for this purpose external interference is not at all necessary; change in the political regime and all systems of social relations can take place from above, if the political and economic elite, having been gradually reconstituted, takes on this task. Radical changes in the political and economical structure of the state, effected by the ruling elite in correspondence with its new system of values, are possible precisely in a totalitarian political structure, in which there is no possibility of societal influence on the selection of political leaders and the taking of decisions of crucial importance for the country. That such a revolution took place in Dagestan is shown by the fact that radical transformations with catastrophic effects on most layers of society and especially on those who determine the character of the development of contemporary industrial society – i.e. qualified workers and technicians, highly qualified specialists (doctors, engineers, teachers, university lecturers, scientists, etc.) – practically did not affect the top layer of society (the political, economic and cultural elite of the country), which remained almost entirely as it was, 'on top'.

In the meantime, however conscious and purposeful this process, once embarked upon, it unavoidably called into being developments which the initiators of *perestroika* did not expect. Such is the nature of social process: it can never be completely assessed and controlled. New tendencies, developing unobserved in the social system, unexpectedly begin to reveal themselves and alter the future which the reformers would like to reach. Already after the 'glorious revolution' the social elite begins to undergo essential changes not only in the course of the natural succession of cadres, but also under the influence of deep-seated and unforeseen changes in society.

In Dagestan and in Chechnya these processes developed as in the rest of the country, but with essential, quite definite peculiarities conditioned by the difference of historical conditions and existing ethno-cultural specificities, which did not reveal themselves in any way within the framework of the totalitarian communist regime, but with its collapse burst out and began to build new political relations.

The general nature of the elite's structural changes in the new post-Communist society was that the main development was not the replacement of representatives of the 'old guard' by the leaders of a new formation, but the swelling of their number by the *nouveaux riches*, which Soviet society had not known. Previously, advancement 'upwards' as a rule proceeded by moderate steps under the strict control of high Party and state authorities. Special principles for the selection and positioning of cadres were consciously framed by a large number of formal requirements and procedures (for instance by the composition of a *nomenklatura* of responsible workers of different levels and the supervision of their advancement), which it was formally impossible to avoid. The sharp increase in the total number of state bureaucrats in the country speaks vividly of the fact that in the new conditions a unification of the old elite with the new took place. While it seemed that the fall of the giant Soviet communist regime should have lead to the simplification and rationalisation of the institutions of state governance, the opposite occurred: according to estimates, the total number of civil servants increased in Russia by 50 per cent, and in Dagestan by 100 per cent.

In Chechnya these processes developed differently, beginning with the fact that the political history of these two republics in the socialist system differed significantly. At the end of the 1920s in the North Caucasus the young Bolshevik regime, after putting down the uprising of the Imam Nazhmudin Gotsinskii and Sheikh Uzuna-Khadzhi Saltinskii in Dagestan (subsequently to be taken up by the inhabitants of Chechnya), proclaimed the formation of two 'autonomous' multi-ethnic republics: the Dagestani and the Gorskii Soviet Socialist Republics (SSR).

For the first three years the political fates of these North Caucasus state formations appeared diametrically opposed: the Gorskii SSR began to collapse in the first year of its existence and by 1924 had ceased to exist, falling into eight administrative units: six national *oblasts* (Karachaevo-Cherkasskii, Adygeiskii, Kabardino-Balkarskii, Chechen, North-Ossetian and Ingush) and the two cities, Vladikavkaz and Groznyi, became independent administrative units with direct subordination to the recently formed *krai* of 'South-Eastern Russia' with its capital in Rostov-on-Don, part of the Russian Republic of the Soviet Union (RSFSR). Dagestan, in this same period, not only preserved its state status of 'autonomous national republic' but also almost doubled its territory at the expense of Caspian coastal flat lands to the North.

The further history of Chechen statehood is even more dramatic. In 1922 the Chechen *okrug* was separated from the Gorskii SSR and made into an autonomous *oblast* (AO) of the RSFSR. After the complete abolition of the Gorskii Republic in 1924, the Ingush AO was also founded. At the very beginning of 1934 both of these *oblasts* were unified into the Chechen–Ingush AO, which in three years, in December 1936, was finally made into a republic, the Chechen–Ingush Autonomous Soviet Socialist Republic (CIASSR). However, in February 1944 this Republic, under the order of Moscow, was abolished and the Chechen and Ingush peoples were one and all rounded up from their homes, loaded onto railway carriages and sent to remote regions beyond the Urals and in Central Asia. Only in 1957 was the CIASSR restored with the loss of the Prigorodnyi region, left in Ossetia, but the Chechens and Ingush permitted to return to their lands. Finally, in the autumn of 1991, after the fall of the communist regime, and in the course of opposition to the centre for independence, the Chechen–Ingush Republic painlessly and by mutual agreement once again fell apart into the Chechen (independent) and the Ingush ('autonomous', but part of Russia) Republics. In the course of this long period of Chechen and Ingush political formations, the political status of Dagestan did not change once.

The existing difference between Dagestan and Chechnya in the period of communist leadership was also that in Dagestan throughout the whole of its Republican status the highest leaders were, as a rule, representatives of the core nationalities. In the early years after the Revolution and in the period of pre-war economic development in Dagestan, the key posts were given to representatives of local peoples. Many of them had received high-class educations before the Revolution in the universities of St Petersburg, Moscow, and in Germany and France – the Dargin Alibek Takho-Godi; the Kumyk Dzhalalutdin Korkmasov; the Avar Magomed Khizroev; the Lezgin Nazhmudina Samurskii and others. Starting with the post-war period, the primary officials (First Secretaries of the Republican Committee of the Communist Party of the Soviet Union – CPSU) of Dagestan were exclusively Dagestanis. In 1948, after the departure of the Azerbaijani A. Aliev, who lead the republic throughout the Second World War, the Avar Abdurakhman Daniyalov was the head of the Republic until 1967; then the Dargin Magomed-Salam Umakhanov until 1983; the Avar Magomed Yusupov until 1990 and Mukhu Aliev right up to the liquidation of the CPSU in autumn 1991. Apart from this post, all three of the highest positions in the Republic (First Secretary of the CPSU, Representative to the Union of Ministers and Representative to the Upper Soviet) were always, from the post-war period onwards, occupied by ethnic Dagestanis. At the same time, these three posts were formed in such a way as to be always held by representatives of the three different nationalities. In the post-war period the following sequences in the changing 'troika' were arranged as follows: Avar – Lezgin – Dargin; Dargin – Kumyk – Avar; Dargin – Avar – Kumyk; Avar – Kumyk – Dargin. The controlling presence of the Russians was manifested only in the institution of the 'second secretary' of the republican CPSU organisation and the post of the head of the KGB in Dagestan.

In Chechnya–Ingushetia the first time that the highest post in the Republic could be held by a 'national' was only in 1989, in the later phase of Gorbachev's *perestroika*. It was held by the Chechen Doku Zavgaev. At the same time, the First Secretary of the republican CPSU organisation received his post not from the hands of Moscow, as it had been always and everywhere, but contrary to the Central Committee's recommendation, in the course of internal conflicts in the republican CPSU organisation and on a wave of *glasnost* and 'democratisation'.

This aspect of Chechnya's political history, namely that the first Chechen came to power in the Republic only in the phase of breakdown in 'the leading and guiding power' and as one of its manifestations, is usually underestimated by analysts trying to understand the reasons for the 'Chechen phenomenon'. In Chechnya–Ingushetia the communist regime possessed qualities which it did not possess in Dagestan. In Dagestan the Russian component in the creative sphere (science, literature, art) did not have a meaning linked to the exercising of dominion power. Thus, for example, in Dagestan the most authoritative academics in historical studies were ethnic Dagestanis. At the same time, it stands to reason that there was no dominating concept of Dagestani history. After 1956, when the ten-year period of the, imposed from above, historical negative attitude towards the activity of Imam Shamil' ended, the theme of 'the national liberation movement against tsarism of Dagestan and Chechnya's mountain peoples under the leadership of Shamil'' was one of the most researched and widely taught university courses in the Republic.

In Chechnya–Ingushetia in the last period of communist rule the Russian professor V. G. Vinogradov, who was hated by the local intelligentsia, held complete sway in historical studies and generally in the field of ideology. He was the chief ideologist of the republican CPSU organisation, in which the highest post was always occupied by a Russian. His absurd and cynical 'concept' of 'the peaceful and voluntary entry of Chechnya into the Russian Empire' was thrust upon society. He was the censor for all academic activity within the Republic and the chief selector of national cadres for the state-Party *nomenklatura* (Gakaev 1999: 150). Thus, right up until the very end of the communist regime's supremacy, Chechens experienced direct and tangible national–cultural oppression from the centre, which was absent in Dagestan.

It is notable that in Dagestan one of the famous historians Professor Vladilen Gadzhiev also adhered to the theory of the voluntary joining of Dagestan to Russia. He based his point of view on diplomatic documents, which were evidence of the numerous agreements of local Dagestani landowners with Tsarist powers. However, his position was never the only one and never predominated.

Therefore the coming to power of a Chechen in 1989 in Chechnya–Ingushetia was a genuine revolution in the Republic's history, it was viewed by the national intelligentsia and people as a long-awaited liberation from Russian *diktat* and to a significant extent this event determined the character of future events, which so differ from how events developed in Dagestan.

In Dagestan in the course of *perestroika* no particular changes in the cadres of power took place. The CPSU was headed by an Avar, the government by a Kumyk and the so-called representative of (Soviet) power was a Dargin. These three people cooperating and clashing between themselves throughout the upheavals of the *perestroika* process maintained the Republic in a condition of relative calm. Not one of them could be 'extracted' from the system without all the remaining leaders undergoing precisely the same fate.

The first real threat to destabilise power in Dagestan came with the fall of the communist regime (August–September 1991). The Avars (numerically the largest people in Dagestan) as a result of the fall lost the 'highest' (although at that time already significantly dissipated in its influence) post – the leader of the republican CPSU organisation. After a few impressive 'people's demonstrations', which threatened mass inter-ethnic clashes, order was restored; and the former leader of the Republican Committee of the CPSU took the post of the first deputy to the Chairman of the Upper Soviet of Dagestan. The shaken parity of powers was in this way partially restored. Of course, hidden tendencies continued to develop and in the end, essentially transformed the structure of the political elite in Dagestan. To characterise this structure let us begin with the subdivision of the ruling elite in Dagestan in two groups:

- high-ranking officials and bureaucrats;
- authorities in the non-governmental sphere, large-scale entrepreneurs, leaders of social organisations and (or) informal groups, drawing on large financial resources and the mass support of their followers.

The relationship between these categories on the Dagestani Olympus could be thought of graphically as a partial overlapping of two large groups. Thus, the formation of another higher category of ruling elite ran parallel to the formation of this 'binary' structure and within its framework. Speaking visually, this might be located in the area where the two original groups overlap. At the same time, the traditional situation was unavoidably preserved: groups of a few different nationalities, supported even more by the numerous national groups of the 'second echelon', remained in power. The formation of this 'third' (higher) category of ruling elite was brought about by two opposing tendencies:

- the enrichment of high-ranking state bureaucrats, their (new to them) involvement in public political activity and the unavoidable formation around them of latent structures of armed support;
- the acquiring by 'charismatic' figures and nouveaux riches of high-ranking state or economic posts through the procedure of state appointments or democratic elections.

Both tendencies led through a zone of numerous, often extremely embittered conflict situations to the formation of a top political elite consisting partly of representatives of the old regime but mostly coming from the *nouveaux riches* of the *perestroika* epoch. In this way, the general structure of the ruling elite in Dagestan does not consist only of the two original categories, but also of a 'third'. It is very clear that the 'third category' of the ruling elite is made up of the most influential persons, relying on their national groups, and is gradually gaining influence and control and is becoming the dominant group. The numerous members of the two 'first' categories of elite, who have not succeeded in acquiring the qualities of the third category, have found themselves in many ways marginalised. They ended up on the fringes of the ruling class. It is well known that as a result of this divergence in status, members of marginal groups are more radicalised; however, while being divided into 'national quarters' and 'marginals', they were getting themselves involved in the difficult process of political bargaining, but they did not call upon the people to overthrow the existing power regime.

All this did not save Dagestani society from clashes of an extremely bitter character within the Dagestani ruling class: above all, between 'heavyweights', i.e. among the representatives of the 'third' category of elite, but also between the 'third' and the two original categories; between the two original categories; and finally, within these two original categories. In the course of these conflicts an interwoven network of horizontal and vertical relationships of power and subordination formed, the subjects of which were the ethnic monolithic groups. Although there was a tense stand-off between 'heavyweights', they were no less interested in agreeing on a common course of action against a member of the 'second rank'. The 'second-rank' fragments were in the course of internal feuding developing into groups of support for one or the other 'heavyweight'. Simultaneously, representatives of the 'second rank' ('marginals'), trying to get into the higher category or, at least to retain high-ranking offices or material resources, sought support either from 'above' or 'below', building hierarchical chains of patron–client relations.

There were many excesses in Dagestan, but they all had a 'patchy' character, i.e. they did not get prolonged into mass demonstrations and clashes between large groups of people. According to data officially published in June 2001, after a series of attempts on the life of Magomed-Salikh Gusaev, the Minister for Nationalities, Information and External Relations, who is popular in Dagestan there have been eighty-six terrorist acts and other crimes were committed against representatives of power in Dagestan since 1990. From these, there were 160 killed and 300 injured (*Novoe delo* 22 June 2001). All of this did not affect the political stability in the republic of Dagestan in any way.

It was clear that the strongest basis for the formation of this interwoven network of relations between numerous authorities was a difference in *nationality*. The theme of the nationality of leaders and their groups in Dagestan burst into life and became crucial in political discourse for the duration of the transitional period, and remains so. At the same time the Russian component of the Republic's ruling class was completely insignificant.

In Chechnya, it all turned out completely differently. After 'their own' (Doku Zavgaev) came to power the euphoria of national celebrations quickly gave way to the prosaic humdrum of political struggle, for the victory passed to one person alone. The coming to power one of 'their own' in place of a 'Russian' did not bring, and nor could it have brought, a general national unity in the conditions of increasing destabilisation in the country and the previously invisible but now revealed possibilities for enrichment. A new stage of bitter fights for power began, but now among 'their own'.

Under the slogans of national unity and cleaning the authorities of corruption Dogu Zavgaev, like any new leader, began to strengthen his personal power. In this connection the highly characteristic action of the new highest Party leader was called the 'Spring Fall' among the people. In February–March 1990 in all the rural regions of the Republic there was a wave of meetings and demonstrations of people's protest demanding the dismissals of the *raion* CPSU First Secretaries. This time it was a question not of Russians, but of Chechens and Ingush. In one month, seven First Secretaries and the majority of responsible CPSU and soviet bureaucrats, workers and law enforcement agencies were dismissed, and most of them were of Chechen nationality. Everywhere Zavgaev was able to put his people in the vacated posts and only in one *raion* (Achkhoi-Martanovskii) did the leader of a local informal movement (Sh. Gadaev) succeed in becoming leader (Muzaev and Todua 1992: 35–36).

Analysts assert that there is no doubt that the 'people's demonstrations' were organised by Zavgaev himself in order to strengthen his power. As the well-known Chechen historian Dzhabrail Gakaev writes in his article cited above: 'the wave of meetings, which occurred in the rural regions of the CIASSR in February–March 1990 was initiated by Zavgaev with the help of the People's Front.' Furthermore Gakaev expresses the important idea: 'It did not remain unnoticed that Zavgaev used the people's discontent and meetings in the regions for the dismissal from power of people in the rural regions of the Republic who were unwelcome. Soon, Zavgaev's political opponents employed just such a device against him' (Gakaev 1999: 153).

The device used by Zavgaev was also actively employed in Dagestan. However, there, where power is traditionally shared between representatives of the different nationalities of a multi-ethnic society, the consequences of such actions turned out completely differently. In Dagestan all actions linked to the substitution of leaders of the central team require agreement and adequate compensation in order to preserve the balance. In Chechnya, all actions which reinforced the leader of the Republic led to the reinforcement of discontent and to resistance on the other pole – in the irreconcilable opposition camp. This binary polarisation of all political forces (on the one hand those in power, and on the other the opposition to those in power) in a transitional and transforming society can easily 'swap poles' and as a result of this become even more unstable.

Soon, Zavgaev laid his hands on the duties of the Presidium of the Upper Council of the CIASSR, both preserving for himself the dying Party power and forming from his people the whole pyramid of power, which in Dagestan, owing to the reasons noted above, could not have been accomplished. In this way, in Dagestan we have revealed an elite, which one can divide into two, mutually intersecting categories: on one side high-ranking officials and state bureaucrats and on the other authorities in the sphere of non-governmental activities, etc. which, in the course of mutual opposition, forms a new higher stratum of groupings led by representatives of different nationalities which oppose, but also cooperate between, themselves. In Chechnya something completely different came about. Here, the two given, primary categories have begun to disperse to two different poles. Moreover, power turned out to be built as a pyramid, without tension and counterbalances. There was no room for any kind of separate and opposing groupings within the system of power.

It also proved to be important that both opposing forces in the struggle against each other appealed and sought support not in different segments of society, but in one target general to both – the Chechen people. This led to the 'echoing' of nationalist feelings. Those in power explained all their actions as being in the interests of the Chechen nation, which the opposition also did in the struggle against those in power. In every case the raising of nationalist feelings may be nourishing opposition forces from without, i.e. most often Russia.

However, the ethnic 'monolithic' character of the Chechens, which brought such an easy and painless 'divorce' from the Ingushetians, concealed, for the time being, the explosive force of traditional Chechen clan structures (*teips*) and other associations (see below). Zavgaev could not but use the force of cohesion within the clan in the course of reinforcing his personal power; already, then,

111

internal *teip* solidarity had awoken to political life. Subsequently, it tore the whole of Chechen society apart.

Nationality, *dzhamaat* and *teip*

Dagestani nationalities, just like the Chechens, even in the recent past hardly existed. Imam Shamil' in his struggle against the Russians did not know of any nationalities in Dagestan and did not formulate any 'national' tasks. For him and his brothers-in-arms at that time the subjects of political confrontation were completely different. The political discourse of that time in Dagestan distinguished between 'orthodox Muslims' and 'those, who called themselves Muslims, but were not' as the central political opponents. Avar, Dargin, Kumyk, Lezgin, Lak, etc., 'Dagestani nationalities' from an ethnographic point of view, existed objectively far more clearly then than they do now, however at that time they were not meaningful elements of socio-political discourse, they did not contribute to social consciousness, they were not a means of ideological reflection on events taking place and the motivation of the actions of their participants.

Occasionally one can read in the text of the chronicle that someone 'cried out in the language of Ansali' or that 'Shamil'' spoke to them through a translator', but a person's nationality – which has become for contemporary Dagestanis practically the most important attribute of a person's identity – remained outside the field of vision of the enlightened person of that time.

At the same time, in the very same chronicles of the Caucasian wars, Chechens appeared for all the Dagestani chroniclers as something whole and different from 'Dagestanis'. It was stipulated that in Chechnya there were no politically differing compact territorial formations, analogous to the Dagestani 'unions of free societies' – or 'republics' as the Russian military correspondents called them – or authoritative 'principalities': *shamkhalates, khanates, utsiinates,* etc. But the clan structures of Chechens in the conditions of strict Shariat, and generally all mountain peoples, were established by Shamil' as an enemy in the face of the '*gyaurs*' (unbelievers), and they were in this political context absolutely inseparable.

The development of different 'nationalities' –Avar, Dargin, Lezgins, Kumyks, Laks, Tabasaran, Nogay, Tats, Rutul, Aghul, Tsakhur but also Chechens and Ingush, took place first in the period of the communist regime. This process took place in a framework developed by the Bolsheviks, with the understanding of nation and people enforced by violence, and in the context of a national policy of 'the self-determination of peoples'. It is true that the understanding of 'national self-determination' was then emptied of any authentic political meaning, and instead was filled to the brim by a whole wealth of ethnographic material.

The contemporary nationalities of the mountain peoples developed 'from above', pre-empting a national consciousness, as a result of decisions taken by the authorities relating to the establishing of a 'scientifically founded' *nomenkla-tura* of nationalities and their registration in all civil documents, bureaucratic forms and passports. Of course, in doing this attention was paid to objective eth-nographic characteristics and to ethnic identifications developing in the con-sciousness of the population. It must be said that signs of ethno-cultural proximity or ethnic relatedness did not necessarily constitute factors in deter-mining the motivation of national self-identification. They may have proven to be the idea of political conjuncture, the communist leadership's changing polit-ical blows in the direction of 'ethnic processes' (the 'dawning' or 'rapproche-ment' of Soviet peoples) or, let us say, the nationality of high-ranking officials or other social, political and far from ethnographical factors.

The communist regime, propagating proletarian internationalism in this phase of its formation, in the following phase initially underwent unavoidable nationalist erosion precisely in the elite; to start with in the artistic elite, then carefully supported by the scientific and political elites. The history of the last twenty-five–thirty years of the USSR was marked by a growing social awareness of nationality. Because, as the regime decayed, personal relations of trust which, as is well known, are easier to establish among persons of a common ethnic origin, started to acquire more and more importance among the ruling class in the centre and the republics, and a hidden nationalism began to put down strong roots.

Similarly in Dagestan, with its particular multi-ethnic structure, mono-ethnic groupings of mutual dependence and support not perceivable on the surface of public life started to form, especially among the elite. The process of strengthening national bonds vertically and horizontally initially remained in the shadows, but immediately after the collapse of the communist regime in August 1991 the forces which had formed, based on intra-ethnic solidarity, revealed themselves in all fields of political struggle. The peculiarities of the Dagestani ethnic structure detailed above began under the new conditions to determine the direction of political process in Dagestan. The ruling elite of the Republic, consisting of representatives of the basic Dagestani nationalities, having lost their base in the power structures which had collapsed, re-established it in the systems of confidence between personal friends, relatives, co-regionalists and especially among co-ethnics.

The national organisations of the respective peoples, emerging and gaining strength and authority in the population, actively opposed the republican authorities, thus forcing the old ruling elite to strengthen vertical intra-national ties. This is why the subsequent political process in Dagestan consisted of the extension of the political elites' influence on the national movements of their peoples. High-ranking officials tried to become the leaders of their peoples, and the informal leaders of the national movements and the *nouveaux riches*, who stepped forward completely unexpectedly, endeavoured to become members of the ruling elite. To a certain extent both goals were realised. As a result, in the course of the transformation of the 1990s the multi-ethnic structure of Dagestan turned into a decisive political factor.

The mobilisation of political forces in the republic did not take place on the basis of ideological differences and political parties, but of identities, at the core of which were traditional ethno-cultural values. Nationalities, which quite recently still did not play any political role and were merely objects of the 'national politics' of an authoritarian and essentially centralised state, were now transformed into the determining subjects of the political process.

In Chechnya–Ingushetia ethnic processes ran differently. From the very beginning, Chechens and Ingush, as an integral unit, differed distinctly as independent peoples, and in their political history within the framework of the communist system. This was reflected in the administrative divisions of the 1920s, which were directed from above. Subsequently, they were universally exiled from their homeland and found themselves in extreme living conditions in an alien ethnic environment. Chechen and Ingush representatives of the Soviet political–administrative, military and intellectual elites were torn out of the communist establishment and began, in the heart of their people, to try and get a niche in the informal leadership of the traditional clans and religious '*aksakals*' and to integrate with them. In the conditions of exile, the Chechen and Ingush traditional clan structures failed to weaken, and gained an even greater definition and a significant source of functional stability. Parallel with this, the general national self-awareness of their peoples grew stronger.

Returning to the homeland after the amnesty in 1957, the Chechens and Ingush found a completely occupied socio-political space and they had to fight it and first of all the Russians little by little. The region where they lived and where their Republic was restored, at that time, thanks to Groznyi oil, became in industrial terms the most developed in the North Caucasus. Chechens and Ingush started once again to create a political–administrative elite and intelligentsia, and to obtain for themselves an increase in political weight in their Republic. But nevertheless, right up until the fall of the communist regime, the ethnic Russian component continued to dominate in political and civil institutions of the Chechnya–Ingushetia Republic. The transformation of the regime, as we have already shown, continued there, by contrast to Dagestan, primarily in the general national movement for liberation from Russian guardianship.

However, it seems strange that nationalism, for all its importance in the social consciousness of Dagestani peoples and Chechens has, in both places, its own peculiar limits of diffusion. In Dagestan, we see that leaders of one and the same nationality bitterly clash among themselves, and often ally with groups of other nationalities. In Chechnya we see equally bitter struggles between authoritative leaders, the grounds for which serve personal ambitions and mercantile motivation and prevail over general national state interests. Why is this so?

114

In Dagestan, political practice bears witness to the fact that although people do not stop talking about nationalities they have, as a rule, become of secondary importance or have completely lost their importance when it comes to the solution of serious problems. For example, popular leaders of national movements, whose mass authority is based on the clear expression of historical and contemporary grievances, and the needs and demands of their respective nationality, do not succeed in even gathering the necessary number of signatures for registration as a candidate for the republican parliament. If some of them do manage to break through to the ruling class, then it is probably at the price of defending the interests of their respective peoples and owing to other qualities, unrelated to nationality issues. Alternatively, for example, the leader of one nationality 'unexpectedly' forms a political alliance with an authoritative figure of another nationality against a second leader of his or her own nationality.

In Chechnya the overthrow of Doku Zavgaev happened exclusively with support from the centre, in as much as the influential 'Moscow Chechens', for their own personal aims, supported the growing internal opposition of the 'new' Chechens. Subsequently, the fragility of Chechnya's political structure remained the same: a universal change in the ruling class with Dzhakhar Dudaev, and the formation of a new irreconcilable opposition of all who were now out of power.

With all of the pro-Chechen political action and nationalist rhetoric of Dudaev, his power not only failed to strengthen, but actually lessened from the beginning of his leadership. Only the crude and foolish interference from Moscow turned Dudaev into an all-nation leader. On 7 November 1991, Yeltsin with his presidential decree No. 178 'introduced' a state of emergency in Chechnya, on the evening of 8 November Chechnya found out about it, on 9 November the triumphal inauguration of President Dudaev took place and on 10 November 1991 Yeltsin cancelled his ridiculous decree. The threat of a new deportation of Chechens and the crude interference from without rallied the Chechen nation around their new leader. Henceforth Dudaev again gradually began to lose the authority of a national leader and met with growing opposition up until the moment when Russia attacked the mutinous Republic. The war from 1994 to 1996 once again made the Chechens into a monolithic nation fighting an external enemy, but after the end of the war and the gaining of *de facto* independence, Maskhadov, the victor in the war and in all-nation alternative democratic presidential elections, did not manage to establish effective control over the situation in the country. The leaders of the Chechen people in their narrow mercenary struggle among themselves gave up themselves and the Chechen's national interests, and in the end, on the eve of civil war, and in order to avoid it they found a new supply of national unity in an external enemy: they attacked the neighbouring Republic – Dagestan.

Something is clearly hiding behind the nationalist discourse both in Dagestan and Chechnya. A deepened analysis of the practice of confrontation in the top political leadership of Dagestan, studying the mechanisms of appointment to high office, the formation of political groups, research into the electoral behaviour of the population and the adoption of campaigning technologies and much else allows one to draw the conclusion that the nationalist discourse, which dictates to the public conscience the forms and means of thinking about what is happening, does not reveal but hides the genuine structure of political relations which have formed here. In Dagestan the situation usually pictured is such that in the concrete political process in the republic the respective nationalities assume the role of agents of the opposition. However the real subjects in the Dagestani political scene turn out to be structures, which are not present in political discourse and which thus seemingly do not exist in reality. However, they can be uncovered if one turns one's attention from what is happening at the front of the stage to follow concrete internal political events.

These latent organised structures can be provisionally named 'ethnoparties', in as much as they possess all the formal attributes of western European parties:

- a degree of common thinking and corporate interest indispensable for the mobilisation of social forces;
- an organisational structure, consisting of one or several authoritative leaders and a sufficient number of activists to carry out the necessary activities;
- financial support from representatives of the highest property elite and the mass support of certain segments of the population.

The difference is 'merely' in the fact that the leaders of these 'parties', the mass and financial support of their activity, as a rule, are realised by the representatives from one subnational ethnic community at the level of rural villages or groups of closely situated villages, historically linked with each other, i.e. that which in Dagestan has long born the name '*Dzhamaat*'.[4] Among the functionaries of the ethno-parties one can even meet persons of other nationalities, however the key components of these political formations (leaders, financial and mass support) are composed of persons of a single traditional community, more organised than the national groups. Thereby not one Dagestani nationality has a single political centre, i.e. one ethno-party. They serve the interests of particular groups and thus cannot embrace the whole nationality. The leaders of these 'parties' often not only do not unite with other groupings of the same nationality, but even ally themselves with the ethno-parties of representatives of other nationalities against 'their own people', if it seems necessary to them.

What has been said here can be illustrated by the results of election campaigns. The opinion that Dagestanis vote for the representatives of their own nationality and the ruling elite consolidates along ethnic lines is axiomatic in the public consciousness of the Republic, but these ideas do not correspond with actual practice, which can be reconstructed from concrete sources.

For example, at the election to the Duma in 1996 in the Makhachkalinskii constituency (comprising all of northern and central lowland Dagestan), four authoritative Avar leaders hindered each other in winning the elections and a representative of the relatively sparse Lak nationality, Nadir Khachilaev, became deputy with only 27 per cent of the votes. The Lak population in this constituency comprises not more than 8 per cent of the population.

The election campaign and the elections of the mayor of the Republic's capital, Makhachkala, equally vividly conforms to the thesis that the genuine subjects of the political process are not the nationalities, however much this might seem obvious in everyday perception, but rather concrete 'parties', the basis of which form a denser traditionalist community, acting in a complex system of political relations with other similar structures. In this case the basic struggle developed between the Dargin Said Amirov and the Avar Sheruchan Gadzhimuradov. In the capital of Dagestan the Avar population is considerable larger than the Dargin, but they do not account for more than 26 per cent of all inhabitants of Makhachkala. For some reason, two candidates of Avar nationality lacking even the slightest chance of victory joined the struggle between the two main pretenders. In the end, Said Amirov won with an overwhelming majority (71 per cent of the votes).

In the by-election for a Duma deputy's mandate in 1997 the Lezgin Magomed-Fazil' Azizov won instead of the Avar Ramazan Abulatipov, appointed by the then Vice-President of the Russian Federation in the Buijnaksii region. In the course of the election campaign the following attracted attention. After the well-known Avar leader Gadzhi Makhachev – a figure who would have undoubtedly gone through – for some reason withdrew his candidacy, the 'Avar Popular Movement' which he headed took the decision to support not the candidacy of the Avar Magomed Aliev, who realistically aimed for victory and was supported by the former deputy for the constituency Abdulatipov, but rather a different Avar, Arkadii Ganiev, whose chances were unanimously rated as nil. The real struggle unfolded between the Avar Aliev and the Lezgin Azizov, and the latter won with an impressive result – 54 per cent of the votes. In this region Lezgins constitute only 22 per cent of the total population. Of course, the victor could secure himself the block voting of his fellow Lezgins. Indeed, in the five deeply 'Lezgin' districts of Dagestan (Magaramkentskii, Kasumkentskii, Kurachskoii, Achtynskii and Dokusparinskii) he received around 60,000 votes, and his basic rival Magomed Aliev only 150. All in all, in southern Dagestan, which additionally includes Rutul'skii, Aguk'skii, Hivskii, Tabasaranskii and Derbentskii *raions*, Azizov got more than 130,000 votes and his main rival only 20,000. We observe the mirror image of this in the basically 'Avar' districts. From ten such districts belonging to the constituency Aliev received only 74,000 votes, but Azizov 'captured' from him 11,000 Avar votes. Thus, in the 'purely' Avar district of Gubetovskii out of 7,000 voters, 4,000 voted for the Lezgin Azizov. Azizov's final victory was handed to him by the 'Dargin' districts of the republic. In them, Azizov received 53,000 votes and his main opponent 24,000. Azizov came second to Aliev only in the 'Dargin' district of Kaitagskii (4,800 votes to 5,200). In the Lakskii district the share of the vote went Aliev's way (4,500 to 2,800).

All these and other examples of real political practice bear witness to the fact that Dagestan has not gone down the road of national segregation and that nationalism here, in the final analysis, did not become the catalyst for political confrontation. Although if one were to follow the social–political discourse of this entire period, everything apparently comes down to the problem of national solidarity, of the 'rights' of nationalities to their share of political power, to 'their' land, etc. Why did nationalism yield in the real political process to a different type of solidaristic relationship, constituting the basis of the structure we refer to as ethno-parties? The explanation must quite clearly be sought in history of Dagestan.

From as far back as the early Middle Ages in Dagestan, clan identity was replaced by a political identity, which did not embrace the whole settlement area of ethnographic collectives with a common origin. In the historical chronicles of that time we do not come across clans, but rather well-defined political formations (Derbetskii emirate, Serir, Khaidak, Zerikhgeran, Shandan, Filan, Zuklan, Karakh, Tabasaran, Gumik, Lagz) (Gadzhiev, Davydov and Shikhsaidov 1996: 234–254).

Subsequently from the fourteenth and fifteenth centuries onwards a complex system of independent, but inter-related political formations with norms of self-government developed – the so-called *dzhamaats*. The ethno-cultural (tribal) uniformity of large areas, which outside observers detected easily, from antiquity up to the present day, already had no political meaning in Dagestan, at least from the fifteenth or sixteenth century onwards.

The social–legal structure of the *dzhamaats* were essentially uniform throughout Dagestan, but of course with numerous nuances. The *dzhamaat*, first and foremost, strictly separated its citizens from all outsiders. Belonging to a *dzhamaat* constituted the strongest identification for a Dagestani and was supported by written laws. The highest degree of punishment was expulsion from the *dzhamaat*, which led to the loss of its protection and almost certain death or disaster. Every *dzhamaat* comprised a few (at least three) clan groups, or '*tukhums*'. The *tukhum* (a large community of blood-ties) did not possess any common property and or an inherited leadership (leader of the family). New settlers could be taken into the *tukhum*, families could move from one *tukhum* to another and even broader redistributions of the population of a *dzhamaat* could take place between *tukhums*. At the same time, civil arrangement of the internal life of a *dzhamaat* was such that the energy of natural internal *tukhum* solidarity between members of one clan group was strictly limited and regulated by written *dzhamaat* laws (*adat*).[5] The membership of a *dzhamaat* member in a certain family group (*tukhum*) was constituted 'from above' as an institution which, alongside other measures, secured public order. The *tukhum*, in its essence, was a mechanism (a conductor) with the purpose of effectively transmitting decisions of the authorities to the individual members of the *dzhamaat*. The entire adult male population of the *dzhamaat*, excluding temporary settlers, guests and prisoners of war, were equal before the law. Ownership of land and all other property was divided up exclusively into *dzhamaat* (woods, pastures and hayfields), private (farmed plots and gardens) and *vakuf*, i.e. the formerly private land, inherited or presented by the mosque of the *dzhamaat*. The basic social cell of the *dzhamaat* was the family, usually extended, as occurs quite often up to the present day. There was a well-established institution of individual private property, especially land. Property rights regarding land were scrupulously determined by *dzhamaat* laws and were limited only in cases of the sale or gifting of land to another *dzhamaat*.

In this way, the *dzhamaat* was the civil and political unit of the traditional social organisation of the Dagestani population. It possessed distinct territorial boundaries. Its land was protected not only with military resources, but also by legislation regarding the rights to buy and sell land. In essence the *dzhamaat* was a city-state, a polis.[6] In a certain sense contemporary Dagestani nationalities, founded in the course of the 'socialist settling of the national question', are a bureaucratic 'reanimation' of ancient clan communities, the basis of whose construction was ethno-cultural similarity, i.e. general ethnic characteristics, which can be easily ascertained by objective examination. The total number and list of nationalities, which in the final analysis were institutionalised in the period of communist rule, were (1) the Avars, (2) the Dargins, (3) the Kumyks, (4) the Lezgins, (5) the Tabasarans, (6) the Rutuls, (7) the Aghuls and (8) the Tsakhurs.

The bureaucratic authority which had established this structure of nationalities, only had to disappear and disorder break out for the structures of the traditional political organisation of the Dagestanis to start to revive.

Judging by all of this, traditional social structures have also been revived and involved in the contemporary political process in Chechnya. And here we turn to the deepest difference between Chechnya and Dagestan, the *teip* (clan) system of Chechen society.

Dagestan, beginning in the fourteenth and fifteenth centuries with the formation period of the main, unified, numerous clan groups (*tukhums*) and settlements (*dzhamaats*), went down the path of forming compact territorial political identities of a civic type. Clearly, this depended on the stormy and all-enveloping development of Islam in the region at the same time. Islam at that time in Dagestan was turning into the most important component of the ideological, legal–political and cultural life of every single *dzhamaat* and, at the same time, was the basic formation of the whole system of internal Dagestani economic, political and cultural relations: the process of *dzhamaat* union formation, their upper unions, the unified common market system, single language and ideology. In this century (fifteenth–sixteenth) the understanding of 'Dagestan' as a separate and distinct political–cultural entity took shape, different to Christian Georgia, Shiite Azerbaijan and heathen Chechnya.

In Dagestan the laid-down structure of a traditional society consisted of the following elements: the family (nuclear or extended); the *tukhum* (the clan society of close relatives through the male line, existing exclusively within the framework of a given *dzhamaat*); the *dzhamaat* (a politically autonomous and territorial unit, organised with the help of civil laws); the 'voluntary society' or 'principality' (political union of a fixed majority of compactly located *dzhamaats*, on the principle of either equality or inequality, on the basis of a republican or authoritarian regime); Dagestan (a whole economic–cultural and historical–ethnographic society).

Chechen traditional society was built differently: the family – *dyuozal, d'ezal* (nuclear or extended); *dzha* (the extended family, kin, a few closely related families, living nearby); *nieke"ii* (clan society, the aggregate of related kin, not dependent on the place of residence); *gar* (the aggregate of related people with distant but genuine common ancestors); *teip, var* (the aggregate of related *gars*); *tukuam, tukkhum* (the tribe, the aggregate of the identified relations, *teips* and *vars*); *k"am* (the whole people, Chechens) (see Nash Dagestan 1995).

In particular, evidence of the deep differences between Dagestanis and Chechens in the organisation of life is that among Dagestanis it is permissible and even encouraged for cousins to marry, whereas Chechens are still categorically opposed to marriages even within the same *teip*, i.e. between relatives through the father's line, the unity of which can be traced deep into antiquity, over the distance of ten–fifteen generations; there cannot be marital relations as they are still considered 'brother' and 'sister'.

The structure of traditional Chechen society, built on a 'clan' principal, has inescapably turned out to be highly intricate. Thus there is no one opinion on the quantity of *teips* and *tukkhums*; sometimes no difference is made between these two categories and sometimes it is particularly emphasised. Sometimes one also hears that one or another *teip* or *tukkhum* is 'impure' or 'not Chechen', etc.

The war with Russia which unified all Chechens could not halt the process of stratification of Chechen society into '*teips*'.[7] The structures of military units (the army) headed by 'field commanders', to a large extent, reflect the *teip* structure of contemporary Chechen society.

The coming to power of the first Chechen (Doku Zavgaev) in 1991 switched on a mechanism for internal power struggles in the Republic. With the collapse in the legal and ideological system of the communist regime and open power struggle, the Chechen traditional clan identity should have inescapably become the most important resource for the regulation of social relations. If in Dagestan ethno-parties were built on the foundations of traditional *dzhamaat* identity, then it is clear that Chechen ethno-parties stand on *teip* solidarity. However, the difference is that *dzhamaat* is a distinct fragment of a given nationality – that is, that social category which is openly controlled and regulated in the system of political relations in Dagestan. As far as *teip* structure is concerned, it does not exist existentially (it is present in the consciousness of Chechens) so it is not possible to imagine how it could be taken into account.

The Dagestani model of 'consociational democracy'

The new Constitution of the Republic of Dagestan was passed on 26 July 1994, after three years of tortuous searching for the political structure most acceptable to the republic. For the entire duration of its preparation the key idea of all concepts, which determined the direction of the search and fuelled the basic conflicts and disagreements, was the observation of the 'rights of nationality'. A broad class of social and political activists and specialists – members of the 'Group for the Composition of a New Constitution', grappled with a solution to the problems of organising power in the republic, which could offer guarantees for the rights of all the peoples of Dagestan to 'their' respective land and 'their' natural resources, and secure a just representation of every nationality in the organs of state power and in organisations responsible for material production, education, science and culture. However it was impossible, for very understandable reasons, to find public agreement in the solution of such questions.

On the other hand, the highest political leaders, who were to decide what the Constitution of the Republic of Dagestan would look like, were interested in an organisation of power, which would exclude the possibility of its concentration in the hands of one person. All these efforts led in the end to a quite original political structure in Dagestan.

Thus, according to the new Dagestani Constitution, the organ of the supreme executive power consists of fourteen people. These are the members of the State Council, and they are not elected directly by the people, but by a special institution, the Constitutional Assembly, which assembles exclusively for such cases and also for constitutional amendments. It comprises members of the Parliament and also a number of members specially elected by representative assemblies of district and city organs of self-government.

According to the Constitution of Dagestan, 'not more than one representative of a single nationality' can be a member of the State Council, consisting of fourteen members (Article 88).[8] Members of the State Council cannot be parliamentary deputies, members of the government or judges, but are allowed to combine executive functions with work as procurators, lecturers, managers or employees of corporations or state organisations or enterprises.

Initially the chairman of the State Council – the 'head of state' according to the Dagestan Constitution (Article 92) – is elected secretly by the Constitutional Assembly. A second member of the State Council takes his seat without being elected – this is the Prime Minister, who takes up his post at the suggestion of the

Chair of the State Council and after confirmation by Parliament. The Prime Minister, in this way, automatically becomes a member of the State Council and, what is more, the first deputy of its Chair. Subsequently, when the nationality of the two aforementioned members of the State Council is known, the procedure of electing the remaining twelve members begins in the Constitutional Assembly. Every member of the Constitutional Assembly independent of his own nationality has the right to recommend a candidacy for the State Council of any nationality for the remaining twelve seats. After the lists of forwarded candidates (who do not necessarily have to be members of the Constitutional Assembly) are drawn up, grouped by nationality, a first secret vote picks out two candidates from each nationality, chosen according to the largest number of votes received. A secret vote then determines which of these two remaining candidates per nationality become members of the State Council.

The Parliament of the Republic (The People's Assembly of the Republic of Dagestan) consists of 121 deputies, elected by universal, direct and confidential ballot in territorial constituencies. At the same time, the Constitution of the Republic of Dagestan ordains that 'the representation in Parliament of all nationalities of Dagestan be guaranteed' (Article 72), and the mechanism for the realisation of this constitutional norm is secured by the law 'On Elections to the People's Assembly of the Republic of Dagestan'.

According to this law the mechanism for securing national proportionality consists of the following: the territory of the republic is subdivided into ethnically uniform territories (mainly the mountainous regions of Dagestan, which are populated by compact masses of Avars, Dargins, Lezgins, Laks, Tabarasans and other nationalities) and ethnically mixed territories, the cities of the Republic and the rural districts of the plain. In ethnically uniform regions there are no restrictions on the nationality of parliamentary candidates. In the ethnically mixed regions and the cities the Law 'On Elections' gives the Republican Electoral Committee the right to establish special 'national territorial constituencies', in which only candidates from one nationality can campaign. At the same time, the electorate of these multi-ethnic constituencies are in no way subdivided according to nationality; the entire population of the constituency votes for candidates belonging to a single nationality. This is done so that the electoral campaign between authoritative leaders does not go outside of one nationality, and so that for the multi-ethnic electorate of such a constituency the nationality of the candidates is meaningless and has no bearing on the results of the election.

Thus, in the first election in 1995, of the 121 constituencies, sixty-six were nationally defined, i.e. each of them was designated to a certain nationality taking into account the necessary proportion of national representation.[9] For this purpose twelve Avar, twelve Kumyk, ten Russian, seven Dargin, five Tabasaran, five Azeri, four Lezgin, four Chechen, three Lak, two Tat constituencies and one Tsakhur constituency were created from the multi-ethnic districts and all cities.

One other constituency was allowed to have candidates of any nationality. This made it possible to avoid the problem of legislative discrimination of members of nationalities apart from the fourteen (for example Armenians, Jews, Georgians, Ukrainians, etc.). These quotas, combined with elections in constituencies with ethnically uniform populations (of which fifty-five remained) made it possible in the end to obtain a parliamentary body which adequately reflected the national composition of the republic's population. The parliamentary election of 1999 took place according to an analogous arrangement.

This entire system succeeds in functioning within the norms of the Constitution of the Republic of Dagestan: 'Everyone has a right to freely choose and indicate his national belonging. No one should be forced to choose and indicate his national belonging' (Article 31).

Apart from the rules regulating the national composition of supreme state institutions, there is also a norm securing the protection of the most important attributes of nationality. Article 81, part 33 of the Constitution of the Republic of Dagestan ordains something resembling the power of veto: 'In the consideration of questions regarding changes in the established administrative–territorial structure and also the demographic, linguistic, socio-economic and cultural environment of the people of Dagestan, in the case of disagreement with the drafted motion of a deputy or a group of deputies from a given territory a decision must be passed with a two-thirds majority in the National Assembly.'

Such a system of taking into account national representation is exposed to constant criticism from the numerically few, but active liberal intelligentsia. The basic flaw is seen to lie in the fact that this system contradicts the rights of a citizen to vote in the constituency in which he wishes to vote. The 'medieval restrictions', in their opinion, establish the regulation of people by national characteristics, which cannot correspond with the norms of the equality of citizens.

Many rules regulating the national balance, although not supported in articles of the Constitution, in laws or in any written rules at all, are strictly carried out in practice. Thus, according to an unwritten rule, the senior figures in the supreme institutions of authority (The Chair of the State Council and of Parliament and of the Prime Minister) have to belong to different nationalities. The Prime Minister's deputies are selected so that representatives of different nationalities are present and, if possible, not more than one belongs to any single nationality. The situation with the deputies of the Chair of the People's Assembly, the leaders of parliamentary committees, the Administration of the State Council, etc. is the same. National representation is also taken into account regarding the senior figures in higher institutions of education and science.

The Dagestani model of political structure was formed free of any influence from the concept of consociational democracy (Lijphardt 1977). At the same time, it is clear that it can be considered to count as such a type of political arrangement.

The fact that in Dagestan it is not nationalities which oppose each other but ethno-parties signifies a greater pluralism of political forces then it might seem if only nationalities were to be singled out in the Dagestani political structure. That also signifies a more complex intertwining of variegated alliances of political groupings, but at the same time the multiplication of possible causes of confrontation between them. All these circumstances taken together secure political stability in Dagestan and, more importantly, discredit in the public consciousness the nationalist discourse with which representatives of the elites, as a rule, justify their efforts to mobilise 'popular' support for their benefit.

NOTES

1   In Dagestan live more than thirty ethnic groups. Fourteen are regarded as 'basic' in Dagestan. Traditionally, the political elite is recruited from the four largest groups Avars (28.0 per cent), Dargins (15.8 per cent), Kumyks (13.1 per cent) and Lezgins (11.5 per cent).The overall population is about 1.77 million. (Figures as of 1989, *Natsional'ny sostav naseleniia SSSRpo dannym Vsesoiuznoiperepisi naseleniia 1989 goda* (Ethnic Composition of the USSR's Population according to the All-Union Census of 1989), Moscow: Finansy i Statistika, 1991.)

2   Imam Shamil' was a Dagestani Avar from the Gimra *dzhamaat*. Shamil' was the third leader of the movement (*imam*) after the Avars Gazimagomed and Gazatbek. The beginning of the opposition to Russia was organised under the leadership of the *imams*, but opposition also started in 1830 on the territory of Dagestan and not directly against the Russians, but against their stronghold in the mountains – the Khunzakh sovereigns (of the Avar khans). Only after defeat at the hands of tsarist forces in a long and bloody battle on the Akhul'go mountain in 1839 was it necessary for Shamil' to leave and hide in Chechnya, where he got shelter and support. In 1840, when the Chechens yet again rose up in answer to Russian punitive expeditions, Shamil' succeeded in organising their spontaneous demonstrations as a holy war against the unbelievers.

3   Used here in the sense of the Soviet term '*nacional'nost''*, referring to an officially recognised ethno-national group.

4   'Dzhamaat' is an Arabic word, meaning 'society', a distinct organised collective of people. In traditional Dagestan there was no common term, signifying a state formation. They all had their own names (Achty-para, Akusha-dargo, Nutsal' (Chunzach), Utsmiist (Kaitagsk), Antsuch, Agul, etc.). General terms, when they appeared and began to spread, were borrowed from Persian, Arabic or Turkish.

5   *Adat'* (the Arabic for custom) signifies the usual law of the peoples, which opposes Islamic law – the Shariat. However, the use of this term to refer to the so-called 'Dagestani Adats' is mistaken. The written 'constitution' of the Dagestani political *dzhamaat* formations ('free societies' and 'unions of free societies') were written and adopted by the mountain people in their time as Muslim Shariah statutes. The perception of them as '*adats*' appeared only at the beginning of the nineteenth century amongst Dagestani Myuridist ideologists, who in the course of the war with Russia expanded the struggle with independent *dzhamaats* for the unification of Dagestan. The demand for the establishing of 'pure Islam' on the whole of Dagestan's territory unavoidably converted the 'constitution' of independent *dzhamaats* into '*adats*', with which to confront the Shariat. The Russian colonial administration and historiography accepted this 'Myuridist' conceptual framework, but in the struggle with this terrible ideological force in Dagestan, they relied on the return of the '*adat*'.

6   City-state' and 'polis' are used here although these terms are not used by historians
     writing about the political history of Dagestan. The generally accepted terms for the polit-
     ical formations of traditional Dagestan outlined here are now 'rural society' or 'feudal
     society'. Shikhsaidov calls the process of development of political formations of the *dzha-
     maat* type in Dagestan in the thirteenth and fourteenth centuries a 'process of develop-
     ment of large villages', 'a period of intensive formation of large settlements', 'the
     formation of new administrative-territorial units (large settlements)'; Shikhsaidov writes:
     'These processes [the growth of villages] also coincided with a time of noticeable strength-
     ening of old and the emergence of new unions of rural communes, with changes in the
     social structure of Dagestani society' (see Gadzhiev, Davydov and Shikhsaidov 1996:
     318–319). The historical phenomenon of the Dagestani 'polis' is so original that until
     now no term has been found to describe it. Mamaichan Aglarov (1988), who has reflected
     more than anyone on the phenomenon of Dagestani traditional 'society', writes that
     Russian soldiers, officials, travellers and historians discovered the principal difference
     between Dagestani 'societies' and traditional peasant communes. Thus, I. Gerber, one of
     the best-informed authors, called them 'territorium', similar to the feudal regions of
     Dagestan, and I. A. Gil'denshtedt (at the end of eighteenth century) termed them 'dis-
     tricts', thus terminologically not differentiating them from political formations, governed
     by personal rulers. P. G. Butkov (at the end of the eighteenth century) writes about the 'the
     unions of private regions' similar to fiefdoms. A. I. Achverdov, a young officer at the end
     of the eighteenth century was the first to call them 'republics', after which this term
     becomes dominant in military and business correspondence in Russian. Thus, the
     Commander-in-Chief in the Caucasus General-Major Graf Pauluchin in reports to the
     armed forces minister Rumyantsev in 1812 calls the unions of *dzhamaats* 'the republican
     societies of the Lezgin'. S.M. Bronevskii (at the beginning of the nineteenth century)
     writes of the 'federative republics' in Dagestan. Thereby all these terms are applied exclu-
     sively to Dagestan, and not at all to the regions, populated by the mountain peoples of the
     northern Caucasus. Only with the beginning of the national-liberation war in Dagestan
     did the 'republics' in Russian business texts change into 'fiefdoms'. This last term stays
     generally accepted up to the present day (see Aglarov 1988: 6–11). Much new and inter-
     esting material regarding the *dzhamaat* political construction in Dagestan can also be
     found in Aglarov (1998).

7   In this case we are using the term '*teip*' as a generalised category of clan identity of any
     level significant for Chechens.

8   Fourteen nationalities are regarded as 'basic' in Dagestan (in order of size): Avars,
     Dargins, Kumyks, Lezgins, Russians, Laks, Tabasarans, Azeris, Chechens, Nogays, Rutuls,
     Aghuls, Tsakhurs and Tats. It should be emphasised that this list is not fixed in any legis-
     lative acts. However there are indirect, but weighty indications to treat them as the 'state-
     forming' nationalities of Dagestan. Two constitutional conditions, i.e. 'the fourteen
     members of the State Council' and 'one from each people' necessarily point to this choice
     of nationalities. As we have seen, Russians, Chechens and Azeris are included among the
     'Dagestani nationalities'. The fact that these nationalities have a historically rooted rural
     population on the territory of Dagestan can serve as another indicator of the choice of this
     number of and of these nationalities.

9   The constitution of Dagestan does not provide for the election of deputies by party lists.
     All 121 members of parliament are elected by a majority system in single-mandate con-
     stituencies.

125

REFERENCES

Aglarov, M. A. (1988), *Sel'skaya Obshchina v Narodnom Dagestane v XVII-XIX v.* (Moscow).

Aglarov, M. A. (1998), *Etnogenez v svete politantropolgii i etnomii v Dagestane. Politica-ethnica* (Mahachkala).

Aliev, B. G. (1999), *Soyuzy sel'skikh obshchin Dagestana v XVIII-pervoi polovine XIX v.* (Mahachkala).

Dogan, M. and D. Pelassi (1994), *Sravnitel'naya politicheskaya sotsiologiya* (Moscow).

Gadzhiev, M. G., O. M. Davydov and A. R. Shikhsaidov (1996), *Istoria Dagestana s Drevneishikh vremen do kontsa XV veka* (Mahachkala).

Gakaev D. (1999), 'Chechnya i Rossiya: obshchestva i gosudarstva', in D. Gakaev, *Put' k chechenskoi revolyutsii* (Moscow).

Jaspers K. (1991), 'Istoki istorii i ee tsel'', in *Smysl i naznachenie istorii* (Moscow).

Lijphart, A. *Democracy in Plural Societies* (New Haven).

Matericly Vsesoyuznoi perepisi naseleniya 1926 goda po Dagestanskoi ASSR (1927), *vyp. 1. Spisok naselennych mest Dagestanskoi ASSR* (Mahachkala).

Muzaev, T. and Z. Todua (1992), *Novaya Checheno-Ingushetiya* (Moscow).

Nash Dagestan (1995), 'Chechnya ot Mansura do Dzhokhara', *Nash Dagestan*, No. 174–175 (Special Edition).

Takhir al-Karakhi, M. (1941), *Chronika Muchammeda tachira al-Karachi o dagestanckich vcjnach v period Shamilya*, trans. A. M. Barabanova (Moscow and Leningrad).

7

Civil wars in Georgia: corruption breeds violence

Pavel K. Baev

Introduction

GEORGIA MAKES AN incredibly rich and uniquely complicated case for the analysis of modern civil wars. It is a newly independent state that appeared with the collapse of the USSR, but it also has a long history of statehood. It is a relatively small state, but it occupies a key geopolitical crossroads which has acquired strategic importance with the new development of hydrocarbon resources in the Caspian area. Its population is small and declining but the ethnic composition, cultural and religious traditions are extremely diverse. From the moment that Georgia restored its independence, it has found itself engulfed by political violence organised along several separate but criss-crossing tracks, with destabilising impulses spreading unchecked. In 1992–93, Georgia came breathtakingly close to collapsing as yet another 'failed state', however, all major violent clashes had terminated by the end of 1993. Despite serious international efforts to assist peace processes and internal reforms, to date none of the conflicts has been resolved, generating occasional skirmishes and, more importantly, significant uncertainty regarding Georgia's ability to survive as an independent state.

It is obvious that the civil wars in Georgia in 1990–93 erupted as a consequence of the break-up of the USSR;[1] however, in most Soviet constituent republics the inevitable destabilisation resulting from that cataclysm did not take such violent forms. Many regions in Central Asia (the Fergana valley), in the North Caucasus (Dagestan, see Chapter 6 in this volume) and in Georgia itself (Ajariya) had explosive combinations of risk factors but remained relatively peaceful. The collapse of the USSR, therefore, cannot in itself be the explanation for the Georgian wars, but should instead be seen as their macro-context and environment. Similarly, the interference from Russia cannot be interpreted as the all-dominant force;[2] Russia's involvement and influence were certainly significant factors but they were not the determinants of the violent escalations of internal crises in Georgia. The main assumption of the following analysis is that the main causes of Georgia's troubles should be sought in the anomalies and distortions of its own society, political institutions and elites. And the main source for these distortions is presumed to be not in the ethnic grievances, or past injustices, or Communist legacies – but in the all-penetrating shadow economy and corruption.[3]

What makes the Georgian case particularly interesting, and maybe even unique, is the parallel development of three major political conflicts – the struggle for power at the state level, the secession of South-Ossetia and the secession of Abkhazia – which occurred with significant overlaps in the space of just four years, from November 1989 to October 1993. They will be analysed here as separate civil wars; however, since such isolation could lead to significant deficiencies in the analysis, every effort will be undertaken to trace the interplay between them.

Background: it is the stupid economy!

There is neither space nor, presumably, need to provide here detailed information on Georgia's history, geography and demography (see Aves 1997; Corley 1999); it is, perhaps, sufficient to say that the rich history of Georgia was remarkably conflict-free and that with its broad ethnic diversity and strong national identity, Georgia had a record of peaceful coexistence of indigenous and immigrant ethnic groups. There might be, however, a need to present some basic economic data, both for Soviet Georgia and for the new republic, with inevitable reservations about the highly unreliable nature of all statistics.

The fundamental problem with economic data on the period immediately preceding the wars in Georgia (1985–89) is that the only source is Soviet economic statistics with all their deficiencies; the problem of accurate measurement of GDP of the USSR (and its constituent republics) has not been resolved even retrospectively.[4] As the USSR was sinking into an economic abyss during the second half of the 1980s, the official statistics maintained fewer and fewer connections with reality.

Another part of the problem is that the 1980s were a decade of fast growth of the 'shadow' economy in the USSR, and Georgia was, quite possibly, one of the leaders in this area. There were several objective reasons for this leadership: the mild subtropical climate provided Georgia with a natural monopoly on the production of citrus fruits (mandarins) and flowers (mimosa) that were of great demand on non-state markets; the Black Sea coastline from Gagra to Batumi provided a booming tourist industry, with significant unregistered elements. But it was political and societal factors that determined the fast spread of illegal activities. Georgia's political elites were purged by Stalin with particular brutality, and then unceremoniously reshuffled during the 'de-stalinisation' campaign, which created quite mixed feelings in the Georgian society. Those who came to power in the late 1950s were real survivors, with few ideological illusions but with clear understanding of the structures of power and networks of influence.[5] The elites were redefining the norms of affluence and success, and the society was eager to embrace those and develop grass-roots entrepreneurial skills, that formally were equal to criminal activities.

Growing in affluence during the 1960s, Georgia acquired an unsavoury reputation for corruption; the appointment of Eduard Shevardnadze as the republic's leader in 1972 was intended to arrest this trend. Shevardnadze duly purged corrupt officials but in fact his reign (which lasted until March 1985 when the newly arrived Soviet leader Mikhail Gorbachev made him the Soviet Foreign Minister) was marked by a steady growth of clan-based corruption culture.[6]

Overall, while the official figures for Georgia from the mid-1970s to the mid-1980s showed a slow growth of the so-called 'Net Material Product' (NMP) and *per capita* income, in fact in that decade more wealth was generated 'informally' than was registered in the accounts. By the late 1980s, the real level of income and the standard of living in Georgia were significantly higher than the average for the USSR.

The collapse of that economic prosperity was unprecedented in its devastation across the former USSR. In 1990, NMP declined by 11.1 per cent, in 1991 by 20.6 per cent, in 1992 by 43.4 per cent, and in 1994 by further 40.0 per cent; the GDP estimates (corrected retrospectively), show a decline of 35.0 per cent in 1994 and a total decline from 1989 to 1994 of more than 70 per cent; the World Bank estimates that Georgia's GDP declined at an annual average of 26.9 per cent in 1990–95. Modest recovery started in 1995, and in 1996–98 GDP showed annual growth of 11.2 per cent; however, in 1999 growth slowed down to just 3.0 per cent and in 2000 to 1.8 per cent. Official government figures now include adjustments for 'unrecorded activity' which amount to 40 per cent of the total.[7]

The almost complete disappearance of the 'official' economy in 1992–94 meant first of all the total paralysis of two key sectors: heavy industry and tourism. Georgian industry had been based on complicated cooperative ties with other Soviet republics; the disintegration of that system led to the 'sudden death' of heavy industries in Georgia – the share of industrial production in GDP was just 13 per cent in 1998–2000, and most of it was in food processing. Tourism used to be a massively profitable sector, with 1.5 million officially registered tourists coming to Georgia annually (another million can safely be added for unregistered visitors) and it has disappeared entirely. Agriculture was also in deep crisis as Georgian fruit and vegetables, tea and tobacco, wines and mineral waters could not compete on the Russian markets owing primarily to high transportation costs. The privatisation of land in 1991–92 actually weakened the potential for market production and fostered a reorientation towards subsistence agriculture.

Sharp economic decline was accompanied by deep financial crisis. Russia's price liberalisation in January 1992 led to a jump in inflation, but also necessitated the introduction of a national currency. The first attempt at this with the coupon, undertaken by Tbilisi in spring 1993, resulted in monthly inflation reaching 100 per cent by the end of the year. The second attempt with the *lari*, undertaken in autumn 1995, was more successful, but the stability of the new currency was entirely a function of external borrowing which has accumulated a debt of $1.6 billion (41 per cent of GDP for 2000).[8] One result of this financial catastrophe was a sharp demonetarisation of the economy; another was the even sharper fall in personal income. By mid-1994 the average monthly salary was estimated at $0.5; while by mid-1996 the average monthly household income was estimated at $160, only a quarter of it came from salaries; in 1999, *per capita* income was estimated at $620.

Even with the approximate character of these figures, they paint a picture of an economy that contracted massively in the first half of the 1990s, and then – after a short recovery – stabilised at half its previous level. Even if estimates of the size of the 'shadow' economy as 80 per cent of GDP are accepted, the total value of the Georgian economy would still be about 2 per cent of the Russian economy, and the government revenues in 2000 would be only about 0.5 per cent of the Russian government's revenues. This means that neither Georgia's 'official' economy nor its 'shadow' economy were able in 1992–95 to generate profits sufficient to sustain significant military activities and later were not able to support a serious military build-up. The picture had not changed that much by 2002; the defence budget of about $22 million can barely sustain the armed forces of about 12,000 – and the caricature mutiny of a National Guard unit in May 2001 (which ended in two days after Shevardnadze promised to pay back salaries) confirms this (see Broladze 2001). The most profitable economic sectors (for both the state and the mafias), like tourism or export agriculture, have been devastated beyond rehabilitation, and the new sources of income, like Western aid or oil transit, are low-volume.

It can be assumed, with hindsight, that the 'conflict entrepreneurs', who pushed for the escalation of civil wars in Georgia at the start of the 1990s, had unrealistically high expectations of future revenues. The blossoming of corruption and the 'shadow' economy in the 1980s created a peculiar quasi-market mentality among the political elite who took high profits from the natural rent for granted. However, partly as a result of drastic changes in the economic environment and mostly owing to the violent conflicts themselves, the object of the claims – the ability to control profitable enterprises – has shrunk; the loot has therefore practically disappeared.

Struggle for power in Tbilisi

Three different and slightly overlapping phases in this struggle can be easily identified: the wresting of political power from the Communist Party apparatus led by Zviad Gamsakhurdia (April 1989–May 1991); the ousting of President Gamsakhurdia from power (September 1991–November 1993); and the consolidation of power in the hands of Shevardnadze (October 1992–November 1995). While it is only the second phase that qualifies as a civil war, the paramilitary organisations created in the middle of the first phase continued to play a role up to the end of the third phase, as well as figuring prominently in two other Georgian wars (see Nodia 1996; Zverev 1996; Ozhiganov 1997).

At the starting point of the Georgian 'time of troubles', in early April 1989, there were demonstrations in Tbilisi, perhaps 15,000 strong but without any semblance of organisation, unarmed but violent. In late November 1989, more organisation was visible, when a column of 20,000–30,000 marched from Tbilisi to Tskhinval (some 120 km); it was still unarmed and was easily blocked by a few hundred Soviet Interior troops, but some paramilitary groups were already present and the first blood in the first war was spilled. The group which claimed the honour for this dramatic event, the Legion of Georgian Hawks, never appeared in the political arena again, but the organisational resources for the march came from a different source: it was the leader of the Georgian Communist Party, Givi Gumbaridze, who, together with Gamsakhurdia, led the column and also provided the logistics.

The chaotic and disorganised parliamentary elections of September–November 1990 showed more passion and enthusiastic networking than structure-building, but one of the first laws adopted by the new Parliament on 15 November 1990 declared the conscription of Georgians into the Soviet Armed Forces illegal – and that prepared the ground for organising a proto-army, called the National Guard. The corresponding legislation was approved during the second half of January 1991 and it authorised the build-up of a 12,000-strong force on the basis of conscription. Owing to the sharp conflict with the Soviet authorities in Moscow, the Georgian government had extremely limited resources at its disposal and was unable to allocate sufficient funds to the National Guard. Instead of conscription, it actually had to rely on volunteers who enlisted to serve with their own weapons – and they also had to rely on these weapons to feed themselves. The Commander of the National Guard, Tengiz Kitovani, a man with no military experience but with strong entrepreneurial skills, had few doubts about squeezing various 'shadow' businesses, in fact he built his forces through 'soft' extortion rackets.

A different paramilitary organisation was growing alongside (and, perhaps, one step ahead of) the National Guard: the so-called *Mkhedrioni* (the Knights) led by a prominent criminal 'authority' Dzhaba Ioseliani. This organisation had few connections with the competing political forces and was built as a combination of criminal groupings and urban teenage gangs. It relied entirely on illegal sources of income (targeting particularly petrol supplies) and exploited connections with the Georgian underworld in Moscow. By mid-1991, the National Guard and the

Mkhedrioni had about 10,000 members each and focused their attention on getting access to arms, buying or seizing them from Soviet military garrisons.

The turning point in the chaotic internal struggle for power in Georgia was set by the *coup* attempt in Moscow (19–21 August 1991), when Gamsakhurdia was so scared by the demand from the 'Emergency Committee' (GKChP) to disband all armed formations that he did indeed order the National Guard to disarm. Kitovani flatly refused to follow the order and moved his forces (some 2,000 troops) outside Tbilisi, setting up a military camp that became the base for the opposition. Gamsakhurdia, aware that his control had been eroded by a series of minor clashes, attempted to restore control by the means of 'patriotic' mobilisation and provoked a new escalation of the war in South-Ossetia. However, by autumn 1991, the chiefs of the National Guard and the *Mkhedrioni* had become quite certain that they had nothing to gain from capturing the already looted South-Ossetia, so they effectively sabotaged the mobilisation campaign. The decisive escalation of the crisis came in late December 1991, when Kitovani led his forces (by then, perhaps, only 500 troops) into Tbilisi and besieged the parliament buildings. Gamsakhurdia failed to organise forces for resisting the coup and after a week of fighting in central Tbilisi he fled the country.

It is possible to conclude that the struggle for power in Georgia degenerated into a civil war primarily because of the inability of the new post-Communist leadership to control the newly created paramilitary forces. The broad and quarrelsome coalition of democratic forces that sought to remove the Communist *nomenklatura* from power saw a strong need for military instruments owing to the threat of forceful interference from Moscow and brewing conflicts in the ethnic autonomies. However, the only resource base for building and sustaining a paramilitary organisation was taxation of the 'shadow' economy, but this inevitably determined the criminalised character of the armed forces. While the personal features of the new leadership did play a role (the ambitious and unbalanced Gamsakhurdia quickly alienated most former supporters), the main purpose of seizing political power by the National Guard and the *Mkhedrioni* was to secure their monopoly on extortion rackets and to find new loot. This explains why the scale of such a decisive battle was so miniscule (perhaps, 500 people were fighting in Tbilisi on both sides) and why the number of casualties was so low (not more than 200 people were killed in the initial phase of the civil war).

The *coup* in Tbilisi in early January 1992 brought a significant change in the character of the struggle for power: it became regional as its focus shifted to western Georgia (Mingrelia) where Gamsakhurdia found a support base. In Tbilisi, the victorious opposition faced a serious problem with legitimising its power; at the same time, the rapidly shrinking resource base undermined the sustainability of both the National Guard and the *Mkhedrioni* – and set the scene for a potential clash between them. The first problem was partly resolved by inviting Eduard Shevardnadze to chair the newly created State Council. The second problem had no solution, but at least the clash was avoided by carefully dividing the spheres of control, so that the *Mkhedrioni* got a monopoly over the distribution of fuel, while the National Guard sought to profit from arms trading. Neither organisation managed to find stable sources of income, but both remained loyal to their leaders (see Fuller 1993).

Initially Shevardnadze was squeezed between these two warlords (Kitovani and Ioseliani) and focused his mid-term game on the parliamentary elections scheduled for October 1992. Meanwhile, he tried to connect both paramilitary forces to the state, presenting the National Guard as the 'official army' (and making Kitovani the Defence Minister) and the *Mkhedrioni* as the interior forces (making Temur Khachishvili, one of Ioseliani's lieutenants, the Interior Minister). The task of keeping western Georgia under control was assigned to the *Mkhedrioni*, which duly looted and burned several villages there. But it was the National Guard that in mid-August rolled its newly acquired tanks into Abkhazia, seeking to profit from a new war. Despite this emergency, Shevardnadze pushed forward with the elections, which produced a very divided parliament but, most importantly for him, a strong personal mandate for leadership.

The war in Abkhazia turned out to be much more protracted and much less profitable than Kitovani budgeted for, and this gave Shevardnadze a chance to replace him as the Defence Minister with the young and dynamic Giorgi Karkarashvili. The devastating defeat in Abkhazia in September 1993 led to a pro-Gamsakhurdia uprising in western Georgia, which neither the demoralised National Guard nor the disorganised *Mkhedrioni* was able to check. Shevardnadze was forced to appeal to Russia for help, and several Russian battalions took effective control over western Georgia in a matter of a week.[9] This, essentially, was the end of the civil wars in Georgia; Gamsakhurdia died in late December 1993, and several minor uprisings in Mingrelia (for instance, the one led by Akaki Eliava in 1999) were of no great threat.

However, Shevardnadze still had a long way to go in consolidating his power. It was the sustained erosion of the resource base for the paramilitary organisations that helped him most, together with the removal of the immediate threat of a new escalation of wars. From late 1993, relying mostly on aid from Russia, Shevardnadze started to build security forces, answerable to new State Security Minister Igor Giorgadze, and soon was able to take assertive steps. In February 1994, the weakened *Mkhedrioni* was formally transformed into a Rescue Corps; in May 1995 this organisation was ordered to surrender its arms; and after the August 1995 assassination attempt on Shevardnadze it was disbanded and its leadership arrested. Even before that, in January–February 1995, Kitovani was provoked into attempting a new march on Abkhazia; this attempt was then presented as mutiny and duly suppressed by security forces. In autumn 1995, Shevardnadze also managed to get rid of Giorgadze, which left him the sole master of Georgia's 'power structures', feeble as they were (see Aves 1996; Fuller

1997). Even with military aid from the United States and Turkey, Georgia could not build combat-capable armed forces; its army of about 8,500 (including the National Guard of 1,600) had some 5,500 conscripts and was more a source of risk then a security provider.

The struggle for power in Georgia involved various participants and had several sharp escalations, which marked a civil war period of about three years (autumn 1991–autumn 1993). The total number of casualties is estimated at up to 2,000 (mostly in western Georgia). Perhaps the most remarkable feature of that war was the swift destruction of its resource base, so that the cost-efficiency of hostilities diminished and the sustainability of paramilitary organisations declined. In the final tragi-comic act of the war, a rebel force of about 1,000 threatened to conquer the country – but was miraculously dispersed by an external intervention. The post-war reconstruction of the devastated state has proceeded without a clear sense of direction and with much uncertainty. The 'shadow' economy continues to concentrate and redistribute the bulk of the resources. While Shevardnadze has very carefully constructed a situation where there is no political 'alternative' to his leadership,[10] resting on a system of corrupt and semi-criminal networks, he has in fact become the central part of the problem – but not of a solution.

The war in South-Ossetia

The conflict in South-Ossetia escalated into violence earlier than most other conflicts in the Caucasus; this was unexpected because in relations between Tbilisi and Tskhinval there had never been such tensions as there had been, for instance, in the Abkhazian case. The core of the problem was that the rise of the democratic movement in Georgia was directly linked to the struggle for restoring independence and this fuelled the nationalistic trends – and many Ossetians saw these as worrisome and even threatening.

The largely symbolic decision of the Georgian Parliament in August 1989 to strengthen the status of the Georgian language triggered the public campaign in South-Ossetia for upgrading their status from that of autonomous *oblast* to autonomous republic. It was a newly created organisation, the *Adamon Nykhas* (People's Assembly), that championed this cause, but the decision of the South-Ossetian Parliament on 10 November 1989 sparkled a sharp public protest in Tbilisi (although at that moment no secessionist claims were advanced). Gamsakhurdia's march on Tskhinval, blocked by Soviet Interior troops, led to the mobilisation of Ossetians around the *Adamon Nykhas* and helped this organisation to build an armed grouping (by seizing light weapons from the helicopter regiment based in Tskhinval). But it also allowed for the build-up of a Georgian paramilitary organisation known as the Merab Kostava Society which took control of several Georgian villages in South-Ossetia.[11]

The local resource base for the conflict was very shallow, as South-Ossetia had always been one of the poorest regions in Georgia with no 'lootable' natural resources. The escalation/de-escalation of the war was at every stage driven by the political struggle in Tbilisi. Since regional parties were banned from the parliamentary elections in Georgia in October 1990, South-Ossetia boycotted those and in early December 1990 held its own elections. Following these, the new Georgian parliament decided to abolish South-Ossetian autonomy altogether. This prompted Moscow to declare a state of emergency in South-Ossetia, which had very little effect on the situation. The Gamsakhurdia government enforced an economic blockade of South-Ossetia, cutting off the electricity and gas supplies, and in early January 1991 it made several attempts to take control over Tskhinval with militia forces, which were repelled in fierce street fighting.

South-Ossetia's defiance was sustained less by interference from the Soviet centre (in fact, Moscow remained mostly neglectful) than by support from North-Ossetia (a part of the Russian Federation). Some 320,000 Ossetians lived there (of the total population of 630,000), compared with just 60,000 in South-Ossetia, so the arrival of a few hundred armed volunteers made a big difference at the key point of the conflict in Tskhinval. It should also be noted that even during the lull in the hostilities in the first half of 1990, the nationalistic pressure on the Ossetians living in Georgia created some 20,000 refugees who mostly moved to North-Ossetia.

Conclusions about the eruption of war in South-Ossetia point directly to the strategy of the Georgian opposition, which aimed at winning power by mobilising society around the independence programme, which contained a design for a unitary centralised state. This programme inevitably involved the separation of South- and North-Ossetia by a state border, so the first forceful steps in its implementation provoked violent clashes – used by both sides for mobilisation. It is impossible to identify any significant economic causes for the war, since South-Ossetia with its backward economy was by no means a prize, and the mobilisation took place on a very shallow resource base. Nevertheless, by the end of 1990 both sides managed to build up and deploy paramilitary forces of 4,000–5,000 troops (most of them part-time combatants).

The war in South-Ossetia remained remarkably static, if brutal, throughout its course and had several peaks of intense fighting. After the eruption of hostilities in January 1991, the economic blockade was maintained throughout the winter, with only sporadic clashes and the looting of a few villages. In early March, Gamsakhurdia outlined his programme for resolving the crisis through restoring 'rightful authorities' in Tskhinval and reducing South-Ossetia's status to that of 'cultural autonomy'. After this, South-Ossetia voted strongly in favour of the preservation of the USSR in Gorbachev's referendum of 17 March 1991 and refused to participate in Gamsakhurdia's referendum on restoring Georgia's independence of 31 March 1991. Two days before the vote, Gamsakhurdia – obviously seeking to bolster public support for full independence – sharply escalated the propaganda war and ordered the newly formed National Guard to move into South-Ossetia. After a couple of weeks of more intensive clashes, the National Guard retreated from the area, leaving the local paramilitaries of the Merab Kostava Society to keep the war going.

For the rest of the spring and the whole summer of 1991 the level of hostilities remained relatively low, but it is during this period that most of the 80,000–85,000 Ossetian refugees arrived in North-Ossetia from Georgia. The next escalation started in September, when Gamsakhurdia – facing increasingly determined opposition after his blunder during the August *coup* in Moscow – again ordered the National Guard to move into South-Ossetia. His plan was probably aimed at strengthening his hand by scoring an impressive victory, but the National Guard saw very little incentive in engaging itself in protracted irregular warfare in the province which had no 'lootable' resources. A few detachments loyal to Gamsakhurdia did indeed attempt several attacks, but these were repelled by better-organised Ossetian forces.

The coup in Tbilisi created an opportunity to de-escalate and then resolve the conflict; the referendum on independence and 'reunification' with Russia held in South-Ossetia on 19 January 1992 was hardly a major obstacle to this. Indeed, Shevardnadze initiated a series of talks, seeking to put the blame for the war squarely on Gamsakhurdia. Much more unexpected was the massive attack on Tskhinval in early June. At first, the Georgian government tried to present the new escalation as the initiative of the local paramilitaries, but then had to admit that it was the National Guard that had burned down and destroyed by artillery fire up to 80 per cent of the city's housing. The aim of this 'last push' was to achieve not so much a decisive victory but rather a position of strength in the final round of negotiations that were held in Sochi on 24 June 1992 and concluded an agreement signed by Shevardnadze, Yeltsin and the representatives from South- and North-Ossetia. This agreement established a ceasefire that was to be monitored by a joint peacekeeping force for which Russia contributed a battalion of 700 lightly armed troops (see the relevant chapters in Baev 1994, 1996).

This agreement marked the end of the war, but the political conflict, nevertheless, remains unresolved and South-Ossetia continues to exist as a quasi-independent unrecognised entity outside any control from Tbilisi. It is essential to emphasise that it was not the intervention from Russia that terminated the hostilities, Russian peacekeepers constituted merely a symbolic and isolated force that was not even able to rely on any direct support. Throughout the war, the 34th Army Corps of Soviet/Russian Armed Forces based in Georgia remained 'neutral' and did not perform a single operation either towards South-Ossetia or in the struggle for power in Georgia.

The war in South-Ossetia lasted for about eighteen months and resulted in

700–1,000 casualties, of which perhaps two-thirds were on the Ossetian side. The Georgian authorities were never able to raise forces capable of capturing a substantial territory with a hostile population or at least to launch an assault and keep control over the capital. It is even unclear whether there ever was such an intention, since the war in South-Ossetia was on every escalation point linked to a certain agenda in the internal struggle for power in Georgia. The hostilities produced up to 100,000 refugees, only a few thousand of which (mostly Ossetians) have been able to return to their homes. The war from the very start had a very shallow resource base and by June 1992 had exhausted it completely. While resisting an attack is always a more cost-efficient form of warfare, the better organisation of the fighting force (while no larger than 5,000 fighters) on the South-Ossetian side was to a large degree the result of direct material support from North-Ossetia.

The war in Abkhazia

Tensions in Abkhazia had been evident long before the eruption of hostilities and in fact the April 1989 demonstrations in Tbilisi that were the starting point of all troubles were held in part in protest against Abkhazian 'secessionism'. The strongest warning about the forthcoming conflict was the violent clash in Sukhumi in July 1989, provoked by the attempt to divide the University into two parts, one of which was to become a branch of the Tbilisi University. While both sides have strikingly different narratives of the immediate causes of the conflict, and indeed its historical roots,[12] it is obvious that the source of the tensions was control over lucrative agricultural and tourism-oriented businesses (the University itself was a money making machine). Local clans with heavy connections with the blossoming 'shadow' economy were eager to grasp more direct executive power, but Tbilisi was equally eager to preserve its control; the previous decadal round of *nomenklatura* elite rotation had taken place (with serious tensions) in 1979–80, so it was quite predictable that 1989–90 would bring new trouble.

Abkhazia managed to stay away from the escalation of war in South-Ossetia and from the internal struggle in Georgia (effectively abstaining from participation in the March 1991 referendum on independence), but the collapse of the USSR made it imperative to define their position towards the independent Georgian state. The risks at that moment were higher than before because two wars had already erupted and clearly destroyed the peaceful heritage of previous decades. The situation was further complicated by the support that the evicted Gamsakhurdia was gathering in western Georgia. Kitovani's National Guard moved into Abkhazia and entered Sukhumi, seeking to deter an escalation of the rebellion. This prompted the newly elected Abkhazian Parliament to approve the decision to create its own National Guard; before then there had been hardly any effort to build up a paramilitary force, the activities of the *Aidgilara* (People's Forum) had been centred on the Parliament. While some financial resources were available locally, more came from well-connected diaspora and some sources in Moscow. The key problem was that there were not enough Abkhazians with even elementary military training; support, therefore, was sought from the recently created Confederation of Caucasian Mountain Peoples (this loose organisation held its congress in Sukhumi in November 1991).

After a short lull in tensions, the Abkhazian National Guard in mid-June 1992 made its first move and occupied the Interior Ministry in Sukhumi, which had been under Georgian control. On 23 July 1992, the Abkhazian Parliament (the Georgian members boycotting the work) restored the republican Constitution of 1925 and effectively proclaimed Abkhazia an independent state. That demonstrative move might have passed without serious repercussions, but hostilities in western Georgia again escalated and several Georgian officials were kidnapped. On 14 August 1992, some 5,000 soldiers of the Georgian National Guard moved into Abkhazia and entered Sukhumi; another 1,000 guards landed in Gagra, blocking Abkhazia's border with Russia. The Abkhazian Parliament retreated north towards Gudauta and mobilised against Georgia's 'invasion'; its armed forces (perhaps, only about 1,000 strong) took up defensive positions along the River Gumista, with the Russian airbase to their immediate rear.

It was – and still is – unclear to what degree Shevardnadze was in charge of the situation in Tbilisi in summer 1992 and whether Kitovani acted largely on his own initiative. What is clear is that the National Guard in July 1992 received a large amount of heavy armaments, including some fifty tanks, from the former Soviet bases which Russia had taken under its control. With this new strength, the National Guard was ready to claim new loot – and Abkhazia was the most promising prize.

It is possible to conclude that the war in Abkhazia erupted as a result of deliberate escalation of political tensions by both sides, and the instability in western Georgia served mostly as a catalyst. While there were some legal grounds for making the case for independence and while both sides applied ethnic mobilisation techniques, the main cause of the war was gaining control over the highly profitable 'shadow' economy. It is in this war that the miscalculation by the rivals is particularly obvious: as the violence escalated, the tourist industry was destroyed beyond repair, and as transport communications were interrupted, agriculture lost its markets. Abkhazia was ruined for the next ten years.

In a matter of a few weeks after the *Blitzkrieg* of 14–15 September 1992, the war turned out to be a much less profitable and more resource-consuming proposition than the National Guard had budgeted for. The looting of Sukhumi had to be restricted since the Georgian authorities wanted to keep a semblance of order in the capital city; the supply base in the Gali region was enough for feeding the troops but did not produce many volunteers or paramilitaries, since the political sympathies there were mostly on Gamsakhurdia's side. The troops that had landed in Gagra found themselves surrounded and Kitovani was not able to organise their supplies using only marine lines of communications. By the end of September, up to 1,000 volunteers arrived from the North Caucasus via mountain passes to support the Abkhazian government, so on 2–3 October 1992 a surprise attack was launched towards Gagra and the isolated Georgian grouping was completely defeated. After restoring control over the main lines of communications with Russia, the Abkhazian government managed to stabilise the situation and started to build up its forces.

The key factors determining the outcome of the war were to be found outside Abkhazia, and the most controversial of these was the position of Russia.[13] The Russian government consistently tried to mediate the cessation of hostilities on the basis of a compromise, although it was not so much concerned about the fate of Abkhazia as Russia was about its control over the North Caucasus. One part of the Russian military, particularly the Command of the Trans-Caucasus Military District, supported Georgia and supplied it with heavy weapons and ammunition. Another part of the Russian military, first of all the forces based in Abkhazia around the airbase in Gudauta, directly supported the Abkhazian side, perhaps with the implicit consent of the Defence Ministry (see Baev 1997). The main source of military support to Abkhazia was the republics of the North Caucasus, where volunteers were openly recruited and financed through the Confederation of Caucasian Peoples. Chechnya, which since autumn 1991 existed outside any control from Moscow, was the most active party, and the Chechens were fighting in Abkhazia side-by-side with the Cossacks and even volunteers from Trans-Dniestria. The sources of financial support to this motley force were highly diverse: from the Abkhazian diaspora in Turkey to Russian ultra-nationalists in Moscow.

It was barely possible to sustain this support for more than a year, so the Abkhazian side from June 1993 started to increase its military activities, undertaking a strong offensive in mid-July and launching the decisive attack on Sukhumi in mid- September. While Russia was the guarantor of the ceasefire agreement of 27 July 1993, attention in Moscow was entirely consumed by the sharp internal crises (culminating in the forceful suppression of the violent revolt in Moscow on 2–3 October 1993). Despite the desperate efforts of Shevardnadze, Sukhumi fell on 27 September 1993 and by the end of the month Abkhazian forces had driven the demoralised National Guard south of the River Inguri, establishing control over the whole territory of Abkhazia and forcing some 200,000 Georgians to flee. That was the end of the war, but the negotiations on the resolution of the conflict remain deadlocked, and this has led to the occasional resumption of hostilities, most seriously in May 1997 and October 2001.

The war in Abkhazia lasted just thirteen-and-a-half months but was the fiercest of the Georgian wars. Up to 20,000 fighters took part in the clashes from both sides and the total number of casualties could be as high as 20,000 (the lowest estimate is 6,000). While Abkhazia was the richest province of Georgia in the 1980s, by 1992 its economy had been weakened (there still were tourists on the beaches when tanks rolled into Sukhumi) and there was no local basis for sustaining the hostilities on such a scale. The external sources of support that Abkhazia was able to mobilise were only short-term which necessitated efforts to achieve a decisive victory. The deployment of Russian peacekeepers in July 1994 (about 3,000 troops) under the CIS mandate and UN monitoring (by the 100-strong UN Observer Mission in Georgia – UNOMIG) has not helped in setting an effective framework for the peace process. The clan of Abkhazian President Ardzinba has established very efficient control over what little is left of the economy and expects to benefit from ties with the newly dynamic Russia (see Baev 2001).

Conclusions

Georgia's wars had remarkable similarities in their duration and timing: one secessionist war started right after another one had ended, while the violent struggle for power escalated in the middle of the first war and subsided right after the end of the second. All three wars were ended after a military victory of one side and both secessionist conflicts are frozen in internationally illegitimate stalemates, while the negotiations are deadlocked. It appears reasonable to assume that these similarities are caused by the presence of the same factors in the politico-economic structure of each war. This analysis argues that the main cause of the wars was the struggle between competing elite groupings for control over lucrative and profitable resources. The short duration of the wars is then explained by rapid depletion of the resource base, since the very possibility of extracting rent was destroyed by the escalation of violence. The deadlocks in resolving the frozen conflicts result from the inability of the central authorities to mobilise sufficient resources for building up the necessary military organisation.

It could be argued that these deadlocks are also the result of the consistent implementation of state building projects in quasi-independent Abkhazia and South-Ossetia;[14] the latter has even acquired a semblance of an electoral democracy, while the former makes an example of a centralised corporate entity which is based exclusively on the 'shadow' economy but maintains sufficient integrity.[15] The success of these state projects should be measured not in absolute terms, but in comparison with the stagnant rump of Georgia; Abkhazia and South-Ossetia have perhaps even fewer resources at their disposal (including foreign aid), but their population is only approximately a half of the pre-war levels. Combining the informal taxation of various semi-legal businesses with permanent mobilisation plans, the authorities in Tskhinval and Sukhumi are able to cover the basic needs of their societies and sustain sufficient military capabilities.[16] For that matter, the recurrent violent clashes in Abkhazia, like the ones in the Kodori Valley in October 2001, help the Abkhazian authorities to maintain the mobilisation preparedness, while they resonate quite painfully in Tbilisi.[17]

The central issue in both the political economy of Georgian wars and the post-war reconstruction is corruption, which penetrates into all spheres of social organisation and corrodes all state structures to a degree of complete functional stupor. There are certainly many forms of corruption and many links between it and the 'shadow' economy, which is also a complex phenomenon, which includes both the informal survival-oriented networks and the criminalised underworld. What is typical for Georgia is proliferation of micro-size businesses that redistribute the small extra product of the subsistence economy and are taxed informally by local administrative structures which then redistribute the profits upwards. On top of that there is some smuggling and narco-trafficking, but not of Central Asian proportions.[18]

Georgia is unlikely to find much comfort in the fact that it does not make it into the Transparency International Corruption Index;[19] according to various measurements of corruption undertaken by the World Bank, Georgia is one of the leaders in the category of administrative corruption.[20] Shevardnadze's numerous promises to combat this evil and the setting up of various high-profile commissions have brought negligible results; the commissions are typically disbanded the moment they approach the activities of the commissioner's own family clan.

It may seem that since 1995 the internal situation in Georgia has significantly stabilised, but in fact the country is trapped in a vicious circle of low legitimacy and fundamental inefficiency, where corruption is the main curse. The semblance of stability is entirely a function of Shevardnadze's ability to manoeuvre among weak opponents and the opposition's inability to mobilise any resources owing to their general scarcity. The long overdue departure of the 'father of the nation', necessary as it is, may prove to be a major source of instability, not so much in terms of restarting the wars in Abkhazia and South-Ossetia, as in terms of general state failure, which might include disintegration and new secessions of, for instance, Adjaria and Akhalkalaki.[21] In the context of the new global situation, driven by the US-led anti-terrorist campaigns, Georgia cannot expect much international attention to its problems, dire as they may become. It will not even be able to resort to the habitual cure of blaming Russia, because this uneasy neighbour may turn out to be its only hope.

NOTES

1 For a provocative comparative analysis of the disintegration of the USSR and Yugoslavia, with more attention to the latter, see Lukic and Lynch (1996); for a competent and insightful analysis of the role of ethnic factors in the Soviet collapse see Tishkov (1997); for a useful analytical framework for analysing post-Soviet conflicts, see Arbatov (1997).
2 Martha Brill Olcott, making a list of counterproductive assumptions about the Caucasus,

includes there the view that all problems are caused by the behaviour of the regional hegemon – Russia – and can be solved only by Russia as well (Olcott 2001).

3   This chapter builds on the author's research on Georgia's civil wars for the project on 'The Economic of Political and Common Violence' conducted by the Development Economic Research Group (DERG) of the World Bank. While the author cannot fully subscribe to the set of hypothesis advanced by Paul Collier and Anke Hoeffler (see, for instance, Collier and Hoeffler 2001), their basic approach to civil wars as economic enterprises is certainly helpful and productive.

4   The debates and disclosures at the conference on CIA analysis of the USSR in 1947–91 provide a good illustration of this point: the CIA experts were more successful in estimating the scale of Soviet military efforts than in measuring the size of the USSR economy, either in absolute or in comparative terms. The collection of documents can be found at www.foia.ucia.gov/historicalreport.htm.

5   It could be said that owing to the accelerated rotation the Georgian elites were just one step ahead of the rest of the Soviet nomenclatura in rejecting 'the two fundamental taboos – engaging in nationalism and private accumulation'. See Derluguian (2000: 215).

6   For excellent accounts of the social and political consequences of the growth of the shadow economy in Georgia, see Fuller (1987a, 1987b).

7   Most of this economic data comes from the *Eastern Europe and the CIS* 1994, 1997, 1999 and the World Bank estimates, available at www.worldbank.org/data/countrydata/. See also Stone and Weeks (1998).

8   In spring 2001 the IMF and the World Bank jointly prepared a report on external debt and fiscal sustainability in Armenia, Georgia, the Kyrgyz Republic, Moldova and Tajikistan, which can be found at http://eb18.worldbank.org/ECA.

9   Vladimir Baranovsky (1995: 195), noting that the campaign in western Georgia 'was closer to farce than to large-scale tragedy', explains that 'Shevardnadze's opponents were contesting control of a system which had almost completely fallen apart and was in a state of virtual paralysis'.

10   For some current reflections on that see Baran (2002).

11   This war has generally received much less attention in Western academic studies then most other conflicts in the former USSR. For useful presentations, see Herzig (1999: 73–76) and MacFarlane, Minear and Shenfield (1996).

12   For a multi-perspective presentation of the conflict, see Cohen (1999); for an attempt to focus academic research on the search for solutions, see Coppieters, Darchiashvili and Akaba (2000).

13   For early reflections, see Dale (1993); for a more balanced view, see Herzig (1999: 102–108); for a more economy-oriented perspective, see Avakov and Lisov (2000).

14   For a sharp and solid argument on the stability of these quasi-states, which in fact suits the interests of all parties to the conflict, see King (2001).

15   On the 'shadow' economy as the source of tensions in the Gali region, see Billingsey (2001).

16   For a telling picture gallery of present-day life in South-Ossetia, see Novikov (2001).

17   A competent assessment of Abkhazia's military capabilities can be found in Mukhin (2001); see also an interview with Abkhazian General Dbar in *VestiRu* (2001).

18   On the scale of the problem of production and transportation of narcotics in Central Asia, see Olcott and Udalova-Zvart (2000).

19   This Index is estimated on the basis of perceptions, so Georgia, presumably, would hardly rank there much higher than Azerbaijan who currently shares the 84th to 87th places (out of 91) with Bolivia, Cameroon and Kenya. See Transparency International (2001).

20   This category estimates the amount of revenues that businesses had to pay in bribes and

other unofficial payments. Georgia scores 4.3, as compared with 5.7 in Azerbaijan and 2.8 in Russia. See Hellman, Jones and Kaufmann (2000).

21 On the peculiar situation in the latter region, where a Russian military base has become the functional centre, see Lieven (2001).

REFERENCES

Arbatov, A. (1979), 'A framework for assessing post-soviet conflicts', in A. Arbatov, A. Chayes, A. H. Chayes and L. Olson (eds), *Managing Conflicts in the Former Soviet Union* (Cambridge, MA), 19–24.

Avakov, R. M. and A. G. Lisov (eds) (2000), *Rossiya i Zakavkazye: Realii Nezavisimosti i Novoe Partnerstvo* (Moscow).

Aves, J. (1996), *Georgia: From Chaos to Stability?* (London).

Aves, J. (1997), 'Georgia' in *Eastern Europe and the CIS*, 3rd edn (London).

Baev, P. (1994), 'Russia's experiments and experience in conflict management and Peacekeeping', *International Peacekeeping*, 1:3, 245–260.

Baev, P. (1996), *The Russian Army in a Time of Troubles* (London).

Baev, P. (1997), *Russia's Policies in the Caucasus* (London).

Baev, P. (2001), *Russia Refocuses Its Policies in the Southern Caucasus*, Caspian Studies Program Working Paper, No. 1, Harvard University (July).

Baran, Z. (2002), 'The Caucasus: ten years after independence', *The Washington Quarterly*, 25:1, 221–234.

Baranovsky, V. (1995), 'Conflict developments on the territory of the Former Soviet Union', *SIPRI Yearbook 1994* (Oxford), 169–203.

Billingsey, D. (2001), 'Security deteriorates along the Abkhazia–Georgia ceasefire line', *Jane's Intelligence Review* (September), 18–20.

Broladze, N. (2001), 'Gruzinskie Voennye Dovedeny do Otchayaniya' (Georgian Military Are Brought to Despair), *Nezavisimaya gazeta* (29 May), www.ng.ru/2001-05-29/ (24.01.2002).

Cohen, J. (ed.) (1999), *A Question of Sovereignty: The Georgia–Abkhazia Peace Process*, *Accord*, No. 7 (London).

Collier, P. and A. Hoeffler (2001), 'Greed and grievance in the Civil War', *DRG Research Paper*, www.worldbank.org/research/conflict.

Coppieters, B., D. Darchiashvili and N. Akaba (eds) (2000), *Federal Practice: Exploring Alternatives for Georgia and Abkhazia*. (Brussels).

Corley, F. (1999), 'Georgia' in *Eastern Europe and the CIS*, 4th edn (London).

Dale, C. (1993), 'Turmoil in Abkhazia: Russian responses', *RFE/RL Research Report*, 2:34 (27 August), 48–57.

Derluguian, G. M. (2000), 'The process and the prospects of soviet collapse: bancruptcy, segmentation, involution', in G. M. Derluguian and S. L. Greer,*Questioning Geopolitics* (Westport, CT and London), 203–225.

Fuller, E. (1987a), 'Georgia in 1986', *RFE/RL Research Note*, 12 (7 January), 1–5.

Fuller, E. (1987b), 'Georgia two years after Shevardnadze: the economy', *RFE/RL Brief*, 318 (28 July), 1–4.

Fuller, E. (1993), 'Paramilitary forces dominate fighting in Transcaucasus', *RFE/RL Research Report*, 2:25 (Special Issue), 74–82.

Fuller, E. (1997), 'Georgia stabilizes', *Transition: Year in Review, 1996*, 3:2 (7 February), 82–83.

Hellman, J. S., G. Jones and D. Kaufmann (2000), *Seize the State, Seize the Day*, Policy Research Working Paper, 2444, The World Bank Institute, www.worldbank. org>/wbi/governance.

Herzig, E. (1999), *The New Caucasus: Armenia, Azerbaijan and Georgia* (London).

King, C. (2001), 'The benefits of ethnic wars: understanding Eurasia's unrecognized states', *World Politics*, 53 (July), 524–552.

Lieven, A. (2001), 'Imperial outpost, social provider', *Transition OnLine* (22 March), www.tol.cz.

Lukic, R. and A. Lynch (1996), *Europe from the Balkans to the Urals: The Disintegration of Yugoslavia and the Soviet Union* (Oxford).

MacFarlane, N., L. Minear and S. D. Shenfield (1996), *Armed Conflict in Georgia: A Case Study in Humanitarian Action and Peacekeeping* (Providence, RI).

Mukhin, V. (2001), 'Sukhumi Gotov ko Vsemu' (Sukhumi is ready for everything), *Nezavisimoe voennoe obozrenie* (19 October), www.nvo.ng.ru.

Nodia, G. (1996), 'Political turmoil in Georgia', in B. Coppieters (ed.), *Contested Borders in the Caucasus* (Brussels).

Novikov, S. (2001), 'Zhizn s Nadezhdoi na Rossiyu' (Life with hope for Russia), *Nezavisimaya gazeta* (30 May).

Olcott, M. B. (2001), 'Challenges which lie ahead', in *Promoting Institutional Responses to the Challenges in the Caucasus*, Favorita Papers 1/2001 (Vienna), 41–46.

Olcott, M. B. and N. Udalova-Zvart (2000), *Drug Trafficking on the Great Silk Road*. Working Paper, No. 2 (Moscow).

Ozhiganov, E. (1997), 'The Republic of Georgia', in A. Arbatov A. Chayes, A. H. Chayes and L. Olson (eds), *Managing Conflicts in the Former Soviet Union* (Cambridge, MA).

Stone, S. and O. Weeks, 'Prospects for the Georgian economy', *CACP Briefing*, No. 15 (London, March).

Tishkov, V. (1997), *Ethnicity, Nationalism and Conflict in and after the Soviet Union: The Mind Aflame* (London).

Transparency International (2001), *Global Corruption Report*, www.transparency.org.

VestiRu (2001), 'Nam Prigodilis By Patrony' (We could use some more ammunition), interview with General Sergei Dbar (8 November), www.vesti.ru.

Zverev, A. (1996), 'Ethnic conflicts in the Caucasus', in B. Coppieters (ed.), *Contested Borders in the Caucasus* (Brussels), 13–72.

8

The art of losing the state: weak empire to weak nation-state around Nagorno-Karabakh

Jan Koehler and Christoph Zürcher

The conflict around Nagorno-Karabakh offers an insight into the rules and processes that governed the transformation of a weak empire into even weaker nation-states. More than other conflicts escalating into collective violence during the demise of the USSR, Nagorno-Karabakh had connotations of civil and interstate war, heavily involved official central and local Soviet institutions and led to the creation of new local institutions. The Nagorno-Karabakh conflict was midwife to the different ways three post-Soviet entities organised their (recognised or unrecognised) statehood.

This chapter deals with the interdependence of institutional weakness of states and the organisation of conflict. Institutional weakness of statehood is at the same time both cause and consequence of violent conflict. On the one hand the escalation of conflict into violence is connected with the local exploitation of organisational voids in the official Soviet institutions. On the other hand, re-institutionalising non-violent conflict after war and forced exchange of population has proven to be a formidable challenge to weak post-Soviet statehood.

What is it all about?

Usually, when writing about a conflict, the first thing to do would be to introduce the object of and parties to the conflict and to offer a bracket around time and place. In the case of the Nagorno-Karabakh conflict these parameters themselves are strongly disputed. According to the position of the Azerbaijani government, part of its territory is occupied by the neighbouring state of Armenia and the conflict is therefore a problem between two sovereign states. To official Armenia and, for that matter, also to the unrecognised Nagorno-Karabakh government, it is a struggle for independence and self-determination by the Armenian population of Nagorno-Karabakh against Azerbaijan.

A rather anecdotal result of these differences in the interpretation of what the conflict is about and who is party to it is the fact that diplomats concerned with the conflict bear official titles too long to fit on any business card. There is, for example, a 'Personal Representative of the Chairperson in Office of the OSCE on the conflict dealt with by the Minsk Conference'.

These neatly clear-cut and opposing perceptions of the Nagorno-Karabakh conflict soften and blur in a diachronic perspective that not only relates to the positions formulated in the international arena. In the beginning the ultimate normative frame of reference was 'Moscow' rather than international law and the conflict was played according to the Soviet rules of the game. The key administrative initiatives at the beginning of 1988 focused on either keeping the *status quo* (i.e. Nagorno-Karabakh autonomous *oblast* (AO) remaining a subordinated administrative region inside the Azerbaijani Soviet Socialist Republic (SSR)) or changing its association (i.e. transferring Nagorno-Karabakh AO as subordinate administrative region into the Armenian SSR). The Soviet institutions involved initially respected the hierarchy of competence; the first official requests for a transfer in February 1988 were addressed by the local Nagorno-Karabakh AO Soviet to the Supreme Soviets of the Republics and further to the Supreme Soviet of the USSR. At this early stage nobody of consequence raised the question of upgrading the status of Nagorno-Karabakh AO instead of transferring it from one Union Republic to the other.

However, the proximate objectives of the parties directly involved changed over time:

- The evolving Armenian leadership of Nagorno-Karabakh initially moved away from demanding the transfer of the territory to Armenia to a (temporary) transfer to the RSFSR or, alternatively, to direct administration from Moscow. The demand for, from the Armenian point of view, a re-unification with Armenia was later changed to the current official viewpoint of independent statehood.

- The positions of the Armenian Karabakh Committee and later leadership of independent Armenia also changed over time and was only slightly different from the Karabakh positions: from transfer of the AO to unification with Armenia after independence and finally to the *de facto* independence of Nagorno-Karabakh. For some time the question of official acknowledgment of the Nagorno-Karabakh Republic as an independent state by Armenia remained a sticking point between factions in the first government of Armenia.

- The position of the Azerbaijani authorities changed from maintaining the *status quo* to favouring direct rule by Baku and the annulment of autonomy altogether, to the current official position of offering Nagorno-Karabakh maximum autonomy within Azerbaijan.

The question of a starting point in space and time for the conflict became as disputed as the question of what the conflict is over and who is fighting.

According to the official Azerbaijani perception, Armenian inhabitants of Nagorno-Karabakh AO started the conflict in February 1988 by unilaterally demanding the transfer of the *oblast* to the Armenian SSR. Armenians, on the other hand, consider the escalation of violence against their ethnic compatriots in the industrial town of Sumgait some 30 km north of Baku at the end of February 1988 as the immediate starting point of the conflict.

In the course of seeking ultimate justification for their objectives, the ideologists of the conflicting parties pushed the question of when the conflict was started decisively backwards in time. It has been increasingly linked to the question of 'who was first to settle on the territory of Nagorno-Karabakh'. This question gained importance in relation to the dispute over the legitimacy of borders and administrative status established in the early days of Soviet rule (Goldenberg 1994: 159–160; Jacoby 1998a: 71–76). Whereas the latter issue touches upon the general problem of the legitimacy of borders decided by colonial powers (Swietochowski 1995: 161–168), the first issue has been raised by both sides as a fundamental claim to ethnically defined ownership of land and tended to drift from population statistics around the turn of the last century backwards via pre-Russian, pre-Ottoman and pre-Persian history to pre-history itself.

Volker Jacoby's view on the somewhat absurd dilemma of the intellectual game of 'who was first, wins' cuts through the futile debate (Jacoby 1998b: 238, translated by the author):

> The territorialisation of questions of origin is in any case highly problematic. The line of argumentation of 'we were here before you' does not decide the question of origin; the latter depends on the time frame applied in order to assess autochthony or allochthony. Is the frame of reference 100 years, 200 years, 4,000 years or 1.5 million years? In the end even zoological evidence needs to be consulted to prove a point.

Violent conflict in word and in deed

Generally speaking, the search for rules governing social processes is complicated by two factors when dealing with society in violent conflict: (1) the widening divide between the rationale of action and the normative narratives assigning sense to deed *ex post* and (2) the increasing relevance of informal institutions, often hidden in the coat-tails of their official hosts and dressed in fancy gowns sewn by the ideologists of conflict.

The bulk of journalistic and, in part, also scholarly writing on the present Nagorno-Karabakh conflict concentrates either on the emic conceptualisations of the causes of conflict or on geopolitics and outside interference in the conflict.[1] While most observers come to the conclusion that the mutually exclusive dogmatic positions of the parties to the conflict cannot be taken at face value they tend to assume that the core problem of the conflict lies in these mutually exclusive normative narratives of 'us' and 'them', of historical injustice and grievance.

147

The impact that the way people make sense of themselves and the other has on conflict and in particular the sense made of violence endured and inflicted, is not denied here. However, making sense of a social process (like violent conflict) and the social process itself are not the same thing and require different approaches for analysis (see Laitin and Suny 1999).

Concerning external interference, while outside interests certainly do play a role in the politics of the Nagorno-Karabakh conflict today,[2] outside influence has sometimes been grossly overestimated for the phase of hot conflict itself (for the very limited impact of various external mediation efforts, see Mooradian and Druckman 1999). This is also true for Russia, which became an external rather than internal force at the end of 1991, although it did play a role in terms of supplying weapons and training at different stages to all parts of the conflict. Before the dissolution of the USSR outside interference was either difficult to define (in the case of interference from the centre) or was irrelevant (as in the case of diaspora support for Armenians).

Unless an outside power directly intervenes it has to play to a large extent by the local rules of the game, making use of lobbies and interest groups existing on the ground. Focusing only on the normative transcript of a violent conflict blurs the crucial analytical line between socially controlled conflict and conflict beyond the bounds of a society's toolbox of regulation. Collectives capable of formulating distinct interests while sharing limited resources are bound to conflict with each other. But only when conflict breaks the boundaries of its social embedding, when it takes place in a space not penetrated by the rules set by society, is it perceived as disruptive and dangerous (see the classic concept of social conflict elaborated by Coser 1956: 121–128; compare also Hirschman 1994: 297–299). The focus of analytical scrutiny should therefore not concentrate so much on who started the conflict between Armenians and Azeris or whose normative claims appear to be justified but rather on the process of disintegration of the institutions that controlled conflict and negotiated order between the distinct groups.

In practice, under the condition of a functioning statehood, the social self-organisation between different communities is usually less mutually exclusive than the normative narratives of those communities may suggest. Since the ideal order of (imagined) communities is usually transported in the sphere of values and believes these normative tales may easily imply cultural clashes as the core of conflict. In the way Armenians and Azeris conceptualise the Karabakh conflict a notion of mutually exclusive 'culture' or 'civilisation' occupies a prominent place next to versions of historic truth among nationalist intellectuals (on primordial concepts of 'ethno-nations' propagated by (post-) Soviet intellectuals, see Tishkov 1994: 450–451). However, in order to understand the decisions and behaviour of people in conflict it is not sufficient to take into consideration only the normative discourses on identity. Media and especially the entrepreneurs of communitarian identities (be they cultural, national, ethnical or the like) are selling this excluding story of 'us' and 'them'. In situations governed by violence and fear the war-mongers may succeed in officially turning the normative identity into a total identity, not only subordinating, but denying other strategies of orientation for individuals and groups inside the we-group.[3] Here the radical exclusiveness of identity is rather the result of dynamics of violent conflict than its cause. As long as the Soviet state functioned in the sense that it prevented violent strategies of conflict-resolution between social groups, 'culture' as ability to command *various* social languages (from local over Caucasian to Soviet codes) was rather a means to connect, communicate and do business with each other (Koehler 1999: 43–46).

Undeniably, however, late Soviet statehood ceased to function for decisive social forces in and around Nagorno-Karabakh AO and it is this fact, rather than ancient history, cultural superiority or who fired the first shot which should serve as starting point for the analysis of the escalation that followed.

Stages of Nagorno-Karabakh conflict escalation

Usually the Nagorno-Karabakh conflict is divided into two phases defined by change in the level of violence from low-intensity to all-out war and roughly coinciding with the dissolution of the USSR in the second half of 1991. Instead of concentrating on a subjectively perceived degree of violence, the conflict process will be subdivided into stages defined by changing social modes of conflict control and organisation of violence (cf. Waldmann 1999: 70–76). The capacities of the USSR in the periphery and the post-Soviet states to emerge serve as starting point of discussion:

> In October 1987 the regional administration of the Azerbaijani town of Chardakhly in the vicinity of the Armenian border took the decision to transfer some land from one *kolkhoz* (collective farm) to a neighbouring one; the former *kolkhoz* was administered by Armenians, the latter by Azeris. When the Armenian workforce refused to comply, the RAICOM (regional committee of the Communist Party) fired the Armenian director of the *kolkhoz*. This measure led to demonstrations by Armenian farmers and escalated into a violent confrontation with security forces (allegedly units of the KGB) from the Azerbaijani SSR in which at least one official was injured. Thereafter Special Forces surrounded the village in the *kolkhoz* and physical reprisals against some inhabitants reportedly took place (Jacoby 1998b: 169). When the news broke, the first public demonstrations took place in Stepanakert (Nagorno-Karabakh) and Yerevan, demanding the transfer of Nagorno-Karabakh and Nakhichevan to the Armenian SSR. (Fuller 1987)

In a nutshell, here is a model picturing the initial protagonists of the mystery play 'dawn of the Soviet empire', repeated in various interpretations all over the peripheries of the former USSR.

As in the case of the first violent clashes in Abkhazia around the introduction of a branch of Tbilisi University as a competitor to the existing Abkhaz-controlled Sukhumi University (Gelaschwili 1993: 91–92), the initial conflicts were not new nor about ethnic belonging. Instead they were about the control of lucrative segments of the 'shadow' economy by competing networks of trust – or, more bluntly, as Georgia's witty warlord Djaba Ioseliani put it on many occasions, they were about 'the legal entitlement to steal' (here as quoted in Gelaschwili 1993: 91).

Since the 1960s illegal economic activity, intimately linked with official functions in the Soviet state-run society, increasingly began to structure those parts of the social space in which the organisational voids of the official system were most obvious. Thus a sophisticated system of parallel rules emerged in the shadow of the official institutions. This system became known as the 'parallel' economy of the *kombinaty* (industrial complexes), *kolkhozy* and *sovkhozy* (state collective farms), the 'shadow' economy in general, the 'economy of shortages' and the 'administrative market'.[4] By the 1980s, especially in the southern periphery of the empire, these shadows had merged into a parallel social order and had a tendency to 'catch up and overtake' the official order as incentive structures for the relevant participants in the society.[5]

Serious and well-organised illegal business needs to address one crucial deficit: the deficit of trust. Trust is essential in any long-term and far-ranging business operations involving the transfer of commodities and cash flows, in operations based on unspecific reciprocity rather than direct exchange of goods or favours. In the official world this future reliability is usually achieved by contracts between institutions rather than individuals (guaranteed by national or international law and backed by the sanctioning power of functioning states) and reinforced by the threat of sanctions involving reputation (spoiling the prestige of a company in the relevant market segment).

Obviously, in the illegal business activities of *apparatchiki-biznesmeny* (Soviet entrepreneurs) trust could not be generated by written contracts, taking the cheating business partner to a Soviet court or ruining his reputation by complaining to a '*tovarishchskii sud*' (court of comrades) about breaking an informal agreement, were not options.

There were a number of more or less effective ways of generating trust in the shadows of Soviet statehood (cf. Koehler 2000: 75–104); the most important for the development of conflict control in the region of interest were (ethnic) kin and '*zemlyachestvo*'. In the writing of journalists and political scientists these two frames of reference are often merged and called 'clan', a term more concealing than revealing unless clearly defined.[6] '*Zemlyachestvo*' refers to solidarity from a notion of community, of the same local or regional upbringing, usually irrespective of ethnic or religious belonging.[7] Kin, by contrast, was the most important social institution in the Caucasus that remained very sensitive to ethnic and religious belonging. Mixed marriages in the bigger cities did take place; however, they were the exception to the rule and very often accompanied by serious conflicts in the extended families (Anderson and Silver 1996 (1983): 494–96; for the Georgian case, see Koehler 2000: 73, 97).

It would be misleading, however, to assume that from ethnic connotations of kin a principle of solidarity among ethnic groups followed; for the network of trust based on an emic notion of kinship, the point of reference was rather the extended family than an imagined ethnic community. In the case of patrons in the 'shadow' economy (the soviet entrepreneurs we call *apparatchiki-biznes-meny*), their identity was closer to a socio-professional group that relied, as key resource for trust, on interpersonal relations with relatives belonging mostly, but not exclusively, to one ethnic group. These were not ethnic networks of trust but patron–client networks that were frequently dominated by one ethnic group as a by-product of informal constraints on interethnic marriage.[8] These networks cooperated or competed with other networks of the same socio-professional group, as in the above example of the 'Armenian'-administered and 'Azeri'-administered *kolkhozy*. Except in cases where a strict (informal) ethnic division of labour had been implemented for some time (e.g. Azeris as shepherds in Armenia or Kurds as street-cleaners in Tbilisi), contact in this important informal world may have been as rare and as insignificant as it was in public life.

Kinship as one of the key resources for knitting networks of trust to secure economic or social advantages in the Caucasus is by no means a private matter, a pre-modern cultural leftover in opposition to or retreat from the state, as implied by some authors (cf. Theisen 1999). Family business in this sense was (and is) closely integrated into the way both the Soviet and post-Soviet states functioned in the Caucasus. 'Tradition' has been a flexible resource to react to chances and deficits of the official order and proved to be – in a non-normative sense – a creative social and political asset (cf. Platz 1995). Taking into account the interplay between state, kinship and neighbourhood, the 'privatised' Caucasian network-state may appear rather post- than pre-modern.

During *perestroika* the well-established relationship between official Soviet institutions and the 'shadow' economy with its entrenched networks of trust were shaken by two developments. First, the legalisation of some private economic entrepreneurship (the blossoming of cooperatives, usually under the patronage and on the territory of existing Soviet industrial complexes and *kolkhozy*) helped to institutionalise economically interested networks of trust officially. The second was the public development of a nationalist frame of reference to explain success and failure, hardships and difference, first in semi-official, later in official local media outlets. This sense-generating filter was not entirely new – before *perestroika* the normative nationalist discourse had simply rarely left the kitchen and the occasional piece of '*samizdat*'. Going public with nationalist ideology was the domain of those provincial representatives of the intelligentsia, who had been rehearsing this hidden code on their informational island of marginalised dissidence.

What is significant in the above *kolkhoz* incident is that a conflict over which group controls legal (and, probably more relevant, illegal) revenues from two *kolkhozy* was *publicly* taken up as a national discrimination issue in administratively unconnected entities (the centres of the neighbouring autonomous *oblast* and the Union Republic) and was then connected to fundamental questions of revising administrative borders between Soviet republics.

Hidden transcript into public transcript: dissident nationalists leave their informational island

> What actually has been the most striking feature of Armenian politics since independence is a lack of ideology rather than ideological differences. Had the survival of African elephants been a popular issue in Armenia, there can be little doubt that the same individuals who formed the Karabakh Committee would have been members of a ' Save the Elephants Committee" if this would have given them chances of coming to power. (Simonian 2001: 377)

A common feature of late-Soviet mass movements in the peripheries of the empire was that initially most of them appeared in public as pro-*perestroika* environmentalist movements. This holds true for the first rallies that were organised in Armenia, after details of the ecological problems were published, in Yerevan in summer 1987 up until the first mass demonstrations there on 16 February 1988. Even the above-mentioned demonstration of October 1987, in which about 2,000–4,000 demonstrators raised the issue of Nagorno-Karabakh and Nakhichevan, had developed as a splinter group from a larger demonstration under ecological banners (Platz 1996: 98).

News – but more often rumours – of violent incidents between Azeri and Armenian individuals, *kolkhozy*, villages or communities in Nagorno-Karabakh and some border regions in Armenia with large Azeri populations were spreading at that time in Armenia and Azerbaijan. Before the end of February 1988 these rumours had not turned into the official transcript of the Armenian movement but remained mostly under the cover of the official ecological motto. As stated above, a situation in which local incidents between individuals or collectives have been interpreted along ethnic lines – independent of the actual background of the concrete conflict – was not new to the kitchen gossip of Armenian and Azeri households. What, indeed, was new in Armenia was the galvanised atmosphere of mobility of a rapidly evolving public with the organisational know-how of the new masters of those masses. This situation in the Armenian capital was in stark contrast to the reality in Baku where no public was fermenting into a movement independent from the organisational potential of official Soviet institutions, yet.

During the last ten days of February 1988 the tide turned and the hidden code of a nation under dire threat went public. The two crucial events, which are usually used as markers of the beginning of the Nagorno-Karabakh conflict, took place: [9] on 20 January 1988 the Armenian delegates of the Soviet of Nagorno-Karabakh AO (Azeri delegates did not participate) passed a resolution to the Supreme Soviet of the USSR, the Azerbaijani SSR and Armenian SSR requesting the transfer of the *oblast* to the Armenian SSR; and between 26 and 29 February a mob rampaged unhindered by Soviet law enforcement agencies through predominantly Armenian inhabited quarters of Sumgait, an industrial city in the vicinity of Baku.[10] On 24 February 1988 a group of organisers of the 'ecology' movement had already reinvented themselves as (first) Karabakh Committee (Jacoby 1998b: 172).[11] On 27 February it had declared a moratorium on demonstrations after assurances from the Politburo in Moscow.[12] Instead, on 4 March 1988 the Karabakh Committee issued a declaration branding the violence in Sumgait a genocide against the Armenian people and thereby linking it to the genocidal massacres and deportations Armenians suffered during the First World War under the cumbling Ottoman Empire (Jacoby 1998b: 180). In Stepanakert on 3 March the Krunk Committee was founded by representatives of the Armenian intelligentsia, the local Soviet and by local patrons (the directors of *kolkhozy* and industry) to coordinate and informally represent the interests of the Armenian population of Nagorno-Karabakh. This cocktail of newly invented institutions, a prestigious intellectual establishment, a vitalised Soviet institution of democratic representation and influential official patrons from important informal networks quickly developed into an organised formidable adversary to the central control of the CPSU (Communist Party of the Soviet Union) in Nagorno-Karabakh and in Armenia. It proved to have the power and will to reframe existing rules of conflict and, ultimately, withstand and organise sustained violence.

Those last ten days of February resulted in a paradigm shift that rapidly rocked the region and finally the USSR on three different levels:

- The canon of Armenian historical experience, trained over decades as a hidden transcript of an officially suppressed discourse of national identity among provincial intelligentsia, was breaking into the open discourse of an organised public. The ritualised dogmas of this canon were (a) the latent danger of again being subject to genocide at the hands of the Turks (who in this discourse equal Azerbaijanis) and (b) the historical experience of being left in the lurch, even betrayed, by a supposedly friendly power (Russia). The programmatic term 'genocide' was used in a vast variety of connotations: as 'white genocide' or 'white massacre', referring to the repression, assimilation or eviction of Armenians from their (claimed) historical homelands by non-violent means; as 'biological/ecological genocide' referring to the level of pollution caused by Soviet infrastructure in Armenia and, after Sumgait, as physical extinction (Platz 1996: 96–97). This formerly hidden discourse of permanent victimisation rapidly developed into the new and mighty normative transcript of the national cause, publicly administered by the Karabakh Committee.

• On the official level a taboo had been broken in Stepanakert by formally absolutely legal means: the irrelevant and powerless institution of a local Soviet had, like a zombie, come to life and dared to place a nationalist demand, bypassing (and eventually even 'bringing to heel')[13] parallel local CPSU and executive control (the RAIKOM and IZPOLKOM) against the traditional top-down command line. There had been territorial administrative changes before in the USSR – but always the decisions were cooked up and finally taken by the centres of power. The problem was not of a legal matter – formally, when both the involved Union Republics were in favour of a territorial transfer and the Union Centre had no objections, they were free to do so. The problem was that a local institution which had never been charged with significant power by the centres of Soviet might, took the initiative and thus had indisputably come to life – and no one knew how to put it back to sleep (for the different approaches discussed in the Politburo, see Gorbachev 1996: 333–340).

• Sumgait became the first widely publicised example, in a long list of similar failures to come, in which the Soviet state grossly undermined its very basis: the legitimate monopoly of violence (and of collective violence in particular). The disintegration of the USSR has shown that the legitimacy of modern statehood, not only in western free-market democracies, essentially rests on two principles: the convincing defence of its monopoly of violence and the implementation or at least facilitation of procedures fit to deal with the conflicting interests of its citizen in a non-violent way on a day-to-day basis. The USSR performed poorly on the level of official procedures and delegated a good part of those functions to informal institutions; the legitimate monopoly of violence, on the other hand, was functional and undisputed. The agony into which the Soviet state was sliding was a combination of lacking official institutions to deal with publicly ethnicised conflict in a sovereign and calm manner and at the same time (from ignorance, arrogance or outright panic on the part of the central decision makers) the failure to at least deliver what people had come to rely upon: a strong, decisive but in effect rather neutral central force consistently suppressing the collective use of violence on a local level (with the possible exception of General Lebed's performance in Moldova/Transdnestr). When Soviet law enforcement not only failed to intervene for days during the rampage in Sumgait, but was even widely suspected of having encouraged the violence in order to deliver a warning to Armenians with their unheard-of nationalist demands, Soviet legitimate authority exposed itself to a rapid undermining in the eyes of perpetrators and victims alike.

It is no coincidence that it was in Armenia that the interpretation of multi-faceted conflict first 'switched' to a radically simplifying nationalist paradigm in public discourse. Following the concept of 'hidden transcripts' developed by James Scott (Scott 1990) for the organisational potential of hidden discourses in oppressed societies,[14] it is shown that behind the curtain of the officially pre-scribed discourse of '*druzhba narodov*' (friendship of the peoples) most peoples of the USSR practiced some variations of national identity in private space.[15] Not every private discourse on identity has the potential to be a hidden transcript, the potential to function as a code for sudden unified resistance against the official order upon its public expression. In the Armenian case, the first differentiating criterion of hidden national discourse was its level of integration: national belonging and 'Armenianness' were not a question of individual interpretation but an individual obligation in the most ethnically homogeneous of the Soviet republics (Platz 1996: 192–197). The second and maybe even more important qualifying criterion was the normative, internally unquestionable and therefore dogmatic code that connected national identity to the historical experience of genocide. The public redefinition of political and social conflict (on pollution, control of resources, communal violence in another Union Republic) as poten-tial or actual genocide taking place connected to a uniform normative code indi-vidually rehearsed in thousands of Armenian kitchens and triggered off a truly national change of public discourse on the world. The physical survival of the nation appeared once again to be at stake and a repetition of the failure of 1916 not to perceive this threat and not to take decisive countermeasures in time to head off the threat would be committing the ultimate crime against the nation.[16] 'Any problem connected to Nagorno-Karabakh is connected to the question of the existence of our people' (position paper of the Karabakh Committee delivered in summer 1988, quoted by Jacoby 1998b: 265).

On the official discourse level the dominating normative narrative of social-ism had been replaced by nationalism among Armenians in Nagorno-Karabakh and Armenia.

Conflict breaking out of its social embedding

The essential breakdown of societies' capacity to deal with conflict in a non-violent way or at least to avoid an escalation of violence does not take place on the level of discourse. It takes place on an institutional level – or, more precisely, when conflict loses its social embedding and finds itself re-embedded in institu-tionalised violence.

The problem with the USSR confronting public reinterpretations of conflict along national fault lines was that the state had not established the rules of a game that was considered taboo by the CPSU (i.e. nationalist demands from a subordinate entity). The institutions formally designed to deal with the conflicting interests of communities on a local level – most prominently the local Soviets with elected representatives from the different professional and ethnic communities – were practically dependent on the decisions taken by their counterparts in the centre and more generally on guidelines transmitted by the local branches of the most powerful hierarchal Soviet institution – the CPSU. Therefore the local Soviets (and for that matter the Soviets in general) were unable to take significant decisions by due, reliable procedure and were more of a place representing a ritual power generated by other institutions. With opponents of *perestroika* gaining ground in the CPSU, Gorbachev increasingly relied on the popular support organised in the Soviets and therefore cleared the way for reviving those dormant pseudo-Parliaments.[17]

After February 1988 the local Soviet in Stepanakert was *de facto* taken over first by the Armenian majority of deputies, then detached from the informal power line connecting it to the RAIKOM and simultaneously connected to the informal, agenda-setting Krunk Committee.[18] Attempts by the Central Committee of the CPSU to regain its local influence by replacing functionaries of the RAIKOM proved unsuccessful.[19] This logic of reactivating dormant but existing institutions rather than destroying them and inventing new ones was a trait followed on a grander scale some months later in Armenia.[20] Here the powerful informal Karabakh Committee called the shots but left the procedures of the Supreme Soviet unharmed. It implemented its will through existing rules of the game, a practice that – quite like events in the Baltic republics – proved functional in providing for an internally non-violent transition to independent statehood.

In the course of consolidation by nationalist radicalisation, any official or informal institution that might have had a mediating effect thanks to cross-cutting ties and interests was brought to heel, driven out, or outright 'nationalised' (including inter-regional segments of the criminal world and 'shadow' economy, explicitly targeted by Minister of the Interior Vano Siragedian in 1993–94). An unavoidable by-product of unification by radicalisation were the new fault lines inside the nationalist camp. The pressure on moderate positions in the ranks of the Karabakh Movement increased in the course of their ascent to power. First conflicts appeared between Levon Ter-Petrosian's so-called pragmatism in relations with Turkey and concerning the question of recognition of the Nagorno-Karabakh Republic and representatives of diaspora-backed positions like the ruling Dashnak party in Stepanakert or co-founder of the Karabakh Movement Vazgen Manukian in Yerevan (Goldenberg 1994: 147–150; Jacoby 1998b: 257–291).[21] Until the end of the war in Nagorno-Karabakh these rifts inside the new Armenian political leadership and even between the, at times, very different interests of the Armenian state and Nagorno-Karabakh Armenians did not lead to a major political crisis and were kept under the cloak of national cause and unity.

The discourse of existential national urge entertained by urban intellectuals found a sturdy and reliable manifestation in the Karabakh Armenians willing to hold on by all means to the land they lived on. This 'war-nationalism', a mixture of rehearsed nationalist cause and concrete existential exterritorial threat, disciplined Armenian politics as long as the war was going on and delayed the infighting between informal networks that was to haunt the country for the rest of the 1990s (cf. Dudwick 1997: 89–91; Iskandaryan 2001).

The way in which the binding power of the official Soviet institutions deteriorated in the capital of Azerbaijan was quite different, though no less significant, for the further development of the conflict. The most visible difference is marked by the fact that:

- a popular mass movement (that only by July 1989 became known as the Popular Front) emerged only a year after its Armenian counterpart (Croissant 1998: 31) and there was no rapid and all-encompassing switch in public discourse from communism to nationalism, and
- the emerging national movement did not succeed in taking over Parliament (the Supreme Soviet) and then eventually the government by playing by the rules of existing institutions. It was rather the communist leadership's attempted to control the opposition movement by a combination of concessions and manipulation, like falsifying elections, abolishing institutions (temporarily the Supreme Soviet) and inventing new ones (*Milli Shura*), that lead to uncontrolled change.

If the Nagorno-Karabakh conflict served to integrate national dogma for Armenian politics – a factor that soon even centrally appointed CPSU secretaries had to fall in line with – in Azerbaijan the conflict instead served to gain and lose the highest portfolios on sale in the corridors of power of Baku. Ayaz Mutalibov was installed as First Secretary of the CPSU of the Azerbaijan SSR in the aftermath of the 20 January 1990 military crackdown on the opposition in Baku ordered by Moscow. This change of CPSU leadership was the last in a series of general attempts of the Central Committee of the CPSU to keep the situation in Azerbaijan and Armenia under control by well-established means (i.e. by installing new local leaders of the CPSU first in Stepanakert, then in Yerevan and finally in Baku).

Up to this point official Baku, in relations to the Nagorno-Karabakh problem, had followed a script which it seemingly never even came close to controlling and one that was hardly influenced by the official measures taken. As in the case of serious and highly symbolic incidents of inter-communal violence in February 1988 in Sumgait and January 1990 in Baku no matter if and how the authorities in the Azerbaijani capital were involved in providing for actual escalation (Altstadt 1997: 122), the initiative and control of the consequences were never with the authorities. In both cases the Armenian side made 'innovative' administrative moves through decisions taken in the local, respectively Supreme Soviet (in the first case formally requesting the transfer to the Armenian SSR, in the second by the Supreme Soviet of the Armenian SSR deciding to include Nagorno-Karabakh in its budget). The corresponding Azerbaijani institutions in both incidents officially reacted by condemning the decisions. Right after these decisions, gangs rampaged through the Armenian quarters in Sumgait and Baku, respectively, undisturbed by local law enforcement agencies.

When the centre finally decided to react and sent armed forces into Baku on 20 January 1990, the measure was too late for the remaining Armenian citizens and too heavy-handed for the opposition movements to be interpreted as a central state exercising its monopoly of legitimate force to restore order. The move basically prevented the Popular Front from taking over from the CPSU and provided for the implementation of a handpicked new First Secretary – Ayaz Mutalibov.

Nowhere and at no time in the Nagorno-Karabakh conflict did the central state use its resources decisively and successfully in order to prevent mass expulsion and ethnic cleansing taking place. Even operations that took place in deteriorating situations and under an agenda clearly in line with the core functions of a legitimate state monopoly of violence – such as those to stop violent rioting and plunder in Baku or disarming guerrilla formations north of Nagorno-Karabakh in April–June 1991 – the so-called operation *Kol'tso* (Ring) – the central state authority was seen from all sides more as part of the problem than as a superior and legitimate force (cf. the compilation of material on abuses on the *Memorial* homepage).

Until the dissolution of the USSR and change in government in Baku the communist leadership in Moscow and in Azerbaijan, while reacting strongly to administrative acts and decisions taken in Nagorno-Karabakh and Armenia, seemed to have had no interest in addressing the fact that parallel to the expulsions of Armenians from cities in Azerbaijan all of the Azerbaijani population of Armenia was driven out. It was the Nagorno-Karabakh Armenians who raised this subject by sharply protesting against the resettlement of Azerbaijani refugees from Armenia in the administrative unit to which they laid claim, and on 12 September 1988 a general strike in Nagorno-Karabakh was resumed in connection with this forced transfer of population (Jacoby 1998b: 198). In Azerbaijan the exploitation of this very significant failure of the Soviet state – i.e. protecting minorities against majorities – was left to the propaganda of the opposition groups.

After the installation of Mutalibov, the dynamics of political process in Baku and its relation to the conflict in Nagorno-Karabakh changed. The heavy-handed and short-lived military occupation of Baku left the legitimacy of central Soviet institutions shattered. Mutalibov's attempts at saving his authority by applying a mixture of concessions to the demands of the opposition while at the same time misusing and manipulating new democratic procedures, further added to the rapid decline of statehood itself. The first multi-party elections to the Supreme Soviet in September 1990 were overshadowed by fraud so obvious that after only one year the overwhelming victory of Mutalibov's CPSU was *de facto* annulled by the invention of a new consultative body, the *Milli Shura*, which was made up of members of the opposition and the communist majority of the Supreme Soviet (twenty-five members each) and functioned as a *de facto* 'small' parliament (Altstadt 1997: 124; Goltz 1999: 114). It was a concession of the First Secretary of the CPSU of Azerbaijan to the opposition that in the long run put the newly elected Parliament beyond use. The 'full' parliament was reintroduced with the *Milli Milet* in May 1992 but parliamentary elections did not take place until November 1995 (Altstadt 1997: 124). At the same time – in the aftermath of the August *putsch* in Moscow that the First Secretary in Azerbaijan allegedly initially backed – Mutalibov left the CPSU and had himself elected as first president of the independent republic of Azerbaijan in single-candidate elections. By contrast to his Armenian counterpart he did not achieve this position following an election to first become speaker of Parliament (Supreme Soviet), and then president.

With the state institutions weakened and the opposition excluded from significant responsibility in official institutions and thus confined to the power techniques of a mass protest movement, the Nagorno-Karabakh conflict became the single most important toy in the hands of the political struggle between opposition and government in Baku. The Nagorno-Karabakh conflict grew to be dominant in Azerbaijan not as a nationalist cause of great urgency unifying the political forces as in Armenia; on the contrary, it was simply the most important tool of political infighting in the capital. In a nearly bloodless *coup*, Mutalibov was finally overthrown by the Popular Front in May 1992 after he tried, by manipulating Parliament's procedures, to return to power. His regime had come under increasing pressure after ineptly attempting to cover up the first significant successful and rather ugly[22] military counteroffensive of Armenian forces in Nagorno-Karabakh in late February (Goldenberg 1994: 153; Goltz 1999: 117–130). As an immediate result Mutalibov was forced to resign and temporally cede power to the Speaker of Parliament Yakub Mamedov (nicknamed 'Dollar', allegedly for preferring bribes in hard currency in his former job as director of the republic's Medical Institute). During his three months as acting president Azerbaijan managed to lose the strategically crucial and from a military viewpoint unconquerable town of Shusha to the Armenian forces, resulting in the opening of the Lachin corridor from Nagorno-Karabakh to Armenia (Altstadt 1997: 126). However, the real new president, Abulfez Elchibey, elected in chaotic but otherwise undisputed and free elections in June 1992 with nearly 60 per cent of the votes, only a year later fell victim to the same dynamics of un-institutionalised conflict that had brought him to the top in the first place. Elchibey's credentials as a nationalist and 'pure' patriot were and remained undisputed. His main problem was that he did not have anything even close to a staff of professional bureaucrats (a lack of professionalism in political administration that extended to himself) at his disposal to run the country (Yunusov 1997: 155–156). Since he was not inclined to make use of the just ousted former communist networks he had to seek new alliances with local and regional strong men. The two most important figures to do the networking were the newly appointed minister of the interior and powerful leader of the paramilitary Grey Wolfs (*Bozkurt*), Iskender Hamidov, and Ministers of Defence, former head of the Military Defence Council of the Popular Front and maths-teacher in real life, Rahim Gaziyev, whom Elchibey inherited from the interim president Yakub Mamedov. The crucial objective was to integrate the various armed groups into a disciplined army (cf. Altstadt 1997: 133; Croissant 1998: 83). In the quest of a middle way between pressure and incentive deals were also struck with local big-men of the *biznesmen-patriot* type like Surat Huseinov, warlord in Ganja and former director of a wool mill in Yevlakh. The problem with these kinds of allies was that they continued to be highly unreliable in the way they conducted (or entirely failed to conduct) the war in Nagorno-Karabakh. In effect, the project of creating an integrated army failed; even the early military success of a large offensive Elchibey ordered on 12 June 1992, right after taking office, has been attributed more to the significant amount of military hardware the departing Russian army left behind than to organisational improvements (Croissant 1998: 83–84). The year Elchibey stayed on in power ended with devastating defeats of the Azeri forces in Nagorno-Karabakh. When in spring 1993 the Kelbajar corridor between Nagorno-Karabakh and Armenia was swiftly taken by Armenian forces while Huseinov, who had pledged to defend the region with his well-armed troops and was ordered to do so, was busy requisitioning the military equipment from the leaving Russian army base in his hometown of Ganja, time was up for Elchibey (Goldenberg 1994: 124–125; Goltz 1999: 345, 357–359). The problem was that on 8 February Huseinov was dismissed from his self-styled position as 'commander of forces of the northern front', coinciding with the sacking of Minister of Defence Gaziyev (Altstadt 1997: 128). But instead of succeeding to call the warlord to order that very *biznesmen-patriot* decided to have his men march on Baku to make sure the people responsible for trying to bring him to heel would be punished. When Elchibey finally called the high-profile Soviet leader Heydar Aliev to the rescue, military operations in Nagorno-Karabakh were conducted by a state that in effect no longer existed.

Physical loss of the state's monopoly of violence

The most obvious aspect of conflict spinning out of control is the state physically losing its monopoly on violence and enforcement. The deterioration of the legitimacy of this functional monopoly has been discussed above as one aspect of the failure of core state institutions. However, without the emergence of organised armed groups challenging the state, conflict does not escalate into civil war.

State control over the material and organisational resources of violence are essential assets of statehood and were provided for by the Soviet state. With the sense of security and trust in state capability and willingness to protect its citizens from collective violence fading, Armenians in Nagorno-Karabakh and the region of Shaumian to the north started organising self-defence units at a very local level, individual courtyards, tower blocks, or streets; armed with primitive weapons like sticks, knives or hunting rifles. In a situation of mistrust, the lack of state guarantees of security and the lack of reliable information, it is generally impossible for collectives to differentiate between the aggressive potential and the defensive intention of such armed groups (a situation political scientists call a 'security dilemma') and some local Azeri communities reacted accordingly. In other regions, quarters of cities and towns with compact ethnic settlements, the option taken by the minority was virtually everywhere 'exit' rather than 'voice' – Azeris in Armenia and Armenians in all other parts of Azerbaijan left without organising significant resistance and without being protected, backed or organised by any state agency.

Military equipment entered the scene with the emergence of armed gangs in Armenia 'organising' weapons from local police and army units through illegal trading and raids, a process that gained velocity in 1990 and resulted in the declaration of a state of emergency by the Supreme Soviet of Armenia on 29 August 1990 in order to disband the armed groups (Zverev 1996; Croissant 1998: 38–39). These groups had been organised on a nationalist pretext of backing their ethnic brethren in and around Nagorno-Karabakh but soon became a serious problem for internal stability in Armenia (cf. Dudwick 1997: 78, 83) before being more or less successfully disarmed or merged into semi-official formations loyal to the government. At the time of the declaration of independence in September 1991 the Armenian National Army (ANA), was the most formidable among the unofficial groups, a semi-officially institutionalised proto-armed force of Armenia. The various guerrilla groups were finally disbanded or absorbed into the official army only after the ceasefire in 1994.

On the Azerbaijani side, police and army units obviously possessed serious weapons from the outset and were – when under local command – taking part with a strong Azeri bias. However, like the Azeri population in Armenia, the Azeris of Nagorno-Karabakh seem to have relied more on Soviet troops and law enforcement for protection than their Armenian counterparts did. This difference in local organisational resource proved to be of decisive impact on the conduct and outcome of the war: from the onset the local Karabakh Armenian population was clearly the highly motivated backbone of the fighting while the military action of the opponent was organised by a fluid gathering of Soviet apparatchiks, nationalist intellectuals and *biznesmeny-patrioty* infighting for power in far-away Baku (Kechichian and Karasik 1995: 62–63; Petrosyan 2000a).

With diminishing discipline on the side of the official local and central armed forces, weapons became increasingly available also in Azerbaijan to informal armed gangs only nominally under any official command (as in the cases of the private armies of Surat Huseinov or the *Bozkurt* of Iskender Hamidov already mentioned). In effect the late Soviet state and the succeeding republics of Armenia and Azerbaijan deteriorated in Nagorno-Karabakh into one armed gang among others. After the break-up of the central state, this situation has been characterised by the hesitant and, in effect, unsuccessful attempt in Azerbaijan to form an integrated national army since autumn 1991 and the overall reluctance of Ter-Petrosian in Armenia to embark on transferring the various gangs into an official state army, a process that finally took off in 1992–93 (Zverev 1996). There may have been a number of reasons for Mutalibov and Ter-Petrosian being less than enthusiastic about establishing an effective and inte-grated armed force in the brand new states they found themselves governing. One may have been the fear of confrontation with the institution of real firing power – the still deployed former Soviet, then Russian Army. An internal and no less significant reason may have been the intuition of those leaders recognising that it is highly unlikely for 'instant armies' to be loyal to an, in effect, as yet non-existent state and that it is far from clear that the leaders of those armed forces (particularly if they were Soviet professionals or, worse, nationalist hotheads) would show any personal loyalty to the presidents. If the state is weak, armed forces with a functioning central command can be quite threatening to a fragile political leadership. For Armenia, another factor played a role: officially the country was not involved in the fighting in Nagorno-Karabakh. The situation of having (after initial differences on the practice of raiding before independence) *de facto* control over by far the strongest informal force, the ANA, while abstaining from organising an official force that might get involved and trigger off an inter-state war, probably made a lot of sense to the political leadership weary of the long-term goal of international recognition for the Armenian cause.

Finally, with the clashes escalating to warfare including the use of heavy artillery and tanks it was the (former) Soviet Army, pulling out of Azerbaijan, which made supplies available to both sides, certainly not always according to agreement or central control from headquarters in Moscow (Zverev 1996; Malek 2000: 11–13).

The fact that the Armenian 'informal' forces towards the end of the conflict proved much more effective than their 'official' Azeri adversary is also owed to an important organisational advantage (Petrosyan 2000a): both newly indepen-dent states had recalled their conscripts and professional soldiers from the (suc-cessors to the) Soviet Army. Of the professionals who answered the call, as a rule the Armenians were much higher in rank and 'battle-readiness', because pro-portionally more Armenians made careers in the Soviet Army than did represen-tatives of Muslim republics. Conscripts of those republics usually served not in combat units but rather in the notoriously undisciplined *stroibaty* (construction battalions) (Altstadt 1997: 127). The Azerbaijani defeat was also associated with the fact that professional soldiers and officers proved reluctant to offer their skills under the dubious command and increasing ranks of warlords with no military education whatsoever. In Armenia the situation was different in two regards: as long as the all-encompassing nationalist hype imitated statehood (cf. Iskandaryan 2001) it kept a notion of an urgent common cause alive and internally disciplined the armed gangs. Also as the going got increasingly rough (around 1991–92) highly qualified officers like '*Commandos*' (Arkadi Ter-Tadevossian) were granted the authority they requested by the *biznesmeny-patrioty*. When the war came to a victorious end, this authority was again taken from the professional soldiers and in many cases they were left offended by their unprofessional colleagues driving Jaguars and Mercedes 600s in the ranks of generals with salaries of around $US 80 a month. It therefore came as no surprise that '*Commandos*' was asked in May 2000 to lead the competitor veteran organisation ('Union of Veterans of the Liberation Struggle' – UVLS), which was designed to reduce the power of war veterans and war profiteers organised around *Yerkrapah*,[23] founded and led until his death by Minister of Defence, then Prime Minister Vazgen Sarkisian (Petrosyan 2000b; Ter-Saakyan 2000). '*Commandos*' quit after a few months, arguing that it was impossible to keep the organisation out of politics (Fuller 2000b).

The end of violence

Violence ended with a radical reduction in the complexity of the conflict, which was implemented on the ground: the Armenian side in and around Nagorno-Karabakh achieved maximum gains on the battlefield, including a sizable buffer zone, sealed by a handpicked Line of Contact around a completely ethnically cleansed and physically wrecked territory (Mooradian and Druckman 1999: 723–724). Armenia had rid itself of all its Azeri population and no Armenian minority was left in Azerbaijan.

Violence stopped because one side won the war over the control of territory and both sides consistently reduced the social complexity of the conflict to a military question of high, electrified fences keeping people, commodities and information apart.[24] Even during the period of violent clashes there was more contact between local commanders and the heads of neighbouring local administrations on both sides than after the ceasefire.[25]

The real challenge for the three entities considering themselves states began when they had to embark on institution building without war. It proved to be especially challenging because the war was won or lost, respectively, not by disciplined armies but by a motley gathering of entrepreneurs of violence, unprofessional volunteer fighters, nationalist believers and few (though decisive) professional officers and soldiers from the former Soviet army. The returning *biznesmen-patriot* type of 'big men'[26] proved to be the greatest challenge for stabilising post-war state institutions, particularly in the Armenian case where they returned victorious and were conscious of the fact that in any functioning state system their education, abilities and recent personal history of professionalising in violence would, at best, bring them back to till the fields they came from, and at worst they might end up in jail or die a violent death.

In Azerbaijan it took the new political heavyweight Heydar Aliev about a year to get rid of the most ambitious *biznesmen-patriot*, the former Soviet wool 'merchant', unruly warlord and short-lived Prime Minister, Surat Huseinov in October 1994. The destabilising 'Huseinov Factor' stayed for some time in Azerbaijan's internal politics and ceased to be a real threat only after forces loyal to president Aliev put down a mutiny of special police forces under Rovshan Dzhavadov in March 1995. Some last remnants of the influence of former warlords have kept flaring up, the last one in early 2000 when the local 'big man' Aga Akperov, a pharmacist turned major, was ousted from his position as head of local administration in the Goranboy district, and his son, Colonel Rasim Akperov and commander of an infantry brigade, threatened to overthrow the authorities if his father was not reinstated. The son was arrested on different charges on 9 February 2000, just one day after his father had been sacked by the president (Fuller 2000a).

In Armenia and Nagorno-Karabakh it proved much more difficult for a political establishment that did not owe its power directly and solely to the organisation of violence in the war to regain some influence. Already during the long demise of the Ter-Petrosian regime people like the physical education teacher, Vazgen Sarkisian, founder of the Armenian army and of the politically, economically and militarily extremely influential organisation of veterans (*Yerkrapah*), were in control of vital institutions of the state by means exceeding their official posts (for Sarkisian the Minister of Defence, and then Prime Minister).[27] His deputy in the organisation and former lorry driver, Manvel Grigorian, had a notorious reputation as a 'fund raiser' by any means among the directors of factories and former *apparatchik-biznesmeny* in general, who were persuaded to share the burden of building up the armed forces and backing the campaign in Nagorno-Karabakh by donations in cash and in kind. Grigorian succeeded Sarkisian as acting leader of *Yerkrapah* (the deceased Sarkisian was elected eternal president) and became Deputy Minister of Defence (Danielyan, Khachatrian and Melkumian 2000). The hybrid official and informal network of power around Vazgen Sarkisian dramatically ceded influence to the new Karabakhian key leaders of Armenia – President Kocharian (the former 'president' of Nagorno-Karabakh) and Minister of National Security, then Minister of Defence Serzh Sarkisian – only after he was killed together with five other leading politicians, two members of parliament and one journalist in the massacre in the Armenian Parliament on 27 October 1999.

The internal political situation in Nagorno-Karabakh resembles Armenia on a smaller scale. This is owing to the fact that both political entities, though officially separate (Nagorno-Karabakh is not even recognised as a sovereign state by Armenia), are informally intrinsically connected and maintain interdependent relations (Panossian 2001). The budget of Nagorno-Karabakh is almost entirely secured by Armenia. Their armed forces are closely related and in part integrated, including both command and conscript levels. Karabakhians that need to travel abroad receive passports of the Armenian Republic. From the very beginning these relations, as obvious as they may be, have never been fully officially admitted and have always taken place on an informal level.

The most important test for the professional politicians ('professional' in that they are not essentially connected in their power to the legacy of war) thus far was reducing the influence of the *biznesmeny-patrioty* turned politicians and replacing the high-ranking warlords in the army with professional soldiers. Samvel Babayan was removed from his posts as Minister for Defence in June 1999, and on 17 December 1999 with the hands-on backing of the Ministry of Defence from Yerevan also as Supreme Commander of the armed forces of the would-be state (Khachatrian and Atanesian 1999). His replacement was Lt Gen Seyran Oganyan, a professional soldier who received a good part of his professional training at the Military Academy in Baku. On 22 March 2000 the president of the statelet, Arkadi Gukasian, was seriously wounded in an attempt on his life. This assassination attempt was immediately linked to Samvel Babayan and he, his clan in part and his associates (altogether around thirty people) were arrested in the days following the incident. The authorities in Nagorno-Karabakh successfully used the possibility to demolish the 'system Babayan' and bring the assets of this system under their own control, including the relevant segments of the army loyal to their former commander and decorated hero of the Karabakh war. To this end, just like in Armenia after the sudden and violent death of 'big man' Vazgen Sarkisian, a new veteran organisation was set up in competition with the powerful *Yerkrapah*, controlled by popular war heroes considered loyal to the political leadership.

To gain and keep control over the lower ranks and conscripts as well has never been an easy task in post-Soviet armies in general and in the region in particular: crucial authority in the units is exercised by an institution of informal authorities in principle inherited from the Soviet Army but tainted with a particular underworld understanding of honour and aspects of the idealised 'big men' of the warlord system of the civil war (cf. *Snark* 2000). The widespread and highly institutionalised informal substructure of authority among the conscripts in the Soviet Army was called '*dedovshchina*' (Lewada 1993: 126–139). It has proved difficult to eliminate the institution in the post-Soviet armies and the high rate of non-combat deaths in Armenia and Azerbaijan are to a large extent attributed to the fact that this 'school of cruelty', as it was called by the sociologist Jurij

Lewada, survived in one form or other (*Snark* 2000; Ali 2001). In Armenia the authorities of this system are now called 'observer' instead of the '*ded*' (grandpa) of the '*dedovshchina*' and are exercising authority that the officers are also unable to ignore. Often officers have to negotiate their orders with or via the informal authorities. For ordinary soldiers to survive this parallel system of command physically unharmed they (or their family) either have to bribe official and unofficial authorities (these payments may be outright extortion from the families of recruits) or to prove themselves as 'good lads', capable of withstanding and applying violence. Random shootings often occur because of peer pressure and inner-group violence in those small units of directly associated young men.

Paying bribes or using relatives (doctors, military ranks) to avoid service was common practice not only in the Transcaucasian republics in the late Soviet period. The extortion of money seems to be a new phenomenon, though, connected to the fund raising practice of the Karabakh war.[28]

The situation in the Azerbaijani forces seems to be different insofar as the official authorities (officers, commanders) managed to 'take over' the financially interesting part of the informal system of authority, not to abandon it but to exploit it materially for their own benefit.[29]

Endnote: farewell to arms

The peace process – or the re-institutionalisation of non-violent conflict as a norm – has been more off than on ever since violence came to an end. This process, loosely equipped with an international diplomatic toolbox called the Minsk Process in the framework of the OSCE, is influenced by a number of factors on the ground, factors intimately connected with the process of conflict escalation and the way violence came to an end.

From the perspective of the Armenian and Azerbaijani leaders involved, there has been an informal timeframe pending over the principal chances for peace. On the one hand a political decision maker must feel confident enough at home that he politically, or even physically, will survive a deal based on mutual compromises. This situation has never been fully achieved in Armenia and Karabakh ever since they reached their objectives on the battlefield. Some observers even consider that it is not in the interest of the present (Karabakh) leadership of the Republic Armenia to strike any deal because only the situation of 'no war, no peace' guarantees their power (cf. Shakhnazaryan 2001). On the other hand the deal has to be done before age, health, the constitution or poorly manipulated democratic elections force a leader capable of delivering a peace deal out of office and trigger a race for power and the resources of competing networks that may well paralyse or even destabilise the state for an unforeseeable period. As stability in Azerbaijan depends on a single person, the age and health of Heydar Aliev are the core variables in Azerbaijani politics.[30] The question of striking a peace deal including painful compromises in Azerbaijan has not so much been a question of whether Aliev could deliver; it is more a question of how long he will still be around to deliver and, connected to this, of how long a deal guaranteed in effect not by a state, but by a strong patrimonial network with ailing super-patron, can last.

Both states, Armenia and Azerbaijan, are states with decisive institutional weaknesses even though they present themselves as authoritative states (and often are perceived even by their citizens as authoritarian).[31] The institutions and procedures defining statehood have in effect been taken over by informal pressure groups, networks and institutions that are not taken into account by the way the state is formally constituted. The fact that influential patrons occupy key positions in the state and keep services to some degree functioning, conceals to some extent the absence of a *raison d'état*. It conceals a situation in which the official part of the state is run in many cases as a non-profit organisation, a noble NGO-engagement of *apparatchiki-biznesmeny* turned *biznesmeny-patrioty* pursuing network interests rather than common or national interests.

NOTES

1   The level of narratives and geopolitical circumscription in Armenia is explicitly targeted by Volker Jacoby, and narratives and making sense of change by the anthropologists Nora Dudwick and Stephanie Platz (Dudwick 1994; Platz 1996; Jacoby 1998b). All three dissertations are excellent first-hand accounts of Armenian society in the late 1980s and early 1990s, respectively. Engaged journalists and scholars may take a less critically conscious approach to the view of the world from within (e.g. Chorbajian, Donabedian and Mutafian 1994; Mamedova 1995; Soljan 1995). Notable exceptions to this are the few first-hand accounts by journalists who stayed for a long period of time in the region and are, for some part, describing social processes rather than discourses on processes (e.g. Goldenberg 1994; Goltz 1999).

2   An obvious example would be the initially unaccounted for and later admitted Russian weapons delivery amounting to about $US 1 billion to Armenia in 1993–96 (Malek 2000: 11–13); more general but often-quoted topics are the US oil interest in assumed but for the larger part not yet proven Azerbaijani oil reserves and ambitious pipeline projects bypassing Russia (Lieven 1999–2000); also last but not least the radicalising factor of Armenian diaspora influence on the interpretation of conflict and (long-decreasing) financial support.

3   Scheffler (1995) convincingly makes the point that this strategy of unifying by force is always ambivalent: a violent claim to total identification with a group always creates lines of division, uncompromisingly separating 'others' (like traitors, unbelievers, dissidents and the like) outside and inside the defined group. In situations where expectations of decisive gains (e.g. in the case of administrative privileges) or losses (e.g. in the case of administrative discrimination or even suppression) are not formally connected to the way a person defines their identity, people do not seem to care too much about a limiting definiteness in defining their belonging. Choice is radically limited as soon as people are being convinced that they will not be able to master their everyday life if they do not unambiguously define their identity.

4   Different from the first two anonymous terms widely used in the USSR the latter two have

'name-tags' attached to them: the economy of shortages was introduced by Kornai (1980) and the concept of the administrative market by Kordonskii (1995).

5   For an extensive portrait of the patronage and parallel networking in Soviet Azerbaijan, see Willerton (1992).

6   See for example Kechichian, Karasik (1995). In social anthropology the term 'clan' usually refers to a group of people defining themselves by a notion of common decent, that is by an emic concept of extended kinship, usually drawing on a mythical common ancestor.

7   In the case of, for example, the often-quoted Nakhichivanian 'clan' of Heydar Aliev (Kechichian and Karasik 1995: 60–61; Altstadt 1997: 142) as an important power base for his political career, the question of breaching ethnic or religious borders does not arise since the point of territorial reference is, in an ethnic sense, homogeneous.

8   Katerine Verdery links the concept of 'economy of shortages' in her case study of Romania directly to ethno-nationalism, rather than treating it as a by-product; her view concentrates more on 'whom to favour' with deficit goods than on 'whom to trust' with illegal activity (Verdery 1993: 173–175); the latter seems much more important for the larger-scale and longer-term business relations the *apparatchiki-biznesmeny* in the Caucasus were seeking.

9   Sometimes cited by Karabakh Armenians as the first deadly incident but neglected here (for lack of general symbolic weight) is the clash between Armenian and Azerbaijani demonstrators close to Askeran (Nagorno-Karabakh AO) on 22–23 February 1988 that resulted in the death of two Azeri demonstrators and fifty people injured on both sides; the Armenian version maintains that a primitively armed Azeri mob marched on Askeran and Armenians defended their settlement.

10 According to the final official account thirty-two people were killed, six of them Azeris, the remaining Armenians (Jacoby 1998b: 178).

11 This first committee, dominated by activists also with a explicit irredentist nationalist agenda in relation to Turkey, was replaced in May–June by the group of leaders that became known as 'The' Karabakh Committee and founding fathers of the Armenian National Movement (ANM) (cf. Dudwick 1997: 78–79; see Shakhnazaryan 2000). The new committee put considerable effort into separating the general ideological issue of '*Hai Dat* (the Armenian cause) from the struggle in Karabakh.

12 The events have been reconstructed here drawing on detailed accounts of Platz (1996), Croissant (1998), Jacoby (1998b) and, in some cases, interviews with eyewitnesses of that time, conducted in 1996 and 2001 by the author.

13 Only a day after the local Soviet placed its request on transfer of the AO, the OBKOM of the CP in Stepanakert agreed overwhelmingly (80:10) to the resolution. Informal local pressure and incentives proved to be stronger than the attempts of the Central Committee in Moscow to rein in their comrades in the outpost.

14 James Scott focuses his discussion on the conditions of development of hidden transcripts on the part of the weak and powerless (Scott 1990). According to Scott 'hidden transcripts' are identity exercises or discourses of power(-lessness) of the weak behind the curtain of the official discourse of power (public transcript). Hidden transcripts may serve as an unrecognised breeding ground for mostly passive resistance. Scott considers open resistance to be rarely successful over longer periods of time. However, the relevant case here is not only a hidden transcript going public but also being successful and turning into the next dogmatic public transcript.

15 One prominent earlier outbreak took place on 24 April 1965 in Yerevan in the realm of semi-approved mass demonstrations about the fiftieth anniversary of genocide (Goldenberg 1994: 139).

16 The most important accusation against the Dashnak party was that they missed the opportunity to organise effective resistance by trying to reach agreement with the demands of the Ottoman, then Young-Turk government of that time; this devastating criticism of being partly responsible for the genocide of one's own people by failing to engage in civil war was reactivated in the showdown between the Dashnak party and Levon Ter-Petrosian in late 1994 that ended with the (temporary) ban of this important Armenian party of the diaspora in December of that year (Jacoby 1998b: 287).

17 On 15 September 2000 in an interview with BBC's Tim Sebastian, Gorbachev regretted (again) not having cooperated with local movements more as an alternative to the unre-formed CPSU.

18 On 23 March 1988 Krunk was banned by the authorities, but as an alternative Karabakh Armenians organised a 'Council of Directors of Enterprises'. Krunk and the Council of Directors of Enterprises were banned between 12 January and 28 November 1989, in the period of central administration of the Special Administrative Committee.

19 Most importantly the replacement of the First Secretary Boris Kevorkov with Henrik Pogosian on the initiative of the Politburo in Moscow was executed via an especially founded PARTAKTIV (special task force of the CPSU) in Nagorno-Karabakh (25 February 1988).

20 The same futile attempt to regain the central initiative occurred some months later in Yerevan, when the Central Committee decided to replace Karen Demirchian with Suren Harutyunian as First Secretary of the CPSU in Yerevan.

21 For a critical assessment of an oversimplifying division taken by former members of the Ter-Petrosian government into pragmatists (like Ter-Petrosian) and ideologists or hardlin-ers (like the early Kocharian or Manukian), see Simonian (2001). To him pragmatism or ideology in Armenia is not an opposing conviction but rather a situative strategy of accessing power.

22 The strategically important village of Khochaly was taken on 25 February 1992, in an operation that left a large number of civilians dead.

23 *Yerkrapah* was originally founded as unpolitical association of Karabakh war veterans but quickly developed into the most powerful informal organisation capable of turning the fortunes of ministers and even presidents (as in the case of the ousting of Levon Ter-Petrosian in 1997–98) and claiming the last say in any peace deal (Seyranian, Melkumian and Zakarian 2000). The influence of *Yerkrapah* has been diminishing after the death of their paramount founding father and leader Vazgen Sarkisian.

24 This radical segregation is implemented only at the official level – informal exchanges do take place on small scale, e.g. some Azerbaijani products are available in Stepanakert; more significant is the semi-official inter-regional market in Sadakhlo, a region in Georgia inhabited mainly by Azeris and bordering Armenia where business mainly takes place between Armenians and Azeris (de Waal 2000).

25 This was a frequent complaint of local administration and commanders in conversations during visits in the vicinity of the Line of Contact during 2000, who pointed out that it was easier to settle common local problems during conflict than after; compare Mooradian and Druckman (1999: 725).

26 For the classic classification of the political entrepreneur, securing influence by control-ling violence and the redistribution of goods, called the 'big man' of non-state-societies, see Sahlins (1963) and Strathern (1991).

27 For an insight into the most important patrons of powerful networks around the mid-1990s, see Dudwick (1997: 90–91).

28 Information on this subject is, to best of the author's knowledge, scarce (cf. Dudwick 1997: 91 on the amounts to be paid for exemption of active service in Armenia). The

author's information is therefore not representative – it was gathered in a number of informal conversations with (former and active) conscripts and their families. It is a fact, though, that even international employers in negotiating the salary with their local staff are sometimes taking these considerable and regularly paid 'health-insurance taxes' into consideration.

29 As a Baku-based officer related to the author off the record in late 2000, referring to the better-off field commanders: 'Do you believe they would allow anyone else to collect money from their soldiers?'

30 In September 2000 Aliev's health politics became known as the 'Cleveland games' when the president chose unexpectedly for the public and, as it seemed, most of his own team, to prolong his US visit and have a check-up in a favourite Cleveland hospital. When fresh pictures were absent for some days and a Russian newspaper reported the death of Aliev even the diplomatic corps was getting a little nervous. A well informed high-ranking diplomat related to the author that it is possible that only the Minister of Defence, Head of Presidential Administration and Aliev's son knew exactly what was going on, in order to enable the President to check on the loyalty and faith of the rest of his men (cf. Lelyveld 2000).

31 Commenting on the preoccupation of international observers with formal and rather superficial indicators of democratisation Nora Dudwick observes for Armenia: 'for its own citizens, life in Armenia has become a disturbing mixture of chaos and authoritarianism' (Dudwick 1997: 69). This assessment would be as accurate for the situation in Azerbaijan with the qualification that the Azerbaijani Ministry of Foreign Affairs is putting less effort and resources into selling a story of genuine democratic achievements to western politicians and observers.

REFERENCES

Ali, K. (2001), 'Azeri army death-wish', *IWPR Caucasus Reporting Service* (25 September: 99), online edition, www.iwpr.net/index.pl?archive/cau/cau_200109_99_3_eng.txt (accessed 20 January 2002).

Altstadt, A. L. (1997), 'Azerbaijan's struggle towards democracy', in K. Dawisha and B. Parrott (eds), *Conflict, Cleavage, and Change in Central Asia and the Caucasus* (Cambridge), 110–155.

Anderson, B. A. and B. D. Silver (1996 [1983]), 'Population redistribution and the ethnic balance in Transcaucasia', in R. G. Suny (ed.), *Transcaucasia, Nationalism, and Social Change. Essays in the History of Armenia, Azerbaijan, and Georgia* (Ann Arbor), 481–506.

Chorbajian, L., P. Donabedian and C. Mutafian (eds) (1994), *The Caucasian Knot: The History and Geo-Politics of Nagorno-Karabakh* (London).

Coser, L. A. (1956), The Functions of Social Conflict (London).

Croissant, M. P. (1998), The Armenia–Azerbaijan Conflict: Causes and Implications, (Westport, CT).

Danielyan, E., R. Khachatrian and H. Melkumian (2000). 'Kocharian promotes Yerkrapah leaders in major army reshuffle', *RFE/RL Armenia Report* (14 March), online publication, www.rferl.org/bd/ar/reports/archives/2000/03/140300.html (accessed 20 January 2002).

de Waal, T. (2000), 'An uncommon market in the Caucasus', *The Economist* (3 June), online edition.

Dudwick, N. C. (1994), Memory, Identity and Politics in Armenia (Ann Arbor).

Dudwick N. C. (1997), 'Political transformations in postcommunist Armenia: image and realities', in K. Dawisha and B. Parrott (eds), *Conflict, Cleavage, and* Change in Central Asia and the Caucasus (Cambridge), 69–109.

Fuller, E. (1987), 'Armenians demonstrate for return of territories from Azerbaijan', *Radio Liberty* (20 October), 441: 87, 1–3.

Fuller, L. (2000a), 'Azerbaijani officer's arrest highlights broader problems', *RFE/RL Caucasus Report* (17 February), 3:7, online publication, www.rferl.org/caucasus-report/2000/02/7-170200.html (accessed 8 February 2002).

Fuller, L. (2000b), 'New Armenian veterans' union deplores leader's resignation', *RFE/RL Newsline* (17 August), 4: 158/1, online publication, www.hri.org/news/balkans/rferl/2000/00-08-17.rferl.html#01 (accessed 8 February 2002).

Gelaschwili, N. (1993), *Georgien. Ein Paradies in Trümmern* (Berlin).

Goldenberg, S. (1994), Pride of Small Nations. The Caucasus and Post-Soviet *Disorder* (London).

Goltz, T. (1999), Azerbaijan Diary. A Rogue Reporter's Adventures in an Oil-Rich, War-Torn, Post-Soviet Republic (New York and London).

Gorbachev, M. *Memoirs* (New York and London).

Hirschman, A. O. (1994), 'Wieviel Gemeinsinn braucht die liberale Gesellschaft?', *Leviathan*, 2, 293–304.

Iskandaryan, A. (2001), Desyat' let nezavisimosti na Yuzhnom Kavkaze: Uspekhi i krizisy transformatsii', paper presented at the *The Second International Sakharov Congress*, available online, www.sakharov-congress-hall.ru/sc2/session/viewarticle.xtmpl?id=10&sn=8 (accessed 13 January 2001).?

Jacoby, V. (1998a), 'Geschichte und Geschichtsschreibung im Konflikt um Berg-Karabach', *Ethnos-Nation*, 6, 63–84.

Jacoby, V. (1998b), Geopolitische Zwangslage und nationale Identität: Die Konturen der innenpolitischen Konflikte in Armenien, (Frankfurt/M.), online publication http://zaurak.tm.informatik.uni-frankfurt.de/diss-cgi/show/meta?signatur= 00000148&seite= (accessed 10 January 2002).

Kechichian, J. A. and T. W. Karasik (1995), 'The crisis in Azerbaijan: how clans influence the politics of an emerging republic', *Middle East Policy*, 4: 1/2 (September), 57–71.

Khachatrian, R. and V. Atanesian (1999), 'Karabakh military will not oppose Babayan's sacking', *RFE/RL Armenia Report* (20 December 1999), online publication, www.rferl.org/bd/ar/reports/archives/1999/12/201299.html.

Koehler, J. (1999), 'The school of the street: organising diversity and training polytaxis in a (post-) Soviet periphery', *Anthropology of East Europe Review*, Special Issue: Reassessing Peripheries Post-Communist Studies, 17: 2, 39–52, http://condor.depaul.edu/~rrotenbe/aeer/aeer17_2.html.

Koehler, J. (2000), Die Zeit der Jungs. Zur Organisation von Gewalt und der Austragung von Konflikten in Georgien, 64 (Münster, Hamburg and London).

Kordonskii, S. (1995), 'The structure of economic space in post-perestroika society and the transformation of the administrative market', in K. Segbers and S. de Spiegeleire (eds), *Post-Soviet Puzzles. Mapping the Political Economy of the Former Soviet Union*, 1 (Baden-Baden), 157–205.

Kornai, J. (1980), *Economics of Shortage* (Amsterdam).

Laitin, D. D. and R. G. Suny (1999), 'Armenia and Azerbaijan: thinking a way out of Karabakh', *Middle East Policy*, 7: 1,online edition, www.mepc.org/journal/9910_laitinsuny.html (accessed 6 January 2002).

Lelyveld. M.. (2000), 'Azerbaijan: misleading reports in Russian press on Azerbaijan', *RFE/RL Features* (29 September), online publication, www.rferl.org/nca/features/2000/09/29092000192114.asp (accessed 6 January 2002).

Lewada, J. (1993), *Die Sowjetmenschen. 1989–1991. Soziogramm eines Zerfalls* (München).

Lieven, A. (1999–2000), 'The (not so) great game', *The National Interest* (Winter), 69–80.

Malek, M. (2000), *Determinanten der Sicherheitspolitik Armeniens* (Köln).

Mamedova, F. (1995), 'Ursachen und Folgen des Karabach-Problems. Eine historische Untersuchung', in U. Halbach and A. Kappeler (eds), *Krisenherd Kaukasus* (Baden-Baden), 110–128.

Memorial (2002), 'Human rights violations during the April– June 1991 military operations in Nagorno-Karagbakh and neighboring regions by USSR Interior Ministry troops, Soviet Army and Azerbaijani Interior Ministry, online publication www.memo.ru/hr/hotpoints/karabah/GETASHEN/ENG/chapter1.htm. (accessed 12 January 2002).

Mooradian, M. and D. Druckman (1999), 'Hurting stalemate or mediation? The conflict over Nagorno-Karabakh, 1990–95', *Journal of Peace Research*, 36:6, 709–727.

Panossian, R. (2001), 'The irony of Nagorno-Karabakh: formal institutions versus informal politics', *Regional and Federal Studies, Special Issue*, 11:3 (Autumn), 143–164.

Petrosyan, D. (2000a). 'Review and outlook: what are the reasons for Armenians' success in the military phase of the Karabakh conflict (1991 to mid-1994)?', *Armenian News Network/Groong* (1 June).

Petrosyan, D. (2000b), 'Review and outlook: "New Yerkrapah" face problems', Armenian News Network/Groong (18 August).

Platz, S. (1995). '"We don't have capitalism . . . We have kinship": the state, the family, and the expression of Armenian identity', *Anthropology of East Europe Review, Special Issue: Culture and Society in the Former Soviet Union*, 13:2, online edition, http://condor.depaul.edu/~rrotenbe/aeer/aeer13_2/Platz.html (accessed 11 January 2002).

Platz, S. (1996), *Pasts and Futures: Space, History, and Armenian Identity, 1988–1994* (Chicago: 1996).

Sahlins, M. D. (1963), 'Poor man, rich man, big-man, chief: political types in Melanesia and Polynesia', Comparative Studies in Society and History, 5, 285–303.

Schefler, T. (1995), 'Ethnoradikalismus: Zum Verhältnis von Ethnopolitik und Gewalt', in G. Seewann (ed.), Minderheiten als Konfliktpotential in Ostmittel- und Südosteuropa (München).

Scott, J. C. (1990), *Domination and the Arts of Resistance. Hidden Transcripts* (New Haven and London).

Seyranian, S., H. Melkumian and A. Zakarian (2000), 'Yerkrapah wants final say on Karabakh peace', *RFE/RL Armenia Report* (7 February), online publication, www.rferl.org/bd/ar/reports/archives/2000/02/070200.html (accessed 21 January 2002).

Shakhnazaryan, D. (2000), 'Armenia na poroge XXI veka. Vlast' naprasno ishchet budushchee svoei strany v ee proshlom', *Nezavisimaya gazeta* (26 January), online edition, http://cis.ng.ru/words/2000-01-26/3_armenia.html (accessed 23 January 2002).

Shakhnazaryan, D. (2001), 'Armeniya upodoblyaetsya Yugoslavii, govorit s trevogoi byvshii ministr natsional'noi bezopasnosti RA David Shakhnazaryan', *AZG* Armenian Daily 92 (22 May).

Simonian, H. H., (2001), 'Review: Gerard J. Libaridian, *The Challenge of Statehood: Armenian Political Thinking Since Independence*, Watertown, MA: Blue Crane Books, 1999, xii, 16', *Nationalities Papers*, 29: 2, 375–379.

Snark (2000), 'Armenian rights group concerned about bullying, criminal elements in army', *Snark* Armenian news agency (11 December).

Soljan, S. (1995), 'Entstehungsgeschichte und aktuelle Probleme des Karabach-Konfliktes', in U. Halbach and A. Kappeler (eds), *Krisenherd Kaukasus* (Baden-Baden), 129–160.

Strathern, M. (1991), 'Introduction', in M. Godelier and M. Strathern (eds), *Big Men and Great Men* (Cambridge).

Swietochowski, T. (1995), 'Der Streit um Berg-Karabach. Geographie, ethnische Gliederung und Kolonialismus, in U. Halbach and A. Kappeler (eds), *Krisenherd Kaukasus* (Baden-Baden), 161–178.

Ter-Saakyan, K. (2000), 'Karabakh veterans split by conflicting loyalties', *IWPR's Caucasus Reporting Service* (6 October) 52, online edition, www.iwpr.net/index.pl?archive/cau/cau_200010_52_04_eng.txt (accessed 6 January 2002).

Theisen, S. (1999), 'Mountaineers, racketeers and the ideals of modernity: statebuilding and elite-competition in Caucasia', in O. Højris and S. M. Yürükel (eds), *Contrasts and Solutions in the Caucasus* (Aarhus), 140–158, also online http://caucasus.dk/publication10.htm.

Tishkov, V. A. (10994), 'Inventions and manifestations of ethno-nationalism in Soviet academic and public discourse', in R. Borofsky (ed.), *Assessing Cultural Anthropology* (New York, etc.), 443–452.

Verdery, K. (1993), 'Ethnic relations, economies of shortage, and the transition in Eastern Europe', in C. M. Hann (ed.), Socialism. Ideals, Ideologies, and Local *Practice* (London and New York), 172–186.

Waldmann, P. (1999), 'Societies in civil war', in G. Elwert, S. Feuchtwang and D. Neubert (eds), Dynamics of Violence. Processes of Escalation and De-Escalation in Violent Group Conflicts (Berlin), 61–83.

Willerton, J. P. (1992), 'Azerbaidzhan and the Aliev network', in J. P. Willerton, Patronage and Politics in the USSR (Cambridge, 1992), 191–222.

Yunusov, A. (1997), 'Azerbaydzhan v postsovetskii period: problemy i vozmozhnye puti razvitiya', in Severnyi Kavkaz-Zakavkaz'e: problema stabil'nosti i perspektivy razvitiya (Moskva), 144–165.

Zverev, A. (1996), 'Ethnic conflicts in the Caucasus 1988–1994', in B. Coppieters (ed.), *Contested Borders in the Caucasus* (Brussels), online edition, http://poli.grmbl.com/publi/ContBorders/eng/ch0101.htm (accessed 6 January 2002).

9

Conflict management in the Caucasus via development of regional identity

Olga Vassilieva

Introduction

THIS CHAPTER CONSIDERS the preconditions for and possibilities of Caucasian integration as a way of conflict management in the region. The 1990s has revealed that a common Caucasian identity might be used for 'constructing' a regional security community. To testify to this thesis, a significant part of the chapter addresses the question of how different identities have influenced the development of nationalism and cooperation, conflict escalation and conflict settlement since 1990. It analyses the impact of different cooperative organisations on conflict management, both directly and via the changes in governmental policies towards ethnic conflict and the identities which fostered it. Of special interest are the current policies of the 'external' powers (Russia, Turkey, Iran and western countries) and the possible changes in their policies towards the region, which might promote the construction of a regional security community and, as a consequence, conflict management in the Caucasus.

A high conflict potential in the Caucasian region, and in the North Caucasus specifically, is conditioned by 'natural' causes of conflict such as a poly-ethnic and poly-cultural population, the scarcity of resources (primarily territory), a high population growth rate, extensive migrations and, at the same time, the preservation of compact ethnic communities. Soviet national policy based on the idea of ethno-federalism smoothed ethnic tensions and provided inter-ethnic peace during the industrialisation period, but it also created the conditions that promoted ethnic competition in poly-ethnic autonomous and 'union' republics since the 1960s. Among these conditions were the recognition of an ethnic identity as a national one (i.e. ethnic nationalism versus civic nationalism), the promotion of the ethnic cadre and 'intelligentsia', and the creation of a hierarchy of quasi-sovereign national-territorial units.[1]

Social mobilisation during Gorbachev's *perestroika* turned into ethno-national movements under slogans calling for the restoration (or the creation) of national autonomy for the 'historical territory of a particular ethnic group' that, in turn, fuelled inter-ethnic conflicts all over the Caucasus as several ethnic groups considered the same territory to be their 'ethnic motherland'.

However, together with the development of competitive ethno-national movements, different coalitions of these movements have also been created in the Caucasus: (1) at the republic level, for the purposes of settling inter-ethnic conflicts (the Congress of Dagestani Peoples) and/or to coordinate the activity of the opposition to communist leaderships in the North Caucasian republics; (2) at the regional (North Caucasian) level, to resolve common problems (the Confederation of Mountain Peoples of the Caucasus – CMPC); (3) although the idea of the Common Caucasian Home had never been realised in practice, it has been discussed: cooperative organisations had contributed to conflict resolution in the Caucasus.

Both processes – the growth of competitive ethno-national movements and the development of different cooperative organisations – reflect a multi-level choice of identity among the population of this region, who ascribe themselves to a local community, to a tribe, to an ethnos, and to particular religious or political movements. But what unites all these peoples now living in different states, is the common Caucasian identity based not on a common language but on shared myths, traditions and values.

Ethnic identity has played a key role in the development of ethno-nationalisms and as a consequence, in conflict escalation, in considering the scarce resources and mutual claims. Caucasian identity resulted in the development of cooperative movements, which contribute to conflict resolution, although their influence on conflict development was much weaker than was the contribution of ethnic identity to conflict escalation.

In explaining the formation of ethno-nationalism, scholars have proposed two basic approaches – 'primordialistic', which explains ethno-nationalism via the universal and natural character of ethnicity (i.e. 'loyalty to one's own ethnic group, culture or place of origin'); and 'constructed', which considers ethnic culture and nation to be primarily social constructs, subjects for manipulation by elites in their competition for wealth and power. These were named 'imagined communities' by Benedict Anderson (Bogdanor 1987: 210).

In reality, however, it is impossible to find a scholar of nationalism who subscribes to 'primordialistic ideas'. Even Anthony Smith, who stressed that pre-modern ethnicity is the root for modern nationalism, did not claim the 'naturalness' of an ethno-nation, as Craig Calhoun notes in his comprehensive review of modern approaches to ethno-nationalism; the 'primordialist' approach is, in many respects, political myth and belief (Calhoun 1993).

A reasonable question arises from this conclusion: if politicians are so successful in 'constructing' ethno-nationalism, what should be done in order to construct successful regional cooperation or a security community in the

Caucasus? Who are the political entrepreneurs interested in such a social construct?

Karl Deutsch defined a 'security community' as an integrated group, where:

> By integration we mean the attainment, within territory, of a 'sense of community' and of institutions and practices strong enough and widespread enough to assure, for a 'long' time, dependable expectation of 'peaceful change' among its population. By Sense of Community we mean a belief on the part of individuals in a group that have come to agreement on at least this one point: that common social problems must and can be resolved by processes of 'peaceful change', By peaceful change we mean the resolution of social problems, normally by institutionalised procedures, without resort to large-scale physical force. (Deutsch *et al.* 1957: 5)

The Caucasus has demonstrated a strong sense of community and a Caucasian identity, which has deep cultural and historical roots. The development of cooperative organisations in the region show the possibility of establishing 'institutional procedures' for the peaceful resolution of social problems. Strong ethno-nationalism resulted in a short life for integrative associations.

What is presented here is an idealistic attempt to implement 'pure theoretical conclusions' from studies of [ethno-]nationalism to conflict management in the Caucasus, i.e. it is an attempt to suggest possible strategies for the construction of a security community in the Caucasus, using its 'primordialistic' all-Caucasian identity, the construction of which may become the basis for peace making and peace building efforts in the region.

For these purposes, how different identities have influenced the development of nationalism and cooperation, conflict escalation and conflict settlement in the Caucasus within the last decade have all been considered. The impact of different cooperative movements on conflict management directly, and via the changes in governmental policies towards ethnic conflict and the identities which fostered it, have also been analysed. Of special interest are 'the external' powers (Russia, Turkey, Iran and western countries), their current policy (or how it is perceived among Caucasian people) and possible changes in their policies towards the region, which might promote integrated communities and, as a consequence, conflict management in the Caucasus.

A multiple choice of identities and their impact on conflict development

A multiple choice of identity defines the different means of consolidation and mobilisation during the second wave of nationalism in the Caucasus.[2]

'Natural' sources for ethnic identity and 'Soviet constructivism'

An ethnic identity, which differentiates between 'them' and 'us' on the basis of criteria such as common cultural traits, common history, language and attachment to a certain territory has provided a high degree of group solidarity in the Caucasus. In many situations, it has overlapped identities on the lower level, such as loyalty to a local community (on the level of small villages) or ethnic subunits (*teips* (clans), tribes and so on). It has also destroyed common territorial identities (at a republican or regional level), and political identities ('pro-democratic' movements), which revealed themselves in the Caucasus in the 1990s.

The fast and mass ethno-national consolidation during *perestroika* resulted from the presence in the Caucasus of both important factors in ethnonationalism: the strong loyalty of the population to a particular ethnic group and a class of political entrepreneurs ('national intelligentsia', 'national cadre', 'national bureaucrats').

In comparison with other national regions of the former Soviet Union, the special importance of ethnic loyalties has been conditioned by the traditionalism of Caucasian societies which, in turn, can be explained by several factors. Throughout the centuries, the topography of the Caucasus has fostered the high level of diversity among local communities and the preservation of their compact settlements and their traditional economic and social life. Owing to a geographic position on the crossroads of major routes between Europe and Asia, the Caucasus became a battlefield for great empires and has been exposed to invasions by nomadic tribes. The wars and invasions prevented attempts at self-organisation and the formation of modern states and resulted in a 'primitive' economic life and the conservation of traditional political institutions for many years.

Russian colonisation and the modernisation of the Caucasus did not significantly change the traditional structures of society, especially in the North Caucasus, which resisted Russian invasion until the beginning of the twentieth century. Local communities considered loyalty to traditional institutions and the traditional way of life a resistance to Russia's colonial policy.

Soviet national policy also failed to significantly modernise traditional life and ties. Moreover, its essence was based on the recognition of national identity as an ethnic identity. 'The support of and development of national cultures' in the form of creating national theatres, film production, national academies of science and humanities, etc. helped not only to create a whole system for the reproduction of ethnic myths, but also to promote the preservation of ethnic identities. For many small ethnic groups, this policy resulted in the creation of the 'political entrepreneurs' of ethno-national movements during *perestroika*, and the 'national intelligentsia' and 'national cadre'.

Policies of assimilation and resettlement (other elements of 'social constructivism') often had the same effect: they provoked the resistance and, in many cases, promoted the re-establishment of traditional institutions. Svetlana Alieva, a daughter of a well-known Karachaev writer who had survived during the years of deportation (1943–57), notes that it was during the deportation that '*stareishiny*' (the older Karachaev men) prohibited marriages between Karachaevs and non-Karachaevs, which had been widespread during the 1920s and 1930s.

Urbanisation and economic modernisation could have influenced the transformation of traditional ties in a society. However, the Soviet policy of levelling the standards of economic development was carried out by means of intensified industrialisation; it did not affect the traditionally agricultural occupations of the local population and required the regular import of qualified manpower from other regions of the Soviet Union. As a result the local population worked in agriculture and was employed in the upper echelon of power, while immigrants, who were concentrated in the cities, were employed in industrial production and the medium echelon of administration.

The specific system of employment fostered the conservation of traditional ties, structures and, as a consequence, ethnic identities. The Soviet policy of recruiting national cadre was based on the class principle (representatives from among the peasants, agricultural workers and industrial workers were preferred for the administrative services) and on the national 'representative-ness' principle (all different national groups had to be represented in power bodies). Having got a position in the Soviet administrative system, new bureaucrats strove to help people from their local communities to get a position in administrative hierarchy. In the poly-ethnic autonomous regions of the Caucasus, such an approach exacerbated inter-ethnic competition and provided a large number of collective grievances. The different statuses in the Soviet hierarchy (being a union and an autonomous republics, or an autonomous *oblast* and *okrug*) defined different access to resources, and also promoted competition among ethnic elites and the conservation of ethnic identities.

Thus, the Soviet national policy directed at creating a new social construct, '*Homo Soveticus*', in reality fostered the development of both the essential elements for ethno-national mobilisation: the preservation of traditional ethnic identities and the creation of ethnic entrepreneurs, which included national bureaucrats, national intelligentsia and national managers of small and medium-sized enterprises (SMEs).[3] All these groups considered *perestroika* a chance to significantly change the ethnic balance in administrative structures in favour of their ethnic groups and to get access to additional resources. The weakening of the central authorities and the elimination of the Communist Party of the Soviet Union, which broke the ethnic balance in administrative structures, accelerated ethnic mobilisation, especially in the regions where strong ethnic grievances had persisted – such as regions with resettled ethnic groups (oppressed peoples, many peoples of Dagestan, etc.); regions with a territorial hierarchy of ethnic units (Georgia, Azerbaijan); or with an administrative hierarchy for ethnic groups (especially, in dual-ethnos autonomous regions such as Kabardino-Balkaria and Karachaevo-Cherkesia).

The development of ethno-national movements pushed the countermobilisation of neighbouring ethnic groups and strengthened tensions between local communities. The ethnic mobilisation and countermobilisation, as well as the competitive purposes of ethno-national movements resulted in a wave of violent interethnic conflicts all over the Caucasus.

Cooperative associations at the republican level, or 'democratic constructivism'

Cooperative organisations in the North Caucasian republics were conditioned not only, and not so much, by the traditional common Caucasian identity, but also by the common political 'pro-democratic' or 'self-determination' stance of the leaders of national organisations. Certainly, the adherence of leaders of the so-called 'informal movement' to democratic values was much weaker than their strong ethnic loyalty. However, the joint struggle against the Communist Party leaderships in the republics explains the cooperation among new political elites, which resulted in the settling of several inter-ethnic conflicts.

The cooperation was conditioned by the history of the 'informal movement', which had developed at the end of the 1980s around ideas of democratisation and human rights. Most upcoming organisations tried to unite activists irrespective of their nationalities. National parties were closely connected with 'pure political' (democratic) organisations and were often headed by the same leaders. Their programmes declared citizenship for all those living on the territory of would-be republics. Inclusive nationalism at this stage was caused by a number of factors. In some regions, the informal movement, including national parties, stemmed from the dissident movement of the 1970s which was based on the idea of individual human rights rather than group rights. In other cases, the leaders of ethno-national movements strove to get support for their nationalist slogans from other ethnic groups, living on the same territory. Sometimes, the devotion to a local community (an incompleteness in ethno-genesis) influenced the delay in ethno-national mobilisation.

Certainly, associations and joint ethno-national organisations with opposing and competitive aims were weak and were doomed to a rapid disintegration. However, from time to time, the confrontation between old 'communist' elites, which had stayed in power, and new 'democratic' parties promoted cooperation between competing ethno-national organisations. These attempts included the creation of electoral clubs to support non-communist candidates in the parliamentary elections of 1989 and 1990; the formation of small democratic factions in the republican Supreme Soviets in 1990; and the coalition of democratic and national organisations under the slogans of 'democratisation' and the re-election of the Communist republican leadership, which supported the *coup* in August 1991. None of the coalitions of the ethno-national organisations and movements in the republics, except Dagestan, declared conflict settlement to be among their goals. However, they created the environment, a workshop for 'interactive problem-solving', which fostered negotiations and personal contact among leaders of competing ethno-national organisations that, in turn, positively influenced conflict resolution (see Chapter 6 in this volume). The role of the 'third party' was usually played by leaders of other ethnic associations.[4]

The associations of new political parties of different ethnic groups had an additional impact on conflict settlement. Fears that the opposition could unite on the democratic platform and challenge the former communist elites stimulated official leaders to search for a compromise on such issues as the ethnic 'representative-ness' of power structures and control over resources. The proposal of the Congress of Peoples of Dagestan to elect parliament according to ethnic quotas and to provide for the rotation of power structures was reflected in the 1994 Constitution of Dagestan and its electoral law. The parity of ethnic groups in the power structures of Adygeya, Karachaevo-Cherkesia and Kabardino-Balkaria became a compromise among acting officials.[5]

Sociological surveys showed that a significant part of the population in the North Caucasian republics supported such an approach. During an all-North Caucasian survey in 1996, 54.4 per cent of the surveyed people in Adygeya were satisfied with how their ethnic groups were represented in the legislative branch of power and 53.6 per cent evaluated the 'representative-ness' of executive power positively. In Dagestan, it was 37.9 and 35 per cent, respectively, in Ingushetia 63 and 59.8 per cent, in Kabardino-Balkaria 55.2 and 50.8 per cent, in Karachaevo-Cherkesia 50.0 and 43.8 per cent, and in North-Ossetia 55.2 and 53.2 per cent.[6] The balance in the political 'representative-ness' of ethnic groups and some degree of public consensus testified to the realisation of some forms of consociational democracy in the republics.[7]

The consensus among ethnic elites resulted in attempts to redefine the notion of nationhood; although an ethnic approach still dominated, it is possible to find signs of a transfer to a civic, inclusive nationalism in the North Caucasian republics. Both notions of a 'Dagestani people' and 'Dagestani peoples' are present in the Constitution of Dagestan. 'The people of Kabardino-Balkaria' are mentioned along with the 'Kabardin people' and the 'Balkar people' in the Constitution of Kabardino-Balkaria. Although a mixture of approaches has dominated in political discourse, transition away from an ethnic notion of nationalism is important for conflict transformation and the construction of regional identities.

The 'Common Caucasian Home'

The idea of the 'Common Caucasian Home' is the essence of a common Caucasian identity. This identity is also based on common values, beliefs and traditions. Moreover, these traditions formed around the idea of conflict resolution and mediation. An ethnic and religious mosaic, the scarcity of resources as well as the preservation of primitive forms of political and economic life, especially in the mountains of the Caucasus, often led to conflict. These conflicts could last a very long time, considering the Caucasian terrain, the use of primitive weapons and the roughly equal balance of capabilities, which did not allow one party to win overall and establish a new political regime. In these conditions, the peoples of the Caucasus elaborated rules to mediate conflicts via meetings of the elders from warring tribes, the invitation of third-party mediators, people's diplomacy and many other elements of pre-modern conflict resolution techniques. To prevent conflict, many traditions were established like, for example, sending children to grow up in a neighbouring tribe, hospitality for travellers, protection even for enemies if they came to the house, blood revenge, and others.

During the 1990s, there were several attempts to create regional organisations, with the final goal of creating a 'Common Caucasian Home'. All these organisations have defined the boundaries of this house differently, some of them considered it to be only the North Caucasus; others included Transcaucasian states. The reasons for this stemmed from recent Caucasian conflicts and reflected alliances which developed over centuries or under the pressure of current political conditions.[8]

The North Caucasian level: traditionalism as a regional ideology

There were several attempts to create cooperative movements at the level of new political leaders as well as among the official elites of the North Caucasian republics and administrative regions of Russia. Among them only the Confederation of Mountain Peoples of the Caucasus (CMPC) created in the summer of 1989, and the North Caucasian Economic Association of Local Councils and Executive Bodies of the Regions of the North Caucasus (the Economic Association) founded in the summer of 1991, have worked for a relatively long time and influenced conflict resolution in the region.

The main objective of the CMPC, incorporating sixteen national movements, was defined as the coordination of activities for solving the problems of 'small' Caucasian peoples, namely, (1) inter-ethnic conflicts (providing conditions for negotiations between the confronting sides), (2) political lobbying (for solving the problems of the oppressed peoples, enhancing the prestige of national movements at the regional and federal levels, etc.) and (3) assisting the cultural integration of the North Caucasian peoples.

The sphere of CMPC activity was limited from the very beginning. First, the competition among ethno-national movements at a republican level influenced the activities of competing ethnic movements in the CMPC: if Adygean (Kabardin, Cherkess, Adygean, Abazin) and Ossetian national movements defined the CMPC's actions, Karachaev, Balkar and Ingush leaders participated in the CMPC round tables only from time to time. Another reason for the unequal participation was central federal policy, specifically the Federal Rehabilitation Law, which was approved in 1991 and guaranteed territorial rehabilitation. The national movements of the oppressed peoples considered the federal centre the main and most powerful ally in achieving their purposes. The federal centre, in turn, made every effort to destroy the CMPC, which expressed support for Chechnya's demand for independence.

Secondly, the covert struggle of the different blocs for the leadership of the CMPC (e.g. between Adygeans and Vainakhians, Chechens and Ingush), the contradictory objectives of national movements and the personal ambitions of leaders had circumscribed the range of the CMPC's major programme guidelines. The CMPC as well as the other cooperative associations was in fact used by its members to defend the interests of their ethnic groups: e.g. Ingush hoped to use the CMPC to make Ossetians recognise their rights to territorial rehabilitation; Ossetians, in turn, strived to repel Ingush territorial claims. Chechens, who were interested in support for their national aspirations, considered the CMPC a 'first step' to independence for the Caucasus.

Thirdly, the consolidation of the CMPC became possible due to external factors: Georgian policy towards South Ossetia and Abkhazia as well as Russian policy towards Chechnya. This factor defined the geographic boundaries of cooperation. For example, the CMPC did not accept the membership of Svan and Megrel organisations (western Georgian subethnic groups) which, in turn, influenced the transition of Abkhazian-Georgian tensions to military actions in 1992–93.

Despite all the internal controversies, the CMPC provided the mechanism for negotiations in ethnic conflicts in all North Caucasian republics. The inability of the CMPC to settle the Ossetian–Ingush conflict was conditioned by the fact that this military conflict developed as a conflict between the Ingush national movement and the official leadership of North-Ossetia, which had had no personal contact or grounds for negotiations. The Ossetian national movement failed to halt the development of the conflict, as (1) it was involved mainly in the long-running Ossetian–Georgian conflict and (2) it maintained an unofficial status that prevented it from having any influence on the North-Ossetian authority. Besides which, after the approval of the Rehabilitation Law, Ingush leaders preferred to appeal to Moscow directly, and did not participate in regional organisations.

The CMPC was successful in initiating the negotiations between the national movements of mountain peoples and the Cossack Hosts in the South of Russia (they are dispersed through Rostov, Stavropol and Krasnodar territorial units, as well as in national republics of the North Caucasus). 'Round tables' managed tensions between Cossacks and 'Caucasians' in the Caucasus in 1993–94.

The idea of the Caucasus as a Common Home for Cossacks and mountain peoples provided the basis for their cooperation. Traditionalism (using the traditional methods of conflict resolution among peoples in the Caucasus and foster-ing the ideas of common history and roots) became a peculiar analogue of nationalism at the regional level, and it possessed the main features of national-ism, i.e. heedfulness of a common past, hopes for the future, and a specific role for the poly-ethnic Caucasus as a bridge between two civilizations – Muslim and the Christian, between the West and the East.

Despite the popularity of the idea, the common Congress of the Peoples of the North Caucasus had been postponed several times. Pressure from the Russian federal centre, which feared the strengthening of separatist tendencies in the Caucasus, was one of main influencing factors. Traditionalism and the appeal to the past also resulted in the failure of the initiative: the shadows of the Caucasian War against Russia in the nineteenth century to a great extent con-tributed to the failure of this initiative. The decrease in popular support for the political movements led to a situation where the initiative naturally expired.

The contradictions and competition among national movements speeded the decline of the CMPC. Besides, the CMPC failed to elaborate common con-structive approaches to the Caucasian Federation. The idea of Caucasian unity outside the Russian Federation, which was proposed by the Chechen leadership, exacerbated the internal tensions in the CMPC; although many peoples criticised Russian policy towards the Caucasus and the military intervention in Chechnya, few in the North Caucasus supported the idea of independence from Russia. However, the declarations to build a united Caucasus outside Russia resulted in a situation whereby the Russian leadership began to consider any cooperative movements created without its sanction as a threat to Russian interests in the Caucasus and undertook actions to destroy such cooperative movements. The transformation of the population's political activity to the economic sphere also influenced the decline of the CMPC during 1995–96.

The federal centre itself tried to use the idea of a common Caucasian iden-tity and initiated several cooperative organisations. The North Caucasian Democratic Congress, the Assembly of the Peoples of the Caucasus, several round tables of representatives of ethno-national parties were held under the aegis of the Nationality Soviet of the Russian Supreme Soviet (1993) and the Ministry for National Affairs and Regional Policy between 1993 and 1995. However, these attempts enjoyed little, if any, support in the region, and their impact on conflict resolution was insignificant. They incorporated small and unknown organisations, the leaders of which hoped to increase their status at local and regional levels through their participation and federal financial support. An uncohesive and unclear Russian policy towards the Caucasus forced national movements to keep away from the Federal centre, which had enjoyed their support in 1989–91.

The North Caucasian Economic Association of the Local Councils and Executive Bodies of the Caucasian Regions reflected, primarily, the idea of the geographic and economic unity of the region. The Association did not consider conflict settlement a central objective of its activities. Members of the Association have adhered to the principle of non-intervention in 'internal' affairs and the refusal of mutual territorial claims.[9] However, the Association contributed to conflict settlement in the Caucasus where many ethnic groups were divided by administrative boundaries. Joint economic activities and project development might create an economic basis for the development of a supra-ethnic, Caucasian unity.

The Caucasian community

One more level of Caucasian cooperation is the unity of the Caucasus on both sides of the Caucasian range. In recent years, this idea has developed from pure declarations of the Common Caucasian Home breaking away from Russia (the role of the new integrating centre in such a 'home' was assigned to either Tbilisi or Grozny) to an elaborated concept considering cooperative institutions and regional ideology.

Alexander Kukhianidze, a Georgian political scientist, proposed, for example, the model of 'Caucasio-central' democracy (Kukhianidze 1995). In his opinion, inter-Caucasian relationships should be based on the ideology of centrism, counting on 'reaching mutually acceptable decisions'. This principle could become 'the Caucasian reply to the globalisation and separatism that destroy a national state from the top and from the bottom'; it would reflect 'modern tendencies in state inter-connections: the formation of regional democratic communities'. The structure of this cooperation should include an all-Caucasian two-chamber Parliament, in which one chamber would incorporate national authorities (three Caucasian states and Russia); the other would join representatives from autonomous republics, regions of South Russia and national minorities. In Kukhianidze's opinion, the right to veto for both chambers would have to guarantee the balance of national and local interests. It might resolve tensions between authorities of Transcaucasian states and Russia, on the one hand, and state, local authorities and national minorities, on the other. The model should also include some executive bodies as well as regional peacekeeping forces created 'not on the basis of nationality', that could be used only in the case of ethnic conflicts or natural disasters.

Obviously, however, the realisation of this model would face significant problems, which were not considered in the scheme. For example, it would be difficult to elaborate norms for representation: should Russian or Armenian minorities in every subject of the Caucasus be represented in the Parliament? Also, who can be considered national minorities? The combination of representatives from state-like autonomous republics and a part of the population (national minorities) would inevitably produce tensions. Beginning the discussion of such issues, however, would promote the development of this initiative.

In 1998, several attempts to organise the Meetings of the Heads of the Caucasian States, Republics and Regions were undertaken. However, this cooperative initiative was short-lived. Several factors influenced the inability to move towards stable regional cooperation. Modern Caucasian conflicts weakened the cooperative potential. The participation of external actors (Russia, Turkey, the international community) and their competition for influence in the region exacerbated tensions among Caucasian states and peoples. The contradiction of international approaches to state sovereignty (self-determination versus the inviolability of state boundaries) also influenced centrifugal tendencies in the Caucasus. Joint economic projects, which could promote peace in the future, have resulted in competition for foreign investment and for the pipeline itinerary from the Caspian Sea. Besides, fearing the recognition of sovereign status for their autonomous republics, the Transcaucasian states are not ready to participate equally with representatives of minorities and local republics authorities.

The current situation in the Caucasus

Excluding Chechnya, the current situation in the Caucasus can be best described by the formula 'no peace, no war.' The unstable balance might be easily broken.

Internal conditions

At present, most conflicts in the Caucasus are frozen. The implementation of specific forms of consociational democracy could settle ethnic tensions in autonomous republics of the North Caucasus. Ethnic cleansing along with the separation of conflicting groups by a third-party intervention stopped conflicts in North-Ossetia, Georgia and Azerbaijan, although inter-ethnic peace there might turn into a new conflict at any time.

In the North Caucasus, both the major tendencies of a return to the confrontation between the ethno-national movements and the transition to more stable forms of consociational democracy, may come about with almost equal probability. The realisation of one of them will depend on the combination of many factors: the ability of the federal centre and local authorities to overcome socio-economic crisis; the development of cooperative institutions and rules accepted by all of the major political actors; the openness of the decision making process, especially in conflict regions; and the transfer of significant power to the local level.

The East Caucasian region has the most unfavourable economic, social and demographic conditions in comparison with other parts of the Caucasus. The Ossetian–Ingush conflict led to the ethnic cleansing of the Ingush population from North-Ossetia, but Ingush hope to return to their houses in the future. The federal centre might solve this problem by buying the properties, but owing to the corruption at different levels, the population itself has not received a significant part of any aid. In Dagestan, consensus among major ethnic groups on power distribution and ethnic quotas in the government and parliament was confirmed in the 1994 Constitution. The Russian wars against Chechnya (1994–96 and 1998 onwards), although preventing the development of other conflicts, have also threatened the stability of the region in the long run.

Although socio-economic conditions in the West Caucasus are more favourable, preconditions for new ethnic mobilisation are also preserved in Kabardino-Balkaria and Karachaevo-Cherkesia. These republics failed to elaborate their own models of ethnic representation in power structures, and disputes among ethnic elites arise from time to time. These disputes can lead to the mass mobilisation of ethnic groups, as happened, for example, in Karachaevo-Cherkesia after the 1997 presidential elections, when a Karachaev representative won. After numerous Abazin and Cherkess protest meetings, the federal authority annulled the results of the elections. In Adygeya, the political dominance of the titular ethnic group guaranteed by the Constitution has led to tensions between Adygeans and Russians, which numerically dominate the republic.

In the Transcaucasian states, the 'freezing' of some conflicts resulted from the fact that the central governments of Georgia and Azerbaijan *de facto* lost control over republics. This situation can easily turn into inter-ethnic conflict again. For example, the central government and political forces in Georgia are not ready to recognise the federal structure of the Georgian state (this provoked conflicts in the 1990s); in turn, the Abkhazian and South-Ossetian governments have insisted on independent status, after the 'victory' and expulsion of the Georgian population. The fragile balance might be easily broken if the central governments try to restore control by using military forces.

External powers

The activities of external powers have also helped preserved the 'no peace, no war' situation. First of all, however, it is very difficult in some cases to define 'external factors'. Whether Russia, for example, should be considered an external or internal factor in the Caucasus, remains a question. Politically and geographically the North Caucasus is a part of the Russian Federation. Should the participation of North Caucasians in Abkhasian–Georgian and Georgian–Ossetian conflicts be considered part of Russian official Caucasian policy? In turn, how should the leaders of the Transcaucasian states involved in direct negotiations with political elites of North Caucasian republics of Russia be considered? How should the participation in conflicts of officers of the former Soviet (now Russian) army who have stayed in the Caucasus, and whom the local authorities have continued to consider a reliable help in all situations, be considered? Could this explain the involvement of Russian military forces in inter-ethnic conflict and political struggle in the Transcaucasus (e.g. Georgia in 1992)?

Frozen conflicts in the Caucasus, in many respects, result from the uncertainty of a transitional phase. The relationships among neighbouring countries and peoples, which became 'foreign' in 1991, are, in many respects, defined by common historical experiences, common values, ethnic ties between peoples of the North Caucasus and the Transcaucasus (Abkhazs and Adygeans, Ossetians, Avars, Lezgins, etc.), and even personal contacts among the members of the Communist Party Central Committee Politburo (Boris Yeltsin, Eduard Shevardnadze and Heydar Aliev).

Meanwhile, the disintegration of the Soviet Union, led to the involvement of other countries in the region after two centuries of the Russian domination, mainly neighbouring Turkey and Iran, which had actively participated in Caucasian politics for centuries. The ethnic proximity of Turks and Turkic language-speaking Caucasian peoples makes other ethnic groups fear Turkey's involvement in regional affairs. Russia, where about twenty Turkic language-speaking peoples live, is apt to see Turkey's turn to the North as *malice prepense*.

Western countries that had abstained from active involvement in the region's affairs for a long time began to show some interest in the region – from the supervision of peacekeeping operations (currently fulfilled by Russian military forces under the supervision of the United Nations in Abkhazia and of the OSCE in Karabakh) to the oil potential of the region.[10]

Only the West has not got a negative image among peoples in the Caucasus because of its traditional remoteness. It could have promoted peace in the region. However, the West does not seem to be ready to invest resources in peace making and peace building processes in the Caucasus. Criticising Russian unilateral involvement, the West carefully avoids getting involved in operations, as in the Balkans.

Considering the existing contradictions between the right to self-determination and inviolability of borders, the West would be in a difficult position to try and define its policy towards the Caucasus. All parties in Caucasian conflicts have different expectations from external interventions: some talk about the right to self-determination, others about the inviolability of borders. Georgian and Azeri governments are seeking external support to restore control over rebellious autonomous regions. Karabakh and Abkhazia, in turn, hope for recognition of their independent status, having insisted that 'the legacy of newly independent states like all over the world are based only on the empire past' (Katz 1996: 29).[11] Until now, judging by events in Somalia or Rwanda, the West, and the international community as a whole, has no solution for weak or failed states if these states are not in the zone of someone's strategic interests.

External powers have essentially influenced conflict development (in both escalation and management) not only, and not so much, by their direct policies towards the Caucasus, but also, and mainly, owing to the expectations of Caucasian peoples. Caucasians have traditionally considered themselves as living at the crossroads of civilisations and, thus, are the focus of attention for the rest of the world; this myth has fostered both ethno-nationalism and region-alism. The image of traditional competition between Russia, Turkey and Iran overcomes its real potential. Political elites in the Transcaucasian states are apt to see discrepancies of interests in terms of the continuation of the Cold War between Russia and 'the West' and try to use 'domino-logic' in their foreign policy decisions. Perceptions of external powers have influenced the political behaviour of Caucasian elites, sometimes more than real policies and actions.

A pluralistic security community in the Caucasus

A few will argue that peace in the Caucasus can be achieved only by the partici-pation of Caucasians in peace building. Initiating peacekeeping and peace making operations, external forces are able to stop a violent conflict but not to resolve it. External interventions might even aggravate conflict in the future because they often support mutual suspicions that the external forces are bias in favour of the opposite side.

Attempts to resolve any particular conflict in the Caucasus will have limited success. Owing to the ethnic proximity of many ethnic groups, often living in separated territories, the Caucasus demands an all-in-one treatment rather than a single operation in a particular zone. The Caucasus really needs to be inte-grated into a pluralistic security community (Deutsch *et al.* 1957). Although in many respects the decade of development of modern cooperative organisations was an unsuccessful experience, it showed that regional integration is not as utopian as it first seemed.

On the basis of an in-depth analysis of ten historical cases, both successful and failed security communities, Karl Deutsch defined two conditions essential for the development of pluralistic security communities, namely, the compat-ibility of major values and mutual responsiveness. Both of these conditions have existed in traditional but not political life in the Caucasus. Despite relig-ious, ethnic, economic and political tensions, as well as numerous deadly conflicts throughout history, the Caucasus has demonstrated adherence to a common identity and common values. Sharing democratic values might strengthen the 'compatibility of common values'. Mutual responsiveness has been historically characteristic of the Caucasus, and is one of the major ele-ments of traditional cultures. Although it would be difficult to construct them in the Caucasus, considering the socio-economic and political situation in the region, a move in this direction would have a good chance of success (Deutsch *et al.* 1957: 123–132).

Five other conditions, which Deutsch designated as 'helpful' for the development of pluralistic security communities, might be created in the Caucasus. Among these conditions are the expectation of joint economic reward, a wide range of mutual transactions, the broadening of elites, social communications links, and greater population mobility (Deutsch 1957: 133–154).[12]

Owing to the recent common past, 'social communications links' and the common language, which is not a necessary but is a useful precondition, are a positive legacy of the Soviet period. Some of these communications links are broken as a result of conflicts; others often become the reasons for complaints and considered 'foreign interventions . These links have to be redefined to provide 'effective channels of communication both horizontally and vertically'. Caucasian traditions might work well in favour of such development.

The 'expectation of joint economic reward' has already demonstrated its power for conflict settlement: oil projects in Azerbaijan and oil transportation has provided real conditions for the ceasefire in Karabakh, and for improving the attitudes of Georgians to Azeris living in eastern Georgia. At the same time, projects implemented in such a way that they would benefit only several ethnic groups might foster a rise in new competitions and grievances. For example, an oil pipeline built round Armenia might cause the situation in Karabakh to deteriorate. A variant of regional economic cooperation like the North Caucasian Economic Association, but including Transcaucasian states, might become the first step to economic growth via a 'wide range of mutual transactions'.

Currently, mutual transactions in the Caucasus mainly exist only at the level of individuals involved in shuttle trading in the territory devastated by conflicts and war. Economic ties in the former Soviet Union were developed without the consideration of regional benefits, therefore the economic ties of factories in the remaining industrial complexes were orientated outside the region. The Caucasus has to develop new economic ties within the region, using a traditional division of labour. Considering the current lack of financial resources and instruments, these ties might be developed in the form of state insured barter.

Economic development and cooperation might foster 'greater population mobility'. The collapse of the economy in the region has led to a situation where many Caucasians have moved to Russia in search of jobs and education. Economic projects might create possibilities for finding work without leaving the Caucasus.

The 'broadening of elites' is another element helpful for constructing a security community. It implies two processes – the inclusion of representatives from broad range of ethnic groups into management as well as a transfer of power and responsibilities to local authorities (at the level of small districts and even villages, when considering the size of ethnic communities in the Caucasus). North Caucasian republics are making the first steps towards the realisation of consociational democracy. These attempts, along with the essential decentralisation of power, have to be continued.

Cooperation, external powers and future peace in the Caucasus

Although the Caucasus has the preconditions and a shared regional identity for being 'successfully integrated', it seems not to have the other important element for 'constructing' regionalism and cooperation – political entrepreneurs. Obviously, only one group – current or future political elites – may be considered possible candidates. Meanwhile, the 1990s revealed that Caucasian politicians seem not to be ready for the essential self-limitation and laborious search for compromise, without which the realisation of any model of the regional, and especially the Caucasian, community is impossible. Caucasian historians have treated the common history in different ways and promoted negative images of neighbouring peoples. The socio-economic situation in the region may be described as devastation. In such conditions, the policy of the international community towards conflict settlement in the Caucasus and Caucasian integration becomes of greater importance.

Michael Brown has given several reasons why outsider powers should care about ethnic war, even though these wars do not create direct threats to their strategic interests (Brown 1993). Ethnic war 'poses a direct challenge to important international norms of behaviour', they create 'chain reaction effects', and the problem of refugees is among them. The international community, and not only neighbouring states, might be interested in a policy promoting peace in the Caucasus. Support for integrating efforts could be one of the main applications of such policy.

Countries involved in Caucasian affairs (the West, Russia, Turkey and Iran) should coordinate their political and economic activities and avoid fostering competition among the Caucasian elites. Cooperative efforts are in need of technological and information support about experience and best practice in resolving problems and tensions as they arise. Considering the necessity of multi-level integration, the support of non-governmental sector networks might be an essential element of international assistantship.

During the past decade, the political elites in the autonomous regions of the North Caucasus began moving towards consociational forms of democracy. For many reasons, however, this tendency is weak and controversial. The governments need special expertise and help in the development of consociational democracy in developing countries. This expertise might be implemented in many other regions. The idea of all-Caucasian integration, arising difficulties and successes should be discussed widely during international conferences on regional problems. At the same time, local politicians and political scientists should get the opportunity to study world experience on relevant issues.

Obviously, however, Caucasian integration will be necessary for several decades to come or even more. But this approach to peace development in this region has no alternatives.

NOTES

1 There were no unique rules or criteria in the decision to confer autonomous status. Sometimes, this decision by the Central Communist Party Committee was defined by the successful or unsuccessful actions of an ethnic cadre, sometimes for other political reasons (the autonomous regions of oppressed peoples between 1943 and 1956, the change of Karelia's status, etc.). Different statuses in the hierarchy provided a different degree of control over resources (primarily, control over the regional economy) and welfare distribution.

2 The first wave was a rise in nationalism in the Caucasus at the beginning of the twentieth century.

3 SMEs were usually republican or joint republican-central property.

4 The method of the 'interactive problem-solving workshop' was introduced by Herbert Kelman (see, for example, Kelman 1991). A significant difference with the Caucasian situation is that leaders of ethno-national parties developed or used conflict resolution techniques themselves (without any training or third-party intervention), on the basis of Caucasian traditions.

5 The Congress of Peoples of Dagestan was elected by the representatives of national movements on 24 October 1992 on the basis of an ethnic quota which reflected the ethnic composition in the republic: Avars, Kumyks, Lezgins and Dargins got seven mandates, Laks and Tabasarans five, Chechens three, Tats two, and two mandates were reserved for Cossacks. The federalisation of Dagestan, which was supported by the Kumyks, Lezgins and Nogays, became the most controversial issue for this cooperative movement.

6 In Adygeya, 22.5 per cent thought that the peoples of the republic were disproportionally ('unjustly') represented in administrative bodies and 21.8 per cent said the same about representative bodies of power, in Dagestan it was 28.6 and 31 per cent, respectively, in Ingushetia 24.4 and 22.8 per cent, in Kabardino-Balkaria 20.4 and 22.9 per cent, in Karachaevo-Cherkesia 25.6 and 32.5 per cent and in North- Ossetia 21 and 21.7 per cent, respectively (Khoperskaya 1997: 221–222).

7 Lijphart introduced the notion of consociational democracy as 'particularly suitable for the governance of plural societies, that is societies which are deeply divided by religious, ideological, linguistic, regional, cultural or ethnic differences'. Consociational democracy is defined in terms of two essential principles, executive power-sharing and a high degree of autonomy for the all segments, and two helpful principles, proportionality and the minority veto (Bogdanor 1991:137).

8 A variety of approaches were characteristic for the Caucasus at the beginning of the twentieth century. 'The Alliance of United Mountain Peoples of the North Caucasus'; 'the South-Eastern Alliance of the Cossack hosts, Mountain Peoples of the Caucasus and Free Steppe Peoples', 'the Transcaucasian *Seim*'; 'the Republic of the Union of Mountain Peoples of the Caucasus'; 'the Tersk People's Republic' and other attempts to realise the idea of a Common Caucasian Home after the February Revolution of 1917 proposed different forms of political and geographic unity for the Caucasus.

9 The official leadership of Ingushetia has recognised the moratorium on territorial rehabilitation, but has insisted on the complete fulfilment of the Law on Rehabilitation.

10 The population and political elites of the Caucasus do not distinguish between western countries because the existing policy of the West towards the Caucasus seems united in comparison with policy towards conflicts in the former Yugoslavia. Only during voting on the Karabakh problem in the OSCE in 1994 did France vote against the condemnation of Armenia. But this case has not influenced the united image of the West.

11   Mark Katz has researched this problem for other cases of newly independent states (Katz 1996: 29).
12   Conditions such as 'the necessity of core areas and their capability' (Deutsch *et al.* 1957: 137), which was more appropriate in a 'pure realist world' before significant changes in international environment, has been omitted. Although until now foreign policy has reflected a realist approach, it is not only this approach that defines international relations. European integration testifies that the security community is possible without core areas. Two conditions here have also been conflated, namely 'superior economic growth' and the 'expectation of joint economic rewards', because, in my opinion, these are two successive stages of one process. The 'compatibility of major values' condition and the 'distinctive way of life' which Deutsch proposed to consider differently, implying again the specific Cold War situation of a different economic and political life between the East and the West, have also been joined as one condition (Deutsch *et al.* 1957: 134).

REFERENCES

Bogdanor, V. (1987), *The Blackwell Encyclopaedia of Political Institutions* (Oxford).
Bogdanor, V. (ed.) (1991), *The Blackwell Encyclopaedia of Political Science* (Oxford).
Brown, M. E. (1993), 'Causes and implications of ethnic conflict', in M. Brown (ed.), *Ethnic Conflict and International Security* (Princeton).
Calhoun, C. (1993), 'Nationalism and Ethnicity', *Annual Review of Sociology*, 19, 227–228.
Deutsch, K., S. Burrell, R. Kann, M. Lee, M. Lichterman, R. Lindgren, F. Loewenheim and R. Van Wagenen (1957), *Political Community and the North Atlantic Area. International Organisation in the Light of Historical Experience* (Princeton).
Katz, M. (1996), 'Collapsed empires', in C. A. Crocker and F. O. Hampson with P. Aall (eds), *Managing Global Chaos: Sources of and Responses of International Conflict* (Washington, DC).
Kelman, H. (1991), 'Interactive problem solving: the uses and limits of a therapeutic model for the resolution of international conflicts', in V. Volkan, D. Julius and J. Montville (eds), *The Psychodynamics of International relationships*, II (Lexington, MA), 147–152.
Khoperskaya, L.(1997), 'Developing legitimate notion of ethnos as a law subject in the North Caucasus', in l. Khoperskaya, *Developing the Relationship Between the Center and Regions in Russia: From Conflict to Consensus Search* (Moscow).
Kukhianidze, A. (1995), 'Caucaso-central conception of democracy', *Nauchnaya mysl Kavkaza* (Tblisi), 4, 66–72.

10

Bringing culture back into a concept of rationality: state–society relations and conflict in post-socialist Transcaucasia

Barbara Christophe

RECENTLY, THE VAST number of contributions to the vivid debate on 'ethnic' violence have been classified according to their underlying theoretical assumptions (Brubaker and Laitin 1998). Approaches which follow the culturalistic turn of sociology are counterpoised with more conventional concepts, based on the premises of rational choice theory. But the constant failure to relate empirical studies to one of these competing models has revealed the confusing ambivalence of the discourse. To analyse the rational strategies of ethnic entrepreneurs, who are suspected of having an interest in the provocation of inter-group conflict as a means of strengthening their position in intra-group competition for power, does not necessarily mean ignoring the cultural logic of mobilisation. A combination of elite centred top-down approaches, exposing the highly selective and functional use of ethnic symbols for rational purposes, with bottom-up approaches, drawing attention to the reasons for society's responsiveness to mobilisational efforts, thus seems to offer the most promising results.

The following attempt to read the hidden transcript of ethnic conflict in post-Soviet Transcaucasia is obliged to an intellectual tradition, that tries to reconcile culturalist and constructivist approaches with rational actor models. But at the same time it suggests a quite unorthodox way of bringing culture back into a concept of rationality. Instead of referring to cultural constraints on goal setting or manipulation of discourses as a technique of mobilisation, it introduces historically evolved and culturally embedded patterns of state–society relations as a key variable.[1] A specific mode of state building, adapted to and shaped by a culturally mediated social structure, is analysed as a crucial precondition for the proliferation of ethnic violence.

The analysis is based on five theses. Starting from the secure ground of more or less commonly accepted knowledge on conflict analysis, the chapter finishes with considerations of a rather speculative character. Owing to a lack of sufficient empirical data the chapter is confined to drawing the blueprint of an analytical framework, that may serve as a guideline for further comparative research on state collapse and state building in Transcaucasia.

The phenomenology of 'new war'

The first thesis directly contradicts assumptions which are still widespread in the literature on Transcaucasian affairs. This region is commonly analysed in terms of a naive culturalistic paradigm. Conflict and violence seem to be triggered either by the aggravation of objective ethnic grievances or by the clash of contrasting concepts of ethnic identities. The main players in the political arena appear to be collective actors – that is peoples, nations, ethnicities. These assumptions can be objected to on two levels. Firstly, it is not ethnicity, but rather the collapse of virtually all modern state structures into anarchy and lawlessness that provides the key variable in explaining the violent escalation of conflicts (Fairbanks 1995). Secondly, the stage of action is not particularly dominated by collectivities, integrated by a declared commitment to national symbols. In what Mary Kaldor termed 'new wars', it is instead necessary to deal with private actors, more or less loosely integrated by a mixture of personal ties and utilitarian considerations (Kaldor 1999). Making use of and even encouraging the dissolution of state power, these actors reap substantial profits from the removal of any kind of institutional constraint on the pursuit of self-interest at the expense of the public. The Transcaucasian mode of warfare, described in various reports from international organisations such as Human Rights Watch (Human Rights Watch 1995), provides a wide range of empirical illustrations for the validation of this thesis.

All these wars involved a permanent blurring of the distinction between organised violence for political purposes and organised crime. This statement not only refers to paramilitary groups and criminal bands, but also holds true for the so-called 'regular forces'. First, despite differences in status they all stood out for their surprisingly low degree of professionalism. Secondly, nearly all of them lacked a clear chain of command, which might have ensured a certain level of discipline. For example, in sharp contrast to the internal structure of conventional armies it is hard to find the rank of sergeant in these units, which normally serves as a crucial link between officers and common soldiers (Jones 1996). Thirdly they were typically not linked to an organised logistical system, funded by the state. The arbitrary seizing of military bases was therefore quite a common means of obtaining weapons.[2] Looting became a sheer necessity for survival. Under these conditions the combatants sooner or later turned into pre-modern brigands. All these features amounted to an effective feudalisation of warfare. Soldiers were more engaged in making money by stealing, selling their arms, dealing drugs or extorting transit fees from refugees, than in fulfilling military tasks Consequently, analyses have to account for low-intensity conflicts, marked by a clear avoidance of battles. To further complicate the situation, the state sometimes even played on these motives. For instance the Georgian government released prisoners in exchange for their agreement to take part in the Abkhazian war. Very often a further escalation of conflict was provoked by the arbitrary moves of warlords, who acted beyond political control. As a rule they took to arms when a possible solution became apparent: an example of this would be Kitovani's march towards Suchumi in August 1992 (Fuller 1993, see also Chapter 7 in this volume). Occasionally these troops even turned their weapons against what remained of the weakened state – like the Zviadists in Georgia at the peak of the Abkhasian war or Surat Huseinov in Azerbaijan, who did not hesitate to reject the government of Elchibey during a period of intense fighting in Karabakh (see Chapter 9 in this volume). The ease with which these warlords shifted their alliances (Kitovani, for example, was suspected of collaborating with the Russians as well as with the Zviadists) seems to indicate that their behaviour was not so much motivated by a dissident notion of national interest. They do not interfere with politics for political reasons, but were instead interested in the perpetuation of anarchy as an ideal precondition for realising essentially private goals.

The legacy of the weak socialist state

To replace nationalism with state collapse as the main factor behind the proliferation of violence in Transcaucasia not only provides answers, but also raises many questions. The second thesis seeks to resolve one of them. It identifies the destructive dynamic of the socialist system as the driving force behind the withering away of the post-socialist state. The notion of 'state weakness' used here refers to Jadwiga Staniszkis' distinction between the modern regulatory state, which gains strength by adhering to the rule of law, and the negative power of the socialist production state, which is based upon a destruction of autonomous regulatory mechanisms (Staniszkis 1992). The rationality of control, which motivated the destruction of society's capacity for self-regulation, condemned the state to a permanent intervention in the organisation of social and productive relations, a necessity that clearly overstretched its capabilities and thus undermined its very ability to exercise efficient control. In attempting to compensate for the ever-increasing loss of control, the socialist state was forced to seek remedy in neopatrimonial strategies of incorporating those it was unable to subordinate to its own rules into its own power structures. It thus destroyed the very notion of public interest and unintentionally opened the door for a colonisation of the state by society (Nee and Stark 1989).

In a study on Soviet Transcaucasia, Gerald Easter has shown that state building efforts in that region already in the Stalinist period relied heavily on the incorporation of clientelistic networks, integrated by personal ties and predominantly opportunistic considerations, into the chain of command (Easter 1996). From a wide range of theoretical literature, dating back to Max Weber, it is clear that the very character of patrimonial administrative structures, vesting power in persons more than in rules or offices, unavoidably weakens state capacity. Resources tend to be diverted to members of the ruling elite. Thus the tacit privatisation of the state, which ended in the total destruction of the very notion of public interest, had already started under communism. The fragmentation of power structures, so characteristic of post-socialist Transcaucasia, can be explained as the logical result of socialist techniques of exercising power, which were designed to stabilise the system in the short term, but proved to be increasingly destabilising in the long term.

The legacy of tradition

Reference to the socialist legacy of state weakness by itself suggests a far too general argument as to permit an understanding of the peculiarities of the Transcaucasian situation. Why the breakdown of the Soviet state produced a great variety of different outcomes is a question which must necessarily be addressed. The following theses are therefore based on comparisons drawn between different regions of the increasingly heterogeneous post-Soviet space. Post-socialist development in Russia, on the one hand, and in Georgia and Armenia, on the other, are contrasted first. In all cases it is necessary to address a dramatic decrease in the rule setting and enforcing capabilities of the state. But despite these similarities, the quite different strategies applied by particularistic actors in exploiting the advantages arising from the absence of institutional constraints should be noted. The Russian scene is dominated by powerful players alternatively called 'oligarchs', 'political entrepreneurs' or 'rent seekers' (Christophe 1998). All these competing labels refer to specific patterns of accumulation. Profit seeking, based upon a sober calculation of costs and benefits, is replaced with rent seeking, based on the externalisation of costs and asset stripping. The techniques applied for this purpose range from the deliberate stimulation of inflation to the spontaneous usurping of state property and the exploitation of political influence in order to obtain privileged access to economic resources and to exclude competitors from organised markets. In Transcaucasia the framework of action was shaped by a different kind of actor, engaged in a much more primitive form of accumulation. The political entrepreneur of the Russian type, which profits from the marketisation of political decisions about the redistribution of resources, is pushed into the background by the entrepreneur of the Georgian type, who reaps benefits from the dissolution of the state monopoly of violence which is promoted by inter-ethnic or civil war. Under these conditions it is the marketisation of violence which may be observed. It is the control over the privatised means of violence that was turned into a productive force, successfully exploited by means of looting, extortion or the commercialisation of a genuine public good like the procurement of protection.

It was therefore not accidental that economic activity in Georgia as well as in Armenia was concentrated around the so-called 'power ministries'. But it should be borne in mind that they did not act as representatives of the state. Even financially they were no longer dependent on the state. With the dramatic decline in revenues from taxation, they increasingly relied on so-called 'non-budgetary funds', that is, on resources accumulated by rendering services to private actors in exchange for cash (Fairbanks 1995). Three inter-related factors account for these differences and are explored below.

First, the scope of corrupt networks in Georgia, incorporated into official structures, was much wider than in other parts of the Soviet Union. To give a slight indication of scale, more than 180,000 people were tried for the abuse of official positions and the misuse of state property in Georgia between 1958 and 1972 (Gerber 1997). Control over the flow of resources was weakened to a much greater degree. Despite the fact that Georgia was among the least successful of all Union Republics in terms of economic growth rates, it showed private saving rates of twice the Soviet average (Schröder 1983). A similar pattern may be seen in the distribution of durable consumer goods. This has crucial implications for the post-socialist option of asset stripping. Owing to the diversion and diffusion of resources into a dense system of networks deeply embedded in society, strategies of asset transfer were not directed at the state as a target of first priority. Instead they were aimed at the dispossession of society as the real locus of wealth. Thus the illegal profits of pyramid schemes in Georgia were estimated to be as high as $30 million (*Georgian Chronicle* 3: 1995), thus nearly equalling the tax revenue of the Georgian State in 1994 (Gerber 1997). This imposed a quite different rationale on actors, who may be characterised as prey seekers instead of rent seekers. In contrast to rent seeking, prey seeking does not depend on the penetration of state structures. Instead it is facilitated by a war of everybody against everybody else as the ideal pretext for primitive accumulation.

Secondly those mechanisms of control that were built into the Soviet system to restrict the disintegrative effects of neopatrimonialism did not work that efficiently in the Transcaucasus. This refers primarily to the principle of *nomenklatura*, the centrally controlled appointment of cadres. While in the rest of the former Soviet Union a person's access to scarce resources and therefore their position in informal networks of exchange was determined by their status in the official power structures, Georgian career patterns revealed a quite different logic. A person's potential for networking was the crucial precondition for being recruited to positions of power, which could not have been exploited for obtaining resources otherwise (Mars and Altmann 1983). So it is the very origin of power, embedded much more directly in social status and prestige, which accounts for the Georgian deviation from the Soviet norm.

The third factor that contributed to the acceleration of institutional collapse in post-Soviet Transcaucasia was the limited ability of the socialist state to penetrate the rural periphery of society. This phenomenon manifested itself in the preservation of a multitude of informal traditional practices, dwelling behind the façade of formal institutions and inside the paradoxes of the self-subverting system. Ethnological research on rural life in Soviet Armenia (Kilbourne Matossian 1962) and Georgia (Dragadze 1988) points, for example, to the reproduction of the structures of a village economy, at least in remote areas. In large parts of both countries the brigades, as the new Soviet-style working units were called, consisted predominantly of close relatives. Even traditional patterns of distribution survived. In many cases Soviet principles of rewarding peasants could not gain a foothold. Agricultural workers were not paid according to the highly differentiated Soviet system of evaluating work, but according to social status or the amount of land they or their families brought into the collective farm (Kilbourne Matossian 1962).

These processes of informalisation did not restrict themselves to the control of resource flows. They even caught hold of the means of violence, which were manipulated and occupied by traditional actors for purposes openly contradicting the officially declared rationality of the socialist system. To give just one example – Mary Kilbourne Matossian describes the case of a collective farm, whose chairmen handed over a peasant to the NKVD for refusing to accept a negotiated marriage between his daughter and the chairman's son (Kilbourne Matossian 1962).

To summarise, the socialist legacy of state weakness is much more acute in the Transcaucasus, which had much more dramatic consequences after the implosion of the socialist system. The lingering decay of the socialist state resulted from the attempt to adapt to the conditions of self-produced complexity and modernity by relying on pre-modern modes of state building. Striving to stabilise official institutions of rule setting and rule enforcement, the Soviet elites tried to reinforce them with a dense network of more reliable personal relations. Without any institutional mechanism to assure against opportunistic behaviour, the Soviet bureaucracy soon degenerated into a neopatrimonial structure that was integrated by private purpose. The very notion of impersonal rules, claiming validity independent of the context and the status of the persons involved, was destroyed. Thus there was no space left for a concept of public interest, capable of imposing constraints on particularistic actors' strategies of enhancing power, prestige and wealth at the expense of the society as a whole.

Moreover socialism in Transcaucasia was somewhat special. State structures were not only re-embedded in neopatrimonial structures of clientelistic relations; these clientelistic networks were grounded in traditional institutions, much more resilient to the detraditionalising interventions of the Soviet state. Consequently it is necessary to examine three and not two different patterns of institutionalising rules in that specific region, stabilising and subverting each other at the same time. These more complex forms of hybridisation accounted for the notorious failure of central efforts to cope with the disintegrative effects of the tacit privatisation of control. Large sections of society, especially in the country-side, were fenced off against the corrective intervention of the socialist state. At the same time these loopholes allowed for a more or less uncontrollable accumulation of resources, which were fed into clientelistic networks. Thus these networks not only confined themselves to the function of intermediary between centre and periphery, but also obtained a greater degree of independence as gate-keepers, controlling not only resources, but access to resources as well.

Nationalism and clientelism

Referring to a more specific notion of institutions, which emphasises the abstract and impersonal character of the underlying rules, we can analyse the destructive dynamics of the socialist system in terms of an ongoing process of deinstitu-tionalisation. This perspective leads to a conceptualisation of transformation that differs in quite crucial aspects from the common use of that term. What seems to be at stake is not the transition from plan to market, from one-party rule to democracy or the replacement of previously applied mechanisms of steering and controlling social relations with more effective ones. It is not even the intro-duction of new rules designed to deal with new forms of conflict. The central task can be defined in much more radical terms as the institutionalisation of rules as such, which are understood as guidelines of action independent of context variables (Lepsius 1996).

This should aid precision in defining the factors accounting for the failure or success of transformation. Once again the problem will be approached by means of comparison, but now focusing on the Baltic and the Transcaucasus, the two regions in the post-Soviet space that mark extreme poles of contrast with regard to progress in institutionalising an effective post-socialist order. Despite striking similarities – both regions proved to be exceptional in terms of the strength of their national movements and both were among the first to break the Communist Party's monopoly of power and to secede from the Soviet Union – they represent quite different models of development. The remarkable success in the Baltics (Christophe 1997a) stands out in sharp contrast to the gloomy perspectives of the Transcaucasian region, which suffers from the violent escalation of conflicts, political uncertainty and economic decline (Hunter 1994). This would seem to reject interpretations which refer to nation-alism as a key for understanding post-Soviet conflicts. Producing quite different outcomes in different contexts, nationalism is far too ambiguous a category to fit into the role of 'independent variable'. But the fact that it plays various roles does not necessarily mean that it plays no significant role at all. Modifying the previous argument, it is therefore now suggested that nationalism should be treated as a dependent variable.

From a theoretical perspective, it is the Baltic case that raises less suspicion. In seeking the preconditions of successful modernisation, historical sociology has always pointed to the enormous integrative potential of nationalism, which promises to rebuild society on a new foundation. The rise of national consciousness transforms the very nature of social integration and thus contributes to the emergence of new trust generating mechanisms. Instead of being confined to the boundaries of face-to-face communities and resulting from the everyday experience of concrete social interaction, trust is now based on the belief of belonging to a community of people who share the same values. It is this notion of generalised trust between individuals, who do not necessarily know each other, that forms the backbone of the modern nation as an imagined community (Anderson 1996).

In recalling the substantial contributions nationalism has rendered in laying the foundations of modernity, the challenge of explaining why this recipe failed to work in the Transcaucasian case needs to be met. Common sense usually points to two factors: the intensity and the content of nationalist discourse in that specific region. However, a comparison with the Baltic experience makes this argument appear less convincing. Content analysis of public debate at the peak of national awakening in Lithuania (Christophe 1997b) and Georgia (Gerber 1997) reveals that Georgian nationalists touched upon the same issues as their Lithuanian comrades in spirit. Both spoke about ethnic discrimination, the distortion of national history and memory, and the subjection to foreign rule, which had encouraged alienation and a cynical attitude towards the state. Even corruption appears to be a prominent theme in both cases. In order to find differences, it is therefore necessary to examine the structural dimension of nationalist arguments. Corruption provides a good example. In Lithuania, the debate concentrated on the incorporation of the whole society into corruptive networks as a means of undermining the moral self-esteem of the nation. This kind of understanding prepared the ground for a conceptualisation of 'nation' as a symbolic construct, which could bring about a break with the personalist logic of socialist neopatrimonalism, at least at a normative level. National revival was meant to imply a return to the principles of generalised reciprocity. To call up the memory of national glory was a means of overcoming informal practices which helped each individual member of the nation to adapt to the incentive structures of the socialist system, but which was actually devastating for the nation as a whole.

A similar way of reasoning cannot be found in the anti-corruption rhetoric of the Georgian national movement. The populist attacks of Gamsakhurdia, for example, were predominantly directed against certain sections of society, especially the urban intellectuals, who were suspected of having enjoyed privileged access to resources under socialism (Jones 1993). But the deformations which caught hold of the society as a whole due to the clientelistic mode of integration imposed on it by socialism were hardly ever mentioned. Therefore the discourse called for the restoration of a substantial form of justice instead of backing the demands for the introduction of procedural norms as a guideline for the distribution of resources. This resulted not only in a reproduction of a socialist mode of reasoning, but paved the way for a very arbitrary mode of exercising power. For example, the police chief of a provincial Georgian town, when asked to comment on the immediate aftermath of Gamsakhurdia's takeover, started to talk about a group of armed young men, totally unknown to him, who entered his police station and demanded the sudden release of prisoners as well as the handing over of money (van der Leeuw 1999).

Obviously the national movement in Georgia did not really succeed in replacing the clientelistic structures of the socialist society, which reinforced persisting traditional patterns of social integration with a modern, that is national, mode of integration, based upon procedural norms. It kept on conceptualising social relations in terms of personal ties. In sharp contrast to the internal coherence of the Popular Fronts in the Baltics, their Georgian counterpart fell into competing factions very quickly. The emerging cleavages can hardly be explained in terms of programmatic differences. Instead they were rooted in personal rivalries, for example, communists were being scattered about the whole spectrum of political organisations. Again it is the arbitrary logic of personal ties that accounts for this phenomenon. Thus, the breakaway of the Socialist Party from the coalition with the ruling Citizen Union in summer 1997 had nothing to do with programmatic differences. Instead it was the result of a violent clash of the commercial interests, represented by these parties (Kjeldsen 1999).

Thus it was the weakness and not the strength of Transcaucasian nationalism that proved to be harmful. Owing to these fundamental shortages it obviously failed to overcome the legacy of socialist neopatrimonialism. This amounts to no less than a failure in nation building. More than this – the very project of nation building was captured and aborted by particularistic actors. More or less consciously, all of them used a nationalist rhetoric as a disguise for the promotion of exclusively private goals, thus leaving no space for the articulation of a public interest, which might have otherwise served as a symbolic point of reference for an institutional breakthrough to modernity.

Stabilisation without stability

This section covers the developments in recent years. The actual situation in the Transcaucasus obviously differs from the chaotic and anarchic picture drawn above. The intensive fighting on the various battlegrounds of 'ethnic' conflict in the region has ceased. However fragile, ceasefires have proved to be quite effective. Remarkable progress in the consolidation of state power seems to contradict the explanatory model employed here, which instead points to the structural obstacles to successful state building. In an effort to account for these recent trends this section therefore concentrates on the example of Georgia, which seems to provide the most challenging provocations.

The same warlords who had benefited from the dissolution of statehood by turning violence into a productive force, re-entered the scene as supporters of a policy aimed at the restoration of a minimalist version of law and order. Having ousted President Gamsakhurdia in a strange coalition with members of the old *nomenklatura* and representatives of the privileged intelligentsia, they voluntarily ceded power to Shevardnadze. Although the former Party Secretary initially respected a kind of power sharing agreement, Shevardnadze soon took on the task of disarming his former allies. At first glance the Georgian entrepreneurs of violence thus seem to have taken part in a destructive move against the system of criminal accumulation upon which their very existence depended. This course of events poses two serious questions, which hardly appear to be answerable within the framework of the explanatory model used here. The first refers to the underlying rationality of this seemingly self-destructive decision. The second asks about the organisational mechanisms which were installed to achieve what is termed here 'stabilisation' without stability.

Common sense would probably point to a miscalculation on the part of the losers, to a lack of capability in anticipating the unintended consequences of what was meant to be only a tactical move. But such explanations unquestionably take on the perspective of the winners, who legitimised their ascent to power as a decisive move towards the consolidation of statehood and engaged in the simulation of reform to justify themselves in the eyes of their international patrons. This interpretation can be rejected on the basis of two inter-related observations.

Firstly, the system of rule established by Shevardnadze did not really mark a break with the dominant prey seeking logic. Instead it stands for the adjustment of its underlying rationality of extraction to self-produced change. The main achievement of the previous years consisted of the attraction of urgently needed grants and credits from the international donor community. Far from encouraging authentic change, the opening up of access to international aid instead assured the survival of a self-exhausting social order, that was incapable of self-reproduction and therefore highly dependent on the permanent input of external resources.

Secondly, the institutional and organisational mechanisms applied in the course of the so-called 'normalisation' were clearly reminiscent of the neopatrimonial strategies of rule that had weakened the rule setting capabilities of the Soviet state. The 'success' of the Shevardnadze regime was actually accomplished by the more than skilful combination of two classical techniques of exercising rule by a tacit feudalisation of power.[3] On the national level of horizontal power relations, relative autonomy was retained by a permanent play on internal frictions between competing groups of warlords. Shevardnadze reached a high degree of mastery in allying with one faction in order to isolate the other and thus step by step managed to eliminate all his rivals. In an attempt to prevent the accumulation of independent power resources not subverted to his control, he repeatedly reshuffled the leading positions of various state agencies. The conscious creation of a multitude of state institutions, with ambiguously defined and intermingling realms of jurisdiction, served the same purpose.[4] On the level of vertical relations of subordination a fragile hegemony at the centre was reestablished by the incorporation of local leaders into the power structure.[5] In conceding them privileged access to state controlled resources and simultaneously controlling them through the judicious manipulation of the central right to appointment, centrifugal tendencies could have been tamed, without really running the risk of penetrating the periphery and thus provoking irreconcilable resistance.

As a gatekeeper to international capital injection the centre has obviously succeeded in altering the balance of power in the informal networks of patron–client relations, which emerged in the period of unrestrained warlordism. In accordance with a consequent strategy of venality as a mode of state building it has reinvested the rents, and it has acquired in the shape of development aid, in the strengthening of its hegemony. Potential power brokers were allured to subordinate and cooperate by giving them a share in revenues as well as in the exercise of power, which additionally provided them with a vast range of opportunities for extortion. The ability to take part in looting was thus no longer dependent on the command of independent means of violence. Instead it became an officially sanctioned right that was confined to members of the state apparatus. State officials from tax inspectors and the traffic police to ministers are entitled to demand payment alternatively for the rendering of services which are officially free of charge or for their readiness to grant exemption from the enforcement of regulations, which seem to have been imposed with the sole purpose of creating opportunities for bribe-taking.[6] Heads of local administrations, which are heavily involved in the illegal transfer or export of state property, enjoy the support of the centre in the defence of their claims against rivals. The case of a west Georgian, Gamgebeli, who was more or less openly charged with both organising the smuggling of timber from the state-owned forest to Turkey and with the distribution to his clients of credits from the local budget that will never be paid back, but who nevertheless survived a vote of no confidence in the local parliament, provides an eloquent example.[7] The fact, that ministers are often engaged in business activities precisely in the sphere which they are supposed to regulate points in the same direction. Obviously the Georgian state has paid for consolidation with the total abandoning of every claim to a central feature of modern statehood: the capacity to set the rules of the game. The state even encourages the arbitrary manipulation of rules by his agents to their personal advantage as a means of ensuring the internal coherence of his power structures.

The anarchic forms of prey seeking in Georgia, that characterised the early years after independence, have thus been successfully replaced by more hierarchically organised methods, already well known from Soviet times. As in the good old days of stagnation, the institutionalisation of corruption left a bureaucracy that was only superficially integrated, more as an arbiter than an executive of power. Nevertheless the means that were employed to strengthen the state's control over of the flow of economic resources, differ significantly. State property as an institutionalised form of subordinating economics to politics was replaced by a more subtle repeal of the legally recognised institution of private property that is constantly undermined by the logic of personalistic ties. In Georgia the problem is not only restricted to the phenomenon of insider privatisation. The fact that private property is not protected against a permanent encroachment of individual state agents weighs much more heavily in this context. Enterprises belonging to clients of the ruling elites, who decide to change their affiliation and desert to the opposition camp, are frequently pushed into bankruptcy by bureaucratic 'spoon-feeding'.[8] This not only refers to the most profitable branches, where high rents are extracted, but also to less lucrative spheres of economic activity. The experience of a petty trader, whose merchandise was confiscated by the police, because he refused to agree to the price dictated by his political patron, does not seem to be exceptional.[9] In an Imeretian village the author was told, that peasants who do not belong to the mayor's clientele shrink back from land lease for fear of retaliation.[10]

The consequences of the Georgian variant of political capitalism are twofold. On the one hand every entrepreneur who wants to run a successful business is obliged to invest heavily into the preservation of personal relations with individual representatives of the state.[11] On the other hand those who adhere to these tacit laws of the Georgian market, are in exchange rewarded with a wide range of competitive advantages over their rivals. As a rule they are released from the obligation to pay tax and custom duties. These informal profit sharing agreements between entrepreneurs and state officials not only create distorted incentive structures, but also block the rational allocation of scarce resources and thus prevent economic recovery. They moreover incur high fiscal losses for a state, whose capabilities are severely weakened even in the most elementary dimension of extraction. After having incapacitated itself to a critical degree by relying exclusively on venality as a mode of state building, the central government moreover has to accept the permanent siphoning away of taxes on various levels. Local administrations have repeatedly violated legal tax sharing agreements. For many years they have simply refused to transfer the legally prescribed share of certain taxes to central bank accounts. They are able to do this without fear of sanctions for two reasons. Although also formally subordinated to central organs, with regard to such central issues like job security, tax inspectors are, as a rule, much more obliged to the representatives of local power.[12] The situation is aggravated by a striking lack of transparency in accounting procedures. Obviously the central government is not even able to determine how much of the total revenues it has actually received. Consequently it also falls victim to constant cheating on the part of individual tax inspectors.

To summarise these observations, it can thus be asserted that the ruling elite in Georgia succeeded in employing hierarchically organised corruption as a resource for the reproduction of a neopatrimonial state. But compared to the lucky times of Soviet rule these structures are very much reduced. The venal strategy applied for that purpose has not really pacified rival elites. Up to now they have only precluded the formation of a common front against the regime. The political settlement achieved under Shevardnadze was not the victory of a consolidated state over anarchy, but the accommodation of formerly autonomous prey seekers within a single state structure. In allowing them to share in the profits and prestige of the state, it incorporated their interests, which previously were represented through independent institutions, within its structures. The ability to control rested on the ability to conciliate the most powerful rival to state power. The state has thus itself become the site for conflicts among elites. Necessarily this state of affairs is of a highly fragile character. The decreasing ability to satisfy the resource hunger of the incorporated elites – either due to crisis or commitment to real reform, i.e. the efficient allocation of resources – could trigger conflict at any moment.

NOTES

1 In the development of this concept I am very much indebted to Barkey's impressive analysis of conflict and state building in Ottoman Turkey (Barkey 1994).
2 Fieldnotes, Sagarejo, 3 September 1999.
3 Compare Lachmann's (1989) analysis of divergent modes of state building in absolutist France and Britain, which reveals striking similarities with the case of present-day Georgia despite the historical distance of more than 200 years.
4 In his brilliant analysis of the dilemmas faced by national leaders of strong societies with weak states, Migdal (1988) decribes analogous strategies in terms of a 'policy of survival'.
5 The nomination of the Mingrel Otatar Patsatsia to the post of the Prime Minister in August 1993 provides just the most prominent example.
6 To cite just some of the more curious examples, minibus drivers are obliged to take an alcohol test every morning and exchange bureaux must have office space of more than 30m².
7 Fieldnotes, Baghdati, 29 September 1999 and 1 October 1999.
8 Fieldnotes, Kutaisi, 27 September 1999.
9 Fieldnotes, Kutaisi, 24 September 1999.
10 Fieldnotes, Obtscha, 4 October 1999.
11 Compare the World Bank survey of 350 enterprise managers in Georgia, cited in Kaufmann, Pradhan ans Ryterman (1998).
12 Fieldnotes, Sagarejo, 3 September 1999 and Baghdati, 5 October 1999.

REFERENCES

Anderson, B. (1996), *Die Erfindung der Nation. Zur Karriere eines folgenreichen Konzeptes*, (Frankfurt).

Barkey, K. (1994), *Bandits and Bureaucrats. The Ottoman Route to State Centralization* (Ithaca).

Brubaker, R. and D. D. Laitin (1998), 'Ethnic and nationalist violence', *Annual Review of Sociology*, 24, 423–452.

Christophe, B. (1997a), 'Nation und Nationalismus in Litauen', *Ethnos*, 5:1, 139–166.

Christophe, B. (1997b), *Staat versus Identität. Zur Konstruktion von Nation und nationalem Interesse in den litauischen Transformationsdiskursen 1987–1995* (Köln).

Christophe, B. (1998), 'Von der Politisierung der Ökonomie zur Ökonomisierung der Politik. Staat, Markt und Außenpolitik in Rußland', *Zeitschrift für Internationale Beziehungen*, 5:2, 201–240.

Dragadze, T. (1998), *Rural Families in Soviet Georgia: A Case Study in Ratscha Province* (London and New York.

Easter, G. (1996), 'Personal networks and post-revolutionary state-building. Soviet Russia reexamined', *World Politics*, 48, 551–578.

Fairbanks, C. (1995), 'The postcommunist wars', *Journal of Democracy*, 6:4, 18–35.

Fuller, E. (1993), 'New states, new armies: paramilitary forces dominate fighting in Transcaucasia', *RFE/RL Research Report on Transcaucasia*, 2:25 (3 June), 74–82.

Gerber, J. (1997), *Georgien: Nationale Opposition und kommunistische Herrschaft seit 1956* (Köln).

Human Rights Watch (1995), 'Georgia/Abkhazia. Violation of the laws of war and Russia's role in the conflict', *Human Rights Watch Arms Project*, 7:7.

Hunter, S. (1994), *The Caucasus in Transition. Nation-building and Conflict* (Washington, DC).

Jones, S. F. (1993), 'Georgia: a failed democratic transition', in I. Bremmer and R. Taras, *Nation and Politics in the Soviet Successor States* (Cambridge).

Jones, S. F (1996), 'Adventurers or commanders? Civil military relations in Georgia since independence', in C. Danopoulos and D. Zirker (eds), *Civil–Military Relations in the Soviet and Yugoslav Successor States* (Boulder, 35–52.

Kaldor, M. (1999), *New and Old Wars: Organized Violence in a Global Era* (Cambridge).

Kaufmann, D., S. Pradhan and R. Ryterman (1998), 'New frontiers in diagnosing and combating corruption', *Public Management Forum*, 4:6.

Kilbourne Matossian, M. (1962), *The Impact of Soviet Policies in Armenia* (Leiden).

Kjeldsen, S. '(1999), Georgia – a clientelist party non-system: party system theory applied to the Caucasus', *Slovo*, 11, 79–102.

Lachmann, R. (1989), 'Elite conflict and state formation in 16th and 17th century England and France', *American Sociological Review*, 54, 141–162.

Lepsius, R. M. (1996), 'Institutionalisierung und Deinstitutionalisierung von Rationalitätskriterien', *Leviathan, Sonderheft 16*, 57–70.

Mars, G. and Y. Altman (1983), 'The cultural bases of Soviet Georgia's second economy', *Soviet Studies*, 35:4, 546–560.

Migdal, J. (1988), *Strong Societies and Weak States* (Princeton).

Nee, V. and D. Stark (1989), *Remaking the Economic Institutions of Socialism: China and Eastern Europe* (Stanford).

Schröder, G. (1983), 'Transcaucasia since Stalin: the economic dimension', in R. G. Suny (ed.), *Transcaucasia, Nationalism and Social Change: Essays in the History of Armenia, Azerbaijan and Georgia* (Ann Arbor).

Staniszkis, J. (1992), *The Ontology of Socialism* (Oxford).

van der Leeuw, C. (1999), *Storm Over the Caucasus: In the Wake of Independence* (New York).

11

Reconciliation after ethnic cleansing: witnessing, retribution and domestic reform

John Borneman

WHAT ARE THE conditions that might make possible reconciliation after ethnic cleansing? This chapter addresses reconciliation in light of specific ethnic cleansings and 'ethnicisations', with a focus on the most recent example in Bosnia. It neither elaborates a specific case nor makes specific historical–cultural comparisons. The potential contribution is theoretical, specifying psycho-social terms and processes integral to reconciliation after violent conflicts. The arguments presented are therefore relevant for reconciliation after conflicts other than those analysed here, but are restricted to the extreme case of ethnic cleansing. 'Reconciliation' is defined not in terms of permanent peace or harmony, but as a project of 'departure from violence'. To reconcile is an inter-subjective process, an agreement to settle accounts that involves at least two subjects who are related in time. They are related in a temporal sense not in that they necessarily have a shared past or a shared future. Consensus about what was shared in the past or what will be shared in the future, in modern parlance a 'collective memory', is not necessary for reconciliation and its expectation may in fact awaken counterproductive drives to recover a lost whole or to produce a harmonious community. Rather, in order to reconcile, different subjects must agree only to share a present, a present that is non-repetitive (Moore 1987). To agree to a present that does not repeat requires both the creation of a 'sense of ending', of a radical break or rupture from existing relations, and the creation of a 'sense of beginning', a departure into a creative relationship marked not by cyclical or rebounding violence but by trust and care.

Traumatic loss after ethnic cleansing

After ethnic cleansing, victims, and to some extent perpetrators, are not merely engaged in a struggle for survival, for resources such as food and shelter. To find food and shelter after an ethnic cleansing is frequently no small feat, especially given that hostilities and violence continue in some form, but physical survival is a solvable problem. Much less resolvable is a problem located at a deeper, existential level: that survivors are suffering from despair, an agony or melancholy of inconsolable and inexpressible grief. Despair, if we follow Kierkegaard, does not result from an inability to live but from:

> the disconsolateness of not being able to die. The survivor's despair, then, rests not in having lived through the recent confrontation with the deaths that they witnessed (or the murders they committed) but in the fact that they themselves have not died and cannot die. What keeps the gnawing pain alive and keeps life in the pain . . . is the reason why he despairs . . . because he cannot consume himself, cannot get rid of himself, cannot become nothing. (Kierkegaard (1974 [1844]: 342)

Because most survivors cannot die, much to their consternation, they are continually confronted with the psychic, social and political tasks of dealing with the ever-present loss of those who did die. They must, in some way, attempt to recover or redeem this loss. Yet the profound loss suffered in an ethnic cleansing, the unbearable loss of loved ones and the damage inflicted on one's own standards of self, irrespective of whether one is perpetrator or victim, is never fully recoverable. Some sense of the loss continually reappears, if not in consciousness then minimally in dreams and fantasies. Because of this continuous and uncontrollable reappearance of loss, survivors remain, necessarily, in a state of melancholy, unable to detach themselves from the love-object or, as Freud would have it, prone to repetition compulsions.

The possibility of non-repetition, then, rests on the recuperation of losses that are impossible to recover, to reconcile with an end to which there is no end. This paradox is the key to reconciliation after ethnic cleansing. Attempts to recover this loss, or these losses, manifest themselves in many ways. Two common attempts are revenge and physical reproduction. Following an ethnic cleansing, in the face of a loss that cannot be articulated and that is unrecoverable, revenge is a frequent response. Revenge after ethnic cleansing takes many forms, from reciprocating one's own suffering by expelling the expeller, to creating myths about the eternal evil of the ethnic other. However it is conducted, revenge is the enactment of a repetition of the violence, the only difference with the 'initial' violence being that those victimised are, or hope to be, temporarily on the 'winning' side. The alternative to revenge after ethnic cleansing is, as is made clear below, a legal reckoning with the violence, an invocation of the principles of the rule of law to settle accounts, which in turn facilitates the building of networks of trust and principles of accountability.

Recuperation of loss through physical reproduction

A second attempt to recover the loss is the compulsive physical reproduction by victims that follows events of this sort, including most wars. One might think that physical reproduction following ethnic cleansing is a positive transformation of a loss into a life-affirming event. This interpretation of reproduction is dangerous, however, first, because it does not take seriously the impossibility of such recuperation and the fundamental paradox in a project of recuperation, and secondly, it does not acknowledge the likely consequences of trying to recover a loss through physical reproduction. Recuperation is impossible because of the specific nature of traumatic loss, which is experienced as a temporally delayed and repeated suffering of events that can be grasped only retrospectively (Caruth 1996). Loss that becomes traumatic is characterised by not having been experienced at the time of occurrence. In other words, the loss is only, if at all, experienced later, as it returns to the victim unbidden, frequently as a horrifying silence that cannot be spoken. Hence our difficulty in detecting, understanding, or treating such an experience.

The suffering of traumatic loss cannot be stopped or overcome through the possibility of return to a prior state of innocence or fullness. Any recovery from traumatic loss, a recovery that might be a reconciliation, a departure from violence, is possible only if the loss is 'relentlessly mourned and mourned'. To assume a definitive end to this mourning is mistaken. Assuming an end is to place oneself in a limbo, as Serge Leclaire writes, 'in the milky light of a shadowless, hopeless waiting' (Leclaire 1998 [1975]: 3). Waiting for an end to the despair, to the inability to die, is to wait for the deliverance of death, and that comes only with suicide. Yet those victimised are challenged to begin anew without an actual end; they are challenged to create an end and a departure that paradoxically also acknowledges its fictional character, a beginning that does not deny the loss.

Impatient with relentless mourning, to deliver oneself from this waiting, many survivors have babies. The arrival of the child changes the nature of the waiting, but it does not end the despair, the inability to die. A child cannot recover a loss that is unrecoverable. But it changes the waiting by presenting a potential fullness to fill the absence left by the loss. Immediate physical reproduction after ethnic cleansing is the substitution of a child for the loss of a loved one, a living substitute for the dead. It is the displacement of a loss. This child might well be the product of an act of love, and might be thought of as a new beginning, but it carries with it the despair, the inability to die, that motivates much of the survivor's grief. This grief now takes a less private form; the circle of grief is enlarged and includes the new child. Immediate reproduction perpetuates this despair by passing it on to the child, who then grows up bearing the parental expectations, their unfulfilled wishes and hopes, of recovering the loss suffered in the initial ethnic cleansing. The child is brought up in the light of these expectations, 'in the milky light of a shadowless, hopeless waiting'. This 'wonderful child', the child of hope and despair, is asked to deliver the parents from their waiting. But deliver what? Herein lurks a likely repetition of the violence, a strong motive for revenge, for the child to begin a new cycle of what Maurice Bloch (1992) calls 'rebounding violence'.

To be more specific and historical, and situate reproduction after ethnic cleansing within the contemporary global movement of 'ethnicisation', an increase in ethnicisation, a recovery, reinvention, or intensification of ethnic belonging, is observable in much of the world, especially in states that legitimate themselves through ruling majorities, and in places on all five continents. It is also prominent among people who have suffered ethnic cleansing, especially among those who remain at the site of the violence, or who are asked to reconstitute the social in the space of this violence. Individuals who live in dispersed diasporas, such as American Jews, have been specifically excluded from this discussion. This new ethnic identification is often talked about as a kind of 'fundamentalisation', akin to a religious fundamentalism. By this, observers usually mean that the group turns in on itself, engages in a further purification of its principles, a nostalgia for autochthony and obsession with origins, a clear demarcation of itself from other groups. Such a turn inward, an inner purification, not only appears to complete, in a putatively voluntaristic spirit, the ethnic cleansing initially perpetrated on the group, but it also institutionalises a further 'cleansing' of the group by enforcing endogamy on its members (Borneman 1998). No marriage with ethnic 'Others'. No statistics to prove this coerced endogamy are provided here, and such a form of proof may well be impossible to offer. But based on the impressions of others, it is asserted here that this holds true following most of the ethnic cleansings of the 1990s, e.g. in Cambodia, Bosnia and Zambia.

I want to draw attention to the relation of compulsive reproduction following ethnic cleansing to this ethnicisation at the social and political levels. However understandable at a personal level, immediate reproduction after ethnic cleansing permits the fiction of a recuperation of the loss through substitution of the living child for the dead loved ones. New group leaders, who understand their purpose to be the reconstitution of the social, frequently utilise this fiction in order to mobilise followers. Insofar as their authority is tied to an ethnicisation of the group, political leaders encourage the illusion of recuperation of personal loss through substitution of the living child for the dead loved ones. In today's world, where the legitimacy of rule in most states is based on constituting a numerical majority, ruling majorities are most easily created based on ethnic affinity. This is especially true after an 'ethnic cleansing'. Reconstituting the social becomes a project in political ethnicisation that is realised through an endogamous reproductive politics. 'Mixed marriages', as they are called, are the antithesis of this politics of exclusion. Endogamous pronatalism, then, substitutes a demographic argument of numerical majority for an argument based on other more inclusive principles of affiliation. The intention here is to demonstrate how the socio-political logic of ethnicisation feeds off the attempt to recover an individual loss through physical reproduction.

In short, ethnicisation is a politics of repetition and is unlikely to lead to a departure from violence. Recall the discussion of reconciliation above. The precondition of reconciliation is a desire for non-repetition and an appreciation of the inter-subjectivity of the present. Such reconciliation is improbable if not impossible without domestic reform, without a new and more inclusive politics of the domestic group. What is also important to explore is under what conditions women actually refuse reproduction after such violence. This may be the case in Peru, for example, where compulsive reproduction has not followed the violence of the last several decades, perhaps because the active inclusion of women in political life has presented them with opportunities to change the social as a means of recovering losses (Billie Jean Isbell, personal communication, April 1999). Physical reproduction is an altogether different mode of recovery from ethnic cleansing. It tends to create a sense of continuity instead of a radical break or rupture from existing relations. It also relegates women to the presumably apolitical role of mothers of the future. The sense of beginning that might be associated with the birth of a child is an illusion, in this case, since the baby represents the wish to return to a prior state of wholeness and innocence. Especially today, given the political uses of pronatalism to support ethnic majoritarian projects, leaders tend to narrate new children into a story of recovery. Because such endogamous physical reproduction contributes to a denial of the inter-subjectivity of the present, it deflects from the work needed to reconcile and actually increases the likelihood of a repetition of violence. The alternative to ethnicisation is the cultivation of care (in German '*Sorge*', in French '*souci*'), reciprocal but non-egalitarian practices that affirm inter-subjectivity (Tronto 1993; Borneman 1997b). Such care might take the form of a politics of sterility, which necessarily focuses radically on the present. This may be called the ethics of 'caring for the enemy'.

Recuperation of loss through revenge

Revenge, too, increases the likelihood of violence. Revenge is an exchange, a form of taking-turn, in which individuals or groups engage in reciprocal violence. Much like the physical reproduction discussed above, revenge is an attempt to recover a loss. It is often motivated by individual frustration with continued injustice; individuals act to solve their own problems where judicial authorities, or the state, will not or cannot act. In anthropological literature, the principle of revenge is frequently equated with other forms of justice administered by the state, but it distinguishes itself from legal redress in one crucial respect: it is the arbitrary, narcissistic exercise of violence in which there is no accountability except to oneself, and to a personal memory of the dead. That the state frequently fails in its pursuit of justice is admittedly a problem, as is the fact that many states themselves actually initiate violence. But people taking justice into their own hands is simply replacing one problem with another, an arbitrariness of 'rule by men' for a potential predictability in 'rule by law'. It is a politics of repetition.

Here two separate but complementary processes are addressed as alternatives to revenge, as modes of possible departure from violence, part of a politics of non-repetition. The first is witnessing, the second is legal redress of violence, or 'retributive justice'.

Witnessing as cultivated listening

Witnessing after ethnic cleansing is a form of truth-telling, involving the listening and speaking of at least two parties. It is primarily associated with speaking, with giving voice to individuals who have been silenced. Ideally, the silenced voices of victims are brought into discourse, that is, their experiences of harm and suffering, of being victimised in the violence of ethnic cleansing, are articulated publicly. Such articulation most frequently intends to contribute to an identification of causality, ultimately leading to the possibility of making claims on perpetrators, of holding them accountable for their wrongdoing. There are many discourses in which this voicing can have an impact, ranging from familial discussions, to neighbourhood meetings, to legal proceedings.

Witnessing differs from its cousin, confessing, in that the voicing tends to focus on the fate of the victim and not the perpetrator; and it is voluntary, not coerced as frequently are confessions. Most recently, in Latin America and South Africa, the art of witnessing in Truth Commissions has played a crucial role in reconstructing a public sphere where truth itself is given a value. The value put on speaking the truth has, in turn, had a significant impact on establishing what may be called networks of trust, networks that include not only neighbours' relations with one another but also citizens' relations with the state, in particular with the courts and the justice system. The importance of 'living the truth' in the construction of trust was in fact a theme in the plays and essays of Czech leader Václav Havel when, as a dissident, he wrote about life under the repressive state-socialist regime of the 1970s and 1980s. An enduring reconciliation is possible only in a departure from violence through a double rebuilding on the basis of trust: between neighbours and between citizens and the state.

It is worth pursuing the question as to whether and under what conditions witnessing as a process contributes to allocating accountability. Witnessing necessarily involves speaking and giving voice but it must be preceded and followed by listening. To listen is a motivated practice that differs from hearing for it always involves listening *for* something. Following an ethnic cleansing, this involves listening for truth. To listen for everything is to hear a cacophony of sounds, which is called noise. But to listen for truth entails a complex interpretive and evaluative process that goes beyond documenting experience *per se*. Listening as a practice, as an art, is similar to the art of reading or speaking. It is not passive but interactive, involving soliciting and questioning, weighing competing accounts, as well as hearing. Listening can be learned and cultivated, and some individuals are far better at it than others. I am suggesting here that we rethink who might be the practitioners of listening after an ethnic cleansing. They include not only friends, neighbours, anthropologists and historians, but also professional observers such as the OCSE, UN 'monitors' and individuals who work for Human Rights Watch. Such professional observers, at their best, actively cultivate the art of listening for the truth.

The significance of listening is not directly linked to its timing. Preferably, listening for the truth in various experiences would occur at the beginning of any escalation of violence. This is often impossible, however, and observers are then limited to documenting the work of memory or the escalation of violence. The presence alone of professional listeners at a moment of escalating conflict may actually have a cooling effect on potential perpetrators, making them pause before committing acts of violence.[1] When this listening is turned into voicing is a matter of timing. So is the question pertaining to which forums – familial, neighbourhood, television, courts – in which the voicing, and the allocation of accountability, takes place. The timing of voicing claims based on listening requires sensitivity to the specificity of place and context, to the politics of the present. The effect of truth-telling on allocating wrongdoing is highly context-dependent. But the nature of listening is not. Hence the telling of some truths has no effect until years after the actual experiences are heard.

The focus on listening here does not aim to discount the importance of voice but to direct our attention to the ineffectiveness of speaking if no one hears and no one acts on this hearing. One of the serious limitations of many Truth Commissions is that they explicitly make telling the truth a substitute for any retribution. It is necessary to create public forums, including newsprint, radio and television, where participants feel compelled to hear, to weigh and judge competing accounts, and ultimately to openly acknowledge the ambivalence and complicities in the exercise of power, and the power of truth and trust in social relations. Listening, in this sense, as a necessary precondition to giving voice, creates the possibility for departure, for a 'sense of ending', rupture, and break. A sense of ending is possible only by breaking silences concerning the nature of loss and its attempted recuperation as it relates to the sources of violence and modes of its reproduction, and the possibility for fair judgement and punishment. The cultivation of listening as a concrete social practice contributes to making a public sphere that is vigilant, critical and engaged. Moreover, many of the nascent public spheres, in Latin America and Europe, as well as in much of Asia, are peopled by marginal actors, for example women or minority groups, whose interests are diverse and dissentious and hence are not easily appropriated and utilised for the purposes of ethnicisation. The success of interventions by the many international non-governmental organisations (NGOs) in their support of 'civil society' projects may in fact largely depend on their ability to listen to these marginal voices. It is frequently the case that pressures for unity after a war silence voices of difference, displacing violence formerly directed at an external enemy to marginalised groups within a society or even to women and children within one's own domestic group. Listening for the truth of this violence, while itself crucial for long-term reconciliation, must be complemented by a process of legal accountability.

Retribution

Unlike witnessing, which rests on truth-telling and listening, a legal accounting, retributive justice is concerned with symbolically affirming the distinction between right and wrong (Hampton 1992). The timing of legal retribution, as mentioned above, may not be the same as that of witnessing and listening in the public sphere, since courts are only formally independent of the other branches of government. Making judicial appointments, setting the budgets, as well as determining types of criminality, are very much political decisions that rest with executive and legislative actors. Moreover, if courts convict, they need the cooperation of the other branches of government to enforce their rulings and carry out their sentences. Because of its embeddedness in political processes, a legal reckoning with injustices may pragmatically be delayed many decades after the actual occurrence of harm and wrongdoing. Such is the case, for example, with the current prosecution of Chile's General Pinochet. Timing aside, an eventual settling of accounts that involves the punishment of evil and the rewarding of good by a higher societal instance, such as a court, is integral to making possible a departure from violence after ethnic cleansing. It is integral to this process largely because memory can never be put to sleep.

In *Settling Accounts: Violence, Justice, and Accountability in Postsocialist States*, I argued that legal accountability is not just desirable but also necessary only in democracies (Borneman 1997a). Unlike other political forms, democracies require a form of strict accountability. That is, democracies are destabilised to the extent that they do not have formally autonomous legal systems that can invoke principles of accountability and apply these principles to members of the executive and parliamentary branches of government. Such legal accounting is never able to redress all of the wrongs perpetrated; in other words, it also cannot recover all of the losses suffered in an ethnic cleansing. Its role stems not from the efficiency of its prosecutions but from the political efficacy of prosecuting symbolically significant cases. This efficacy results in establishing trust in non-arbitrary institutions of law that stand above individual men and women. These legal institutions, if they make good-faith efforts at justice, produce trust in government and encourage networks of trust among disparate individuals. This trust, in turn, relieves victims of the need to take justice into their own hands; that is, it takes away one of the prime motives for revenge.[2]

A further step in this direction occurred in 1998, as 120 nations agreed to set up a permanent International Criminal Tribunal in The Hague. Fully independent international tribunals are presently at work in establishing accountability for the ethnic cleansing in the Balkans and the attempted genocide in Rwanda. In 1999, an alternative UN joint war crimes tribunal was proposed for Cambodia, in which Cambodian and foreign judges would try former political and military leaders of the Khmer Rouge in a single trial. That these tribunals lack their own effective enforcement powers and are dependent on national judiciaries and armies for exacting compliance with international judgements presents an obstacle that may eventually doom their efforts. So does the fact that such supranational courts are not democratically constituted and hence make no pretence to represent majorities. Without the support of democratically elected majorities, courts risk a legitimation crisis. This is especially so when they base their judgements on 'human rights' in the defence of injured minorities or the cosmopolitan ideas of intellectual elites. Unlike civil rights, human rights have no democratically organised or territorial constituency. Obstacles to enforcement are present for all judicial systems, however, only they are more formidable for those in their formative stages and which lack the naturalised sovereignty claims of state-run legal systems.

Whether these obstacles will make a mockery of the tribunals and prove them to be 'paper tigers' is a question that will be resolved only through a lengthy struggle, as the timing of the prosecution of cases, as mentioned above, is a strategic decision in each and every context. The time lag in the popular reception of legal judgements will undoubtedly affect their efficacy, but not in ways that can be clearly foreseen. Efficacy is a processual achievement, never achieved immediately and once-and-forever. The crucial factor, at present, is that the tribunals, as with national courts, make good-faith efforts, through the time-tested procedures of the rule of law, listening for the truth, witnessing and documenting the harms perpetrated and procuring remedies for them. Passing and enforcing judgements is crucial, to be sure, but it is only the last step in a settling of accounts that itself can never draw a thick line over memory. Retributive justice merely creates a sense of ending by stopping the cycle of rebounding violence, thereby opening the possibility to mourn the losses and articulate alternative beginnings.

Reconciliation and peacekeeping

In sum, it has been argued that reconciliation, as a departure from violence, requires both domestic and governmental initiative. Our ability to imagine departures from violence is hampered by inadequate understanding of both the possibilities of justice and alternative responses to personal loss. The former, the possibilities of justice, alerts us to the potential effects of a system of national and extra-national legal accountability, such as those embodied in the principles of the rule of law, as an alternative to revenge. The latter, responses to personal loss, alerts us to the importance of principles of care, networks of trust and an inclusive political vision that might serve as alternatives to the politics of endogamous physical reproduction and its potential effects as ethnicisation.

Presently local, regional, international as well as transnational actors and organisations are increasingly challenged to respond to the escalation of violence and proliferation of 'ethnic cleansing'. Often this response takes the form of what are called 'international peacekeeping efforts'. Especially for the militaries of the United States and Europe, peacekeeping efforts increasingly supplement, if not replace, coercive military operations. Such efforts are attempts to end 'hostilities' and bring about a 'reconciliation', a non-repetition, after a period of intense violence, at its most extreme after an attempted genocide, within a particular locality. Imagining what departures from violence might look like is essential for their success.

While peacekeepers must open themselves up to understanding the locale in its own terms, or as fieldwork-based anthropologist Urvater Malinowski put it, 'from the native's point of view', that is only a part of their task. They must also understand how they are perceived in these settings, as they are already a part of the imagery of that locale. Once they enter as bodies with money, tools, guns and access to other worlds, they become an integral and internal part of the shaping of local culture.[3] Hence they necessarily play an active role, consciously by way of active listening for the truth, by encouraging legal accountability through governmental reform and by encouraging domestic reform that builds larger networks of care and trust. If 'reconciliation' is to be pursued as a utopian project of 'departure from violence', it must then be conceived as the fundamental paradox of an ongoing recuperation of a loss that is not recoverable. This entails cultivating a vision of inter-subjectivity that is necessarily reflexive and relativist, that requires an often uncomfortable encounter with difference. It challenges us to construct new selves and institutions in terms of relationships of accountability, trust and care for the other, including the enemy.

NOTES

1   The Russian presence in the Caucasus offers an interesting example of the effect of the perception of active listening over intervention. Initially, this presence destabilised relations as it was perceived as a continuation of Soviet hegemony in the region. Later, the presence of Russian monitors helped stabilise the situation. (My thanks to Gia Tarkhan-Mouravi for this insight.)

2   The necessity of redistributive schemes of justice depends on the social and political location of the party claiming injury. Socialist regimes were initially motivated as redistributive responses to unjust distributions of wealth, which they, in turn, tried to rectify by creating public, shared forms of wealth. Their demise everywhere and reintegration into the capitalist world system has meant a re-redistribution of public and private property

and wealth from the historically less well-off to the better-off. The legitimation of postsocialist states has not been less contingent on their new re-redistributive schemes than on democratic and economic reforms. In places like Russia, however, capital re-redistribution to the better-off has been so extreme that it threatens to destabilise democratic reforms. In the transformation of long-standing, authoritarian oligarchies to democratising states, their legitimation might depend on both retribution and a redistribution of property from large landholders to the less well-off.

3   The impossibility of being 'external' was clearly revealed in the position of the US American marines in Lebanon between 1982 and 1984, but one could just as well take the examples of peace makers in Somalia or Bosnia. While the US marines in Lebanon saw themselves as external, neutral peace makers, local parties immediately made them a part of the conflict.

REFERENCES

Bloch, M. (1992), *Prey into Hunter: The Politics of Religious Experience* (Cambridge).

Borneman, J. (1997a), *Settling Accounts: Violence, Justice, and Accountability in Postsocialist Europe* (Princeton).

Borneman, J. (1997b), 'Caring and being cared for: displacing marriage, kinship, gender, and sexuality', *International Journal of Social Science*, 154 (December), 623–635.

Borneman, J. (1998), 'Toward a theory of ethnic cleansing: territorial sovereignty, heterosexuality, and Europe', in J. Bourneman, *Subversions of International Order: Studies in the Political Anthropology of Culture* (Albany), 273–319.

Caruth, C. (1996), *Unclaimed Experience: Trauma, Narrative, and History* (Baltimore).

Hampton, J. (19992), 'Correcting harms versus righting wrongs: the goal of retribution', *UCLA Law Review*, 29, 1659–1702.

Kierkegaard, S. (1974 [1844]), 'Despair', in R. Bretall (ed.), *A Kierkegaard Anthology* (Princeton).

Leclaire, S. (1998 [1975]), *A Child is Being Killed* (Stanford).

Moore, S. F. (1987), 'Explaining the present: theoretical dilemmas in processual ethnography', *American Ethnologist*, 14, 727–736.

Tronto, J. (1993), *Moral Boundaries: A Political Argument for an Ethic of Care* (New York).

12

Intervention in markets of violence

Georg Elwert

Introduction

WARLORDS DESTROY THE backbone of a state, the monopoly of violence. The society loses its cohesion. Behind smokescreens of ethnic, political, religious or other ideological goals appears a new – mainly economic – reference for social action: acquisition based upon violence. Markets of violence are highly profitable social systems, which can remain stable over several decades. The dominant actors in this system, the warlords, combine violent appropriation with peaceful exchange.

Markets of violence generally originate in conflicts of a non-economic nature. The continuation of the violence is, however, based on economic motives or unconscious economic behaviour. From the perspective of the warlords, violence can be used to maximise profit to such an extent that it is on a par with other economic methods. The fact that the balance sheet is far from positive in its effect on the overall system is irrelevant. This inherently rational economic behaviour can continue as long as the warlords are able to exercise their power without the support of the majority.

The expansion in economic potential, the fall in arms prices, the widespread existence of command-state structures and a reluctance on the part of foreign powers to intervene in such situations enables the continuation or even increase in such markets of violence. They can collapse as a result of the monopolisation of violence, the exhaustion of inner resources or a blocking of access to external resources. Only then can peace gain stability, when formal and informal institutions of conflict regulation limit the use of violence.

Markets of violence and policies of help and intervention[1]

Osama Bin Laden, the ghost behind the terrorist attacks of 11 September 2001, came out of a market of violence. Sudan's and later Afghanistan's territories enabled his group to train and organise their troops. Their place was among the warlords; they were respected as partners. The markets of violence, which enabled them to develop their organisational network, were older. Paradoxically it was the violent environment which gave them the time they needed to find, by trial and error, more and more efficient modes of operation for their ideological enterprise. This enterprise, al-Qaeda, shares with other warlords the condition that the income, be it from smuggling/trade, from violence or from donations (which is dominant for al-Qaeda), has to reproduce the power apparatus.

To analyse only the warlords' ideologies leaves the structural conditions of their enterprises in the dark. The protagonists and their representatives cite venerable traditions of hate, revenge and religious–moral obligations as justification for their activities. The long-term basic patterns of these markets of violence are, however, based on rational, comprehensible economic behaviour. Emotions, such as hate and, above all, fear are instrumentalised in this context but are not structurally formative. Actors, who are active within both the internal markets for blackmail and receiving stolen goods and external markets for gold, weapons and drugs, appear to fulfil an organisational function. The leading actors – and not necessarily the fighters who in addition to pecuniary gain are also motivated by other purposes – are primarily characterised by a high sensitivity for the economic rationale of their enterprise. This does not exclude the fact that their personal motives and – in most cases – their propaganda is dominated by an ideological self-representation. The economic aspect is, however, behind the reproduction and self-stabilisation of markets of violence.

The origins of such violent conflicts can be explained by other factors. The disintegration of the monopoly of violence – more precisely: the monopoly of coercion – can be triggered by a series of various motives and situations. The longer the violence lasts, however, the stronger the compulsion to rely on economic imperatives (cf. Waldmann 1999). In many cases, the continuation of the violence can be explained only in terms of the existence of markets of violence.

During the 1980s, the 1990s, and at the beginning of the twenty-first century, markets of violence could and can be found in Afghanistan, Angola, Bosnia, Chad, Columbia, Congo/Zaire, Ethiopia, Lebanon, Liberia, Mozambique, Northern Burma, Northern Mali, Sierra Leone, Somalia, Sudan, Tajikistan, the Caucasus and the Central African Republic.[2] Acquisitive behaviour similar in nature to the markets of violence also plays a role in some other violent situations. Terrorism or military fights in Northern Ireland, the Basque Country of Spain, the southern Philippines, in northern Sri Lanka and some other regions instrumentalise ideological motives to win some popular support but follow a clear economic strategy for its reproduction. The state's monopoly of coercion is severely damaged insofar as it cannot hinder the economic reproduction of para-state structures which finance violence. Although these situations are not (yet) the dominance of a market, a market of violence, over a (civic) society, they may well degenerate into it once the state loses its last protective capacity or once the military and police convert into warlordism.

The concept of 'monopoly of violence' (*Gewaltmonopol*, literally 'monopoly of coercion', Weber 1922) should be central to any reflection about alternatives to markets of violence. In a social structure governed by a monopoly of violence it is not everyone who can use violence. The occurrence of violence is very much restricted. This creates violence-free realms. As Norbert Elias (1978) has shown, such violence-free realms were essential for the development of European civilisation out of the Middle Ages. For a democracy, a monopoly of violence is a necessary condition; but it can also exist perfectly well in undemocratic structures. It may, for example, be a class monopoly of knights and kings. Violence-free realms are more stable if even the persons authorised to use violence are bridled by the law. If they can exert coercion – including violent coercion – only within the limits of legal regulations and legal procedures, then violence-free realms become realms of predictability. Under them, long-term investments in intellectual formation and the means of production also make sense for persons far from the centres of power. The lack of a monopoly of violence produces (under competitive conditions) spaces open to violence – violence fields. In these violence fields, people invest individually in the social and physical conditions of security in much higher proportions. Development, growth or productive innovation are not their preoccupations.

The general practice of state policy towards violence fields organised by markets of violence is that of non-perception masked by humanitarian intervention. Formally, the continuous existence of the states concerned is assumed. Diplomats of the former states transformed into markets of violence are paid by the country of residence or feed themselves through some smuggling. Non-interference is justified with the sovereignty of the country, which once existed. Sometimes neighbouring states let their armies or secret services profit from the situation in order to pursue economic goals, as in the cases of Afghanistan, Sierra Leone or Zaire/Congo. In most cases some western states directly or indirectly send (under the cover of refugee programmes) humanitarian aid, which contributes to the warlords' economies. The influence goes, however, in both directions. These open spaces of violence offer excellent breeding and selection conditions for the evolution of new forms of organised crime and organised terrorism, both of which may also affect peaceful industrial countries.

Markets of violence as systemic process

Markets of violence are understood as economic areas dominated by civil wars, warlords or robbery, in which a self-perpetuating system emerges and links non-violent commodity markets with the violent acquisition of goods. Violent and non-violent trade become so entwined that the system-specific opportunities for profit give direction. A self-perpetuating economic system emerges beneath the surface of a moral world-view and power conflicts – and even in the absence of such attempts at legitimisation. This may be based on the fact that the economic motive of material profit dominates beneath the surface. It is also possible that irrespective of the conscious motives of the actors (such as freedom, honour or revenge), only those actors who pursue economically profitable strategies – irrespective of their intentions – will survive. Markets of violence can emerge in areas open to violence, i.e. where there is no monopoly of violence.[3] The disintegration of a monopoly of violence is not generally caused by directly economic factors. In fact, it is mainly political and not economic motives that predominate in the initial phase.

Areas where there are no rules, which build channels for the use of violence, are open to violence. The unregulated violence may lead to the establishing of routines, it will not, however, result in the formulation of rules. Contracts between the warring parties can also be breached. Violence can even destroy the clientelist relations within a warring party and between warlords, their chiefs and mercenaries. The officer of a warlord may revolt against him or may betray him allying with his enemies. The possibility of murder for the sake of murder cannot be excluded in areas open to violence, even if such a murder would appear uneconomical to most actors.

Thus, to summarise, a market of violence is a field of activity which is mainly characterised by economic aims, in which both robbery and barter and the related activities of collection of ransoms, protection money, road tolls, etc. feature. Each actor has a number of basic options ranging from theft to trade.

The generals, princes, militia chiefs and party leaders who lead the troops in such conflicts are known in the research as 'warlords'. This term is used without any acknowledgement of its connotations with respect to the civil or criminal legal status of these persons. Warlords are understood as entrepreneurs who use deliberate violence as an efficient tool for achieving economic aims. These 'entrepreneurs' differ from normal entrepreneurs in that they also use violence – although not exclusively – as an instrument for the generation of revenue. This image of persons primarily acting on an entrepreneurial level is confirmed by the few academic reports emerging from the centres of such conflicts. In Ethiopia, the same circle of actors who once fought each other now cooperate as peaceful entrepreneurs (Zitelmann 1993). This view does not coincide with the stereotypes largely propagated in the media, which cite emotions and tradition by way of explanation. Unlike pub brawls, modern wars necessitate strategic planning and logistics. The killing cannot be sustained without cool and calculated planning for supplies of weapons, munitions, food and fuel. The planning of strategic action and military logistics requires a cool head and not the sustained evocation of emotion.

Owing to the fact that since the end of the Cold War, the big powers have lost interest in violent interventions in such situations and in the control of weapons sales, an important external factor is no longer present. [4] In Russia the *nomenklatura* even lost interest in controlling the events in its marginal territory Chechnya in the period 1991–94; the wars of 1994 and later years were merely a means to generate symbolic capital within Russian politics (Zürcher 1998: 107, 117, see also Chapter 6 in this volume). Organised crime made use of the situation. Markets of violence will continue to emerge wherever there is a coincidence of areas open to violence, exploitable resources and corresponding markets. Where the external framework conditions remain unchanged (particularly the reluctance to intervene and control the traffic in arms), they are more likely to increase than decrease in number. Whether the intervention in Afghanistan after the terrorist attacks of 11 September 2001 will bring a new policy of internationally coordinated intervention to restore monopolies of violence globally is yet to be seen.

Partial markets and developed strategies

The theoretical perspective presented here is less concerned with revealing economic motives behind conflicts bearing ideological labels, or demonstrating the economic success of individuals in situations previously solely characterised by destruction than with demonstrating the systematic character which lies behind conflicts which otherwise appear to be chaotic in nature. [5] Thus, the observable regular forms of economic behaviour in these areas are focused on first, followed by the external economic forms of stabilisation and, finally, how such markets of violence are formed. The manifold causes of the emergence of the markets of violence do not explain their durability; this lies in their systemic nature.

The players in this game are not only former entrepreneurs or criminals. They may also appear (and subjectively act) as security providers, government officials, politicians or religious leaders. This does not change the need for reproduction, although it may add further sources of income. [6] If a foreign country intervenes – as Russia did in Abkhazia – it may lose money; this is different to the warlords' calculation. [7] The troops financed by this outside support have, however, to avoid deficit, and this does not exclude economic behaviour equivalent to embezzling credit or fraudulent bankruptcy on behalf of the troop leaders. Commanders financed by neighbouring countries, such as Russia and the USA in Afghanistan, have noted this possibility.

The decision whether to steal or obtain certain goods through commercial transactions is basically always open in the markets of violence. The warlords need to win time so that they can make strategic decisions and keep their options open. Thus, the actors are confronted with a strategic triangle of violence, trade and time. The warlord makes calculated moves between these poles, carefully considering and optimising the cost/benefit relationship. Given that it is often not recognisable as such, this calculating rationality is explained below.

It is not suggested that cultural values or emotions have no structurally formative role to play in the social process. In the markets described here, however, optimisation processes are based exclusively on economic imperatives. This does not, however, eliminate the possibility that emotions make a significant impact on the cost aspect of the individual instruments and thus influence the cost structure of the market. Theft and enslavement are particularly obvious in this context.[8] Theft, however, is rarely for personal consumption. Anyone who hauls off refrigerators, video recorders and cars in Bosnia (or removes gold teeth) is not fulfilling a personal need but is reacting to the demands expressed by the receivers of such stolen goods.

The production of violence is also based on economic imperatives. The aim is to reduce the cost of the violence. Weapons, munitions and fuel are indispensable resources and it is not advisable for the warlords to save money by skimping on quality. It makes more sense to economise on the fighters' fees. Thus, 'marauding', i.e. systematic theft by soldiers, is an obvious form of the reproduction of working capacity. Indeed, a market actually develops for the marauding itself. In other words, it is possible to participate in organised robberies for a fee. In Yugoslavia, volunteer organisations made use of the support of 'weekend soldiers' who on Friday afternoons for a suitable fee and the loan of weapons were bussed to the front to return with their rich pickings on Sunday evening. That sadists who have paid their money are also allowed to seek their satisfaction is 'economic' in this sense.

Costs can be reduced by the well-meaning activities of foreigners too, food aid has also been used to supply troops (e.g. in Liberia). Research reports on refugee camps in Africa, describe how they have been converted into barracks full of troops awaiting deployment.[9] A parallel development could be observed in the Afghan refugee camps in Pakistan, which gave birth to the violent movement of the Taliban (Rashid 2001). The intervention of international donors follows a pattern which is instrumental for building up the organisational structures of warring groups and which later provides infrastructures for warlords, as one might have been able to note back in the 1960s, when violence broke out in Congo (cf. Mummendey 1997). The refugee camps in Congo, then established under UN supervision, bore considerable responsibility for the recruitment of the militia which continues to exist in Congo/Zaire. The parties succeeded in creating their armies by terrorising their 'tribal brothers'. Such developments are favoured by the collusion of warlords with organisations active in the distribution of aid. They do not wish to jeopardise the flow of aid as a result of critical reports and the absence of monitoring of the conflict's dynamics (beyond the mere counting of victims and the needy).

Another way in which the warlords can reduce their overheads is by exploiting desire for social prestige. Young men can easily be won over as highly motivated 'volunteers' if involvement in dangerous acts (e.g. multiple robberies) means they will be finally considered 'real men', or if the exercise of violence is one of the conditions of an initiation ritual. In Georgia, the criminal underworld and militant political leaders make efficient use of the prestige rituals of young males (Koehler 2000, see also Chapter 7 in this volume). Threats and acts of limited violence are central symbols of a code which communicates prestige, status and power ambitions. The high level of common violence thus reached several times brought the country to the brink of a dominant market of violence. If a country turns into a market of violence the ensuing chances for income generation through violence then affects the prestige pattern. In Albania in 1997–98, young males engaged in violence as an honourable activity. This activity, in a situation where the monopoly of violence had broken down, generated a considerable income. The exhibition of this wealth and the chance to master the violence under their own order brought the young men a status which the seniority system that had existed until then could not provide for them (Schwandner-Sievers 1998: 75).

In the short term the promise of justice and freedom – or to be more precise, the hope of resolving latent conflicts or overturning despotic rule – can be sufficient to mobilise volunteers (i.e. unpaid actors) and this is particularly important in the initial phase of a market of violence.

The generation of fear is a particularly cost-effective form of mobilising troops. Propaganda is thus an important instrument of production in such conflicts. From an economic perspective, 'senseless violence' can find a meaning in this way. The fear of retaliation on the part of the victims leaves no option open but to join an army or support it for one's own protection. Fear of revenge stabilises the system. Fear of becoming a victim of violence oneself can also motivate to preventive attacks. These are generally not based on strategic planning, can escalate rapidly and end in the slaughter of neighbours with whom the attackers may previously have had close relationships. Reports from Rwanda and Bosnia demonstrate the importance of radio and television propaganda in this context (Bringa 1995; Neubert 1999). In Rwanda, the radio service, which was set up using development aid funding, was responsible for spreading and reinforcing the fear which ultimately provoked the bloodbath.

The main difference between markets of violence today and those in the nineteenth century lies in the way in which propaganda can electronically reach large populations more quickly and cheaply. It can thus convert the fear of people into mass panic or participation in military actions (which are economically profitable for a small minority) on a scale previously unknown. The automation of revenge and fear of revenge creates unanimity where multiple memberships (e.g. based on language or religion) would previously have left people neutral towards the militant actors. This new unanimity means that massacres can take place on a large scale; there is no need to omit individual houses during firing. The militarily meaningful friend–foe distinction can now be ideologically reformed and take the form of 'ethnic cleansing'. The fear of being declared an enemy and thus becoming a potential victim, or fear of revenge, motivates civilians to assume the role of unpaid 'cleansing agents'.

The most important resource for trade is goods, which are easy to transport. For this reason, trade in valuable objects is of disproportionate significance in the market of violence. Precious stones and precious metals assume particular importance as they enable the transfer of large values in a single movement.[10] Drug trading, e.g. opium in Afghanistan (Goodhand 1999), and the weapons trade are not less lucrative. Wherever markets open to violence have developed, trade does not only centre on these valuable commodities but may even be attracted to the area, as could be observed in Tajikistan and the Balkans. Professional protection of the transport of goods by warlords and possibly even *entrepôt* trade (temporary storage in a 'safe' location) can be particularly attractive services for all kinds of illegal trading such as drugs and weapons smuggling. Smuggling routes move into these areas. This leads to consequential feedback processes. Afghanistan's market of violence fostered drug smuggling, which helped to finance violence in Central Asia. The collapse of state structures there, especially in Tajikistan, widened the opportunities for drug smuggling from Afghanistan and stable production structures for drugs could be built (Goodhand 1999). The Bosnian market of violence created relay structures for Kosovo-based organised crime. This, together with the great weapons sale in Albania in 1997, contributed to the abolishing of state structures in Kosovo (see also Chapter 5 in this volume).

The collection of protection money – also referred to as duties – and the taking of hostages have assumed major significance as an intermediary activity between trade and theft in markets of violence. The guarding of goods is today a particularly relevant phenomenon. The 'work' of the diamond and gold smugglers in contemporary Congo/Zaire,[11] *qat* traders in Somalia, emerald smugglers in Columbia and last but not least the protectors of convoys carrying food aid in Sudan, Somalia, Liberia and Bosnia, have made this branch of commercial activity the warlords' most important source of income.

In some markets of violence there is a commodity sold which the buyers do not recognise as such: the sacrifice of human lives for the sake of ideology. Battles are fought in pursuit of an ideal and accompanied by detailed reporting. Lives on both sides of the divide are sacrificed for one product, which is of value to emigrants or foreigners interested in the fate of the world. 'The Free West', 'the Socialist World Revolution', 'the Honour of Our Nation', 'Saving our Islamic Faith' are the issues which appear to be at stake. Considerable resources are transferred into the market of violence from outside if the warlords pay special attention to this commodity through the establishing of a special troop which is trained in rhetoric and international communication. It was in this way that Jonas Savimbi succeeded in selling his battles in Angola as both a sacrifice for the

Maoist socialist world revolution and then later for the defence of the free West against socialism, before turning his attention again to his main activity in Angola's and Zaire's diamond business.

The victims of these sacrifices do not need to be in the market of violence itself. Terrorist attacks steered from within the market but targeted at outside goals can be no less efficient if they receive sufficient publicity. The al-Qaeda of Osama Bin Laden and others managed to win an important share in this donation market. Their annual income is estimated at between US$20 and 50 million. Whereas other violent ideological entrepreneurs are engaged in the market of mass 'charity' (such as the IRA in Northern Ireland), al-Qaeda lives off the market of wealthy organisations and individuals. Each trade has its own rules. Whereas conventional warlords have to seek a military superiority simultaneously with the continuous control of exploitable resources, an ideology entrepreneur such as al-Qaeda requires the protection of a military partnership and has to remind the public from time to time of its existence by spectacular acts. Competition in the donation market among organisations of the same type produces an outbidding in the visibility of symbolic action.

If warlords blend their organisation with the features of a charismatic social movement, they may gain social cohesion and ease compliance with their commands. This is especially important if warriors have to undertake tasks far away from their commanders. In such a movement's atmosphere the perception of hierarchy is covered by the sentiment of living in a community of equals, of 'brothers'. The great utopian goal and the words of the guru create subjective clarity where before there was the mist of an opaque and chaotic future. Thus the hardships of daily life and all the petty conflicts lose relevance before the sentiment of their alleviation. One is in the clouds, flying to higher goals. Bin Laden's al-Qaeda network obviously made use of charismaticism as a resource (Elwert 2001b).

It is possible to observe an accumulation not only in the means of violence and money but also in time options. Time options are created first and foremost by ensuring means of subsistence. Such guarantees can take the form of contracts for food supplies (including those from aid organisations) or the delivery of tributes from enslaved farming communities. Time options are also created through pacts with competitors or opponents. Finally, time is won through negotiations: it is possible to negotiate about non-aggression, the delivery of supplies or pacts without necessarily being primarily (or even 'secondarily') interested in the non-aggression, goods or pact in question. What is important is winning time. Mediators who fail to understand this part of the strategic game become unsure and nervous when local or national rulers hold them in threatening situations. Some internationally noted attempts at mediation ride on concealed propagandist juggling with violence or exchange of goods and also time. Is it better to rob someone, extort a contribution, exchange goods or block everything and play for time? One plays for time, allowing the non-aggression to be bought and then calling it taxation, duty or financing the peace process. Time-wasting can weaken or simply unnerve the other side, making military success easier to achieve.

Stabilisation of markets of violence: 'civil war' as a long-term state

In fields of violence, the areas open to violence, a deregulated market economy develops. Economic opportunities determine who cooperates and who attacks whom. It is not ethnic groups and clans who oppose each other in these civil wars but economic interests. Economic systems based on the use and generation of violence become established, systems which repeatedly erect smokescreens of political or religious legitimisation. They are happy to assume and replay culturalistic interpretations, because this gives their activity a higher moral value and hinders outside intervention from persons sharing the same political or religious orientation.

One consequence of violent situations is that the opportunities for income generation disperse into alternative economic sectors. Trade, industrial production, peaceful commercial activity and agriculture enter crisis and completely collapse when they become dependent on continuous external inputs. Wages and income in these sectors sink. Invested capital is devalued. In many cases, the only way that those dependent on wages, and the self-employed can survive is to become soldiers and/or marauders. Entrepreneurs are well advised to invest their liquid capital in the formation of a troop and the purchase of weapons. Thus, it is not surprising that Somalia's warlords were previously – in times of peace – mainly involved in wholesale trading or as political entrepreneurs, but also as partners in development cooperation. The incipient market of violence makes the (relatively) higher wages and profit opportunities in the violent market sector absorb work force and capital. Warlordism thus becomes established simultaneously with the increasing pressure on alternative income sectors, which for the most part lose their opportunities for reproduction.

Autostabilisation also involves efforts in the symbolic–ideological sphere. Armed parades in front of the cameras of international television crews are as much a part of the successful propaganda methods used by this trade as the demonstrative brutality. The ideological self-presentation, which forces violence to the forefront, is intended to stabilise the position in the market of violence. It facilitates *inter alia* the sale of 'protection' and the influx of donations.

The selection of victims is based on highly complex calculations. Not everyone with possessions is subject to theft. The warlords also need trading partners, supporters and neutral powers. It is helpful to allow the violence to follow clear symbolically delineated lines to enable them to feel safe. Religion, urban or rural costume, regional accents, etc. are all suitable as the basis for distinction here.

They give the impression of ethnic or religious confrontation. However, no trading partner or associate can be sure that they will not fall victim to the covetousness of yesterday's ally. Given the high risk of betrayal of leaders by troops, commanders try to revive proven patterns of authority. These efforts can lead to an 'innovation' which will then undermine the markets of violence. In order to win an easy loyalty, leaders may emphasise the belonging of their subjects, the so-called ethnic or religious 'identity'. This multi-faceted word (not really a precise concept) means in this context that distinctions gain in importance and that a traditional authority is invoked which should bind members of the defined we-group. This may create or recreate ethnonational units with an authority structure and some legitimacy, which produces rule compliance. This may not end but stabilise the violence within clearly defined boundaries (Schlee 1996, 2000; Elwert 2001c). The progression to classic war as well as to a ceasefire between commanders who are representative and capable of entering into an agreement are both possible outcomes.

The widespread hope that the majority of the population which is the victim of violence and impoverishment will rebel against the warlords can materialise only if a monopoly of violence is established from outside. This promise was the strong argument of the Taliban, when they won over other warlord organisations in Afghanistan. Their failure to keep control shows, however, some of the conditions for lasting peace. Free elections and, what is often neglected, the establishment of justice, of peaceful forms of conflict regulation and the circulation of free information can make the monopoly of violence a normality for the state's citizen. It is not in the interests of the warlords to allow this to happen as long as their trade remains profitable. If an end to the violence is actually achieved, a shift in values often occurs within the population, which now places a taboo on the willingness to engage in violence. Thus, whoever establishes a monopoly of violence – whether by democratic or non-democratic means – can be sure of a high degree of legitimacy.

Markets of violence as a breeding ground for evolutionary processes

Nothing is forbidden in the market of violence; there are no bridles on creativity; everything is conceivable in terms of what one can create and maintain by one's own (armed) power. The brutal selection by violence – violence that pays – offers an efficient test for new institutions and new forms of violence. Any organisation unable to secure by its deeds the means to reproduce weapons and to sustain fighters will lose and has to give up. In the selection process the most efficient organisations show up rapidly. Markets of violence enable a high-speed evolution – from dinosaur to modern predator in a decade. If the organisation exhibits different forms it may also survive in different environments.

The al-Qaeda, active from Afghanistan, successfully combines features of a formal organisation with a network structure and, most notably, the features of a charismatic movement. It has changed its targets over time – the Saudi Arabian government, the Soviets in Afghanistan and now the United States. In Uzbekistan's Ferghana valley they started as agitators for the Wahabbist version of Sunni Islam against the region's traditional Islamic rituals. Then, after clear failure, they opted for the vigilant role criticising the 'unislamic' behaviour of some state officials. The means of donation collection, of propaganda and of internal communication have changed constantly, adapting and innovating after each failure. The virtues of systemic differentiation were thus learned. Special staffs were devoted to organisation, fundraising and the technologies of murder. Some specialist services were bought, some troops were rented out. These contractual relations bridged ideological differences. In 1998 some 'Arabs from the Arab peninsula' – probably al-Qaeda – asked the Tamil Tigers if they wished to rent out a brigade of suicide assassins (Elwert 2001b). That this Sri Lankan terrorist group is rather hostile to its own Muslim minority and has an ideology which blends Hindu and Marxist elements, did not hinder the contact. It failed because of the financial terms of the contract, the nationalist limitation of the Tigers necessary for their troops' cohesion, or because of the perishable character of the goods offered.

Warlords learned rapidly how to manage their financial assets. The time of gold-hoarding generals is gone. They launder money at the best European, North American and Caribbean banks. They invest their money in trade and transport and have, as the Elam Liberation Tigers of Sri Lanka have, a special office for asset management. Ironically, the only surviving part of the warlord-ridden Liberian State is its New York-based office of ship registration, which is a useful institution for some warlords' transport business. Bank accounts are held in Liechtenstein, Cyprus, on island dependents of Great Britain and in Canada and the United States. The safety of financial systems protected by a rule of law are largely preferred to the institutions of 'rogue states'.

Given that markets of violence largely destroy the internal institutional structure and production potential of a country, they are highly dependent on clients, suppliers, banks and other services outside of their area. It is easy to overlook the importance of the service sector. Markets of violence need external infrastructure. Somali warlords, for example, make extensive use of educational centres, special hospitals, banks, insurance companies, stock exchanges and commerce arbitration courts in other continents (North America and the Middle East).

Markets of violence do not develop and exist in a vacuum. They grow out of self-organising social systems, which by virtue of their nature depend on an exchange with their environment, and they continue this exchange in (evolving) forms. Exchange across the borders of its own system is, therefore, one of the vulnerabilities of markets of violence. Blockades, i.e. the prevention of this exchange, can destroy them from outside.[12]

In markets of violence organised crime targeting the population of other states finds positive growth conditions as long as it does not seek its victims among the impoverished population of the host country itself. Criminal entrepreneurs in this environment have, however, different working conditions from the classic mafia (cf. Krauthausen 1997). They lack the support of corrupt but so far-reliable state institutions. But they profit from a considerable freedom margin. Warlords, ideological terrorists and organised crime share the same evolution-enhancing environment. What future threats may come out of markets of violence cannot be predicted with precision. It can only be said that the evolution goes on at high speed.

Prevention and the origins of markets of violence

For the sake of prevention it is important to know how markets of violence come into being. A monopoly of violence does not, however, disintegrate suddenly. It is merely perceived suddenly – when it is too late. It crumbles with increasing speed as a result of contraventions which reveal the fragility of the system. The sustaining success of robbers or the obvious violence of despotic local power holders may lead to this perception. In most cases, however, the monopoly of violence disintegrates from within. That means state intervention contravenes the notion of a legitimate use of violence, which exists among the people. These violations legitimate counterviolence or an imitation of this arbitrary violence for a competing despotism. Despotism is a characteristic of the Command State, 'the brother of the command economy'. In this form of government the authority present has priority over laws, contracts and other written regulations (Elwert 2001a). Clientelism and corruption overrule formal laws and they marginalise regulations, which should provide for fair markets.

Conflict as such does not lead to violence. 'Conflict' in the meaning attributed to this concept in the social sciences is any incompatible divergence of interests. Most conflict is dealt with by institutional arrangements providing for arbitration or compromise. Violence is the system's default option. In some societies avoidance may also be a current option. If a higher level of interaction is needed, then avoidance favouring societies will turn more often to violence, since alternative institutional arrangements are weak (Elwert 2001d). Modern societies are characterised by an 'institutionalisation of conflict'. The more conflicts a society can deal with peacefully, the greater its capacity for social transformation. The lack of conflict processing capacity is a major weakness of the Command State.

Arbitration and the security of the legal system can prove too weak or unreliable when they are heavily challenged by economic development. Thus the idea of 'self-help', materialised as violent strife or feuding, appears as a means of achieving justice. This option becomes especially obvious when economic growth necessitates a higher institutional capacity for conflict resolution. This 'self-help' takes violent forms particularly in the vital area of land rights: the expulsion of sections of the population during and immediately after periods of economic growth in Nigeria, the Ivory Coast and Central Asia led to the emergence of temporary or permanent fields of violence. If there is a higher level of economic activity, then people engage in more potentially conflictual interaction. These require a greater processing capacity of the regulating institutions. If these institutions did not grow at the same pace as economic development, then failure is probable and the avoidance of interaction or violence are obvious options.

The temporal coincidence of democracy movements and the increase in internal state violence has led some observers to the conclusion that one is the cause of the other. In actual fact, however, both are a consequence of the end of the Cold War. Large powers and former colonial powers now enjoy less legitimisation for intervention when violence or a power shift occurs in their area of interest. They now allow local actors to prevail in situations, where they would previously have taken immediate action. This can give rise to a situation whereby free elections take place without the monopoly of violence being in the hands of the state. It is also possible that parliaments elected in this way have no *de facto* legislative authority, as the public servants do not feel bound by the laws. The Command State does then also exist in democratic forms. Willingness to compromise is weak when it is perceived as a loss of the prestige – vital for assuring credibility in the future. Violence is the better alternative to compromise as long as the gradual conflict (the more-or-less conflict) does not replace the alternative conflict (the either-or conflict) as dominant paradigm of conflict interpretation.

Liberation movements or a violent opposition, which merely aims to transfer the exercise of the monopoly of violence to other (i.e. their own) hands, actually create a second pole of violence. When violence comes from both sides, the monopoly of violence can quickly collapse and areas open to violence emerge. In the course of further development, the economic motives for the exercise of violence can become dominant in these fields of violence. That is not to deny that politically motivated wars of liberation exist. The transition to an economy of violence is, however, fluid. On the one hand, the guerrillas gain legitimacy from the violent state despotism, a despotism which serves the individual profit of the officials; on the other hand, however, the long-term financing of weapons supply necessitates that the war sustains itself from the war. Thus, ideologically motivated fighters become economically motivated warlords who continue to promulgate the old ideology for the sake of greater legitimacy.

In local societies, which are not subject to central state control, an economic or technological imbalance – e.g. a demand for scouting services to help robbers or gold-digging, or cheap and efficient weapons – can lead to failure in the internal control of violence. In the case of the Ugandan civil war, the Ik, who were previously mainly active as hunter-gatherers, saw the opportunity to enrol as scouts (Turnbull 1972). This brought about the partial disintegration of the internal moral control and produced a famine among the old and the women and children they left behind. In the highland of New Guinea, feuds became war when automatic firearms became available and replaced spears, bows, axes and cudgels. In Somalia, some militias emerged from nomadic self-help units, which needed to obtain access to wells and food without state protection. They obtained their weapons from their trading partners in the cattle trade who were economically dependent on the cattle supplied by the nomads. The young people who – unlike in the traditional clan system – controlled these weapons soon discovered that the taking of hostages, protection and blackmail are also profitable activities. These examples throw light on both the problem of international weapons trading and the necessity of a monopoly of violence guaranteed by a state governed by the rule of law. These two areas were not previously considered basic concerns of development-aid policy; however, they clearly exercise a significant influence on development processes.

The disintegration of the monopoly of violence is a necessary but insufficient condition for the emergence of markets of violence. The future warlords must be at least familiar with the rules of a market economy. This explains why, for example, in the Caucasus and Central Asia the warlords mainly originate from the circles of the former 'shadow' economy. Furthermore, weapons, munitions and fuel must be available at acceptable prices. The fall in the price of the weapons of war which can be observed in Africa since the early 1990s may have contributed to the spread of markets of violence there (Lock 1997). Finally, a certain level of disposable resources must also be available. Extreme poverty of the victims prevents the emergence of markets of violence in situations open to violence (e.g. in the mountain regions of Afghanistan and Tajikistan). A concentration of wealth and access to legally or illegally exploitable resources promotes the emergence of these markets (e.g. precious metals and stones have sustained the markets of violence in Congo/Zaire since the 1960s). Thus, even if the other parameters remain unfavourable, positive economic development can favour the development of markets of violence.

When areas open to violence and the market economy coincide, there may be positive interaction between them; i.e. the market interests are increasingly realised in areas open to violence. Thus, the self-stabilising system of the market of violence is generated.

How it ended: historical experiences on the demise of markets of violence

Markets of violence 'only' ever exist for a few decades. There are several factors, which lead to their eventual demise. Everything is permitted in the radical free market economy, including breach of promise. Thus, anything that can stabilise relationships of trust is particularly in demand. Associations based on religion, language, origins or (secret) associations are created. Efforts are made to mark out small areas of internal morality, areas in which violence is eliminated and trust established within the radical free market, which permits all violence and breach of honour. The invention of an ethnic group or religious community is one way of doing this. In Somalia and Afghanistan, for example, the concept of religious community (*umma*) came to the foreground.

Such moral groupings can lead to underground transformations, which can elude observers focused on violence for a considerable time. At the beginning of the twentieth century, underground secret societies flourished in China, which was torn and divided by warlords. They included groups with high ethical claims (even one Christian lay mission succeeded in becoming established among some of the armed troops). One of the secret societies, which flourished in this underground was based on a particularly successful combination of charismatic obedience, the concept of peaceful Utopia and efficient military organisation: the Chinese Communist Party. Many observers deemed it not contemporary owing to its moral rigour. And yet this was the very characteristic which proved the key to its success.

The disintegration of a market of violence can, of course, also lead to the outbreak of a classic war situation as discussed above. This often has particularly unpleasant consequences for the populations involved. In the 'normal' market of violence, owing to the cost of the violence there are actually fewer victims than in classic wars (e.g. in many phases in the development of the war in Afghanistan). The warlord also sees death in terms of its financial cost. The deployment of 'cheaper' volunteer forces, which are mobilised through fear of the enemy (e.g. fear of the 'enemy' ethnic group) can, however, result in a drastic increase in the number of victims. When the violence is used to serve non-economic aims (such as territorial rule of an ethnic group or the prestige of a nation), when ethnic cleansing becomes an aim along with theft and blackmail, the nature of the activity changes and the number of victims increases. Why should warlords resist the temptation to put themselves in the service of such a 'superior' object if the business continues to be profitable for them (as demonstrated in the Bosnian conflict)?

No market activity is purely based on motives of profit, subsistence and consumption. Market events cannot be consolidated without secondary motivation.[13] Secondary motivations – such as efforts to create a new ethno-national community – can become primary motivations, which then establish a new reference. This was also the European experience: the capitalists of the mercenary armies of the Thirty Years War became both power-accumulating statesmen and peaceful entrepreneurs (Tilly 1985). Then, as today in Lebanon, the exhaustion of resources caused by the violence may have contributed to the establishing of relative peace.

The transition from market of violence to other forms of violence, or to more peaceful states, can, therefore, be achieved through three developments: (a) the exhaustion of resources, especially through the imposition of external blockades, (b) internal shifts in orientation linked to a military imbalance in favour of the carriers of the new ideology and (c) the imposition of a monopoly of violence accompanied by the creation of conflict resolving institutions. An important and typical change in orientation is the establishing of institutions which promote trust, the long-term predictability of the regulations and in addition – like relations – the moralisation of behaviour, or – like a legal system – the regulation of conflict. The transition period is characterised by ambivalent activity. It is as though players of a game seated together at the same table interpret the moves differently. Players judged 'irrational' in terms of the majority can prevail if they manage to gain control over a scarce resource or synchronise their actions with the effects of an external blockade or the exhaustion of internal resources.

Means for developing prognoses about the growth or demise of markets of violence

Even before a violence-free space comes into being, it can be predicted whether or not warlords will dominate the game. A sound prognosis requires first that the (potential) warlords' ideological statements are not taken at face value but as nothing more than a means to win support and deter interference. Analyses have to be based on economic facts and on social patterns. Ten parameters have to be studied with priority.

The patterns of violence

That violence is patterned is an important finding of anthropological research. Violence exists in every society at least as a default option if no other means to pursue power interests are attainable. Violence in every society is contained by a normative arrangement which anthropology calls 'embedding' (Elwert 2002). This arrangement may vary in respect of the functioning or failure of institutions in respect of the changing demands put upon them. The patterns of violence with their historical variations have to be described.

The institutions of conflict regulation

The study of institutions of conflict regulation is necessary in order to assess their efficiency. How far are they capable of processing conflicts in a peaceful way? And to what extent do people feel unsatisfied and opt either for avoidance or for violent solutions?

The actual status of the monopoly of violence

How far is the monopoly of violence respected? In which social and regional sectors does violence occur without the legitimisation of the formal rules?

Self-violations of the legitimate monopoly of violence

As formulated above, the violation of the legitimate monopoly of violence is the most common of all triggers for civil war.

The development of autonomous sanction capacities

A recent study on warmongers and mediators draws our attention to the establishment of autonomous sanction capacities within subgroups as a necessary condition for their transformation into collective violent actors (Eckert *et al.* 1999). Once these groups have established such an autonomous sanction capacity they are 'ripe' for civil strife. Whether they start attacking other groups or defend their own depends instead on the perceived balance of power.

The degree of violence inducing disinformation

As shown above, disinformation may motivate violence out of fear. Disinformation is especially helpful for endo-strategic mobilisation, that is, a mobilisation whereby would-be leaders declare the need to defend their group against assumed enemies.

Mobilisable economic goods

Mobilisable economic goods have to be assessed. The quantities of goods which may be stolen, the money which may be attracted by ransom taking, extortion or hostage taking, or that which may be gained through illegal trade has to be compared with the income sources within the formal and legal sector of market economy. The availability of such goods is a necessary but insufficient indicator of potential transformations into markets of violence.

The potential of violent ideological entrepreneurs

Violent political organisations, which mobilise along ideological lines, may have a high fund-raising capacity outside their country. If the size of the resource flow depends upon spectacular deeds, then terrorism is a likely option.

Labour power assessment

The number and quality of persons who could be mobilised as volunteers, soldiers, mercenaries, as compared with the numbers of such persons in peacekeeping forces is another good indicator.

Resource transfer opportunities

Stolen goods have to be sold, ransoms have to be collected. Profits have to be stored, saved or reinvested. All this requires safe structures for money laundering, transfer and investment. The availability of such structures enhances the chances of warlords dominating the game.

Political options to promote peace from the outside

'Fattening the booty': or the ambivalence of distributing aid

Currently the most common form of intervention in conflicts is humanitarian aid. Doctors and nurses are dispatched to the war zones; food and clothing are distributed to the victims of violence; infrastructures get repaired; for logistic reasons refugees or people suffering from hunger get concentrated in camps. This measure is highly ambivalent, since recruiting troops is made easier rather than more difficult for the warlords (as demonstrated by the example of Rwandan refugees in Congo/Zaire or the Taliban's recruits from refugee camps in Pakistan). Decentralised supply concepts would be more suitable.[14] Warlords use refugee camps not only to recruit but also to regenerate their troops. They may also invite in humanitarian organisations because they can sell them their services as protection forces against the risks generated by other warlords or by themselves. Warlords may as well scale down the violence as long as humanitarian forces distribute food and repair infrastructures, if the population has become too poor to be robbed. Once the 'booty is fattened' the cycle of war starts again. It is impossible to completely avoid aid supplies being diverted from the intended recipients as a result of blackmail, 'duties', payments for transportation, protection or theft. It would, however, be possible to avoid such supplies being used to benefit the warlords more than their victims through monitoring. The 'booty-fattening' effect can be avoided only if humanitarian action also implies the establishing of a monopoly of violence.

Blockade

It is possible seriously to jeopardise the economic interests of warlords through blockades. Smuggling, the investment of the proceeds of trade, theft, blackmail or hostage taking in safe third-party states, weapons and fuel supplies are all vulnerable to intervention. Such blockades are, however, difficult to implement. They may involve extensive manpower and technological resources on the borders of the war zones. They necessitate that the personnel who carry out the border policing are authorised to use weapons in the completion of their duties (unlike in the former Yugoslavia). Such blockades must also be implemented as blockades of services, particularly the movement and laundering of money. This is seen by some states as interference in their 'freedom of banking'.

Armed peacekeeping and the need for support for institution building

In some situations, the market of violence can come to an end only if the intra-state monopoly of violence is guaranteed by external powers for a limited period of time. This policing (and in the sociological sense non-military) task has four prerequisites.

First, the arms and logistics resources available to the intervening powers must be such that they can cope with actors who are potentially violent. Secondly, the use of sanctioned violence must be based on legal state regulations and enjoy institutional back-up and control. If soldiers can abuse their power, the intervening force will degenerate into another warlord. Thirdly, weapons control must be achieved. Fourthly, everyday conflicts must be resolved in peaceful procedures, if violence in the form of self-help 'for the achievement of rights' is not to flare up again; that means building institutions. The linking up with local concepts of justice and local institutions is unavoidable here if the aim is to lay the foundations for the endogenous development of the rule of law by native powers. These institutions may be both formal and informal, e.g. those organising illegal markets (cf. Zürcher and Koehler's Chapter 13 in this volume).

All this is based on an assumption of socio-cultural competence on the part of the intervening party. This is seldom in evidence in the cooperation with developing countries and is sorely missed in situations of violence.

Building civil society at a grassroots level

A monopoly of violence can be established only if violence-free interaction is made a matter of routine in daily life. This normalisation of peace requires changes in what one expects from neighbours and from unknown persons. These changes require four conditions.

First, power abuses by state officers, especially arbitrary violence, have to be controlled. Institutions of justice specialised in this field are a highly efficient tool for ensuring this function. Secondly, criminality has to be curbed. Thirdly, imagined threats, e.g. from witches or from infectious diseases brought by strangers, have to be dispelled by enlightening information. Finally, peaceful forms of conflict resolution have to be low-cost and quick.

Forcing violent actors into moves towards peace

In many examples of peacekeeping through external forces the (former) violent actors are still present. A study of the peacekeeping process in Bosnia shows both the failures and successes of such processes (Gosztonyi 2001). Violence can be effectively scaled down provided that there is a consistent system of positive and negative sanctions, of rewards and penalties. Starting from the *status quo* the relevant parties have to agree in a formal or informal contract on what will be considered an improvement or deterioration in the situation. Sanctions have to be administered consequentially and with a high degree of consistency and reliability in respect of the so defined 'goal corridor'. To achieve this, first of all the donors and intervening forces must be coordinated. If not, they will be played off against each other. Then they have to invest heavily in monitoring what is going on at the local level. Positive sanctions may include investments in welfare, infrastructure and productive assets. Subsidies and bribes should be avoided or at least reduced in the process. Among the negative sanctions is of course the removal of these social or personal benefits. But they must go further. One option may be targeted actions against a warlord's investments in other countries. The use of the mass media in the country itself or in countries whose public matters to the 'warlord-come-politician' can be an efficient tool, a sanction through negative reputation.

Coercive violence – especially the arrest of rule violators or armed intervention to secure the implementation of measures which were part of the contract – must not be excluded. The Bosnian case shows that once such an intervention was delayed, the violence level increased. The predictability of the sanctions and clarity in the agreements are the peacekeepers' virtues; fuzziness and lack of specific consequences for certain actions give them Achilles' heels. We have observed that in situations of unstable peace the risk of misunderstandings owing to delayed action or ambivalent symbols is above average.

Economic opportunities as a means of socio-cultural transformation

Given that states of war particularly reward the values of the warring parties, there is a particular danger that peace will be seen as only a temporary cease-fire. In areas open to violence, a prestige situation specific to violence often gets established which links the opportunity for young men to acquire honour and respect by acts of violence against third parties or revenging the 'infringement of honour'. This prestige is mostly bestowed by informal institutions. Age-specific organisations of young males play an important role. As long as these institutions exist and this prestige situation remains, a reserve army for possible civil war strategies continues to grow, even in peacetime. This is not the only possible outcome in such situations. It is also possible to open new paths to social recognition. The promotion of entrepreneurial ambition in peaceful forms can transform potentially destructive energies and provide both profit and prestige.[15]

As violence is a product of men's social organisation, so are markets of violence. There is thus a chance to undo them.

NOTES

1   This chapter draws on earlier publications of the author. Notes and references are restricted to arguments not yet contained in Elwert (1999). For this version the author has to thank especially Julia Eckert, Kristóf Gosztony, Ulrich Hiemenz, Jan Koehler, Dirk Kohnert, Thomas Zitelmann and Christoph Zürcher for support in the empirical research (especially Julia Eckert, Kristóf Gosztony, Dirk Kohnert, Jan Koehler, Thomas Zitelmann) and style (especially Ulrich Hiemenz, Christoph Zürcher).

2   It is important to note that in all of these countries or regions, areas exist or existed where the use of violence was not a regular occurrence.

3   This system can be described as a 'market' only in the descriptive sense of economic anthropology. In other words, the exchange under this system is based on the exchange value of the goods and unlike reciprocal systems, personal trust between economic partners is not required. The system described here, in which breach of contract, blackmail and theft are the rule, could not be described as a 'market' in the normative sense.

4   The different forms of violence were not, of course, interpreted as revolts against state attacks, robbery or markets of violence during the Cold War era but as the subversive violence of opponents.

5   For more detailed versions of the theory of markets of violence see Elwert (1997, 1999). The first formulations of the theory were presented at a plenary session of the German Sociological Convention in Düsseldorf in 1992 chaired by Gudrun Lachenmann (Elwert 1996), and a workshop at the World Congress of Sociology in Bielefeld in 1994 chaired by Amrita Rangasami. I have to thank both of them not only for the invitation but also for advice and the lively debate.

6   On security firms in Southern Africa, see Misser (1997a, 1997b), on bureaucracies in the Sudan, see Keen (1996).

7   Uganda, which in 2000 was able to balance its budget 'in spite' of the presence of Ugandan troops in the neighbouring Congo, shows that governments may also win.

8   For example, in Mozambique cf. Geffray (1992).

9   For example, in East Africa for troops from Somalia, Sudan and Ethiopia, cf. Allen (1996, 1999); Duffield (1997); Hancock (1997).

10 Diamonds, emeralds, gold, silver and minerals containing rare elements appear on the shopping list. For the diamonds in Sierra Leone example, see Grill (2001), and for emeralds in Columbia, see Krauthausen (1997).

11 Gold trading and protection or extortion of protection money for the gold trade was the speciality of the warlord Laurent Kabila who has been active for over thirty years and has now reached new honour in Zaire/Congo.

12 It is, however, difficult to find examples of successful blockades. Mozambique after the changes in South Africa, which previously provided the external infrastructure for violence, is perhaps such a case.

13 This can be seen in German society, for example, in the prestige awarded for academic work, which is a condition for advancement on the academic labour market.
14 Gerd Spittler developed such a decentralised concept for hunger intervention in the Sahara (Spittler 1988).
15 Thomas Zitelmann observed this in Ethiopia (cf. Zitelmann 1993; Eckert *et al.* 1999).

REFERENCES

Allen, T. (ed.) (1996), *In Search of Cool Ground. War, Flight and Homecoming in Northeast Africa* (Genf).
Allen, T. (1999), 'War, genocide and aid', in G. Elwert, S. Feuchtwang and D. Neubert (eds), *Dynamics of Violence. Processes of Escalation and De-Escalation in Violent Group Conflicts* (Berlin), 177–202.
Bringa, T. (1995), *Being Muslim the Bosnian Way: Identity and Community in a Central Bosnian Village* (Princeton).
Duffield, M. (1997), 'Ethnic war and international humanitarian intervention: a broad perspective', in D. Turton (ed.), *War and Ethnicity* (Rochester).
Eckert, J., G. Elwert, K. Gosztonyi and T. Zitelmann (1999), 'Konflikttreiber – Konfliktschlichter. Erste theoretische Erkenntnisse einer vergleichenden Untersuchung in Bosnien, Bombay und Oromiya Regional State (Äthiopien)', *Sozialanthropologisches Arbeitspapier*, 75 (Berlin).
Elias, N. (1978), *Über den Prozeß der Zivilisation I + II*, 5th edn (Frankfurt/M.).
Elwert, G. (1996), 'Afrikanische Pfade für Europas Zukunft? Gegenwärtige und zukünftige Entwicklungen europäischer Nationalismen/Percorsi africani per il futuro dell'Europa? Sviluppi attuali e futuri dei nazionalismi europei', *Annalisi di Sociologia/ Soziologisches Jahrbuch*, 12: I–II, 123–161.
Elwert, G. (1997), 'Gewaltmärkte. Beobachtungen zur Zweckrationalität der Gewalt', in T. von Trotha (ed.), *Soziologie der Gewalt* (Special Issue, No. 37 of the *Kölner Zeitschrift für Soziologie und Sozialpsychologie*).
Elwert, G. (1999), 'Markets of violence', in G. Elwert, S. Feuchtwang and D. Neubert (eds), *Dynamics of Violence. Processes of Escalation and De-Escalation in Violent Group Conflicts* (Berlin).
Elwert, G. (2001a), 'The Command State in Africa. State deficiency, clientelism and power-locked economies', in S. Wippel and I. Cornelssen (eds), *Entwicklungspolitische Perspektiven im Kontext wachsender Komplexität, Forschungsberichte des BMZ*, Band 128 (Bonn).
Elwert, G. (2001b), 'Rational und lernfähig – Wer die Attentäter des 11. September bekämpfen will, muss zunächst ihre Logik begreifen', *Der Überblick*, 3, i–vii.
Elwert, G. (2001c), 'Primordial emotions and the social construction of we-groups – switching and other forgotten features', in G. Schlee (ed.), *Imagined Differences: Hatred and the Construction of Identity* (Münster).
Elwert, G. (2001d), 'Conflict, anthropological perspective', in P. Baltes and N. Smelser (eds), *International Encyclopedia of the Social and Behavioral Sciences* (Amsterdam).
Elwert, G. (2002), 'Sozialanthropologisch erklarte Gewalt', in W. Heitmayer (ed.), *Internationales Handbuch der Gewaltforschung*, in print.
Geffray, C. (1992), *La cause des armes au Mozambique: anthropologie d'une guerre civile* (Paris).

Goodhand, J. (1999), 'From Holy War to Opium War? A case study of the opium economy in north-eastern Afghanistan', *IDPM Working Paper*, 5 (Manchester).

Gosztonyi, K. (2001), 'International intervention in the Bosnian War', dissertation (Berlin).

Grill, B. (2001), 'Die Chaosmächte Westafrikas', *Die Zeit* (27 July), 3.

Hancock, G. (1997 [1989]), *Lords of Poverty. The Freewheeling Lifestyles, Power, Prestige and Corruption of the Multibillion Dollar Aid Business* (London).

Keen, D. (1996), 'Ein sehr bürgerlicher Bürgerkrieg', *Die Tageszeitung* (7 February), 16–17.

Koehler, J. (2000), *Die Zeit der Jungs. Zur Organisation von Gewalt und der Austragung von Konflikten in Georgien* (Münster).

Krauthausen, C. (1997), *Moderne Gewalten. Organisierte Kriminalität in Kolumbien und Italien* (Frankfurt/M.).

Lock, P. (1997), 'Armed conflicts and small arms proliferation', *Policy Sciences*, 30 117–132.

Misser, F. (1997a), 'Mercenaries or security men?', *New African* (December), 14–16.

Misser, F. (1997b), 'The mercenary as corporate executive', *African Business* (December), 8–14.

Mummendey, D. (1997), *Beyond the Reach of Reason. The Congo Story 1960–1965* (Bonn).

Neubert, D. (1999), 'Dynamics of escalating violence. The genocide in Rwanda', in G. Elwert, S. Feuchtwang and D. Neubert (eds), *Dynamics of Violence. Processes of Escalation and De-Escalation in Violent Group Conflicts* (Berlin).

Rashid, A. *Taliban. The Story of Afghan Warlords* (London).

Schlee, G. '(1996), Traditionelle Totenrituale. Islamisierung und der Islam als Feindbild', in E. Orywal, A. Rao and M. Bollig (eds), *Krieg und Kampf. Die Gewalt in unseren Köpfen* (Berlin).

Schlee, G. (2000), 'Identitätskontruktionen und Parteinahme: Überlegungen zur Konflikttheorie', *Sociologus*, 1, 64–89.

Schwandner-Sievers, S. (1998), 'Wer besitzt die "Lizenz zum Töten" in Albanien? Oder: Fragen zu Gruppensolidarität und Gewaltlegitimation in einer "anderen Modernisierung"', in J. Koehler and S. Heyer (eds), *Anthropologie der Gewalt. Chancen und Grenzen der sozialwissenschaftlichen Forschung* (Berlin).

Spittler, G. 1988), *Handeln in einer Hungerkrise. Tuaregnomaden und die große Dürre* (Opladen).

Tilly, C. (1985). 'War making and state making as organized crime', in P. Evans, D. Rueschemeyer and T. Skocpol (eds), *Bringing the State Back In* (Cambridge).

Turnbull, C. (1972), *The Mountain People* (New York).

Waldmann, P. (1999), 'Societies in civil war', in G. Elwert, S. Feuchtwang and D. Neubert (eds), *Dynamics of Violence. Processes of Escalation and De-Escalation in Violent Group Conflicts* (Berlin).

Weber, M. (122), *Wirtschaft und Gesellschaft* (Tübingen).

Zitelmann, T. (1993), 'Violence, pouvoir symbolique et mode de représentation des Oromo', *Politique Africaine*, 50:3, 45–58.

Zürcher, C. (1998), 'Krieg und Frieden im Transformationsprozess: Tschetschenien', in J. Koehler and S. Heyer (eds), *Anthropologie der Gewalt. Chancen und Grenzen der sozialwissenschaftlichen Forschung* (Berlin).

13

Institutions and the organisation of stability and violence

Jan Koehler and Christoph Zürcher

Post-socialist turmoil in Yugoslavia and in the Caucasus

IN THE CAUCASUS and in Former Yugoslavia the collapse of the socialist empires has caused more hot conflicts and wars than in any other transition region. In each region there were four major armed conflicts. In the Caucasus, there was the disagreement between Armenians and Azeris over Nagorno-Karabakh (1988–93: no political settlement); the wars about Chechnya (1994–96 and 1999–today: no settlement); the internal war in Georgia (1991–92) and Georgia's war with breakaway Abkhazia (1992–93: no settlement); and breakaway South-Ossetia (1989–92: no settlement).

In Yugoslavia, the four major violent conflicts were the short campaign of the Yugoslav Army against the breakaway republic of Slovenia in June 1991; the wars between Croats and Serbs in eastern Slovenia and in the Krajina (1991–95); the war in Bosnia-Herzegovina (1992–95); and the war about Kosovo, which was fought on the one hand between Serbs and Kosovo-Albanians in Kosovo, and on the other hand between NATO and Serbia (1998–99).

Both the Caucasus and Former Yugoslavia are typical high-risk regions. At least four factors commonly held responsible for increasing the risk of violence are present.[1] First, there is the legacy of the socialist system of ethno-federalism (Brubaker 1994; Bunce 1999). Socialist ethno-federalism had linked territories with a titular nation and provided these territories with quasi-state institutions, such as citizenship, borders, symbols, political institutions, and in the case of Yugoslavia, armed forces. Ethno-national mobilisation for independence was thus prepared by the socialist systems. Secondly, in most cases there was also a past history of grievance and conflicts. Armenians and Azerbaijanis, Chechens and Russians, Serbs and Kosovars, Croats and Serbs all have stories and experiences of old animosity. Thirdly, the peoples of Yugoslavia and the USSR experienced economic hardships during the 1980s. Lastly, all polities in Yugoslavia and in the Caucasus (that is, the former Federal Republics and the former

Autonomous Republics) are multi-ethnic territories with a complex ethnic geography.

As a result, there is a wide array of conflict potential in both regions. However, far from all potential conflicts turned into violent conflicts. In other words, similar permissive conditions do not always and not automatically translate into violent conflicts. In the Caucasus, the most surprising case of stability against all odds is Dagestan (see Chapter 6 in this volume). Despite the fact that this tiny mountainous Republic is home to more than thirty national groups, borders war-torn Chechnya and suffers from dramatic economic deprivation, it has managed to avoid large-scale internal violence. But also in Yugoslavia, there are cases of stability against all odds. Voivodina, Montenegro and, until 1999, also Macedonia are such examples.

By comparing Yugoslavia and the Caucasus, differences in the intensity and scale of conflicts may be observed. Fighting in Yugoslavia, as a rule involved more armed people, and more civil victims. This may partly be explained by structural differences between Yugoslavia and the Caucasus, namely by the different structures of the federations, and by the way in which the federal centre was dismantled by the federal units.

In Yugoslavia during the 1980s, the most powerful of the Republics, Serbia, tried to usurp the position of the dwindling federal Yugoslav centre. When it became obvious to the Serbian leaders that they would not be able to hold together the federation, under the leadership of Slobodan Milosevic they switched to a nationalist agenda, trying to secure a 'greater Serbia' at the expense of the territorial integrity of Croatia and later Bosnia-Herzegovina. This triggered wars between nationalising states, although these wars were, as in the Krajina, in east Slovenia and especially in Bosnia, mainly fought by the proxies – the ethnic groups.

By contrast, in the USSR, it was Russia – by far the most powerful republic – that actively opposed (under Yeltsin's leadership) the restoration of the Union. Russia thus became, for a certain period, the natural ally of the breakaway republics. This explains the smooth and relatively peaceful dissolution of the USSR. Secondly, Russia itself is a multi-ethnic federation. Russia's state ideology is not based on Russian (*russkii*) ethno-nationalism, but on the multi-national Russian (*rossiiskii*) state. The Russian Federation was thus able (with the dramatic exception of Chechnya) to contain and defuse ethnic tensions within its territory.

In the South Caucasus, however, the patterns of conflict are similar to those in Yugoslavia. Here, the nationalising process of Georgia, Armenia and Azerbaijan was met with similar nationalising processes in the territories of minority groups within these states. The conflict between breakaway Nagorno-Karabakh and Azerbaijan stopped short of turning into an official inter-state war between Azerbaijan and Armenia and was accompanied by ethnic cleansing on all sides. In Georgia, the nationalising Georgian state was challenged by two ethno-national secessionist movements, in Abkhazia and South-Ossetia, which spiralled into wars accompanied by ethnic cleansing.

Violence, transition and state weakness

Between 1989 and 1991, both federations imploded. How was the emergence of organised violence visible both shortly before and after the break-up linked to this extreme form of state weakness?

The systemic transition that occurred in Yugoslavia and the USSR can be depicted as rapid institutional change, accompanied by a breakdown of hierarchies and by the loss of the state's sanction capacities. Systemic transition increases the risk of violence. Two mechanisms account for this: first, when the state loses its sanction capacity, the costs for breaking the rules fall. Secondly, in situation of transition, the premium for the winner is extremely high, because the winner takes all: what is at stake during transition is essentially the right to write the new rules. The future is at stake. In short, during transition, the costs for breaking the rules and organising violence sink, while the booty is 'fattened' (see Chapter 12 in this volume). The risk for socially 'dis-embedded', violent competition increases.[2]

These mechanisms apply to competition between all sorts of societal actors in transition societies. Relevant for the study of organised violence are, however, two arenas: first, the competition on the ground between two or more ethnic groups within a multi-ethnic polity. Notably, all Yugoslav and Soviet polities (that is, the first-order, Republics and the second-order Autonomies) are multi-ethnic polities.

Secondly, these mechanisms also apply for the competition between incumbent political elite and challenging political elite. Systemic transition always opens up opportunities for political newcomers to challenge incumbent leaders. During such intensified competition, actors may seek to use all available resources. The mobilisation of support by instrumentalising ethnicity can be one of the available strategies. This is, however, a very risky strategy, since it implies the promotion of a negative and threatening perception of the 'Other'. Ethno-radical mobilisation promotes fears of exclusion or even physical destruction, and can thus easily spin out of control.

A second threat to societal stability that comes with transition, state weakness and elite power struggles is the emergence of parallel and competing political institutions. When the entry into existing political institutions is blocked, challengers often create new, alternative *ad hoc* institutions. For example, challengers in Chechnya, Azerbaijan, Armenia and Georgia founded popular national movements. At a certain time, these alternative institutions were assigned so much political power that a situation of parallel power emerged: the formal socialist institutions, in the first place the Party and the Supreme Soviets, were opposed by organised national movements. In Armenia, in a relatively swift and constitutional move, the challengers took over the state and consolidated the new regime. In Chechnya, Georgia and Azerbaijan, however, the competition between the socialist institutions and the newly founded challenging institutions (the 'Popular Front' in Azerbaijan, 'Round Table/Free Georgia' in Georgia and the 'Chechen National Congress' in Chechnya) led to internal instability and eventually to internal war.

State weakness can cause violence. Therefore, it may be assumed that rebuilding state capacities must be a high priority of new leaders. A quite unexpected lesson to be learned from the study of organised violence in Yugoslavia and the Caucasus is that this assumption is not necessarily true. This lesson pertains in the first place to unrecognised would-be states (the formally second-order units). Abkhazia, South-Ossetia, Chechnya and Kosovo have made no significant progress towards strengthening their state capacities, despite their aspirations for sovereignty (Nagorno-Karabakh has to be regarded as an exception because of its very close informal integration with the Armenian Republic). It is argued here that this is not a paradox, but can be the rational strategy of a political elite: international legal sovereignty is a valuable resource. Establishing state capacities, with functioning state bureaucracies, however, is expensive, risky and can even contradict the interests of elites. All of these 'statelets' are governed by highly institutionalised networks of patronage. In order to stabilise these networks, the patrons of the networks have to satisfy the needs of their clientele. Not surprisingly, patrons in such weak network-states usually control access to resources. In order to secure their position, the patrons must prevent access to resources to potential challengers and hinder independent activities outside the network. Therefore, patrons will minimise public goods such as safety, protection, economic opportunities or legal protection; instead they will try to privatise these goods and to make them available only within the network. Patrons artificially minimise public goods. One means of achieving this is by keeping the state weak; another means is by tolerating or even promoting low-level conflict, even within their own state, since this increases insecurity and thus maximises the dependency of political actors (and the population) on the patron's good will. State weakness may thus even be the rational choice of leaders, who base their rule on networks of patronage (see Mappes-Niediek's Chapter 5 on Kosovo; Baev's and Christophe's Chapters 7 and 10, respectively, on Georgia; Koehler and Zürcher's Chapter 8 on Azerbaijan, Armenia and Nagorno-Karabakh; and Kisriev's Chapter 6 on Chechnya, in this volume).

Institutions matter

What accounts for the different ways the various post-socialist societies dealt with the stress of transition? The case studies in this volume look at the institutional framework of these societies for answers. It is argued here that institutions perform three functions which are relevant for the organisation of stability and violence:

First, institutions are accepted, trained and sometimes enforced patterns of interaction which 'embed' conflict. Institutions process competing interests: they offer rules and procedures for the articulation of interests, they provide for a flow of information between actors and they offer binding procedures for determining the outcome of interaction. Institutions, particularly official state institutions, are usually 'protected' – the state has the means to punish defiance. Violation of the procedures is thus expensive as long as the state has the capacity and the will to sanction defiance. The breakdown of such a framework lets conflict spin out of the framework that a society has designed in order to deal with conflicts. Conflict potential may then turn into escalated, violent conflict. The fact that a society has institutionalised procedures for dealing with conflicts in place does not mean that there is no conflict within the society. Conflicting interests are the normal state of affairs in every society.[3] Competing interests can be processed according to accepted rules or according to unregulated power. Internal fragmentation and violence is thus not a result of competing interests, but of unregulated, dis-embedded processing of competing interests.

Secondly, in general the institutional framework provides the incentive structure for actors. The costs of organising violence depend on the institutions at work. When the institutional framework of a society is such that the organisation of violence is cheap, then the risk of conflict increases. When, on the contrary, institutions increase the cost of violence, the risk decreases. In other words, it depends on the design of the institutional framework whether institutions defuse or diffuse violence. A case in point is the socialist system of ethno-federalism. This system, originally designed for processing potential tensions between national groups has, once the tight control of the party weakened, promoted secessionist conflicts and inter-group violence. The socialist system of ethno-federalism has prepared the quest for sovereignty and independence of the federal subjects of Yugoslavia and of the USSR. Ethno-federalism provided the subjects with a set of political institutions such as borders, symbols, a constitution, citizenship, parliaments, media, educational system, a titular nation and a national elite. All these prerequisites of statehood were well in place at the time that the empires broke down. Thus, the cost of state building was relatively low, and the national elite in the republics opted for independence. Likewise, the national elite of the second-order units (the so-called Autonomous Republics) opted for independence from 'their' republics. Not surprisingly, the borders of the second-order units mark the hot spots in Yugoslavia and the Caucasus – in Nagorno-Karabakh, South-Ossetia, Abkhazia, Chechnya and Kosovo.

Thirdly, institutions have distributional consequences. They structure access to resources and define, 'who gets what' in society. The relative power of actors in a society thus depends on the institutional framework. Changes of the institutional framework, accordingly, also have distributional consequences. When institutions cease to work, for example when the state loses its sanction capacity, then the old elite may lose access to resources, or challengers may gain access to resources. This shift in the relative power of 'incumbents' and 'challengers' may lead to an intensified struggle for power. The risk that this competition spins out of control is high, when the sanction power of the state is weakened. Institutions not only regulate access to resources, they are *per se* a resource. Institutions are a set of rules, and some of them have a considerable organisational power. Those who control bureaucratic or military hierarchies, parties, clan networks or networks of patronage can use the organisational power of these institutions in order to mobilise support.

Institutional framework and local know-how

Evidence from the case studies suggests that the presence of risk factors on the ground and the collapsing central state alone cannot explain the variance that may be observed across Yugoslavia and the Caucasus with regard to violent or non-violent social outcome.

An explanation of this variance in the institutional framework of these societies has been sought. But which institutions matter? Social spaces are veined with numerous rules and procedures; stability and violence are consequently a social outcome of many institutions intertwining. There is not and cannot be a general answer to the question which institutions matter, as this may vary significantly from case to case: however, the chapters in this volume present some road signs. First, the usual suspects matter: the formal political institutions of a polity – parliaments, presidency, election laws, parties, property rights or administrative divisions – are important. Significant parts of formal institutions of the USSR and the Yugoslav Federation survived the demise of the central state and were and still are of consequence. The importance of the administrative–territorial division of the ethno-federations has already been stressed. Other important legacies of the socialist system are the party structure and the socialist rubber-stamp parliaments, which acquired real influence during the course of transition. In fact, internal cohesion or internal fragmentation depended a lot on how and by whom these institutions were reused. When elites use existing, 'trained' institutions for conquering or keeping the state, the risk of social fragmentation is lower than when elites invent new institutions, such as round tables, popular fronts, or national congresses. For example, the communist *apparatchik* Milosevic rose by taking over the organisational potential of the Serbian Communist Party and reusing it for his nationalist agenda. The key to his 'success' was combining two central resources of post-socialist spaces, namely the mobilising power of ethnicity and the organisational power of party structures. The price for Serbia's internal stability was paid, however, by its neighbours, because Milosevic proved to be very skilful at externalising conflicts.

An analysis of the institutional framework of society must not be limited to formal state institutions. In challenging widespread state-centric approaches, it has been argued here that the institutional framework of post-socialist societies consists not only of the institutional legacy of 'official' state institutions, but also of the 'shadow' institutions that have emerged as a response to the organisational voids of socialism, and of those locally rooted traditional norms and conventions that survived in the organisational voids of the socialist state. These three analytically distinct sets of institutions – the 'formal', the 'shadow' and the 'traditional'– form together a hybrid, locally distinct framework, which structures incentives, opportunities and constraints of actors on the ground.

The existence of a locally distinct, colourful and largely informal set of institutions clearly contradicts the superficial picture of homogeneous, centralised socialist states fostered by many outside observers, ruling elites and dissident intellectuals alike (compare Hann 1996: 7–10). All chapters in this book stress the fact that the socialist societies were at least in the last decade of their existence socialist only in form, but informal and locally distinct in content.

The socialist state in its last two decades was a rather weak state, although its vertical command lines were functional until the late 1980s. The social institutions compensating for (or simply exploiting) the failures, voids and weaknesses were informal, often even illegal, since the blueprints of the socialist state did not foresee societal organisation outside the realm of the state's control.

These unofficial institutions went largely undetected by political science and sovietology, which focused mainly on 'official' state institutions. Again, it is impossible to name which of these 'shadow' institutions are in general relevant for the explanation of violence. But here, too, road signs exist, and the chapters in this book present some evidence.

Of the issues with which this book is concerned, the most significant organisational void of the socialist state was that it formally banned all open social conflict. On the other hand, it relied on social self-organisation to fill the gaps. Instead of founding its legitimacy on setting the general rules for local institutions regulating conflict, the state condemned those institutions to the shadows of informality or even criminality. Thus conflict was socially embedded in the informal sector but not institutionalised by official state institutions.

By denying the existence of the conflicting interests of social groups the state was unable to provide a framework of checks and balances between identity groups or socio-professional lobbies in a given administrative unit. Competing interests were pushed beneath the official surface and were accordingly dealt with by informal bureaucratic barter at the few 'switchboards' of decision making. Minority groups had therefore no official channels for lobbying their real or perceived grievances. Even lobbying for a change in administrative status (like in Kosovo in the late 1970s or in Nagorno-Karabakh on repeated occasions over the decades after the death of Stalin) had to be organised via informal channels and was usually aimed directly at the corridors of power in the centre, thus bypassing the formal political institutions. The failure of the state to provide for official arenas in which identity groups (here the titular nation and a minority) were able to settle their disputes by procedures aggravated the tendency of radicals of such groups to retreat to what Elwert called 'informational isolates' (Elwert 2001a). This in turn increases the risk of future violent conflict, since these informational islands breed radical and exclusive views of the other group.

One species that grew especially well in the organisational voids of the socialist state were omnipresent networks of patronage (cf. Willerton 1992). After the collapse of the central state, these networks became, in many places, the most cohesive institutional structure, substituting state tasks and concentrating political power and economic resources.

The most powerful and relevant informal networks developed in the shadow of the official socialist institutions and were usually closely linked to administrative functionaries who, by virtue of their official position, had the power to allocate resources, privileges and protection to their clientele. Often, patrons of such networks were the provincial 'strong men' which Koehler and Zürcher in Chapter 8 in this volume call *apparatchiki-biznesmeny*. After the collapse of empire, many of these *apparatchiki-biznesmeny* smoothly turned into *biznesmeny-patrioty*. It has been shown in another study that in all cases of organised violence in the Caucasus, the financial resources that are needed for the – expensive – organisation of violence came from the Soviet 'shadow' economy (Zürcher, Koehler and Baev, 2002). The *biznesmeny-patrioty* that have grown rich in the shadow economy were the most important financiers of the wars in the Caucasus. Raufer and Mappes-Niediek in Chapters 3 and 5, respectively, in this volume reach similar conclusions with regard to the war in Kosovo.

Networks of patronage and trust were especially well suited to exploiting the opportunities that the booming shadow economy of the late socialist state offered the entrepreneurially minded (on the scope and growth of the shadow economy in the former USSR see Baev's Chapter 7 in this volume). Often such networks were built around clans and neighbourhoods in order to inject the measure of trust and cohesion that a successful exploitation of the opportunities of the socialist economy requires. Thus, as a by-product of generating trust, many networks developed an ethnic flavour. Often informal economic activity thus became ethnicised, and the competition for scarce resources was structured by ethnic belonging (see Koehler and Zürcher's Chapter 8 on Nagorno-Karabakh in this volume).

The border between networks of patronage designed for the exploitation of the 'shadow' economy and outright criminal networks is blurred, since all economic activities outside the planned economy of the state were by and large illegal.[4] In addition, one activity of criminal networks in the late socialist state, apart from taxing the informal economy, was to provide services for the *apparatchiki-biznesmeny* such as protection, contract-security and mechanisms of enforcement or sanction.[5] There is little comprehensive research on organised crime in the late socialist state, but evidence suggests that organised crime played an important role in resource generating and organising violence. Koehler and Zürcher's Chapter 8, Baev's Chapter 7, Mappes-Niediek's Chapter 5 and Raufer's Chapter 3 in this volume all support this assumption. They also lend credibility to the notion that closely-knit ties based on kinship with a high degree of exclusiveness were well suited to the organisation of criminal activity. In the former USSR and in former Yugoslavia such normative frames of reference, referred to as 'amoral familism'[6] (Schwandner-Sievers 1998 on Albania), could be found as a parallel legal code in remote regions of Chechnya in the North Caucasus, Abkhazia and Svanetia in the Southern Caucasus and in Montenegro and Kosovo. Under conditions of increasing physical and social mobility (as in growing diaspora communities in remote cities) the exclusive code of such small-scale identity groups sometimes became relevant for the effective organisation of mafia-like criminal networks (see Raufer's Chapter 3 on Kosovo in this volume; compare Jamieson and Silj 1998: 20–39)

Finally, in the organisational voids of the late socialist state a colourful patchwork of 'traditional' institutions may be found, dealing with conflict and negotiating justice and access to resources which had survived socialist homogenisation. 'Traditional' institutions are presented here as local institutions without official character that use narratives of traditional depth as a resource for legitimacy.

Kisriev's Chapter 6 on Dagestan in this volume provides an illuminating example. Stability against all odds in multi-ethnic Dagestan can be explained by the existence of the system of *dzhamaat*. In Dagestan, '*dzhamaat*' denotes a solidarity group, based primarily on neighbourhoods and not on ethnicity that has been in existence since the fifteenth century. In today's Dagestan, the *dzhamaat* forms the core political unit and performs many functions that in western democracies are performed by political parties. Dagestan's constitution and electoral law reinforces the importance of the *dzhamaat*: in Dagestan, only single-mandate electoral constituencies exist, and in each constituency only representatives from one ethnic group can run in elections. Political competition on the local level thus takes place between *dzhamaats*, but not between ethnic groups. Thus, the 'traditional' institution of *dzhamaat* and formal political institutions intertwine and produce societal stability. This example also demonstrates that even in weak states conflict can be effectively socially embedded over long periods of time, thanks to the division of labour between official and informal institutions.

Violent conflict as dynamic process

Conflict escalation and de-escalation is, rather than a temporal sequence of different phases in time, a dynamic process, during which the rationales of the conflicting parties and the incentive structures that govern their action undergo dramatic changes. The initial rationales of a dispute may thus be very different from those that actually trigger the conflict and from those that eventually lead to either the stabilisation of a violent environment or to a departure from violence.

Generalising the material presented in this book, four different stages of the conflict process may be identified, called here 'dis-embedding conflict', 'markets of violence', 'ending violence' and 're-embedding conflict.'

Dis-embedding conflict

'Dis-embedding' is the process whereby conflict spins out of the socially constructed bonds designed to deal with it. There are four significant markers that accompany the dis-embedding of conflict, and each in its own right may serve as an early warning indicator: the loss of the binding power of official institutions; the loss of the state's legitimate monopoly of violence; access to resources for organisers of violence; and the emergence of organised groups that partly substitute the state.

The loss of the binding power of official institutions for the relevant groups in society has been a latent condition in the late socialist state. The socialist state, rather than provide for institutionalised procedures for dealing with conflicts over resources or positions, has pushed social conflicts into the informal sphere. As a result, official state institutions were detached from the relevant spheres of society's self-organisation. Parallel institutions developed or were empowered to back up functions not provided by the state. The weaker the legitimacy of state institutions became, the stronger the capacity and legitimacy of the parallel structures in place grew. This interdependency between the state and its competitors is most straightforwardly demonstrated in the performance of the Serbian state and the reaction of the Albanian community in Kosovo (see Mappes-Niediek's Chapter 5 in this volume).

The second factor that marks the dis-embedding of conflict is the loss of the state's legitimate monopoly of violence. Chapters 5, 7, 8 and 2 on Kosovo, Georgia, Nagorno-Karabakh and Bosnia, respectively, in this volume demonstrate that the state's monopoly of violence is not only endangered by dwindling state capacities; actually, they indicate that the real threat to the state's monopoly of violence is the loss of its legitimacy to use it. Legitimacy may break down owing to unpredictable or regular misuse of the state monopoly (as was the case of the Soviet state in Armenia, Azerbaijan and Georgia) or when it is taken over by one social force that is party to a conflict. A case in point is the attempt to take

252

over the Yugoslav structures (above all, the army) by Serbian nationalist forces. Grandits and Leutloff's Chapter 1 in this volume describes this process from a local perspective in the case of the Krajina.

This loss of legitimacy of the central state was not, with the possible exception of Armenia in the Caucasus and Serbia in Former Yugoslavia, successfully backed up anywhere by the enforcement bodies of the newly independent states. They were seen either as party to the conflict (from the perspective of internal breakaway 'statelets' like Krajina, Nagorno-Karabakh or Abkhazia) or utterly ineffective and atomised beyond any central state control (most dramatically in Azerbaijan and Georgia until 1995).

A third factor that speeds up the dis-embedding of conflict is access to the three resources necessary for the organisation of violence, namely finance, manpower and weapons. The socialist 'shadow' economy provided enough opportunities to the *biznesmeny-patrioty* to acquire the necessary funds and channel them into the organisation of violence. Other sources of income stem from the diaspora and the profits from international crime, demonstrated in the case of Kosovo in Raufer's Chapter 3 in this volume.

Access to weapons is a second significant factor. Mappes-Niediek's Chapter 5 on Kosovo in this volume shows how rapidly the relatively stable and non-violent situation changed once cheap automatic firearms were available from the storehouses of the failing Albanian state. In the Caucasus, weapons came in very large quantities from the storehouses of the disintegrating Soviet Army. Both the newly independent states and challenging rebel formations had no problems in arming themselves with cheaply bought or easily stolen Soviet weapons.

The third factor that helps dis-embed conflict is manpower. The organisation of violence requires the existence of groups of young men[7] detached from state control or the gerontocratic social control of their families. The latter seems very likely in situations where the traditional family structure is either unable to secure a future career (be it official, informal or criminal) for their young males, or young men perceive the participation in gangs outside social control as a real short-cut to access resources traditionally controlled by the older generation. Mappes-Niediek's Chapter 5 in this volume shows the relevance of this condition for Kosovo. The breakdown of social control over young men and weapons has also been a dramatic experience especially for the older generation in Chechnya between the two wars in the 1990s and during the Georgian troubles at the beginning of the 1990s (Koehler 2000: 48–50, 71–74).

Such groups are capable of organising violence only when they possess mechanisms for internal coordination and internal sanction. This is where the last indicator for 'serious trouble ahead' comes into the equation: the existence of gangs or networks, often set up initially by specialists of informal violence (like patrons of organised crime), is the last factor that marks the dis-embedding of conflict. There is a myriad of colourful personalities – most of them now dead or in prison – competing for dubious fame: for Albania, Raufer's Chapter 3 in this volume outlines the cases of Agim Gashi and Princ Dobroshi; from the Bosnian war, violence specialists like 'Arkan', 'Tuta', 'Stela' (Hedges 1996; Wood 2000); and 'Juka', 'Celo' and 'Caco' in Sarajevo (Schork 1994) were important in the initial phase of organising collective violence by mobilising armed youths and then merging business interests with the opportunities of the emerging market of violence. In Georgia, criminal authorities like Djaba Ioseliani and shady *biznesmeny-patrioty* like Tengiz Kitovani even succeeded in temporarily taking over the state (Koehler 1999). In Chechnya, Bislan Gantemirov, former *militsioner* (Soviet policeman) and entrepreneur in the 'shadow' economy, set up the first armed gang in Grozny that was to become the backbone of Dudaev's National Guard.

As stated above, the important characteristic of these groups is that they develop internal sanction capacities: defiance of the group's rules may then often be costlier for the young members than challenging the crumbling state's monopoly of violence. At the same time, such groups offer personal security, protection of private business and trust for their members and clients. In so doing, they may become a highly effective competitor for the weak state and partly substitute state functions.

The establishment of such groups, ready to exploit the new opportunities for acquiring resources of violence and further undermining the weakened legitimacy of the state monopoly of violence and the binding capacity of the official institutions, occurred at some stage in all the cases presented in this volume (explicitly in the conflicts in the Krajina, Kosovo, Georgia and around Nagorno-Karabakh). Those armed groups were made from different raw materials (criminal, ethnic, clan or neighbourhood networks of trust) and usually went under an ideological banner of patriotism, nationalism (as in most cases presented in this volume) or protection of the ethnic kin and freedom as general anti-state approach (as in the cases of Chechnya and Kosovo). As competitors for 'the heart of the state' they were already in place before violence escalated beyond state control.

Both Kisriev's Chapter 6 on Dagestan and Vasilieva's Chapter 9 on the greater part of the North Caucasus in this volume show that the disintegration of central statehood even where weapons are available does not automatically lead to violence spinning out of control. Local institutions in many cases proved capable of not 'dis-embedding' violence and kept evolving violent alternatives to the retreating central state under social control. There may well be other such cases in the Caucasus and in Former Yugoslavia – like Adjaria in Georgia, Ingushetia bordering Chechnya, Montenegro, the Voivodina and (until recently) Macedonia – in which violence has been kept in check by institutions other than the state.

However, the more striking process has the state disintegrating into an armed gang warfare (see the cases of Krajina (Chapter 1), Kosovo (Chapter 5), Herceg-Bosna (Chapter 2), Nagorno-Karabakh (Chapter 8), Chechnya (Chapter 6) and Georgia (Chapter 7) in this volume) and thus heralding the next stage of violent performance.

Markets of violence

Whatever the rationale for escalation may have been, sustained organised violence has a high probability of stabilising as what Elwert's chapter 12 in this volume describes as 'markets of violence'. According to Elwert, markets of violence are 'understood as economic areas dominated by civil wars, warlords or robbery, in which a self-perpetuating system emerges which links non-violent commodity markets with the violent acquisition of goods' (p. 221).

The implication of this development is that no matter what stimuli, noble ideas or justified grievances may have accompanied or even motivated the process thus far, collective organised violence develops its own systemic rules. Once violent conflict is institutionalised as a market of violence, then the process of dismantling state institutions can hardly be reversed. There may be no way back to the *status quo ante*. The institutionalisation of violence as an integral part of everyday life is a change in paradigm that brings along a set of new rules, new types of actors with distinct limits, choices, and rationales; the institutionalisation of a market of violence may be seen as a systemic border after which the rules that governed society are replaced by a completely different logic of action. From the local perspective of the people used to the former institutions, this process has to be perceived as destructive and even traumatic.

While the core of the conflict may still be socio-political, the strategic actions of the entrepreneurs of violence are increasingly structured by short-term economic gains. The organisation of violence is expensive, and sustained violence needs continuous investment. Therefore, entrepreneurs of violence engage in economic activities which characteristically combine legal business activities, organised crime and warfare. This economy tends to be integrated in transnational networks of trade and investment. Entrepreneurs of violence engage in drug or weapons trafficking, in kidnapping, extortion, or in taxing the second economy. Profits are reinvested, or kept in offshore banks. Gradually, short-term economic interests replace long-term political ones, and entrepreneurs of violence become interested in avoiding battles and sustaining profit.

Once a market of violence is established, there is a strong rationale for the warlords to stabilise the *status quo*. If government officials receive a share of the revenues from the market of violence (or are themselves embarking on warlord politics), they might also become interested in prolonging this violence. In such cases sustaining low-level violence becomes a rational objective of both, the 'rebels' and the 'state'. This view contradicts the commonly held view of prolonged conflicts as an 'unintended and anarchical outcome', and it also contradicts the official discourse of governments and rebels. Such a situation is characterised by the lack of real battles between soldiers and rebels. Both sides may pretend to fight a war, but neither side is determined to commit substantial resources in order to win and end the war.

The profit-orientated entrepreneur of violence is at first glance hard to distinguish from the politically motivated rebel. They may share the same political discourse on historical injustices and political motivations, recruit from the same pool of recruits und pursue similar military tactics. However, the profit-oriented entrepreneur of violence has a different ranking of priorities: the main rational is making economic profit. Profit-orientated entrepreneurs of violence go for absolute gains, while the political motivated rebel goes for relative gains *vis-à-vis* the state they are fighting.

Negotiating political solutions to conflicts with entrepreneurs of violence is difficult. Often they have no interest in ending violence because only the escalation of violence brought and kept them in the leading positions and enabled them to keep the loyalty of their armed followers by acquiring booty to redistribute. Entrepreneurs of violence may be very reluctant to agree to any peace settlement. A successful peace settlement may lead to the strengthening of the state and to the re-establishment of a state monopoly of violence. This in turn would destroy the biotope in which markets of violence blossom. In their view, peace settlements are bad for business. Once a conflict zone has turned into a fully developed market of violence, any political solution, even one that fully takes into account the original grievances that caused the conflict, is prone to fail. There are no political solutions for violence that is mainly motivated by private profits. Entrepreneurs of violence cannot be involved in a lasting (and maybe costly) peace settlement by granting political concessions to the group they pretend to represent, since this is not their first preference.

This is not to say that entrepreneurs of violence cannot, in principle, be involved in conflict regulation. But it is vital to understand that their first preference is to make absolute gains. Hence, they even might support a conflict regulation plan that weakens the 'rebel state', if it increases their profit. They can, in other words, be bought. The latter point was most likely relevant in Kosovo since the leaders of the KLA had reason to feel confident that they would play leading roles in post-Serbian Kosovo and retain significant access to profitable resources (not always of the legal kind, as pointed out by Raufer's Chapter 3 in this volume).

On the other hand, the most prominent warlords of Former Yugoslavia, Mladic and Karadjic had no options for political careers in a post-war Bosnia under the auspices of the international community. Consequently, in order to smooth the Dayton process, international negotiators put considerable effort into deconstructing them as possible negotiating partners before Dayton.

All violent conflicts in Yugoslavia and the Caucasus developed for a certain period into markets of violence. In comparison to near 'ideal-types' of markets of violence like Afghanistan, Lebanon, Sierra Leona or the Democratic Republic of Congo this stage was, however relatively brief, except for Chechnya, which has been completely torn apart by rival entrepreneurs of violence after the defeated Russian army left in 1996. The second Russian intervention in 1999 has until now not managed to dry out this market of violence.

Departure from violence

How did the Caucasian and Yugoslav polities depart from large-scale, organised political violence? The first striking observation with regard to this question pertains to the remarkable differences between the Caucasus and the Balkans. In the Balkans, the military defeats of the Serbs in the wars in Bosnia and about Kosovo, which paved the way to the end of violence, were achieved only owing to decisive international intervention. Likewise, the current non-violent situation in Macedonia, Bosnia and in Kosovo and the attempts at reconstructing the state are borrowed from the international community. It was international military intervention that implemented a monopoly of violence. In Bosnia and even more so in Kosovo, state functions are *de facto* executed by the international community. Security and the suppression of violence are exercised by foreign troops and are not an achievement of internal organisation.

By contrast, in the Caucasus, there has been no military intervention by the international community, and the precarious stability in and between the post-Soviet states and 'statelets' is a result of internal organisation and of coming to terms with the consequences of performances on the battlefield.

It is noteworthy that Russia, Georgia and Azerbaijan were all unable to win the wars against their secessionist regions. Nagorno-Karabakh, South-Ossetia and Abkhazia are *de facto* independent 'statelets', and so was Chechnya until the second Russian military intervention in 1999. On the other hand, none of the secessionist regions has been able to gain internationally recognised independence, and none has concluded a peace treaty with the state from which it seceded.

The military victories of rebel territories are statistically rather a rare occurrence, since the central state usually commands more resources than the challengers. In the Caucasus, the success of the breakaway territories may be explained by the weakness of the newly independent states. Both Georgia and Azerbaijan had to organise their state capacities from scratch. They were economically and politically weak states that lacked the resources for intensive warfare, their soldiers were badly trained and hardly motivated to fight a dangerous war in order to keep peripheral regions within the central state. In addition, both Georgia and Azerbaijan were plagued by internal power struggles. Finally, these wars took place in societies that are haunted by a very high level of corruption. When corruption is widespread – sometimes even the single most important source of income for the state administration – people from ministers and high-ranking officers to privates may profit from the state of war. They may then become interested in prolonging the state of war, but have no real interest in fighting, winning and ending the war. Thus, the violent contest between 'secessionist rebels' and 'states' in the Caucasus resembled the competition between two upstarts. In the wars of Azerbaijan against the breakaway Nagorno-Karabakh and Georgia against the breakaway Abkhazia and South-Ossetia, the 'rebel' upstarts proved to be much more efficient in organising violence (including resources form outside) than the 'upstart states' they challenged. Consequently, the 'rebels' won on the battlefield.

Departing from violence requires not only coming to terms with the neighbouring state or the neighbouring groups. It also requires the reconstruction of statehood and state capacities. The post-war polities must, in the first place, execute their legitimate monopoly of violence and integrate or neutralise those groups that have an interested in prolonging conflict.

In Kosovo, Bosnia and more recently Macedonia, this task has been largely outsourced. It is the international community that provides these territories with the most basic state capacities. By contrast, the post-war Caucasian polities had to master their internal post-war consolidation by themselves. A formidable challenge they had to meet was the neutralisation of entrepreneurs of violence returning from the battlefield and aspiring to take over leading positions in politics and business. Not all polities have mastered this task. The most dramatic failure was Chechnya. President Maskhadov's strategy of incorporating key players of the market of violence in his administration only sped up the process of disintegration. By the end of 1998, rivalling warlords had completely dismantled the few remaining state institutions and turned Chechnya into a market of violence.

More successful were the attempts at reconstructing statehood elsewhere. In Georgia and in Azerbaijan, the old guard of professional political patrons incorporated key players of the market of violence into state-run power agencies, only to neutralise or outmanoeuvre them at a later date. As it turned out, extensive Soviet-trained networks of patronage proved to be a resource strong enough to oust the warlords.

This, however, succeeded at the cost of opening significant shares of state resources to the ambitions of the old networks of patrons that guaranteed non-violent stability and at the cost of empowering certain powerful agencies to act as state agents beyond the control of state (the police in Georgia, the army in Armenia and the presidential apparatus in Azerbaijan).

In the case of Armenia, where a dogmatic idea of common national cause with existential urgency remained a paramount integrating factor throughout the war, coming to terms with the returning victorious 'former truck drivers turned generals turned deputy ministers' proved to be a very serious and not always peaceful challenge. Here – as in Nagorno-Karabakh – the Soviet networks that managed to establish a stagnant stability in Azerbaijan and Georgia had a much harder time competing with, first, the new nationalist elite and then the entrepreneurs of violence returning victorious from the war in Nagorno-Karabakh. With the violent death of both the former First Secretary of the CP in Soviet Armenia and icon of Soviet patronage (Karen Demirchian) and the leading strong man (Prime Minister and former Minister of Defence, Vazgen Sarkisian) who were assassinated in the 1999 parliament massacre, a relatively new network of former politicians from neighbouring Nagorno-Karabakh was left to run the state (most prominently President Robert Kocharian and Minister of Defence Serzh Sarkisian).

Re-embedding conflict

The process of conflict spinning out of socially constructed bonds has been called 'dis-embedding'. Re-embedding means therefore taming conflict by (rebuilding) socially constructed bonds that reverse this process.

In the study of violent conflict the problem of institutionalising peace is usually not regarded as a dynamic social process in its own right, separate from the departure from violence. It is either treated as a problem of society after conflict, detaching the question of peace from the dynamics that ruled conflict before, or peace is simply treated as the absence of war.

The approach taken in this book has been different from the outset. By regarding conflict as a crucial, yet very common phenomenon in society the focus was shifted away from tale and content of the quarrel to the question of the institutional embedding of conflict in order to understand the processes of violent escalation or its containment in the Caucasus and Former Yugoslavia. 'Embedding' refers to a conflict being socially controlled by internalised norms and values and dealt with by the existing and reliable institutions a society has in place. The ability for adaptation to changing conditions and innovation proved essential for the societies in transition to keep conflict embedded and avoid passing the threshold of no return and sliding into an economy of violence.

Providing institutions and procedures for handling conflicts in a predictable way according to known rules is essential for the cohesion of a society and can actually be the foundation of the state's legitimacy (Luhmann 1983 [1969]: 100–106). It was the economist Albert Hirschman who convincingly claimed that it is not so much common values that integrate a modern society but the implemented and guarded institutional equipment of reinterpreting either-or conflicts into more-or-less conflicts (Hirschman 1994). The disruptive potential of a zero-sum game where total gain of a winner means total loss for the loser is changed according to the rules provided by a third uninvolved party (the institution, e.g. a court) into a negotiated outcome. In other words those institutions must protect the complexity and graduation of a conflict from techniques of radical simplification by force – power techniques that lead to either-or approaches or even deny the opponent the right to dispute altogether.

The question of re-establishing peace therefore has to be approached in the same basic way. The crucial question is which institutions societies and states have left after sustained violence in order to re-embed conflict, and what capacities they have to build new ones. Societies after conflict must ensure that vital state tasks such as providing security and opportunities are not taken over by organised groups; they must prevent organisers of violence accessing resources; they must re-establish a legitimate monopoly of violence; and they must, finally, provide social coherence by establishing the institutions that integrate a society. These are complex tasks that require time and resources that most post-war societies do not have. The odds that this will happen without external intervention, relying solely on societal self-organisation, are very slim.

A brief overview over the cases presented in this volume shows that none of the post-war societies has until now managed to complete these tasks. All of them are still struggling with the many obstacles on the road to institutionalised peace, and where stability has been achieved, it has come at a price.

Armenia has been the most stable of the Transcaucasian states. The reason for this may be found in the ethic homogeneity and in the perception of a constant threat of national disaster that is both an integral part of modern Armenian identity and a political reality in the post-Soviet period. The price for the relative stability has been the externalisation of conflict, a price that both Armenians and Azeris had to pay. As an Armenian taxi driver in Yervan in the summer of 2000 put it when complaining about the recently aggravated problem of high-level political violence: 'Our problem is our ethnic homogeneity. We have only each other to blame and fight with.'[8]

In former Yugoslavia, reconstruction of statehood has so far been borrowed from the international community, which has invested considerable military and financial resources. The experience in Kosovo teaches us that the task is extremely difficult. Despite the presence of an overwhelmingly and widely accepted military force, and despite the impressive financial resources the European Union is committing to the rebuilding of a working state structure in Kosovo, Bosnia and Macedonia, only extremely benevolent observers would think that the operation has ended successfully. On the contrary – external forces are getting more and more deeply involved in the Balkans, and the chances are very high that conflicts will very soon remerge, were it not for the presence of the externals.

With regard to Kosovo, is very doubtful whether those groups that have successfully organised violence are willing to engage in meaningful state building efforts. The fact that the UCK has been deeply involved in a criminal economy makes it rather unlikely that this group will become the backbone of the state. In addition, Mappes-Niediek's Chapter 5 in this volume reminds us that Kosovars in general place their loyalty and their efforts much more in the extended family than the state. It is not hard to predict that the KFOR and the UN administration of Kosovo will sooner or later have to engage this problem, thereby risking becoming regarded as an occupying force rather than as protector.

The case of Bosnia also provides an important lesson. External intervention does not automatically pave the way for state reconstruction. As Gosztonyi's Chapter 2 in this volume demonstrates, intervention can actually contribute to a diffusion of power. The intervening force's efforts at establishing a monopoly of violence and at holding responsible the local strong men actually makes it rational for local elites to appoint weak leaders and to create an institutional 'jungle' in order to diffuse responsibility. In time, the local elite loses the ability to commit themselves and to deliver – both preconditions for instability and contradictory to the fundamental task of re-embedding conflict. Such counterstrategies of local networks prove effective unless intervening states or alliances are willing to establish a long-lasting protectorate and resume semi-colonial responsibilities – a task that would clearly overstretch the capacities of the international community, even if it wished to do so.

Looking back at a decade of coming to terms with conflict in post-socialist Yugoslavia and the Caucasus, the picture is, as always, neither one thing nor another. On the one hand, all conflicts in the regions are for the time being frozen, with the exception of Chechnya. However, stability in the Caucasus is precarious, as it is, despite the commitment of the international community, in the Balkans. Most successor states of the empires are still far from having established a legitimate monopoly of violence – either it is defunct and working only when the state happens to drive past, or it is rented out from international organisations. And lastly, in many cases the networks of patronage of the late socialist state took over and are in effect running the remnants of the state. Therefore, it would be very wrong to believe that trading the imitation of socialism for the imitation of democracy spares the new states (or the international organisations in charge of implementing state institutions) from the pitfalls of weak statehood.

And finally: a word on methodology

It has been argued here that violence and stability in post-socialist societies cannot be explained without taking into consideration the hybrid institutional framework of the locality under consideration, since it is the local 'traditional' institutions that account for the remarkable variance revealed by comparing the potential hot spots in Yugoslavia and the Caucasus. Such local institutions process the impact of various 'risk factors' and determine whether a society deals with these factors in a non-violent way. Violence, and especially internal and common violence, is organised at the local level. Consequently, it has been argued here that the local institutional framework is the most promising level of analysis. This is not to say that the institutional framework of a polity is not subject to external influences, clearly the weakening of the central state hierarchies; the (intended or unintended) effects of the policies of third countries; the (intended or unintended) effects of the policies of international organisations and spillover of violence ('bad neighbourhoods') all impact upon the incentive structures of local actors. External influence is important, but it needs to be investigated from the local perspective.

How can such micro-politics of violence be captured?

Analytical narratives dealing with the organisation of violence may profit from a multi-disciplinary approach. Since 1980, quantitative probabilistic studies have made significant progress in identifying risk factors.[9] Economic deprivation, a high level of dependence on primary commodity exports, ethnic composition, terrain, previous conflicts, perceived and real grievances and 'bad neighbourhoods' are among the most prominent risk factors. Analytical narratives should watch out for such factors. One should, however, be aware that risk factors do not automatically turn into violence. Statistically measured probabilities inform about risks; but they do not show anything about causal links. For organised violence to emerge, it takes certain social situations in which actors think that the relative costs of violence are lower than the relative costs of nonviolence. Otherwise actors would not engage in the organisation of violence. In other words, the organisation of violence depends on the incentive and opportunity structure in which actors are locked. Often, the most relevant of these structures are not official state institutions, but informal and traditional institutions in the shadow of the façade of statehood. Detecting these requires an intimate knowledge of the local. Conducting traditional ethnographical fieldwork captures unofficial institutions, networks, norms and values systems that help examine local social settings, in which the official (normative) story conceals rather than reveals the 'real' story of why actors act.

To what extent can insights, produced by such a research design, be generalised? What is the potential contribution to theory building of an approach that focuses on the institutional framework of a society? Such an approach would produce more than a story and less than a theory. Such a research strategy would hardly provide the 'parsimonious, elegant models with a high prediction power' of which the political scientists of the 1970s and 1980s dreamed. It would also not produce yet another account of how violence emerged in a specific time in a specific place under specific circumstances. The level of abstraction stops halfway: the 'causes' for violence or stability cannot be generalised, since violence is a strategy that, in principle, can be chosen in every social situation. However, it is possible to generalise aspects of the process of organising violence and stability. Some of these have been presented in this chapter.

NOTES

1   For a useful overview of factors which can increase the risk for ethnopolitical violence, see van Evera (1994); Brown (1997); Gurr and Harff (1995).

2   The fact that institutions usually function within the values and belief systems of a society, i.e. are 'morally embedded' (unlike the institutions of markets of violence), is usually not considered in purist economic definitions of institutions. For the stabilising effect of moral embedding even for commodity markets see Elwert (1989: 459); compare also Norbert Elias' concept of internalised norms as conditions for establishing social space devoid of violence ('*gewaltfreie Räume*', Elias 1992 [1969]: 312–336).

3   It was Lewis Coser's congenial reading and further development of Georg Simmel's approaches to social conflict that laid the ground for an understanding of the significance of conflict and its institutionalisation for the dynamic cohesion and development of society (Coser 1956).

4   This pattern is also applicable to those seemingly authoritarian post-socialist states: if the state is not directly and openly involved in the control of civil institutions (like in Serbia under Milosovic) it necessitates them, just like trade and business, to seek the (illegal) patronage of state institutions. The notion that Command States – to borrow a term developed by Elwert in African case studies – are often weak states in an institutional sense is contradictory only at first sight. According to Elwert's definition, '[t]he Command State is a system of politics and administration characterised by the primacy of present authority in daily life interaction and an ambiguous relation with legal norms, which however define the overall power sharing within the apparatus' (Elwert 2001b: 420). If state institutions are not running in accordance with their own norms – if an only formally democratic or socialist government is, for example, relying entirely on the 'power ministries' (the military, police or secret services) for control and in its legitimacy is relying on informal networks of patrons distributing state resources – they may be considered 'weak'. As in the case of the late socialist states the rules providing stability are borrowed from other institutions.

5   For a differentiation of official, informal and criminal economy on a global scale, see Lock (2001).

6   The term was developed in Mediterranean anthropology (Banfield 1958) and has been criticised as normative derogatory. The concept was, however, applied to analyse family–state relations in Serbia (Simic 1991).

7   For the time being women and children did not play a decisive role in the organisation of violence in the Caucasus and former Yugoslavia. The appearance of groups of female fighters in the course of some conflicts (like, for example, the 'Anahit'-detachment in Nagorno-Karabakh) is the exception to the rule and not a widespread social phenomenon with an impact on the organisation of violence.

8   Conversation with Koehler in June 2000, as remembered.

9   Prominent projects are, among others, the Correlates of War Project (cf. Singer and Small 1994); the State Failure Project (cf. Gurr, Harff and Marshall 1997); the Polity Data (cf. Jaggers and Gurr 1995); the Minorities at Risk (cf. Gurr 1993); The Economics of Political and Common Violence. The World Bank Development Economic Research Group DECRG. (cf. www.worldbank.org/research/conflict/index.htm). The key paper from this project is Collier and Hoeffler (2001).

REFERENCES

Banfield, E. (1958), *The Moral Basis of a Backward Society* (Illinois).

Brown, M. E. (1997), 'The causes of internal conflict: an overview' in M. Brown, O. Coté, S. Lynn-Jones and S. E. Miller (eds), *Nationalism and Ethnic Conflict. An International Security Reader* (Cambridge, MA and London), 3–26.

Brubaker, R. (1994), 'Nationhood and the national question in the Soviet Union and post-Soviet Eurasia: an institutionalist account', *Theory and Society*, 23:1, 47–78.

Bunce, V. (1999), *Subversive Institutions. The Design and the Destruction of Socialism and the State* (Cambridge).

Collier, P. and A. Hoeffler (2001), *Greed and Grievance in Civil War*, www.worldbank. org/research/conflict/papers/greedandgrievance.htm (accessed 12 January 2002) (Washington, DC).

Coser, L. A. (1956), *The Functions of Social Conflict* (London).

Elias, N. (1992 [1969]),*Über den Prozeß der Zivilisation. Soziogenetische und psychogenetis-che Untersuchungen. Wandlungen der Gesellschaft. Entwurf zu einer Theorie der Zivilisation*, II (Frankfurt/M.).

Elwert, G. (1989), 'Nationalismus und Ethnizität. Über die Bildung von Wir-Gruppen', *Kölner Zeitschrift für Soziologie und Sozialpsychologie*, 3, 440–464.

Elwert, G. (2001a), 'Kühl, hochvernünftig und lernfähig. Wie terroristische Gruppen unter dem Dach von Ideologiefirmen effizient arbeiten und Attentäter heranziehen/ Typologische Einordnungen von Georg Elwert', *Frankfurter Rundschau*, online edition, www.asyl-rlp.org/aktuell/terrorfr.html (accessed 11 January 2002) (20 October).

Elwert, G. (2001b), 'The Command State in Africa. State deficiency, clientelism and power-locked economies', in S. Wippel and I. Cornelssen (eds), *Entwicklungspolitische Perspektiven im Kontext wachsender Komplexität. Forschungsberichte des BMZ* , 128 (Bonn), 419–452.

Gurr, T. R. (1993), *Minorities at Risk* (Washington, DC).

Gurr, T. R. and B. Harff (1994), *Ethnic Conflict in World Politics* (Boulder, CO).

Gurr, T. R., B. Harff and M. G. Marshall (1997), 'Codebook: internal wars and failures of governance, 1954–1996', *State Failure Task Force*, online publication, www.bsos. umd.edu/cidcm/stfail/index.htm (accessed 12March 2001).

Hann, C. (1996), 'Introduction. Political society and civil anthropology', in C. Hann and E. Dunn (eds), *Civil Society. Challenging Western Models* (London), 1–26.

Hedges, C. (1996), 'War-bred underworld threatens Bosnian peace', *New York Times* (1 May), 8.

Hirschman, A. O. (1994), 'Wieviel Gemeinsinn braucht die liberale Gesellschaft?', *Leviathan*, 2, 293–304.

Jaggers, K. and T. R. Gurr (1995), 'Tracking democracy's third wave with Polity III data', *Journal of Peace Research*, 31:4, 469–482.

Jamieson, A. and A. Silj (1998), *Migration and Criminality: the Case of Albanians in Italy* (Rome: Consiglio Italiano per le Scienze Sociali and Centre for European Migration and Ethnic Studies) (November).

Koehler, J. (1999), 'The school of the street: organising diversity and training polytaxis in a (post-) Soviet periphery', *Anthropology of East Europe Review, Special Issue: Reassessing Peripheries Post-Communist Studies,* 17:2, 9–52, http://condor.depaul.edu/~rrotenbe/aeer/aeer17_2.html.

Koehler, J. (2000), *Die Zeit der Jungs. Zur Organisation von Gewalt und der Austragung von Konflikten in Georgien,* 64 (Münster, Hamburg and London).

Lock, P. (2001), *Ökonomien des Krieges. Ein lange vernachlässigtes Forschungsfeld von großer Bedeutung für die politische Praxis,* www.peter-lock.de/Neuer%20Ordner/Kriegs% 9Akonomien2.html (accessed 12 January 2002).

Luhmann, N. (1983 [1969]), *Legitimation durch Verfahren* (Frankfurt/M.).

Schork, K. (1994), 'Sarajevo gangsters die as they lived – by the gun', *Reuters Information Services* (5 January), online edition.

Schwandner-Sievers, S. (1998), 'Wer besitzt die "Lizenz zum Töten" in Albanien? oder: Fragen ur Gruppensolidarität und Gewaltlegitimation in einer "anderen Modernisierung"', in J. Koehler and S. Heyer (eds), *Anthropologie der Gewalt. Chancen und Grenzen der sozialwissenschaftlichen Forschung* (Berlin), 71–88.

Simic, A. (1991), 'Obstacles to the development of a Yugoslav national consciousness: ethnic identity and folk culture in the Balkans', *Journal of Mediterranean Studies,* 1:1, 18–36.

Singer, J. D. and M. Small (1994), *Correlates of War Project: International and Civil War Data, 1816–1992* (Ann Arbor).

van Evera, S. (1994), 'Hypotheses on nationalism and war', *International Security,* 18: 4 , 5–39.

Willerton, J. P. (1992), *Patronage and Politics in the USSR* (Cambridge).

Wood, P. (2000), 'Gangster's life of Serb warlord', *BBC News* (15 January), online, http://news.bbc.co.uk/hi/english/world/europe/newsid_605000/605266.stm (accessed 11 January 2002).

Zürcher, C., J. Koehler and P. Baev (2002), *Internal Violence in the Caucasus,* study prepared for The World Bank Development Economic Research Group (DECRG), The Economics of Political and Common Violence (Washington, DC).

INDEX

Note: page numbers given in **bold** refer to main entries.